Contents

Introduction

How this book matches the AQA A AS specification 4

What is special about this book? 6

The AS examinations 7

Types of AS exam questions 8

AO1 – descriptive skills 10

AO2 – evaluation skills, the beginner's guide 12

AO2 – evaluation skills, expert level 14

Extended writing skills – theories 16

Extended writing skills – studies 18

Application of knowledge 20

Revision lists 22

Mock exams for PSYA1 24

Mock exams for PSYA2 26

Chapter 1	**Cognitive psychology: memory**	**28**
	Visual summaries	48
Chapter 2	**Developmental psychology: attachment**	**54**
	Visual summaries	76
Chapter 3	**Research methods**	**82**
	Visual summaries	103
Chapter 4	**Biological psychology: stress**	**108**
	Visual summaries	128
Chapter 5	**Social psychology: social influence**	**134**
	Visual summaries	150
Chapter 6	**Individual differences: abnormality**	**154**
	Visual summaries	174

Mock exam: suggested answers 180

Activities: suggested answers 188

Glossary 200

How this book matches the AQA A AS specification

Specification for cognitive psychology: memory	This book	Page
• The multi-store model, including the concepts of encoding, capacity and duration. Strengths and limitations of the model.	Topic 1 Research on the duration of memory	28
	Topic 2 Research on the capacity of memory	30
	Topic 3 Research on encoding in memory	32
	Topic 4 The multi-store model	34
• The working memory model, including its strengths and limitations.	Topic 5 The working memory model	36
• Eyewitness testimony (EWT). Factors affecting the accuracy of EWT, including misleading information, anxiety, age of witness.	Topic 6 EWT and misleading information	38
	Topic 7 Effect of anxiety on EWT	40
	Topic 8 Effect of age on EWT	42
• Improving accuracy of EWT, including the use of the cognitive interview.	Topic 9 The cognitive interview	44
• Strategies for memory improvement.	Topic 10 Strategies for memory improvement	46

Specification for developmental psychology: attachment	This book	Page
• Explanations of attachment, including learning theory and Bowlby's theory.	Topic 11 Explanation of attachment: learning theory	54
	Topic 12 Explanation of attachment: Bowlby's theory	56
• Use of the Strange Situation in attachment research.	Topic 13 The Strange Situation	58
• Types of attachment: secure attachment, insecure-avoidant and insecure-resistant.	Topic 14 Types of attachment	60
• Cultural variations in attachment.	Topic 15 Cultural variations in attachment	62
• The effects of disruption of attachment, failure to form attachment (privation) and institutional care.	Topic 16 Disruption of attachment	64
	Topic 17 Failure to form attachment (privitation) and institutional care	66
• The impact of different forms of day care on children's social development, including the effects on aggression and peer relations.	Topic 18 Impact of day care on aggression	68
	Topic 19 Impact of day care on peer relations	70
• How research into attachment and day care has influenced child care practices.	Topic 20 Influence of research into attachment on child care practices	72
	Topic 21 Influence of research into day care on child care practices	74

	Specification for research methods	This book	Page
Methods	Experimental method, including laboratory, field and natural experiments.	Topic 22 Experiments	82
		Topic 24 Field and natural experiments	86
	Studies using correlational analysis.	Topic 28 Studies using correlational analysis	94
	Observational techniques.	Topic 29 Observational techniques	96
	Self-report techniques including questionnaire and interview.	Topic 30 Self-report	98
	Case studies.	Topic 31 Case studies and other methods	100
Design	Aims.	Topic 22 Experiments	82
	Hypotheses, including directional and non-directional.	Topic 22 Experiments	82
	Experimental design (independent groups, repeated measures and matched pairs).	Topic 23 Experimental design	84
	Design of naturalistic observations, including the development and use of behavioural categories.	Topic 29 Observational techniques	96
	Design of questionnaires and interviews.	Topic 30 Self-report	98
	Operationalisation of variables, including independent and dependent variables.	Topic 22 Experiments	82
	Pilot studies.	Topic 28 Studies using correlational analysis	94
	Control of extraneous variables.	Topic 22 Experiments	82
		Topic 24 Field and natural experiments	86
	Reliability and validity.	Topic 22 Experiments	82
		Topic 24 Field and natural experiments	86
		Topic 28 Studies using correlational analysis	94
		Topic 29 Observational techniques	96
		Topic 30 Self-report	98

The research methods topics in the orange column are not listed in order and are repeated. This has been done to show how the specification content has been represented in this book.

Design	Awareness of the British Psychological Society (BPS) Code of Ethics.	Topic 27 Ethical issues	92
	Ethical issues and ways in which psychologists deal with them.		
	Selection of participants and sampling techniques, including random, opportunity and volunteer sampling.	Topic 25 Selection of participants	88
	Demand characteristics and investigator effects.	Topic 22 Experiments	82
Data analysis	Presentation and interpretation of quantitative data, including graphs, scattergrams and tables.	Topic 26 Data analysis	90
	Analysis and interpretation of quantitative data. Measures of central tendency including median, mean, mode. Measures of dispersion including ranges and standard deviation.		
	Presentation of qualitative data.		
	Analysis and interpretation of correlational data. Positive and negative correlations and the interpretation of correlation coefficients.	Topic 26 Data analysis	90
		Topic 28 Studies using correlational analysis	94
	Processes involved in content analysis.	Topic 29 Observational techniques	96

Specification for biological psychology: stress	This book	Page
• The body's response to stress, including the pituitary-adrenal system and the sympathomedullary pathway in outline.	Topic 32 The body's response to stress	108
• Stress-related illness and the immune system.	Topic 33 Stress-related illness and the immune system	110
• Life changes and daily hassles as sources of stress.	Topic 34 Life changes	112
	Topic 35 Daily hassles	114
• Workplace stress, including the effects of workload and control.	Topic 36 Workplace stressors: workload	116
	Topic 37 Workplace stressors: control	118
• Personality factors, including Type A and Type B behaviour, hardiness.	Topic 38 Personality factors: Type A	120
	Topic 39 Personality factors: hardiness	122
• Psychological and biological methods of stress management, including stress inoculation therapy and drug therapy.	Topic 40 Psychological methods of stress management	124
	Topic 41 Biological methods of stress management	126

Specification for social psychology: social influence	This book	Page
• Conformity (majority influence) and explanations of why people conform, including informational social influence and normative social influence. • Types of conformity, including internalisation and compliance.	Topic 42 Conformity	134
	Topic 43 Why people conform	136
• Obedience to authority, including Milgram's work and explanations of why people obey.	Topic 44 Obedience	138
	Topic 45 Explanations of why people obey	140
• Explanations of independent behaviour, including locus of control, how people resist pressures to conform and resist pressures to obey authority.	Topic 46 Independent behaviour: resisting pressure to conform	142
	Topic 47 Independent behaviour: resisting pressure to obey	144
	Topic 48 Independent behaviour: locus of control	146
• How social influence research helps us to understand social change; the role of minority influence in social change.	Topic 49 Social change	148

Specification for individual differences: psychopathology (abnormality)	This book	Page
• Definitions of abnormality, including deviation from social norms, failure to function adequately and deviation from ideal mental health, and limitations of these definitions of psychological abnormality.	Topic 50 Definitions of abnormality	154
• The biological approach to psychopathology.	Topic 51 The biological approach	156
• Psychological approaches to psychopathology including the psychodynamic, behavioural and cognitive approaches.	Topic 52 The psychodynamic approach	158
	Topic 53 The behavioural approach	160
	Topic 54 The cognitive approach	162
• Biological therapies, including drugs and ECT.	Topic 55 Biological therapies: drugs	164
	Topic 56 Biological therapies: ECT	166
• Psychological therapies, including psychoanalysis, systematic desensitisation and cognitive behavioural therapy (CBT).	Topic 57 Psychological therapies: psychoanalysis	168
	Topic 58 Psychological therapies: systematic desensitisation	170
	Topic 59 Psychological therapies: cognitive behavioural therapy (CBT)	172

What is special about this book?

This book is part of our 'Companion' series, and shares the same aim of providing a companion to help turn your understanding of psychology into even better exam performance.

There are many features in this book that we think make it very distinctive:

1. INTRODUCTION and skill practice

In the introductory section of this book we have provided activities to help you understand the skills you need in order to to perform well. You might believe that 'doing well' just means knowing the psychology, but that is only really half of the formula for success. You also have to be able to express your knowledge appropriately – i.e. know and follow the 'rules of the game'. Exams are a kind of game – not a playful game but a serious game.

2. Must, could and should

The content in this book focuses on preparing answers to the extended writing questions worth 12 marks. If you fully understand the material AND can answer these questions, then you should be able to cope with all other kinds of questions that are asked.

We have divided this material into:

MUST. For some students this will be sufficient. If you can produce this material in an exam you are likely to get a Grade C.

Once you have mastered the 'must' content, then move on to **SHOULD**. Knowing this extra material should lift your answer to a Grade A.

Some students may wish to tackle the **COULD** section at the bottom of each left-hand page. This is for students who are aiming for A* quality answers.

3. Activities

On the right-hand side of each spread there is a range of activities to help consolidate your knowledge. Some activities aim to help you construct better exam answers. Other activities will help you process your knowledge and enhance your understanding and memory.

Answers to most activities are given at the end of this book.

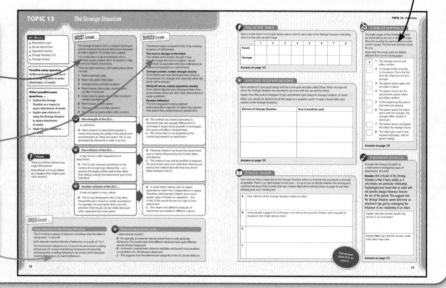

4. Unique visual summaries

At the end of each chapter we have provided visual summaries to make the material more memorable. The use of cartoons or colourful graphics provides an invaluable cue to learning, both during your revision and also when you attempt to recall the material in an examination. We have tried to make them amusing as well (wherever appropriate), but the primary aim of these summaries is to make your revision more effective (and more fun).

Like the material elsewhere in this book, we have divided the summary content into 'Must', 'Should' and 'Could'. The 'Must' material is always complete, but the 'Should' and 'Could' boxes frequently require you to complete the content yourselves to gain a more in-depth understanding of the point being made.

The evaluation material also offers you the opportunity to go beyond the basic critical point (in black type) and complete the sentences that follow (in coloured type). Research tells us that elaborating material makes it more memorable, so that's why we have given you plenty of opportunity to do just that.

Sometimes you are guided in how you might elaborate the material, at other times we offer only the visual cue – the rest is up to you!

5. Other features

There are also some mock exams for you to try, with 'model' answers and examiner comments. And there is also a glossary.

We think this is a very special book, and hope you do too.

There are **two** AS exams: Unit 1 (PSYA1) and Unit 2 (PSYA2).

★ In each exam all of the questions are compulsory.

★ The spaces provided on the exam paper and the number of marks indicated give you an idea of how much to write.

★ You have 1½ hours to complete each paper.

★ The total mark for each paper is 72 marks.

★ This means that you should spend just over 1 minute per mark. For a question worth 6 marks this means you should spend about 7 minutes thinking about and writing your answer, and should probably write about 150 words.

How science works

The theme 'how science works' is a key feature of the Psychology examination.

'How science works' includes your knowledge of the methods psychologists use when conducting research, and the strengths/limitations of these methods. It also includes the issues of reliability, validity and ethics.

Unit 1 PSYA1

Cognitive psychology, Developmental psychology and Research methods

The exam paper is divided into **two** sections, each worth 36 marks.

There will be one 12 mark extended writing question on this paper. Quality of written communication is assessed in this question.

There may be other, shorter 'essay' questions worth, for example, 8 or 10 marks.

Section A Cognitive psychology and Research methods

In this section you will be asked questions on the topic of memory. You will also be given some brief descriptions of hypothetical studies of memory and asked research methods questions ('how science works') in relation to these hypothetical studies. These research methods questions add up to about 12 marks.

Section B Developmental psychology and Research methods

In this section you will be asked questions on the topic of attachment and again will be asked research methods questions about hypothetical studies of attachment that add up to about 12 marks.

Unit 2 PSYA2

Biological psychology, Social psychology and Individual differences

This exam paper is divided into **three** sections, each worth 24 marks.

There will be *at least* one 12 mark extended writing question on this paper. There is no guarantee as to which section it will appear in. Quality of written communication is assessed in this question.

There may be other, shorter 'essay' questions worth, for example, 8 or 10 marks.

Section A Biological psychology

Most of the questions in this section will be on the topic of stress. About 4 marks are allocated to a question or questions on 'how science works' in relation to stress research.

Section B Social psychology

This follows the same pattern as section A – mainly questions on the topic of social influence but there may also be about 4 marks worth of questions on 'how science works', this time related to social influence research.

Section C Individual differences

This also follows the same pattern as section A – mainly questions on the topic of individual differences plus there may be some questions on 'how science works', this time related to abnormality.

There's lots of good exam advice in the podcast 'Exam advice' which is a section of our Audio Companion.

Grade boundaries

Your exam papers (Units 1 and 2) are marked out of 72.

In general if you receive about 53 out of 72 marks (about 75%), this will give you a Grade A. The actual mark changes from session to session depending on the difficulty of the paper (if the paper is difficult in any one year the Grade A boundary will be lower).

In general the Grade E boundary is between 30–35 marks out of 72 (close to 50%).

The bottom line

Grade A = 75% – this means that, if a question is worth 4 marks and you score 3, you're heading for a Grade A (if the same pattern of scoring is repeated across all questions).

Grade E = 50% – this means that, if a question is worth 4 marks and you score 2, you're heading for a Grade E (if the same pattern of scoring is repeated across all questions).

Every mark counts.

Psychology AS
The Audio Companion

Mike Cardwell · Cara Flanagan · Michael Griffin

OXFORD

There isn't a comprehensive list of the questions that might be asked in the AS exam. If questions are too predictable then students tend to focus on memorising answers rather than gaining a good understanding of the specification content.

Therefore the unpredictable nature of the questions should encourage you to focus on the specification rather than being concerned with what questions can be asked.

As long as you have covered the specification you should be able to answer the exam questions.

Having said that the exam questions are unpredictable, it is possible to identify certain question types that are predictable. We have looked through the past AS exam papers and produced a breakdown of the types of questions that you are likely to encounter. Please note that this is not a definitive list!

Knowing these question types should help you to be better prepared for the exam and focus on how to turn your knowledge of psychology into exam success.

On each spread of this book we have indicated likely questions that may be set to assess the topic of the spread.

Question type	Example	Advice
Simple recognition question	The following statements refer to different approaches to abnormality. Select three statements that describe the psychodynamic approach. Tick three boxes only. **A** Holding unrealistic and irrational beliefs about oneself and the world. ☐ **B** Behaviour is caused mainly by the unconscious. ☐ **C** Behaviour is shaped by forces in the environment. ☐ **D** There is conflict between the id and the super-ego. ☐ **E** The human mind is an information processor. ☐ **F** Abnormality is caused by unresolved childhood problems. ☐ *(3 marks)* January 2012 PSYA2	*Questions like this can sometimes be quite easy. But sometimes they can be quite difficult!* *It is worth taking extra time to make sure you have selected the right answer rather than rushing and throwing away valuable marks.* *It is important to read the question itself first before jumping in and trying to select the correct answer.* *Students often lose marks because they haven't followed the instructions – for example selecting four answers where only three were required. In such cases you will simply get 0 marks.*
Short description question	Research has suggested that the encoding and capacity of short-term memory are different from the encoding and capacity of long-term memory. Explain what is meant by encoding. *(2 marks)* January 2013 PSYA1 Cognitive interviews have been developed to improve witness recall. Identify and explain two techniques used in the cognitive interview. *(3 marks + 3 marks)* June 2009 PSYA1 Outline the pituitary-adrenal system. *(3 marks)* June 2012 PSYA2 There are various types of psychological therapy for treating abnormality. Outline what is involved in psychoanalysis. *(3 marks)* June 2011 PSYA2	*The number of marks available indicates the depth required in your answer.* *The amount of space available (lines in the answer booklet) also indicates about how much to write.* *There may be a section in the answer booklet labelled 'extra space' – but this is extra. Don't feel you have to use it.* *Always read the questions carefully – for example 'what is involved' means 'how is it done'.*
Longer description question	Outline the main features of the multi-store model. *(6 marks)* January 2009 PSYA1 Explain how social influence research helps us to understand social change. *(6 marks)* January 2013 PSYA2 Outline the biological approach to psychopathology. *(5 marks)* June 2012 PSYA2	*Again the number of marks available gives you guidance about how much to write.* *The maximum number of marks for any AO1 question is 6.* *You should avoid including any evaluation in response to these questions. This is unlikely to be creditworthy unless specifically asked for.* **The skill of description is explained on pages 10–11.**
Differences	How does the behaviour of securely attached infants differ from that of insecurely attached infants? *(4 marks)* June 2009 PSYA1 Explain the difference between privation and disruption of attachment. You may use examples to help explain the difference. *(4 marks)* January 2011 PSYA1	*You will only gain credit if you actually identify the difference rather than simply defining the two terms.* *You must be explicit about the difference(s) in order to gain full marks.* *Credit will be given for one difference in detail or more than one difference outlined briefly.*

Question type	Example	Advice
Research studies *Questions about research studies have a number of important features. Ignore these features at your peril because you will lose valuable marks.*	**'How' questions** Outline how **one** research study investigated the accuracy of eyewitness testimony (EWT). *(4 marks)* <div align="right">January 2009 PSYA1</div>	*Questions that say 'how' are asking for procedures only. There will be no credit for aims or findings/conclusions.*
	'Show' questions Outline what research has shown about cultural variations in attachment. *(4 marks)* <div align="right">June 2011 PSYA1</div>	*Questions that say 'show' are asking for findings and/or conclusions only.*
	'What' questions Outline **one** study that has investigated stress and the immune system. *(4 marks)*	*When questions don't say 'how' or 'show' then you should include both.*
	Research Describe what research has shown about conformity. *(4 marks)*	*In questions that say 'outline research', if you describe several studies, you will be credited for all relevant material. Whereas in questions that say 'Outline **one** study' you will only receive credit for the details of one study.*
	One-study questions Describe **one** study of the duration of short-term memory. *(4 marks)*	*In all cases studies need to be <u>identifiable</u>. You don't need to have the researcher's name(s) but it does help to make the study identifiable.* *If a question just says 'one' and you write about two studies, then only your best one will receive credit.*
Application of knowledge	Sandy and Vandita play for the same netball team. Two weeks ago, while playing in a competition, they both grazed their elbows. Vandita's wound is healing well, but Sandy's wound is taking much longer to heal. Sandy is very worried about the plans for her wedding and her forthcoming house move. Using your knowledge of psychology, explain why Sandy's wound is taking longer to heal than Vandita's. *(4 marks)* <div align="right">January 2010 PSYA2</div>	*In these questions you will be given an everyday situation (the question 'stem') and asked to use your psychological knowledge to provide an informed answer.* **The skills involved in answering application of knowledge questions are discussed on pages 20–21.**
Evaluation, strengths and limitations	The behavioural approach assumes that abnormal behaviour is learnt through classical conditioning, operant conditioning and imitation. Evaluate the behavioural approach to psychopathology. *(4 marks)* Identify **one** definition of abnormality and explain **one** limitation of this definition. *(1 mark + 2 marks)*	*Be guided by the number of marks available and be careful to answer the question.* *In the first example strengths and/or limitations are creditworthy. There is no requirement for a balanced answer.* *In the second example strengths would not be creditworthy, and writing a second limitation would not be creditworthy.* **The skill of evaluation is explained on pages 12–15.**
Short description + evaluation questions	Abnormality can be defined as 'the failure to function adequately'. Outline and evaluate this definition of abnormality. *(6 marks)* <div align="right">January 2012 PSYA2</div> Discuss research into conformity. *(8 marks)* <div align="right">January 2013 PSYA2</div>	*The terms 'discuss' or 'outline and evaluate' or 'describe and evaluate' signal that there are marks available for both description <u>and</u> evaluation.* *These marks are always equally divided into AO1 and AO2, e.g. 3+3 or 6+6. There is one 12 mark question on every paper but there may be other, shorter AO1+ AO2 questions as well.*
Long description + evaluation questions **The extended writing question**	Describe and evaluate the multi-store model of memory. *(12 marks)* <div align="right">January 2012 PSYA1</div> Outline and evaluate research into the effects of age of witnesses on accuracy of eyewitness testimony. *(12 marks)* <div align="right">June 2011 PSYA1</div> 'Abnormality is very difficult to define. It can be hard to decide where normal behaviour ends and abnormal behaviour begins.' Discuss **two or more** definitions of abnormality. *(12 marks)* <div align="right">January 2010 PSYA2</div>	*Some questions say '**one or more**'. This means that writing about only one explanation can be sufficient for full marks.* *Some questions say '**two or more**'. This means that two of the required things are sufficient for full marks. There is no requirement to write more – but you can if you wish.* *The question may begin with a quotation. The quotation is intended to guide you. But make sure you answer the question, not the quotation.* **More advice about answering extended writing questions is given on pages 16–19.**
Research methods	Suggest **one** reason why the researchers decided to use a field experiment rather than a laboratory experiment. *(2 marks)* Outline **one** strength and **one** weakness of using correlations in stress research. *(4 marks)*	*Research methods questions tend to be related to a 'stem' – some context for the questions. Therefore it is important to relate your knowledge to the context.*

'**Doing AO1**' is a skill. To develop any skill you need to practise to make sure you become proficient. On this spread the key elements of AO1 (descriptive) skills are explained and you are given the opportunity to practise these.

Throughout this book you will be given opportunities to practise these skills.

By the way, 'AO1' stands for assessment objective 1.

What skills are needed for AO1?

Giving psychological information

First and foremost in an AO1 question you are required to present your psychological knowledge. However, many students make the mistake of thinking that's all there is to it – learn a chunk of psychology and then 'dump' it into an exam question. Unfortunately, simply learning the psychology isn't the *only* skill you need.

Showing your understanding

You are marked on your understanding as well as your knowledge. Examples are a good way of communicating understanding. However, consider this answer:

Encoding refers to the way information is stored in memory. One example is visual encoding.

The example used in this answer doesn't really explain encoding and therefore doesn't demonstrate understanding. The following answer would be better:

Encoding refers to the way information is stored in memory. One example is visual encoding, which is when something you see is stored in the brain as nervous impulses.

Including detail

What does 'detail' mean? It is **SPECIFIC** information – not just more information but being precise. Consider these two sentences:

Short-term memories tend to be held as sounds.

Short-term memories tend to be encoded acoustically.

The second sentence has more information – not more words but more detail. When learning your psychology you need to focus on the details – such as psychological terms, psychologists' names, the approximate date of the research and examples.

You don't have to include these details but they improve your mark.

Selecting appropriate material

Students often write much more than they need to in an exam answer and often include material that is not really relevant. It is difficult to decide what should be put in and what should be left out – and that's why it is a skill. You need to learn how to focus on the specific demands of the question and select what is important to include. This makes your answer better than one where someone just writes everything that comes into their head.

Clear and coherent presentation

You are only assessed on your ability to use English and organise information clearly in the extended writing question worth 12 marks. However, this ability matters throughout the exam because the examiner has to understand what you are trying to say. Learning to express yourself clearly is a skill.

AO1 mark scheme

The mark scheme below shows you how the skills on the left contribute to your AO1 mark on a **6 mark question**.

Marks	Knowledge and understanding	Detail	Selection of appropriate material
6	Sound	Accurate and reasonably detailed	Appropriate
5–4	Relevant	Less detailed but generally accurate	Some evidence
3–2	Some relevant	Basic	Little evidence
1	Very little	Very brief/ flawed	Largely inappropriate
0	No creditworthy material		

5 out of 6 marks is a Grade A performance.
3 out of 6 marks is a Grade D or E performance.

For AO1 questions worth 4 or 5 marks a similar mark scheme to the one above is used.

For AO1 questions worth 2 or 3 marks:

- 1 mark for a very brief explanation.
- Further marks for increasing detail/ explanation (which can include an example).

We suggest that 150 words would be adequate for a question worth 6 marks. For questions worth fewer than 4 marks the length is usually less important. One sentence per mark is a useful guideline.

On the right-hand side of most spreads in this book there are activities for you to do.

In order to practise the skill of AO1 we need some content, so we have used content from Chapter 1.

(see pages 22–23)

How many marks?

Below are two answers to the question 'Describe the multi-store model of memory'. *(6 marks)*

How many AO1 marks would you give them? In order to help you in this task:

- Underline key words or phrases.
- Consider how much detail has been included.
- Watch out for material that is repeated.

Alice's answer

The multi-store model consists of three stores. First of all information arrives at the senses (sight, hearing and so on). This is sensory memory which has a very large capacity and very short duration (milliseconds). Then that information is passed to the short-term memory (STM) if attention is focused on it.

In STM capacity is limited to 7±2 items and a duration of less than 18 seconds. Information in STM can be rehearsed, otherwise it decays and disappears. Rehearsal also means it is passed into long-term memory.

Long-term memory has potentially unlimited capacity and duration, and is mainly encoded in terms of meaning (semantic).   105 words

Suggested mark for Alice's essay _____ marks

Tom's answer

The multi-store model of memory was proposed by Atkinson and Shiffrin. They proposed that memory consisted of three stores: sensory memory, short-term memory (STM) and long-term memory (LTM). Sensory memory is the information you get from your senses such as your eyes and ears and nose. When attention is paid to something in the environment it is then converted to short-term memory. Research has shown that the duration of sensory memory is extremely short.

In the multi-store model short-term memory is a store with limited capacity and duration. The process of maintenance rehearsal is used to increase the duration of STM to repeat information and also for converting to LTM. The multi-store model proposes that the more information is rehearsed the longer the duration. If the information is interrupted during rehearsal it may mean that the information is forgotten.

Long-term memory is shown in this model, like short-term memory, to be a unitary store. Unlike short-term memory, long-term memory has unlimited duration and capacity. This means people can remember everything but there may be other reasons why they don't.

One problem with this model is that it is too simple. For example short-term and long-term memory are divided into sub-stores of different kinds of memory.   205 words

Suggested mark for Tom's essay _____ marks

Answers on page 188

Selecting material

Tom included a lot of unnecessary material. So even though his answer was longer, it wasn't as good as Alice's. You can improve his answer by:

1 Crossing out the irrelevant material.
2 Add in a few more details such as the actual duration and capacity.
3 Can you think of any other details that could be added?

Detail and understanding

Choose a key term (see pages 22–23) and write one sentence defining it.

_____

_____

Now see if there is one word that you might change to make the definition sharper/more precise.

_____

_____

Now add an example.

_____

_____

Getting the details

Choose a theory in the specification, such as the working memory model or learning theory of attachment. (There is a list of these theories on pages 22–23).

Look at your textbook or this book.

Identify 6 key words for this theory.

Theory

1 _____

2 _____

3 _____

4 _____

5 _____

6 _____

Optional extra

7 _____

8 _____

Now try to write one or two sentences for each key word.

This is your 6 mark answer.

Getting the details

Choose a research study in the specification (there is a list of key research study topics on pages 22–23).

From your textbook or this book identify 4 key words related to procedures (how the study was done).

1 _____

2 _____

3 _____

4 _____

From your textbook or this book identify 4 key words related to findings and conclusions (what the study showed).

1 _____

2 _____

3 _____

4 _____

Now try to write one sentence for each key word.

Clear and coherent

Try to rewrite the student answer below so it is clearer and more detailed.

Question: Outline **one** feature of the working memory model. *(3 marks)*.

One feature is the central executive. It has little storage. It transfers things.

'Doing AO2'

Students generally find evaluation more challenging than AO1. That's because it is more challenging!

Since it *is* more challenging we are going to take it in two steps. On this spread we tackle the beginner's guide to doing AO2. When you feel ready you can progress to the next spread of doing more 'expert' AO2-ing.

AO2 questions are questions that require criticisms (strengths or limitations).

For example:

Outline **one** limitation of conducting memory research in a laboratory setting. *(2 marks)*

Outline **one** strength of using questionnaires in stress research. *(2 marks)*

Explain **one** criticism of Bowlby's theory of attachment. *(3 marks)*

What skills are needed for AO2?

Understand what evaluation is

'Evaluation' simply means 'What is the value of this thing?'

Think about an orange. How can we think about its value?

One limitation of an orange is that it is awkward to eat.

You probably knew that but wouldn't think of it if you were asked to evaluate an orange. Asking for 'evaluation' is just a different way of asking 'What are the problems (or advantages)?' with something.

State the AO2 point (S)

When you are writing criticisms (evaluations) the first thing you must do is to state the criticism. For example:

One criticism of an orange is that it is awkward to eat.

One limitation of conducting research on eyewitness testimony in a lab is that it's artificial.

Elaborate the AO2 point (E)

The second thing that is required is elaboration. If you look at the mark schemes for AO2 on the right you will see that 1 mark is awarded for identifying a criticism. For further marks, you must supply elaboration.

'Elaboration' means 'to develop thoroughly'. In particular you need to provide **EVIDENCE** or **EXAMPLES** to support your claim. For example:

(S) One criticism of an orange is that it is awkward to eat. (E) This is because it makes your hands sticky.

(S) One limitation of conducting research on eyewitness testimony in a lab is that it's artificial. (E) It is artificial because the participants didn't feel emotionally involved; (E) for example, they would in a real accident.

AO2 mark scheme

2 mark questions	1 mark for identifying a criticism (limitation/strength).	A further mark for elaboration
3 mark questions	1 mark for identifying a criticism (limitation/strength).	A further 2 marks for elaboration.

To be performing at the Grade A standard you really need to gain full marks on 2 mark questions.

If you only score 1 out of 2 marks (50%) that is a Grade D or E performance.

The *DROP IN*

A criticism such as 'one limitation of conducting memory research in a lab is that it's artificial' can be used for any memory study – it can be 'dropped in' any question on memory research.

To get more than 1 mark, you need elaboration.

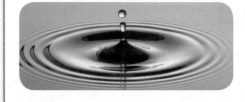

(S) **One problem** with eating an apple is

.

(E) **This is because**

.

(S) **One limitation** of (name a theory)

theory is

.

(E) **This is because**

.

(S) **One strength** of the research study by _____ is

.

(E) **This is because**

.

Answers on page 188

Mark these 2 mark answers

With each of the answers below, decide whether you would award 1 mark or 2 marks. To help you decide, write (S) and (E) where appropriate.

(Note – only award a second mark if the second sentence does actually provide elaboration.)

Aled's answer

> A weakness of correlations in stress research is that they do not show cause and effect. Therefore it may not be the case that stress is the cause of illness but just related to it.

The mark I would give is _____

Naomi's answer

> One strength of the working memory model is that it focuses solely on STM, providing a clear outline of our memory functions.

The mark I would give is _____

Alison's answer

> One limitation of a case study is that it cannot be generalised to the general population because it is based around just one person or case.

The mark I would give is _____

Answers on page 188

Researching past papers

You can check through past papers on the AQA website (type 'AQA A Psychology past papers' into Google) or your teacher may have copies of past papers.

Find some 2 or 3 mark evaluation questions and write them here:

Clear and coherent

There are two things wrong with the AO2 answer below. Can you spot them?

Question: Give **one** limitation of the use of the Strange Situation in attachment research. *(3 marks)*

Rita's answer

> As they are only small, adult informed consent is needed and they must be treated sensitively.

First thing that is wrong:

.

Second thing that is wrong:

Answers on page 188

AO2-ing
Try to improve Rita's answer.

Mark these 3 mark answers

With each of the answers below, decide whether you would award 1 mark, 2 or 3 marks. Write (S) and (E) where appropriate.

Jack's answer

> An advantage of a questionnaire is they are quick to do rather than a face-to-face interview with 100 adults which is very time consuming. Recalling past events may take time and this affects the interviews.

The mark I would give is _____

Shaheen's answer

> One limitation of defining abnormality in terms of deviation from social norms is that norms change. For example, in the past homosexuality was not accepted in society and deemed abnormal. However it is accepted today and therefore this shows that this definition is era dependent and unreliable.

The mark I would give is _____

Answers on page 188

On the previous spread we looked at AO2 questions worth 2 and 3 marks. Such questions say 'Outline one limitation …' or 'Explain one criticism of …'

Exam questions sometimes ask for evaluation rather than specifying 'one criticism'. For example:

Evaluate the multi-store model of memory. *(6 marks)*

Such evaluation questions require that you make several critical points and are marked with the mark scheme below right.

What skills are needed for expert AO2?

Superficial consideration or reasonable depth or greater depth

The most important point to understand is between 'superficial' and 'reasonable depth' (see mark scheme on right).

Grade C answers tend to provide superficial evaluation.

Grade A answers tend to provide reasonable (or better) depth.

Superficial elaboration = state the point (S) + a bit of elaboration (E). You may write 10 critical points but if they are all superficial you will get no more than 3 out of 6 AO2 marks.

Reasonable depth = state the point (S) + a bit of elaboration (E) + further elaboration (E). **E can be evidence, examples, explanation.**

Greater depth = state the point (S) + a bit of elaboration (S) + further elaboration (E) + further elaboration OR a link back (L). **An example of a link back: 'This shows that … '** **where you explain what the critical point demonstrates.**

The activities on the facing page will help you practise these elaboration skills and link back.

> This is the four-point rule = S E E L.

Issues or evidence

What kinds of things count as AO2? The mark scheme says 'issues or evidence'.

Issues include:

- The research methods used, for example a strength of a study might be that it was well-controlled or a limitation might be that it caused psychological harm to participants.
- Arguments for or against an explanation, such as suggesting an explanation is too simple.
- Individual differences or gender differences – not everyone responds the same way but many psychological explanations assume that they do.
- Real-world applications, which provide support for any explanation because they show that the explanation is useful.

Evidence includes:

- Research studies that support or challenge an explanation/theory.
- The strengths or limitations of alternative explanations – a comparison needs to be made between the current explanation and an alternative one focusing on why one is stronger than the other (but for AO2 make sure you don't just *describe* any alternative explanation).

Make it effective

If you *describe* a research study, then you are doing AO1.

If you use a research study as an evaluation it becomes AO2 but only if you say that's what you are doing. Use a **LEAD-IN SENTENCE**. For example:

One study that supports this theory is …

For any AO2 point, effectiveness is determined by:

1 The lead-in sentence (see list on facing page).
2 The amount of elaboration to make your point clear.

> Evaluation includes strengths and/or limitations. You can gain full marks in any evaluation question by giving all limitations and no strengths (or vice versa).
>
> Unless, of course, the exam question specifically requests strengths and/or limitations.

AO2 mark scheme

The mark scheme below shows you how the skills on the left contribute to your AO2 mark on a **6 mark question**.

Marks	Evaluation/ commentary	Depth (elaboration) of issues/ evidence	Selection of appropriate material
6	Effective	Broad range (5) in reasonable depth OR narrower range (3 or 4) in greater depth	Clear and good range, few errors
5–4	Not always used effectively	Range (4) in limited depth OR narrower range (3) in greater depth	Reasonable, some errors
3–2	Basic	Superficial consideration of restricted range	Lacks clarity, some specialist terms, errors
1	Rudimentary	Just discernible	Poor, few specialist terms
0	No creditworthy material		

'Broad range' = 5 critical points

'Range' = 4 critical points

'Restricted range' = 3+ critical points but no elaboration.

For AO2 questions worth 4 or 5 marks a similar mark scheme to the one above is used.

We will start with the **three-point rule**: S E E

Fill in the table with your answer to the questions given:

Outline **one** strength of the multi-store model. *(3 marks)*

State	
Evidence	
Example	

Outline **one** limitation of the multi-store model. *(3 marks)*

State	
Evidence	
Example	

Practise this with other AO2 questions on strengths and limitations.

Further elaboration – S E E L

For each criticism in the box above now write the **link back**.

Outline **one** strength of the multi-store model. *(3 marks)*

Link back	This suggests that …

Outline **one** limitation of the multi-store model. *(3 marks)*

Link back	This suggests that …

> Sometimes the link back may work better to say 'This shows that …' or 'Therefore we can conclude that …'

Different kinds of AO2

Strengths and limitations are not the only way to 'do AO2'. On the facing page we give you some other ideas.

Write down two other possible ways to make an AO2 point:

1 ....

2 ....

Using lead-in phrases for effectiveness

One strength of this study is …	This explanations is supported by …
One limitation of this study is …	This explanations is challenged by …
A real-world application is . …	An alternative explanation could be …
However …	There may be cultural variations …
On the other hand …	This would imply …
Not everyone reacts the same way, for example …	A consequence would be …

You do not have to start an AO2 point by saying 'One strength is …' or 'One limitation is …'. The lead-in phrases above all can be used as a way to start an AO2 point.

Select one of the phrases above and write your own critical point related to the multi-store model.

....

....

....

....

Superficial consideration or reasonable depth or greater depth?

Question: Explain **one** strength of the multi-store model of memory. *(3 marks)*

Each answer provides one AO2 point that could be used to answer this question. Is the AO2 superficial, reasonable depth or greater depth?

Sahil's answer

> Research that supports the sensory store is a study by Sperling (1960). In this study participants had to remember a chart of numbers and some of them just had to remember a line from the chart. The results showed that those who only had to remember a line were more accurate than the other group which shows that information decays rapidly in the sensory memory.

This AO2 is superficial/reasonable depth/greater depth

Anthony's answer

> One strength of the multi–store model is that is gives us a good understanding of the structure and process of the STM. This is good because this allows researchers to expand on this model. This means researchers can do experiments to improve on this model.

This AO2 is superficial/reasonable depth/greater depth

Answers on page 188

Putting AO1 and AO2 together

We have now arrived at the extended writing question where you have to put your two skills together.

For example:

- Outline and evaluate the working memory model of memory. *(12 marks)*
- Describe and evaluate the behavioural model of abnormality. *(12 marks)*
- Discuss the learning theory explanation of attachment. *(12 marks)*

In these questions you are required to write:

6 marks of description (AO1)

6 marks of evaluation (AO2)

Describe or outline = description (AO1)

Discuss = describe + evaluate (AO1 + AO2)
(There are also AO1 + AO2 questions worth less than 12 marks but we will focus on the 12 markers.)

Outlining/describing a theory

In a 12 mark question, there are 6 marks for description (AO1). The mark scheme for 6 marks AO1 is shown on page 10.

You are aiming to:

1 **Give the right amount** – about 150 words of AO1.

2 **Provide detail** – use psychological terms and specific pieces of information, psychologists' names and dates plus examples where appropriate.

3 **Select appropriate material** – make sure you focus on the theory/explanation required.

One way to prepare the appropriate amount of material is to identify key words for the theory.

You **MUST** have 6 key words.

You **SHOULD** have a further 2 key words (= 8).

You **COULD** have 2 more key words (= 10).

Special note

You do *not* get credit for an **INTRODUCTION** to the knowledge part of your answer. For example this is an introduction:

'The multi-store model is one of the main explanations into how and why memory works.'

This would gain no credit. Just go ahead and describe the theory/explanation.

Evaluating a theory

In a 12 mark question, there are 6 marks for evaluation (AO2). The mark scheme for 6 marks AO2 is shown on page 14.

You are aiming to:

1 **Give the right amount** – about 150 words of AO2.

2 **Provide elaboration** – all points should have some elaboration. Present fewer AO2 points but spend more time elaborating each one.

3 **Make AO2 effective** – each AO2 point should begin with a lead-in phrase and form a distinct AO2 paragraph.

How many AO2 points?

You **MUST** have 3 points or 2 points with elaboration.

You **SHOULD** have 4 points in some depth or 3 points in greater depth.

You **COULD** have 5 points in some depth or 4 points in greater depth.

Special note

You do *not* get credit for a **SUMMARY** of your evaluation.

You *would* get credit for a **CONCLUSION** (where you combine two or more points to produce something new). Usually, however, what students write is just a summary, restating what they have already said.

Use paragraphs to show structure

Examiners have to mark thousands of answers in only a few weeks. The clearer your answer is, the better.

For an extended writing answer on a theory:

- Do all your AO1 and then all your AO2.
- Divide the AO1 content into paragraphs.
- Write each AO2 criticism as a separate paragraph.

An examiner who has a lot to mark – using paragraphs in your answer will help her!

Outline and evaluate the multi-store model of memory. *(12 marks)*

For each answer to this question:

- In the description section, underline any **DETAILED** pieces of information.
- In the evaluation sections, number the critical points and insert **(S) (E) (E) (L)** where appropriate.
- Decide on an AO1 and AO2 mark (see mark schemes on pages 10 and 14).

Rebecca's answer

The multi-store model of memory is made of three stores. In the first store environmental stimuli are stored for a very brief time in the sensory store. Then any information is passed into short-term memory (STM) if paid attention to. The STM has a capacity of 7±2 digits and a duration of approximately 20 seconds. By using maintenance rehearsal, for example repeating the information over and over again in your mind, the information can be held for longer in STM and then encoded in LTM. This is done by giving the information semantic meaning, which is related to something else you remember. Your LTM has an unlimited capacity and duration and the information can be retrieved from LTM to STM. 122 words

Detail is reasonable/limited/basic/flawed

AO1 mark _____ out of 6

Strengths of the multi-store model of memory are that it suggests that the STM and the LTM are joined by encoding and retrieval, which can explain how we remember things because they are connected. Another strength is that it is supported by research evidence that shows the STM and LTM stores are separate. This is done by doing brain examinations that show that different sections of the brain are active when STM and LTM are active.

Limitations with the multi-store model are that STM is a single store whereas research suggests that it has separate stores for your different senses. The study of KF is that he suffered from brain damage after an accident but he had trouble with verbal but not visual information. This shows that there are different parts to the STM. Another limitation is that there isn't a lot of research into the sensory store. All that is known is that there are different parts for each sense. We don't know how it works. 168 words

Number of AO2 points is _____

Depth is great/limited/superficial

AO2 mark _____ out of 6

Answers on page 188

Eric's answer

The multi-store model is one of the main explanations into how and why memory works. There are three main parts of the explanation which suggests that memory can be lost if one part of the system for whatever reason fails, this supports the idea of amnesia.

The first part of the multi-store by Atkinson and Shiffrin is sensory memory. This is all memory that is related to your senses – what you hear, what you see, what you smell and taste and so on. When attention is paid to something this excites sensory memory and it is then encoded (changed so it can be stored) into our short-term memory. Short term memory has a duration of up to 30 seconds and can hold an average of plus or minus 7 pieces of information. Long-term memory is the stage after information from the short-term memory is rehearsed. Long-term memory can hold an infinite amount of information. The duration of this is that it can last forever. 164 words

The detail is reasonable/limited/basic/flawed

AO1 mark _____ out of 6

There have been other memory models that challenge this idea by Atkinson and Shiffrin. Ideas that memories are withheld just because of different senses.

The multi-store model is applicable because it explains the idea of many different stages of memory and also fits all memory stages. Also memory problems like amnesia can be supported with this.

However, some may challenge this idea because memories can be lost and not remembered. This explanation does not support this. 77 words

Number of AO2 points is _____

Depth is great/limited/superficial

AO2 mark _____ out of 6

Answers on page 188

Bruce's answer

The multi-store model (MSM) was created by Atkinson and Shiffrin. It is a representation of their beliefs about how memory works and has instigated much research into memory. According to the MSM, a memory is created when environmental stimuli go into the sensory store in the form of the five senses. When attention is given to this information it is transferred to short-term memory (STM). It is kept there by maintenance rehearsal (repeating) until it is either displaced (pushed out by new information) or gone through by repeated rehearsal to the long-term memory store (LTM). Information is retrieved from from LTM to STM if remembering a memory. Each store varies according to duration of the store (how long it stays there), the capacity of the store (how much information it can hold) and the way it is encoded (acoustic, semantic, etc). 113 words

The detail is reasonable/limited/basic/flawed

AO1 mark _____ out of 6

One strength is evidence for STM and LTM stores. This is given studies using brain scans. Beardsley found that when participants were asked to do a STM task the prefrontal cortex was most active. Squire et al. found the hippocampus was most active when participants were doing LTM tasks. This supports the existence of the separate stores.

One limitation is that the STM store is not a unitary store. Brain damaged patients have certain aspects of STM working but not others. Evidence for this is KF (Shallice and Warrington) whose verbal STM was much poorer than his visual STM, suggesting that these are separate things.

A second limitation is that STM actually relies on LTM for chunking. Without LTM, STM would not be able to chunk because learned information is required (semantic information from LTM). This evidence was given by Logie who suggested that participants chunked initials together because of meaning.

So although the MSM has limitations, it has plenty of evidence in relation to encoding (Baddeley), capacity (Jacobs) and duration (Peterson and Peterson). However much of this evidence is artificial and is therefore low in ecological validity. 188 words

Number of AO2 points is _____

Depth is great/limited/superficial

AO2 mark _____ out of 6

Answers on page 188

Improve the answers

Select one piece of descriptive content from the answers above and suggest what other **details** could have been included.

Select **one** critical point from the answers above and rewrite it with more **elaboration**.

Write your answers on a separate piece of paper.

Extended writing skills – studies

Sink or swim

On each exam paper there is ONE 12 mark extended writing question.

If you get 3 out of 12 marks on this question instead of 8 out of 12 marks that probably has cost you a whole grade. The difference between a B grade and a C grade (or a C grade and a D grade and so on) is usually just 5 marks.

You may do quite well on all the other questions on the exam and then get a poor overall grade because you didn't do the extended writing question very well.

Examples of extended writing questions on studies include:

- Outline and evaluate research on the accuracy of eyewitness testimony. *(12 marks)*
- Describe and evaluate research into the effects of day care on children's social development. *(12 marks)*
- Discuss research into conformity. *(12 marks)*

If the word 'research' is used in a question it refers to studies and/or explanations/theories.

Note that research studies can also be used as a way to evaluate a theory (see previous spread).

When you use a research study as AO2 then you must begin with an AO2 lead-in phrase such as 'This research study is supported by …'. This signals to the examiner that the research study is being used as AO2 and not AO1.

You also should keep the 'how' part of the research study to a minimum if the study is being used as AO2.

Outlining/describing studies

When describing research studies remember that both 'how' and 'show' are important:

- **How.** What did the researchers do?
- **Show.** What did the researchers find out and what did this show?

One study

You **MUST** know one study very well in all areas of the specification. See the lists on pages 22–23.

You need to know one study for the 'how' and 'show' questions. This is your **KEY STUDY**.

In a question worth 6 marks – if you describe just one study, your answer would be described as **BASIC** (up to 3 marks).

Second study

You **SHOULD** know a second study less well in all areas of the specification.

In a question worth 6 marks – if you describe one study reasonably well and a second study less well, your answer would be described as **LESS DETAILED** (up to 5 marks).

Third study

You **COULD** know a third study in less detail to gain the full 6 marks. Alternatively, you could gain the full 6 marks by knowing your second study reasonably well.

Use paragraphs to show structure

We can't emphasise enough how important it is to structure your answers using paragraphs. You should do this partly to make the examiner's job easier when marking your answers – but also to help you see what you have included.

The plan on the right would ensure equal coverage of AO1 and AO2 in an essay on research studies, which is vital for top marks.

Paragraph 1	AO1 1st study (70 words)
Paragraph 2	AO2 point and elaboration (50 words)
Paragraph 3	AO2 point and elaboration (50 words)
Paragraph 4	AO1 2nd study (40 words)
Paragraph 5	AO2 point and elaboration (50 words)
Paragraph 6	AO1 3rd study (40 words)
Paragraph 7	AO2 point and elaboration (50 words)

Evaluating studies

The same points apply for evaluating research studies as for evaluating theories:

1. Give the right amount.
2. Provide elaboration.
3. Make AO2 effective.

You **MUST** have 2 or 3 points with some elaboration.

You **SHOULD** have 3 points, all in reasonable depth.

You **COULD** have 4 points, all in greater depth.

Ways to evaluate a study

- **Criticise the research methodology**. Give a strength or limitation of the methods. This must be contextualised, i.e. can't be 'dropped in' as a criticism of any study. It must be specific to this study. For example:
  (S) One limitation of this study was that it was artificial (E) because they used film clips of a car accident. (E) This means it wasn't like being an eyewitness to a real accident. (L) Therefore we can't draw conclusions about the accuracy of eyewitness testimony in everyday life.
- **Compare with another study** that either supports or challenges your AO1 study.
- **Consider real-world applications** – how could the results of the study be used to improve people's lives?

Outline and evaluate research into the effects of age of witnesses on accuracy of eyewitness testimony. *(12 marks)*

For each answer to this question:

- In the description section, underline any **DETAILED** pieces of information.
- In the evaluation sections, number the critical points and insert **(S) (E) (E) (L)** where appropriate.
- Decide on an AO1 and AO2 mark (see mark schemes on pages 10 and 14).

Tony's answer

A study was undertaken where random participants on the street were asked to describe a young woman who had just walked past. Each participant recalled well. This showed little difference, the participants varied in age and gender therefore showing that age didn't affect immediate recall. Although this study was a natural experiment participants may have been aware when being asked to describe a woman as this isn't an everyday task therefore it lacks ecological validity. It also has low ecological validity because it was difficult to control the extraneous variables so it would be difficult to replicate. Throughout many studies a factor called own-age bias was discovered. This would affect recall on eyewitness testimony because if the witness was 17 then they are more likely to recognise a criminal of age 17 due to own-age bias. Again if a 75 year old saw a criminal age 75 they would be more likely to identify them accurately than a 17 year old due to own-age bias. Another study where participants watched a video of a car accident and were told to come back a week later. They recalled information accurately. This study lacked ecological validity because the participants watched a video and therefore weren't emotionally involved. Also it didn't take into account individual differences.   216 words

Number of studies = _____

Detail is reasonable/limited/basic/flawed

AO1 mark _____ out of 6

Number of AO2 points is _____

Depth is great/limited/superficial

AO2 mark _____ out of 6

Answers on page 188

Wei's answer

Eyewitness testimony relies on an individual's account of events in order to try to piece together what has actually happened. For example, witnesses of a murder or bank robbery. Kebble et al. claimed that police and many others relied heavily on eyewitness testimony, despite the fact that there are many factors affecting the account of events being given. Rattner looked at 25 cases of wrongful conviction and found that 52% of them had been down to unreliable eyewitness testimony. One factor that can affect the reliability of a person's eyewitness account could be age.

One psychologist who looked at the effects of age on eyewitness testimony was Yarmey, who staged a bank robbery in front of elderly and younger participants. When asked to recount what had happened 80% of the elderly participants left out the presence of the weapon that one of the robbers had been brandishing. This result was in comparison to the young adults where only 20% of them left out the presence of the weapon.

This proved that although a child's and adult's memory of an event can be similar, the child's memory will suffer over time which can be negative in a real life setting as court proceedings can take months upon months to organise.

This study links into another study about eyewitness testimony. Gordon claimed that a child's eyewitness testimony can hold accuracy but time can cause unreliability.   233 words

Number of studies = _____

Detail is reasonable/limited/basic/flawed

AO1 mark _____ out of 6

Number of AO2 points is _____

Depth is great/limited/superficial

AO2 mark _____ out of 6

Answers on page 188

Emily's answer

There has been a lot of psychological research on the effect of age on the accuracy of EWT. Memon et al. conducted a study which aimed to see how an elderly group of participants performed against a much younger group when recalling an event. One group contained students of between 16 and 33 years of age and the other between 60 and 85 years of age. Both groups were shown a criminal act in a laboratory setting and waited for 35 minutes before being questioned on what they had witnessed. Memon found that there was little difference between the groups' recollection of the event in the short time afterwards. Memon then decided to interview the groups on the event a week later and found that the older group performed significantly worse when accurately recalling the event next to the younger group. The study showed how age can effect an individual's EWT over a period of time and in real life when EWT is used in court it can be up to a couple of years after the evidence was witnessed.

Another study carried out by Brassard et al. studied a child's ability to give an accurate eyewitness account of an event. In this study a group of children under the age of 12 and a group of another age of adults were shown a video of a bank robbery incident. Brassard found the group containing the children were more likely to say what happened in the event whereas adults would try to explain what happened. He therefore concluded that adults were more likely to give accurate EWT as a result of reconstructive memory.

On the other hand a range of psychologists found children are more inclined to change their views of an event when misleading questions are used as compared with adults. Therefore it is hard to draw up conclusions as to how EWT is affected as there is contradictory evidence. However conclusions can be made regarding having worse memory and therefore EWT accuracy is worse. There are also many problems in the way in which research on age and eye witness testimony is carried out. For example Brassard and Memon's research took place in a lab experiment with a video of an event being shown. This situation means that the real anxiety of witnessing an event is lost and so EWT may be different if the event is witnessed in the real world so the studies lack ecological validity. Also individual differences play a big part in the accuracy of EWT as some people have better memories than others and so age may not be the defining factor.   438 words

Number of studies = _____   Detail is reasonable/limited/basic/flawed   AO1 mark _____ out of 6.

Number of AO2 points is _____   Depth is great/limited/superficial   AO2 mark _____ out of 6

Answers on page 188

Do you really understand your psychology?

One way to assess this is to give you a pretend situation and see if you can apply your psychological knowledge to it.

For example:

The stem

Jamie wanted to contact his doctor. He looked up the number in his telephone directory. Before he dialled the number, he had a short conversation with his friend. Jamie was about to phone his doctor, but he had forgotten the number.

Question ➤ **Use your knowledge of the multi-store model to explain why Jamie could not remember the doctor's number.** *(4 marks)*

PSYA1 January 2011

The stem

Psychology students sometimes revise for an exam by reading their notes over and over again. However, psychologists suggest that other memory improvement strategies may be more effective.

Question ➤ **Explain how a student could use their knowledge of strategies for memory improvement (other than repetition) to help revise for a psychology exam.** *(4 marks)*

PSYA1 June 2012

The stem

Brett and Sahil both work for the same company and have been talking about recent changes at work. Brett said that his pay is now dependent on other people's performance and that his department has introduced tighter deadlines and more rigid working hours. Since these changes were made, he has had more days off sick and is concerned that his health is beginning to suffer. There have been no changes in Sahil's department and he said that he hardly ever takes days off sick.

Question ➤ **Explain why Brett might have been affected by the changes in his department. Refer to psychological research into workplace stress in your answer.** *(6 marks)*

PSYA2 June 2012

> The research methods questions on PSYA1 also begin with a stem. These are illustrated in Chapter 3.

> Doing well in the psychology exam is not just about what you know – but about making effective use of it.

> The two-pronged plan …
> Attacking the problem on two fronts …
> An approach that has two parts.

You must make sure that your answer to 'application of knowledge' questions contains two parts:

1 Reference to the material in the stem.

2 Psychological knowledge.

Look at the examples on the left. Each one begins with a 'stem' – a description of how people have behaved in certain situations.

At the end is the question for you to answer. This question generally contains two parts:

1 Reference to the material in the stem.

2 A phrase that asks you to use your psychological knowledge.

In the first example:

Students might explain why Jamie couldn't remember the phone number but forget to refer to the multi-store model.

OR

Students might describe the multi-store model but say little or nothing about Jamie and his difficulty with the number.

Neither approach would get better than half marks.

YOU MUST DO BOTH.

NB It is not enough just to insert the word 'Jamie' occasionally.

- You must engage with the stem included in the question.
- Your answer must demonstrate psychological knowledge.

Jenny was standing at a bus stop talking on her mobile phone. The weather was wet and cold. Two men in the bus queue started arguing. One of the men was stabbed and badly injured. Later that day the police questioned Jenny, using a cognitive interview. They asked her to report everything she could remember about the incident even if it seemed unimportant.

Apart from 'report everything', explain how the police could use a cognitive interview to investigate what Jenny could remember.

In your answer you must refer to details from the passage above.
(4 marks)

January 2012 PSYA1

In the above exam question what are the 'two prongs of attack'?

1 The psychology that is needed:

2 Some information about the context:

Below are four answers to the application question about Jenny above. What mark would you give each of these?

You can check through past papers on the AQA website (type 'AQA A Psychology past papers' into Google) or your teacher may have copies of past papers.

Find some 'application of knowledge questions'.

For each one, identify:

1 The psychology that is needed.
2 Some information about the context.

Example 1 – date of exam paper _____

1 ....

2 ....

Example 2 – date of exam paper _____

1 ....

2 ....

Amalia's answer

A cognitive interview is an interview based on trying to find out as much information as possible. The interviewee must take down every single thing that happens in an interview even though the details may appear unuseful. Also the interviewee will try to change the order of information to see if that provides a different answer. The interviewee must ask for the participant to take on other people's perspective and views on what happened. Also Jenny could be asked to tell the story from one of the men in the argument and could be asked to say what events happened from the end to the start. *106 words*

Mark = _____ out of 4 marks

Melissa's answer

As well as asking Jenny to remember everything they would have to ask Jenny to tell her story from a different perspective. They could ask 'If you were standing on the other side of the road what would you have seen?' They may also ask Jenny to tell the story in a different order, asking 'What happened last?' or 'What started the argument?' The police officers may repeat the story back to her to see that it's correct. *79 words*

Mark = _____ out of 4 marks

Pedro's answer

After reporting everything the police could ask Jenny to alter her mental context and imagine what the victim would have seen. This helps reliability if witnesses are lying because then they have several versions of the report. They could then change the order of the incident to try and gain further information which would help them work out who did what. Finally they could ask her to put the incident in perspective with what other witnesses may have seen. *79 words*

Mark = _____ out of 4 marks

Roy's answer

After report everything, the police can ask her to mentally context everything which happened. Also changing the order/ perspective will help Jenny remember everything. Schemas are also used when memory may be inaccurate. It helps people remember things from previous experiences and expectations of events. *44 words*

Mark = _____ out of 4 marks

Write your own answer

Combine the best elements from all of these answers to produce your own 4 mark answer.

Answers on page 188

Revision lists

These lists indicate what you need to learn for each section of the specification. On the left of the table each section is divided into topics (which match the topics in this book).

The three headings in the table tell you what you need to prepare for each topic.

You need to know one research study well (both 'how' and 'show') and one or two other studies less well.

Topics	Key terms 'What is meant by …' (3 marks)	One research study 'Describe how one study has investigated …' (4 marks) 'Describe what research has shown about …' (4 marks)	Extended writing Describe and evaluate theories/research studies …' (6 marks AO1 + 6 marks AO2)
Models of memory			
Duration	✓	✓	✓
Capacity	✓	✓	✓
Encoding	✓	✓	✓
Mutli-store model			✓
Working memory model			✓
Memory in everyday life			
Eyewitness testimony	✓		
EWT and misleading information	✓	✓	✓
Effect of anxiety on EWT		✓	✓
Effect of age on EWT		✓	✓
The cognitive interview	✓		✓
Strategies for memory improvement	✓		✓

Cognitive psychology – memory

Topics	Key terms	One research study	Extended writing
Attachment			
Learning theory			✓
Bowlby's theory			✓
Types of attachment	✓	✓	
Secure attachment	✓		
Insecure-avoidant attachment	✓		
Insecure-resistant attachment	✓		
Strange Situation	✓		✓
Cultural variations	✓	✓	✓
Disruption of attachment	✓	✓	✓
Failure to form attachment (privation)	✓	✓	✓
Institutional care	✓	✓	✓
Attachment in everyday life			
Impact of day care on aggression		✓	✓
Impact of day care on peer relations	✓	✓	✓
Influence of research into attachment on child care practices			✓

Developmental psychology – attachment

Research methods is different

Candidates should be familiar with the following topics, plus their strengths and limitations	Candidates should be familiar with the following topics	Candidates should be familiar with the following features of data analysis, presentation and interpretation
Laboratory experiment Reliability and validity of laboratory experiments	Aims	Quantitative data, including graphs, scattergrams and tables
Field experiment Reliability and validity of field experiments	Hypothesis (directional and non-directional)	Qualitative data
Natural experiment Reliability and validity of natural experiments	Operationalisation of variables, including independent and dependent variables	Measures of central tendency, including, median, mean, mode.
Experimental design (independent groups, repeated measures and matched pairs)	Pilot studies	Measures of dispersion, including ranges and standard deviation
Studies using correlational analysis	Control of extraneous variables	Positive and negative correlations and the interpretation of correlation coefficients
Observational techniques, design of naturalistic observations, including the development and use of behavioural categories The reliability and validity of self-report techniques	Ethical issues and ways in which psychologists deal with them, awareness of the British Psychological Society (BPS) Code of Ethics	Processes involved in content analysis
Self-report techniques including questionnaire and interview; design of questionnaires and interviews The reliability and validity of observational techniques	Selection of participants and sampling techniques, including random, opportunity and volunteer sampling Strengths and limitations	
Case studies	Demand characteristics Investigator effects	

Topics	Key terms 'What is meant by ...' (3 marks)	One research study 'Describe how one study has investigated ...' (4 marks) 'Describe what research has shown about ...' (4 marks)	Extended writing Describe and evaluate theories/research studies ...' (6 marks AO1 + 6 marks AO2)
Stress as a bodily response			
Pituitary-adrenal system	✓		
Sympathomedullary pathway	✓		
Stress-related illness	✓	✓	✓
Immune system	✓		
Stress in everyday life			
Life changes	✓	✓	✓
Daily hassles	✓	✓	✓
Workplace stress (workload)	✓	✓	✓
Workplace stress (control)	✓	✓	✓
Personality factors: type A and Type B behaviour	✓	✓	✓
Personality factors: hardiness	✓	✓	✓
Psychological methods of stress management			✓
Stress inoculation therapy			✓
Biological methods of stress management			✓
Drug therapy			✓
Social influence			
Conformity	✓	✓	✓
Why people conform			✓
Informational social influence	✓		
Normative social influence	✓		
Types of conformity			✓
Internalisation	✓		
Compliance	✓		
Obedience	✓	✓	✓
Explanations of why people obey			✓
Social influence in everyday life			
Independent behaviour	✓	✓	✓
Locus of control	✓	✓	✓
How people resist pressures to conform		✓	
How people resist pressures to obey		✓	
How social influence research (minority influence) helps us understand social change			✓
Minority influence	✓		
Defining and explaining psychological abnormality			
Definitions of abnormality			✓
Deviation from social norms	✓		
Failure to function adequately	✓		
Deviation from ideal mental health	✓		
Biological approach			✓
Psychodynamic approach			✓
Behavioural approach			✓
Cognitive approach			✓
Treating abnormality			
Biological therapies			✓
Drugs			✓
ECT			✓
Psychological therapies			✓
Psychoanalysis			✓
Systematic desensitisation			✓
CBT			✓

Biological psychology – stress

Social psychology – social influence

Individual differences – abnormality

Model answers are given for Example 1, along with examiner comments, on pages 180–183.

Example 1

Section A Cognitive psychology and research methods

Answer all questions.

1 Psychologists have explained human memory using the multi-store model and the working memory model. Which **two** of the following statements (**A**–**E**) apply to the working memory model? Tick the **two** correct boxes. *(2 marks)*

A	The model was first proposed in the 1960s.	
B	Verbal rehearsal leads to the creation of long-term memories.	
C	Verbal rehearsal is managed by the articulatory process.	
D	There are three separate stores that differ in terms of duration and capacity.	
E	The central executive allocates resources to the other subsystems.	

2 (a) Explain what is meant by misleading information. *(2 marks)*

2 (b) Outline how **one** research study investigated the effect of misleading questions on the accuracy of eyewitness testimony (EWT). *(4 marks)*

3 Beth is a keen supporter of her local animal charity, who look after animals with no owners and try to find them new homes. She has volunteered to do a school assembly about the charity to try to get more volunteers involved. She can't use any notes so has to remember everything she has to say.

Using your knowledge of psychology, explain a suitable method that she might use to help her remember the key points of her talk. *(4 marks)*

4 A psychology teacher suggested that her class might conduct a study investigating eyewitness testimony and age. They decided to compare the performance of young adults (age 16–18) with older adults (aged 30–40). In order to test the accuracy of eyewitness testimony, they tested each participant by showing them a video clip of a rather unpleasant accident and then asking them questions to see how much information they could recall. The dependent variable was the number of correct responses given.

4 (a) Write a non-directional hypothesis for this experiment. *(2 marks)*

4 (b) Explain why the students thought it would be a good idea to conduct a pilot study. *(3 marks)*

4 (c) Explain why the study used an independent groups design rather than a repeated measures design. *(1 mark)*

4 (d) Explain **one** limitation of using an independent groups design. *(2 marks)*

4 (e) Identify **one** ethical issue associated with this experiment. Suggest how psychologists could deal with this ethical issue. *(3 marks)*

5 'The cognitive interview is used as a means of improving the accuracy of eyewitness testimony.'
Describe and evaluate the use of the cognitive interview. *(12 marks)*

Total for this section = 36 marks

Section B Developmental psychology and research methods

Answer all questions.

6 Psychologists use the Strange Situation to assess strength of attachment in infants.

6 (a) Outline the use of the Strange Situation. *(4 marks)*

6 (b) Outline **one** limitation of the Strange Situation. *(3 marks)*

7 (a) Explain the difference between insecure-resistant attachment and insecure-avoidant attachment. *(4 marks)*

7 (b) Identify **one** other type of attachment. *(1 mark)*

8 A psychologist tests the belief that the amount of time a parent spends with a baby is related to security of attachment. In order to conduct this study the psychologist asks parents to estimate how much time both the mother and the father spend with the baby each week. The psychologist then observes each parent with the baby to calculate how securely attached the baby is to the parent.

8 (a) Suggest **two** behaviours the psychologist might observe in order to determine whether the infant has a secure attachment to the parent. *(2 marks)*

8 (b) Apart from ethical issues, identify **one or more** limitations with the design of this study. *(3 marks)*

8 (c) The psychologist finds that parents who spent more time with their children have a more secure attachment with that child (on a scale of 1 to 10 where 10 is very securely attached). What kind of correlation is this? *(1 mark)*

9 A Health Centre is planning to prepare a leaflet for prospective parents about how to offer the best care for their babies.

Suggest **two** pieces of advice they might include in this leaflet. Refer to psychological research on attachment in your answer. *(4 marks)*

10 Research on the effects of institutional care has looked at the behaviour of ex-institutional children later in their life. One study used in-depth interviews with a group of adults who had experienced institutional care for more than one year early in their lives.

10 (a) Write **one** suitable question that could be used in the interview to produce quantitative data. *(2 marks)*

10 (b) Explain **one** strength of using quantitative data rather than qualitative data. *(2 marks)*

10 (c) Explain why it might be preferable to use a questionnaire rather than an interview to collect data in this study. *(2 marks)*

11 Outline and evaluate research into the effects of day care on peer relations. *(8 marks)*

Total for this section = 36 marks

Example 2

Section A Cognitive psychology and research methods

Answer all questions.

1 (a) Explain what is meant by encoding in memory. *(2 marks)*

1 (b) Outline the difference between encoding in short-term memory and encoding in long-term memory. *(2 marks)*

2 Explain **two** limitations of the working memory model. *(3 marks + 3 marks)*

3 The cognitive interview is a technique used by only some police forces. Other police forces continue to use the standard interview which is the traditional method used in questioning suspects or eyewitnesses. A researcher is employed to compare the two interview techniques. To do this the researcher compares two police forces. One force uses the cognitive interview and the other uses the standard interview technique. The researcher shows a set of films to 10 'eyewitnesses' and then the eyewitnesses are interviewed by both police forces. The information gathered is scored for accuracy. The results are shown in the table below.

Table 1

	Mean accuracy score out of a maximum score of 100
Police Force A (uses cognitive interview)	76
Police Force B (uses standard interview)	69

3 (a) Explain what is meant by the cognitive interview. *(2 marks)*

3 (b) Explain in what way this study is a natural experiment. *(3 marks)*

3 (c) Explain **one** limitation of a natural experiment. *(2 marks)*

3 (d) Identify the participants in this study. *(1 mark)*

3 (e) What do the results in Table 1 show? *(2 marks)*

3 (f) Explain why the mean was used to calculate the average score for accuracy. *(2 marks)*

4 Students use many different strategies to help them remember facts for examinations.

Outline **one or more** memory strategies that might be effective when trying to remember facts for an exam. *(4 marks)*

5 Outline what research has shown about the effects of anxiety on the accuracy of eyewitness testimony. *(6 marks)*

6 Outline the multi-store model of memory. *(4 marks)*

Total for this section = 36 marks

Section B Developmental psychology and research methods

Answer all questions.

7 A psychologist conducts a case study in order to consider the effects of disruption of attachment on a young boy who is in hospital for a major operation. He will be in hospital for three weeks. Both his parents have full-time jobs and will not be able to visit their son very much. However they have arranged for a family friend to go in every day for a few hours.

7 (a) What is meant by a case study? *(2 marks)*

7 (b) Apart from ethical issues, identify **one** limitation of using a case study as a method of investigation. *(1 mark)*

7 (c) Give an example of this limitation in the context of this study. *(3 marks)*

7 (d) Psychologists use a range of techniques to gather information in case studies. Identify **one** technique that the psychologist could use in this case study and explain how it might be used. *(2 marks)*

7 (e) Based on your knowledge of psychological research, what do you think the psychologist's results will show? *(4 marks)*

8 Briefly describe the learning theory of attachment. *(4 marks)*

9 Research shows that day care may have positive effects on children's development if the quality of care is good.

9 (a) Identify **two** features of high-quality day care. *(2 marks)*

9 (b) Explain why **one** of these qualities is likely to have positive effects of children's development. *(2 marks)*

10 A study compared the cognitive and social development of children who were adopted either before or after the age of six months. The results are shown in the graph below.

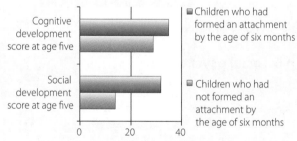

What does this graph show about the effects of failure to form attachment by the age of six months? *(4 marks)*

11 Research into attachment has been conducted in many different countries and cultures around the world.

Outline and evaluate research into cultural variations in attachment. *(12 marks)*

Total for this section = 36 marks

Model answers are given for Example 1, along with examiner comments, on pages 184–187.

Example 1

Section A Biological psychology

Answer all questions.

1 Outline the pituitary-adrenal system. *(3 marks)*

2 The scattergram below shows the relationship between stress and daily hassles.

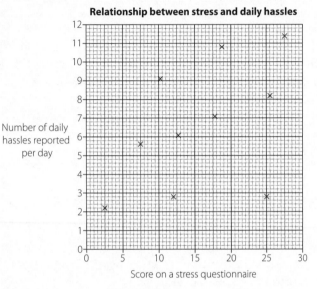

Relationship between stress and daily hassles

Number of daily hassles reported per day (vertical axis, 0–12)

Score on a stress questionnaire (horizontal axis, 0–30)

2 (a) What does the scattergram tell you about the relationship between stress and daily hassles? *(4 marks)*

2 (b) How many people are represented in this scattergram? *(1 mark)*

3 Drug therapies are used as a form of stress management. Evaluate the use of drugs as a form of stress management. *(4 marks)*

4 Discuss research into life changes as a source of stress. *(12 marks)*

Total for this section = 24 marks

Section B Social psychology

Answer all questions.

5 (a) Outline the difference between conformity and obedience. *(4 marks)*

5 (b) Outline **one** study of obedience. *(6 marks)*

5 (c) A researcher interviews students on their attitudes about conformity. Give **one** advantage of collecting information using an interview. *(3 marks)*

6 Outline **one or more** explanations of independent behaviour. *(5 marks)*

7 Attitudes towards women's rights changed in this country over a hundred years ago. In some parts of the world such attitudes are still changing.

Using your knowledge of research into social influence, explain how such change occurs. *(6 marks)*

Total for this section = 24 marks

Section C Individual differences

Answer all questions.

8 Describe and evaluate the deviation from social norms definition of abnormality. *(6 marks)*

9 (a) One psychological approach to the explanation of abnormality is the psychodynamic approach. Outline this approach to abnormality. *(5 marks)*

9 (b) Psychoanalysis is the therapy related to the psychodynamic approach. Outline **one** technique that may be used in psychoanalysis. *(2 marks)*

9 (c) Another therapy that is used in the treatment of abnormality is systematic desensitisation. Explain **one** criticism of this method of treatment. *(3 marks)*

10 Selma has been having many difficulties at home and at work. She feels she has become very depressed and doesn't want to go back to work. Her doctor suggests that cognitive behavioural therapy (CBT) may help her recover.

What information might the doctor give about this kind of therapy? *(4 marks)*

11 A psychologist investigated which methods of treatment were most effective. Thirty depressed patients were given one of three treatments for 6 weeks after which their improvement was assessed on a scale of 1 to 30 where 0 = no improvement. They were assessed again after 1 year to see if the improvements had continued. Improvement rates are shown in the table below.

	Mean improvement score after six weeks	Mean improvement score after one year
ECT	11	12
Drug therapy	17	10
Psychoanalysis	16	23

Explain what these results show about the effectiveness of different therapies. *(4 marks)*

Total for this section = 24 marks

Example 2

Section A Biological psychology

Answer all questions.

1 A psychologist investigated the relationship between stress and personality type. The results were analysed using a correlational analysis.

Explain **two** limitations of studies using a correlational analysis. *(2 marks + 2 marks)*

2 Outline how **one** research study has investigated the relationship between stress and the immune system. *(4 marks)*

3 Desmond has a Type A personality, whereas his friend Sally has a Type B personality.

3 (a) Explain what is meant by Type B personality. *(1 mark)*

3 (b) Using your knowledge of the body's response to stress, explain why Desmond is more likely to suffer negative effects when stressed. *(4 marks)*

4 Outline how stress inoculation is used as a method of stress management. *(5 marks)*

5 Tina's job involves dealing with customers who have a complaint to make about their telephone service. She has to work for long hours without a break and often has to listen to very angry customers when she can't really solve their problems.

Explain why Tina may be feeling very stressed. Refer to psychological research into workplace stress in your answer. *(6 marks)*

Total for this section = 24 marks

Section B Social psychology

Answer all questions.

6 A research study tested conformity levels using a questionnaire. The results are displayed in the graph below.

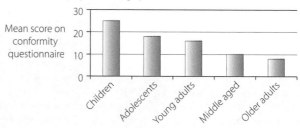

6 (a) What do these results suggest about the relationship between conformity and age? *(2 marks)*

6 (b) Explain **one** strength of using questionnaires in conformity research. *(2 marks)*

7 Outline and evaluate **two** explanations of conformity. *(8 marks)*

8 (a) Explain what is meant by locus of control. *(2 marks)*

8 (b) Outline what research has shown about the relationship between locus of control and independent behaviour. *(4 marks)*

8 (c) Give **one** criticism of the research you described in part (b). *(2 marks)*

9 Children are usually very careful to obey a policeman but may not be as careful to obey what they are told to do by their older sister.

Explain why people obey some people and not others. Make reference to psychological research on obedience in your answer. *(4 marks)*

Total for this section = 24 marks

Section C Individual differences

Answer all questions.

10 Outline how ECT (electroconvulsive therapy) is used to treat abnormality. *(3 marks)*

11 (a) Identify **one** definition of abnormality. *(1 mark)*

11 (b) Explain **two** limitations of the definition of abnormality identified in part (a). *(2 marks + 2 marks)*

12 Two drugs are developed for use in the treatment of depression. Outline how you might conduct a study to demonstrate which of the two drugs is more effective. *(4 marks)*

13 Outline and evaluate the cognitive approach to psychopathology. *(12 marks)*

Total for this section = 24 marks

KEY WORDS

- Duration
- Long-term memory (LTM)
- Retention interval
- Short-term memory (STM)
- Spontaneous decay

Possible essay question ...

Outline and evaluate research on the duration of memory. *(12 marks)*

Other possible exam questions ...

+ Explain what is meant by duration in relation to memory. *(2 marks)*
+ Describe **one** way in which psychologists have investigated the duration of short-term memory. *(4 marks)*
+ Outline **one** research study on the duration of short-term memory. *(6 marks)*
+ Apply this knowledge to ... *(6 marks)*

MUST know ...

Key study: Peterson and Peterson

Duration of STM

How?

The participants were 24 students. Each was tested over eight trials.

On each trial a participant was given a consonant syllable and a three-digit number (e.g. THX 512 or HJS 384).

They were asked to recall the consonant syllable after a retention interval of 3, 6, 9, 12, 15 or 18 seconds.

During the retention interval they had to count backwards from their three-digit number.

Showed?

Participants on average were 90% correct over 3 seconds.

They were 20% correct after 9 seconds.

They were 2% correct after 18 seconds.

This suggests that STM has a very short duration, less than 18 seconds, if verbal rehearsal prevented.

This study lacked ecological validity ...

... because the stimulus material was artificial.

- **E** – Trying to memorise consonant syllables does not truly reflect most everyday memory activities where what we are trying to remember is meaningful.

One problem with this study is that ...

... the findings may be explained by displacement rather than the material only lasting a short time in STM (spontaneous decay).

- **E** – Participants were counting the numbers in their STM and this displaced or 'overwrote' the syllables to be remembered.

SHOULD know ...

Second study: Bahrick *et al.*

Duration of LTM

How?

Bahrick *et al.* tested 400 people of various ages (17–74) on their memory of classmates. There were various tests, including:

- A photo-recognition test consisting of 50 photos, some from the participant's high-school yearbook.
- A free-recall test where participants were asked to list all the names they could remember of individuals in their graduating class.

Showed?

Participants who were tested within 15 years of graduation were about 90% accurate in identifying faces.

After 48 years, this declined to about 70% for photo recognition.

Free recall was about 60% accurate after 15 years, dropping to 30% after 48 years.

- **E** – However, we do sometimes try to remember fairly meaningless things, such as groups of numbers or letters as in a phone number or post code.
- **L** – This means that the study does have some relevance to everyday life.

- **E** – One study (Reitman) used auditory tones instead of numbers so that displacement wouldn't occur. She found that the duration of STM was much longer than in the Petersons' study.
- **L** – This suggests that forgetting in the Petersons' study was likely to be due to displacement rather than decay.

In Bahrick et al.'s study the results ...

... may be due to rehearsal.

- **E** – For example, some participants might have looked at the yearbooks regularly and that's why their recognition/recall was good.
- **E** – rehearsal is acting as an extraneous variable.
- **L** – This means that Bahrick *et al.*'s findings lack validity.

COULD know ...

Third study: Nairne *et al.*

How?

Nairne *et al.* modified the Petersons' technique so that the material to be remembered was the *same* across trials. This was done to prevent one set of items interfering with another, which might affect recall.

Participants were shown five nouns and, after a retention interval, were shown all five nouns in a different order and had to recall the nouns in the correct order.

Showed?

Nairne *et al.* found that items could still be accurately recalled after as long as 96 seconds.

Therefore it seems that information remains for longer in STM if there is no interference from other items.

One criticism of this study is that ...

... words were used instead of consonant syllables.

- **E** – Participants might be better at remembering real words than meaningless consonants or numbers.
- **E** – This means that these results may only apply to some kinds of STM tasks.
- **L** – However, the results still show that forgetting rates in STM vary depending on the presence or absence of interfering materials from prior trials.

DRAWING CONCLUSIONS

The graph below shows the data from the study by Peterson and Peterson.

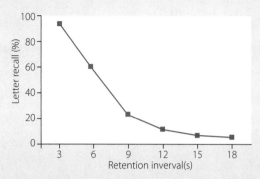

State **two** findings and for each one draw a conclusion (state what the finding shows):

Finding 1:
Conclusion 1: This shows that …
Finding 2:
Conclusion 2: This shows that …

Answers on page 188

 KEY PHRASES

Select key phrases to help you remember the key study by Peterson and Peterson.
A few have been done for you.

How?	Showed?
24 students	90% 3 secs
8 trials	

On a separate piece of paper, use your key phrases to answer the following exam questions.

- Outline how psychologists have investigated the duration of memory.
  (4 marks)
- Outline what research has shown about the duration of memory.
  (4 marks)

 CIRCLE TRUE OR FALSE

T or F Bahrick *et al.* tested participants who were all over 30 years old.

T or F In Bahrick *et al.*'s study recognition memory was 100% accurate when tested after 15 years.

T or F This was reduced to 70% after 48 years.

T or F Peterson and Peterson found that participants only remembered 2% of the information to be remembered after 18 seconds.

T or F Three letters such as HGB are called consonant syllables.

T or F Bahrick *et al.*'s study found that after 48 years memory was about 60% accurate.

T or F Peterson and Peterson showed that short-term memories almost all disappear in under 6 seconds.

Answers on page 188

 JUMBLED SENTENCES

Here are three criticisms linked to the Must and Should studies on the facing page. However, the sentences making up these criticisms have been jumbled up. Sort them into the correct order.

Criticism 1

4	1	This means that the study is not totally irrelevant to everyday life.
	2	Memorising consonant syllables does not truly reflect most everyday memory activities where what we are trying to remember is meaningful.
	3	Because the stimulus material was artificial.
	4	This study lacked ecological validity.
	5	We do sometimes try to remember fairly meaningless things, such as phone numbers.

Criticism 2

	6	This suggests that forgetting in the Petersons' study was likely to be due to displacement rather than decay.
	7	The findings may be explained by displacement rather than the material only lasting a short time in STM.
	8	Participants were counting the numbers in their short-term memories and this displaced or 'overwrote' the syllables to be remembered.
	9	One problem with this study is that …
	10	One study (Reitman) used auditory tones instead of numbers so that displacement wouldn't occur. She found that the duration of STM was much longer than in the Petersons' study.

Criticism 3

	11	In Bahrick *et al.*'s study the results …
	12	Some participants might actually have looked at the yearbooks regularly and that's why their recognition/recall was so good.
	13	In this case rehearsal is acting as an extraneous variable.
	14	May be due to rehearsal.
	15	This means that Bahrick *et al.*'s findings may not be meaningful.

Answers on page 188

KEY WORDS

- Capacity
- Chunking
- Digit span
- Short-term memory (STM)

Possible essay question ...

Outline and evaluate research on capacity in memory.
(12 marks)

Other possible exam questions ...

+ Explain what is meant by capacity in relation to memory. *(2 marks)*
+ Outline the difference between the capacity of short-term memory and the capacity of long-term memory. *(2 marks)*
+ Outline what research has shown about the capacity of memory. *(4 marks)*
+ Apply this knowledge to ... *(6 marks)*

MUST know ...

Key study: Miller

How?
Miller made observations that everyday things come in sevens, e.g. seven notes on the musical scale, seven days of the week.

Miller also reviewed several studies that have investigated the span of STM, e.g. where participants counted dots flashed on a screen or were tested on the recall of words.

Showed?
When dots are flashed on a screen, participants are reasonably accurate when there are seven dots but very inaccurate when 15 dots are shown.

This suggests that the span (or capacity) of STM is about seven items (plus or minus 2).

Miller also observed that people can recall five *words* as well as they can recall five *letters*. They do this by chunking – grouping sets of digits or letters into meaningful units (chunks).

One problem is that ...

... Miller may have overestimated the capacity of STM.

- *E* – Cowan reviewed research on this topic, and found that the capacity of STM is more likely to be about four chunks rather than seven chunks.

There are real-world applications ...

... to the UK postcode system.

- *E* – Baddeley used research on chunking to make recommendations about what combinations of letters and numbers are most easily remembered.

SHOULD know ...

Second study: Jacobs

How?
Jacobs tested digit span.

Each participant first listened to four digits and had to recall these in the correct order. If this was correct they progressed to five digits and so on, until they couldn't recall the order correctly. This determined the participant's digit span.

The same activity was repeated with letters.

Showed?
Jacobs found that the mean span for digits was 9.3 items whereas it was 7.3 for letters.

He also observed that digit span increased with age; eight year olds could remember an average of 6.6 digits whereas the mean for 19 year olds was 8.6 digits.

This might happen because people develop strategies to improve their digit span as they get older, such as chunking.

- *E* – Cowan's finding was further supported by Vogel *et al.* who found four items was about the limit for visual items.
- *L* – This means that the lower end of Miller's range is more appropriate (i.e. 7 – 2 which is 5).

- *E* – Baddeley found that numbers were best remembered if placed between the city code and some random letters. Phone numbers and car licence plates also use chunks.
- *L* – This shows that research on chunking has led to useful applications.

Jacob's study is very old ...

... because it was conducted in 1887.

- *E* – Jacobs may not have adequately controlled the study because research was not as formal.
- *E* – The instructions he used with adults and children might have differed, acting as an extraneous variable.
- *L* – This might explain why adults performed better, rather than there being any real difference.

COULD know ...

Third study: Simon

How?
Simon tested his own recall for one-syllable, two-syllable and three-syllable nouns and also familiar phrases. He read them aloud and then later tried to see how many he could recall.

Showed?
He found there was a slightly shorter span for three-syllable words than one- or two-syllable words.

He also found that there was a shorter memory span for longer phrases than shorter phrases.

This study may lack generalisability ...

... because only one person was involved.

- *E* – However, in this particular situation it may not matter that only one person's data was observed as the findings fit with common experience.
- *E* – The data is more of an observation than a formal research study.
- *L* – However, it refines our understanding of chunking.

A MARKING EXERCISE

Mark each of the student answers below to the following exam question:

Outline the difference between the capacity of short-term memory and the capacity of long-term memory. *(3 marks)*

Celeste's answer

The capacity of STM is very limited whereas the capacity of LTM can last up to a lifetime.

MARK
.... out of 3

Jennifer's answer

The capacity of short-term memory is 7 +/– 2 items. The capacity of long-term memory is unlimited.

MARK
.... out of 3

Answers on page 188

WRITE YOUR OWN EVALUATION POINT

Select one evaluation point from the facing page and write it out in your own words below.

Underline key words to help you remember the AO2 point.

S	
E	
E	
L	

See page 14 for an explanation of how to S E E L.

APPLYING YOUR KNOWLEDGE

Identify the psychology
1
2

A group of students decide to use their knowledge of psychology to help them more effectively learn material for a test. How might they use research on the capacity of memory to learn more effectively? *(4 marks)*

Link to a method they could use
1
2

Answers on pages 188–189

FILL IN THE BLANKS

The key piece of research on this spread is by (1) ....

It is not a single research study but a review of studies that all investigated (2) ....

.... Miller analysed the results of these studies and also observed that many things

come in sevens, such as (3) .... These studies and observations

suggest that the capacity of STM is about seven items. For example, people can count

(4) .... dots accurately when they are flashed on a screen but not (5) ....

dots. Miller also observed that people can remember five words as well as they can remember five

sentences. This is called (6) ....

Answers on page 189

An idea
What is your own digit span? Is it different for letters and digits?

KEY WORDS

- Acoustic
- Articulatory suppression task
- Encoding
- Free recall
- Long-term memory (LTM)
- Retention interval
- Semantic
- Short-term memory (STM)

Possible essay question …

Outline and evaluate research on encoding in memory.

(12 marks)

Other possible exam questions …

+ Explain what is meant by encoding. *(2 marks)*
+ Outline how psychologists have investigated encoding in short-term memory. *(4 marks)*
+ Outline **one** research study on encoding in memory. *(6 marks)*
+ Apply this knowledge to … *(6 marks)*

MUST know …

Key study: Baddeley

How?

- Group A participants were given acoustically similar words (e.g. cab, can, mad, max).
- Group B were given acoustically *dis*similar words (e.g. pit, few, cow, pen).
- Group C were given semantically similar words (e.g. great, large, big, huge).
- Group D were given semantically *dis*similar words (e.g. good, huge, hot).

On each trial five words were read out. After a time interval, participants were shown 10 words and asked to select the correct five words and place them in the right order.

Showed?

When STM was tested, participants with acoustically similar words had lowest recall.

This suggests that words in STM are encoded acoustically.

When LTM was tested (time interval of 20 minutes), the group with semantically similar words had the lowest recall.

This suggests that words in LTM are encoded semantically.

 One limitation of this study was …

… that quite artificial stimuli were used.

- **E** – This means we should be cautious about generalising the findings to different kinds of memory task.

 One limitation of this study was …

… that the LTM memory task wasn't very long term.

- **E** – It was only 20 minutes, which is not the same as remembering information for months and years.

SHOULD know …

Second study: Brandimote *et al.*

How?

Brandimote *et al.* showed participants six picture pairs (see examples at bottom of facing page).

One of each pair was a component of the other.

Participants were asked to 'subtract' the second picture from the first one for each pair.

In the retention interval some participants had to say 'la la la la' to prevent any verbal rehearsal (an articulatory suppression task).

Showed?

Participants' performance was unaffected by the articulatory suppression task.

This shows that the images were visually rather than verbally encoded and that encoding in STM is not always acoustic.

Normally we 'translate' visual images into verbal codes in STM. However, since verbal rehearsal was prevented in this study, visual encoding was used.

- **E** – For example, if people were processing meaningful information they might use semantic encoding even for STM tasks.
- **L** – This means that this study only tells us a limited amount about encoding in STM/LTM.

- **E** – It is possible that different kinds of encoding processes are involved when information is stored over months and years.
- **L** – However, the study does clearly show there is a difference over time.

 Brandimote et al.'s study was supported by …

… other studies.

- **E** – Wickens *et al.* found that STM sometimes uses a semantic code.
- **E** – Frost's study showed that LTM was related to visual as well as semantic categories.
- **L** – Therefore encoding is not simply acoustic or semantic but can vary according to circumstances.

COULD know …

Third study: Frost

How?

This study focused on visual encoding in LTM.

Participants were shown drawings of 16 common objects.

After a 15-minute interval, participants were tested on recall of the drawings and their responses were timed. In some cases the original drawing was presented in a different form – from a slightly different perspective.

Showed?

Participants responded more quickly when the drawings were identical to the original presentation.

This shows they encoded the drawings visually.

 One criticism of this study is …

… that speed of response was important.

- **E** – Psychological research has shown that, when people are required to make quick decisions, this affects the kind of information recalled.
- **E** – Hintzman and Curran found that quicker responses make people more dependent on recognition (which would be visual in Frost's study) than recall (which would be semantic in Frost's study).
- **L** – Therefore, in Frost's study encoding may have been both visual and semantic if speed hadn't been emphasised.

KEY PHRASES

The table below should help you remember the key study by Baddeley related to encoding in STM and LTM. Fill in the second and third columns.

	Example	Affects STM or LTM?
Acoustically similar		
Acoustically dissimilar		
Semantically similar		
Semantically dissimilar		

On a separate piece of paper, use your key points to answer the following exam questions.

- Outline how psychologists have investigated encoding in memory. *(4 marks)*
- Outline what research has shown about the encoding in memory. *(4 marks)*

FILL IN THE BLANKS

One limitation of Baddeley's study is that (1) .... stimuli were used.

This means we should be cautious about generalising the findings to

(2) .... For example, if people were processing

meaningful information they might use semantic encoding even for STM tasks. This means

that this study only tells us a limited amount about (3) ....

One limitation of this study was that the LTM memory task wasn't very long term. The LTM

task only lasted (4) .... It is possible that different kinds of encoding

processes are involved when information is stored for (5) ....

However the study does clearly show there is a difference over time.

Answers on page 189

An idea

The study by Brandimote *et al.* involved asking participants to subtract one shape from another, and then recall the resultant shape.
Draw the images that you get when you subtract item 2 from item 1 in each row.
Try to develop some further test images and use these to conduct your own research.

MATCH THEM UP

1	Duration	A	Transforming incoming information into a form that can be stored in memory.
2	Capacity	B	The length of time memory holds information.
3	Encoding	C	A measure of how much can be held in memory.

Answers on page 189

DRAWING CONCLUSIONS

A group of psychology students repeat Baddeley's study and their findings are shown below.

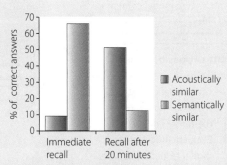

State **two** findings and for each one draw a conclusion (state what the finding shows):

Finding 1:

Conclusion 1: This shows that …

Finding 2:

Conclusion 2: This shows that …

Answers on page 189

KEY WORDS

- Brain scanning
- Capacity
- Decay
- Displacement
- Duration
- Encoding
- Hippocampus
- Long-term memory (LTM)
- Multi-store model (MSM)
- Prefrontal cortex
- Sensory memory (SM)
- Short-term memory (STM)

Possible essay question ...

Outline and evaluate the multi-store model of memory.
(12 marks)

Other possible exam questions ...

+ Give a brief outline of the multi-store model of memory. *(3 marks)*
+ Evaluate the multi-store model of memory. *(6 marks)*
+ Apply this knowledge to ... *(6 marks)*

⭐ **Exam tip**

You will never be asked more than 6 marks' worth of description or 6 marks' worth of evaluation.
6 marks' worth is about 150 words.

MUST know ...

Sensory memory	Duration: Milliseconds Capacity: Very large Encoding: Auditory for hearing, visual for sight, etc.
Short-term memory	Duration: Less than 18 seconds Capacity: Limited, 7 ± 2 items or chunks Encoding: Mainly acoustic
Long-term memory	Duration: Potentially forever Capacity: Very large Encoding: Mainly semantic

 Research evidence supports the MSM ...

... showing the existence of STM and LTM as separate stores.

- **E** – Beardsley used brain scanning and found that the prefrontal cortex is active during STM but not LTM tasks.

Another study that supports the MSM ...

... was the case study of HM.

- **E** – His hippocampi were removed which led to an inability to transfer STM to LTM.

 One criticism is that the ...

... MSM is a very simplified model of memory.

- **E** – STM can be further subdivided into verbal and visual stores, as suggested by the working memory model (see page 36).

SHOULD know ...

In addition to the three stores, there are two key *processes* in the MSM:

1. Attention

Information first arrives at SM.

Attention causes information to be transferred to STM.

2. Rehearsal

Information in STM is in a fragile state. It disappears through decay or displacement:

- It disappears if it is not rehearsed (decay).
- It disappears if new information enters (displacement).

Verbal rehearsal maintains information in STM ((information is repeated over and over again).

Increasing verbal rehearsal leads to transfer from STM to LTM; the more rehearsal of an item the better it is remembered. This is called maintenance rehearsal.

- **E** – Squire *et al.* also used brain scanning and found the hippocampus is active when LTM is engaged.
- **L** – This research shows that different areas of the brain are active when people are doing STM tasks or LTM tasks.

- **E** – HM was still able to remember things that occurred prior to the operation, i.e. his long-term memory was not affected by the operation.
- **L** – This shows there is a distinction between short- and long-term memories.

- **E** – Research has shown that LTM can be subdivided into different kinds of memory, including semantic, episodic and procedural memory (Schachter *et al.*).
- **L** – The MSM just has one STM store and one LTM store.

COULD know ...

Updated MSM

Shiffrin updated the original MSM in response to criticisms about the process of rehearsal.

In the original model, information was transferred from STM to LTM through the process of verbal 'maintenance' rehearsal.

Shiffrin suggested that rehearsal could also be elaborative, i.e. processing information deeply. Such elaboration leads to more enduring memories.

 The importance of elaboration was supported ...

... in a study by Craik and Tulving.

- **E** – In their study participants were given tasks that involved shallow or deep processing – asked whether a word was printed in capital letters (shallow) or asked whether the word fitted in a sentence (deep).
- **E** – The participants remembered more words in the task involving deep processing rather than shallow processing.
- **L** – This shows that elaborative processing is a key process in memory.

COMPLETE THE DIAGRAM

This is a diagram of Atkinson and Shiffrin's multi-store model of memory.

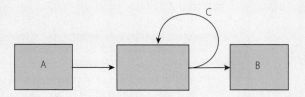

In the list below, fill the correct letter in the three appropriate boxes in the list.

Long-term memory	☐
Encoding	☐
Rehearsal loop	☐
Short-term memory	☐
Sensory memory	☐
Primary memory	☐

Answers on page 189

MATCH THEM UP

1	Beardsley brain scanning	**A**	Visual and verbal stores.
2	STM can be separated into	**B**	Prefrontal cortex active during STM tasks.
3	HM	**C**	Hippocampi removed.
4	Squire *et al.* brain scanning	**D**	Semantic, episodic and procedural memory.
5	LTM can be separated into	**E**	Hippocampus active during LTM tasks.

Answers on page 189

APPLYING YOUR KNOWLEDGE

Mr Bill is a salesman. He visits different companies selling products. It is important that his clients remember all the things he tells them about the advantages of his products and the prices.

Use the multi-store model to explain how he might improve his clients' memory of what he tells them. *(4 marks)*

Identify the psychology	Link to Mr Bill
The MSM suggests …	This means that Mr Bill should …
The MSM suggests …	This means that Mr Bill should …

Suggested answers on page 189

PRACTICE ELABORATION

Fill in the boxes to answer this exam question:
Evaluate the multi-store model of memory. *(6 marks)*

(1) One strength of the MSM is …	Give some evidence or an example.	Link back …
(2) One weakness of the MSM is …	**Give some evidence or an example.**	**Link back …**

SPOT THE MISTAKES

Read this student answer to the following exam question:
Describe the multi-store model of memory. *(6 marks)*

There are 4 mistakes, draw a circle round each.

The multi-store model consists of two stores. One store is short-term memory. Information in short-term memory has a very limited duration of less then 5 seconds. Short-term memory also has a limited capacity. It is said to hold 7 plus or minus 2 items. Once information is in the short-term memory it can be rehearsed and then passed into long-term memory. Long-term memory holds information for weeks, months or years. It never disappears. An important difference between short-term and long-term memory is that information is usually in a semantic form in short-term memory though it may also be visual.

Answers on page 189

See page 20 for an explanation of the 'two-pronged attack' needed to answer 'applying your knowledge' questions.

KEY WORDS

- Articulatory process
- Articulatory suppression task
- Central executive
- Dual-task performance
- Episodic buffer
- Inner scribe
- Phonological loop (PL)
- Phonological store
- Visual cache
- Visuo-spatial sketchpad (VSS)
- Word-length effect
- Working memory model (WMM)

Possible essay question ...

Outline and evaluate the working memory model.
(12 marks)

Other possible exam questions ...

+ Outline the working memory model. *(6 marks)*
+ Outline **one** limitation of the working memory model. *(4 marks)*
+ Apply this knowledge to ... *(6 marks)*

⭐ Exam tip

Students always find the WMM model more difficult that the MSM, yet they are fairly similar – a bunch of different stores. Possibly one of the things that makes the WMM more challenging is the more complex names for the stores.

MUST know ...

Baddeley and Hitch proposed a model for how information is processed and stored when working on *current* tasks.

For example, solving a maths problem or deciding which bus to catch.

Central executive

The central executive monitors incoming data and allocates 'slave systems' to tasks.

It has a very limited storage capacity.

Slave systems

1 **Phonological loop (PL)** – for auditory information, e.g. memorising a list of words.
2 **Visuo-spatial sketchpad (VSS)** – for visual and/or spatial information, e.g. counting how many windows your house has.
3 **Episodic buffer** – integrates information.

 One strength is the research support ...

... such as case studies of brain damaged patients.

- **E** – Shallice and Warrington studied patient KF whose working memory for visual stimuli but not verbal material was intact, e.g. he could recall letters and digits but not sounds.

 Further research support comes from ...

... a study by Baddeley *et al.*

- **E** – They showed that people find it more difficult to remember a list of long words (such as 'association') rather than short words (such as 'table') – called the *word-length effect*.

 One limitation of the WMM is ....

... that some components are not well defined.

- **E** – Cognitive psychologists suggest the description of the central executive is unsatisfactory and doesn't really explain anything.

SHOULD know ...

Dual-task activity

The WMM explains dual-task performance.

For example, performance of a visual task is slower when a second simultaneous task is visual than if the second simultaneous task is auditory.

Two simultaneous visual tasks interfere with each other whereas visual and auditory ones don't.

Baddeley and Hitch proposed the PL is subdivided into:

- Phonological store – auditory information is recorded but decays over time.
- Articulatory process – allows maintenance rehearsal (repeating sounds or words to keep them in WM to avoid decay).

Logie proposed the VSS is subdivided into:

- Visual cache – stores information about visual items, e.g. form and colour.
- Inner scribe – stores the *arrangement* of objects in the visual field.

- **L** – This suggests that just KF's phonological loop had been damaged, leaving other areas of memory intact.
- **E** – However, evidence from brain-damaged patients may not be reliable because it concerns unique cases who have had traumatic experiences.

- **E** – This occurs because there is a finite space for rehearsal in the articulatory process (probably equivalent to about 2 seconds of speech).
- **L** – The word-length effect disappears if a person is given an articulatory suppression task (a repetitive task that ties up the articulatory process), demonstrating the existence of the articulatory process.

- **E** – The central executive needs to be more clearly specified rather than just being described as 'similar to attention'.
- **L** – There may not be just one central executive but instead many separate components.

COULD know ...

More detail for the episodic buffer

This is a temporary store for information, integrating the visual, spatial and verbal information processed by other slave systems.

It also maintains a sense of time sequencing – basically recording events (episodes) that are happening.

The episodic buffer sends information to LTM.

A second limitation of the WMM is ...

... it doesn't offer a full account of memory.

- **E** – The WMM focuses on STM alone and offers no insights into sensory memory or LTM.
- **E** – The WMM also does not explain changes in processing ability that occur as the result of practice or time.
- **L** – However, it does offer a basis of conducting research in order to develop a fuller model.

✓ A MARKING EXERCISE

Read the student answers to the following exam question:
Outline the working memory model. *(4 marks)*

David's answer

The working memory model consists of four features. These are the central executive, phonological look, visuo-spatial sketchpad and episodic buffer. The central executive controls the other three features and holds no information, just distributes it. The phonological loop consists of two separate stores – the phonological store which processes the words you hear and the articulatory loop which processes written words. It is called a loop because it continuously loops words.

Betty's answer

The working memory model was proposed by Baddeley and Hitch. The aim of the working memory model is to describe a more accurate explanation of STM. They said that STM was made up of the articulatory process, phonological loop, central executive, visuo-spatial sketchpad and episodic buffer. The episodic buffer was added more recently and was used to describe a store that could integrate all sorts of different kinds of information.

What mark do you think each answer would get?

Your comments on David's answer:

....

....

....

David would get _____ out of 4 marks

Your comments on Betty's answer:

....

....

....

Betty would get _____ out of 4 marks

Answers on page 189

You can read marking guidelines on page 10.

✐ COMPLETE THE TABLE

To help prepare an answer to the exam question above, fill in the table below:

Component of WMM	Description

✐ FILL IN THE BLANKS

One strength of the WMM is the research support such as case studies of

(1) .... One case study involved a patient called KF

studied by (2) .... KF's working memory was intact for

(3) .... but not (4) ....

Further research support comes from a study by Baddeley *et al.* of the

(5) .... effect. They showed that people find it more difficult

to remember (6) .... than

(7) .... One weakness of the WMM is that some components

are not (8) .... For example, cognitive psychologists

suggest that the (9) .... is unsatisfactory and doesn't really

explain anything.

Answers on page 189

⚙ APPLYING YOUR KNOWLEDGE

The psychology		Link the psychology to the research findings described
Identify and outline a component of the WMM	Research has shown that people perform a visual task more slowly if they are simultaneously required to perform a second visual task. However, their performance is not slower if they have to perform one visual and one verbal task simultaneously.	
	Explain how such research findings can be explained by the working memory model. Refer to different parts of the working memory model in your answer. *(4 marks)*	

Answers on page 189

KEY WORDS

- Eyewitness testimony (EWT)
- False memory
- Misleading information
- Post-event information

Possible essay question ...

Outline and evaluate research into the effects of misleading information on the accuracy of eyewitness testimony. *(12 marks)*

Other possible exam questions ...

+ Explain what is meant by eyewitness testimony. *(2 marks)*
+ Explain what is meant by misleading information. *(2 marks)*
+ Outline what research has shown about the effects of misleading information on the accuracy of eyewitness testimony. *(4 marks)*
+ Outline **one** research study on the effects of misleading information on the accuracy of eyewitness testimony. *(6 marks)*
+ Apply this knowledge to ... *(6 marks)*

MUST know ...

Key study: Loftus and Palmer

How?

Participants, 45 American college students, were shown film clips of traffic accidents.

Questions afterwards included a critical one: 'About how fast were the cars travelling when they <verb> each other?'

There were five groups of participants, each were given a different verb: 'hit', 'smashed', 'collided', 'bumped' or 'contacted'.

Showed?

The group given the verb 'smashed' estimated the highest speed (mean 40.8 mph).

The group given the word 'contacted' estimated the lowest speed (mean 31.8 mph).

This supports the view that misleading information (post-event information) can have a significant effect on memory.

EVALUATION — *The study lacked ecological validity ...*

... because Loftus and Palmer just showed people a film of a car accident rather than seeing how they would respond if watching an actual accident.

- **E** – Participants may not take the experimental task as seriously as they would if they were to witness an actual accident.

EVALUATION — *There are real-world applications ...*

... because EWT is often relied upon by police.

- **E** – A review in 2003 found that mistaken eyewitness identification was the largest single factor in convicting innocent people (Wells and Olsen).

EVALUATION — *The findings were supported ...*

... in a further study by Loftus.

- **E** – Participants were shown pictures of stop or 'yield' traffic signs and then asked questions that were consistent with the pictures (i.e. not misleading) or inconsistent (i.e. misleading).

SHOULD know ...

Second study: Loftus and Palmer

How?

This study followed on from the first study, aiming to see whether misleading information alters storage or retrieval.

Participants were 150 American college students, who saw a film of a car accident and were asked a question about the speed.

There were three groups: one given the verb 'smashed', one given the verb 'hit' and a control group with no question.

Participants were asked more questions a week later, including whether there was any broken glass.

Showed?

Those who heard the question with 'smashed' were more likely to remember broken glass (there was none) than the other two groups.

The responses about the broken glass for the 'hit' and the control group were about the same.

This shows that post-event information affects initial storage.

- **E** – This was supported in a study (by Yuille and Cutshall) where participants witnessed a real-life armed robbery. Interviews included misleading questions yet recall of events was accurate four months later.
- **L** – This suggests that EWT in the real world may not always be inaccurate.

- **E** – Loftus and Palmer's research was important in convincing people that EWT is unreliable and has led to changes in the reliance on EWT in court cases.
- **L** – This demonstrates the value of this research in real-life situations rather than just in the laboratory.

- **E** – Loftus *et al.* found that final identification of the original photos was most accurate when the questions had been consistent.
- **L** – This shows that misleading information (inconsistent questions) does affect accuracy of recall.

COULD know ...

Third study: Braun *et al.*

How?

167 college students were asked to evaluate advertising material about Disneyland. Embedded in this material was misleading information about either Bugs Bunny or Ariel (neither character could have been seen at Disneyland because Bugs is not Disney and Ariel hadn't been introduced at the time of their childhood).

Participants were assigned to the Bugs, Ariel or control condition (no misleading information). All had visited Disneyland.

Showed?

Participants in the Bugs or Ariel group were more likely to report having shaken hands with these characters than the control group.

This shows how misleading information can create a false memory.

EVALUATION — This supports Loftus and Palmer's research ...

... because it shows that storage was affected by misleading information.

- **E** – The misleading information in the ads led participants to alter their existing memories.
- **E** – The 'new' false memories generated expectations about the participants' experiences.
- **L** – Such research on false memories supports the view that misleading information can create unreliable eyewitness testimony.

KEY PHRASES

Select key phrases to help you remember the key study by Loftus and Palmer.

A few have been done for you.

How?	Showed?
45 college students	Smashed was highest
	40.8 mph

On a separate piece of paper, use your key words to answer the following exam questions:

- Outline how psychologists have investigated the effects of misleading information on the accuracy of eyewitness testimony. *(4 marks)*
- Outline what research has shown about the effects of misleading information on the accuracy of eyewitness testimony. *(4 marks)*

MATCH THEM UP

1	Loftus and Palmer's study lacked ecological validity because …	**A**	Mistaken testimony often leads to wrongful convictions.
2	Loftus and Palmer's study …	**B**	How fast were the cars travelling when they <verb> each other?
3	Braun tested the effect of misleading information by …	**C**	Misleading information affects the initial storage of information.
4	In Yuille and Cutshall's study ….	**D**	The car accident wasn't actually happening as participants watched.
5	Research on the effect of misleading information has real-world application because ….	**E**	Give very low speed estimates.
6	The critical question in Loftus and Palmer's study was …	**F**	Real-life witnesses were interviewed.
7	The study where they asked about broken glass showed that …	**G**	Used American college students.
8	The verb 'contacted' led participants to …	**H**	Giving information that suggested Bugs Bunny was at Disneyland.

Answers on page 189

DRAWING CONCLUSIONS

The graph below shows the findings from the second study by Loftus and Palmer.

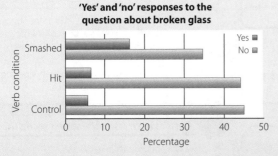

'Yes' and 'no' responses to the question about broken glass

State **two** findings and for each one draw a conclusion (state what the finding shows):

Finding 1:
Conclusion 1: This shows that …
Finding 2:
Conclusion 2: This shows that …

Answers on page 189

 CIRCLE TRUE OR FALSE

T or F The verb 'bumped' was used in both studies by Loftus and Palmer.

T or F Loftus and Palmer found that the verb 'smashed' led to the highest estimates of speed.

T or F Lab studies have shown that eyewitness testimony is unreliable.

T or F Studies of real-life eyewitness testimony have shown that eyewitness testimony is unreliable.

T or F Eyewitness testimony has been found to be the largest single factor in convicting innocent people.

T or F Research suggests that misleading information affects the retrieval of information at the time of questioning.

Answers on page 189

APPLYING YOUR KNOWLEDGE

Mary was a witness to a theft on a train. She was interviewed by the police. Explain why the following question is an example of misleading information:

'How tall was the man who committed this crime?'

Explanation:

Answer on page 189

KEY WORDS
- Weapon focus effect
- Yerkes–Dodson effect

Possible essay question ...
Outline and evaluate research into the effects of anxiety on the accuracy of eyewitness testimony. *(12 marks)*

Other possible exam questions ...
+ Outline how psychologists have investigated the effects of anxiety on the accuracy of eyewitness testimony. *(4 marks)*
+ Outline what research has shown about the effects of anxiety on the accuracy of eyewitness testimony. *(4 marks)*
+ Outline **one** research study on the effects of anxiety on the accuracy of eyewitness testimony. *(6 marks)*
+ Apply this knowledge to ... *(6 marks)*

MUST know ...

Key study: Johnson and Scott

How?
While sitting in a waiting room, participants heard an argument in an adjoining room.

Condition 1 – a man runs through a room carrying a pen covered in grease (low anxiety).

Condition 2 – the man holds a knife covered in blood (high anxiety, 'weapon focus').

Participants were later asked to identify the man from a set of photographs.

Showed?
Mean accuracy was 49% in identifying the man in the pen condition, compared to 33% accuracy in the knife condition.

This shows that high anxiety reduces accuracy of face recognition.

It also suggests that anxiety may focus attention on central features of a crime (e.g. the weapon) and thus reduce recall of details (e.g. of perpetrator's face).

There is research that supports ...

... the weapons focus effect.

- **E** – Studies show that eyewitnesses do look more at a weapon than at other features of the crime scene which would reduce the accuracy of what they recall.

There is evidence that challenges ...

... the view that anxiety reduces accuracy of EWT.

- **E** – Rinolo *et al.* considered the EWT of survivors of the *Titanic*, who were in a state of considerable anxiety, nevertheless their reports were accurate.

SHOULD know ...

Second study: Christiansen and Hubinette

How?
The researchers conducted interviews with 58 eyewitnesses of Swedish bank robberies.

The witnesses were either victims (bank teller) or bystanders (employee or customer), i.e. high and low anxiety respectively.

The interviews were conducted 4–15 months after the robberies.

Showed?
All witness reports were consistent with previous reports to police.

All witnesses showed generally good memories for details of the robbery itself (better than 75% accurate recall). Victims had the best recall of all.

Self-rated emotional anxiety was not related to good memory performance.

This study generally shows that anxiety does not reduce accuracy of recall.

- **E** – For example, Loftus *et al.* used eye-tracking to record eye movements and found that eyewitnesses did look more at the weapon rather than the 'criminal's' face.
- **L** – This shows that raised anxiety may indeed reduce the accuracy information from eyewitnesses.

- **E** – At the time of the sinking 75% of the survivors reported that the ship broke in two when it sank. When the wreck was found the survivors were proved right.
- **L** – This supports the view that anxiety does not necessarily result in inaccurate recall.

Christiansen and Hubinette's study ...

... was flawed in certain respects.

- **E** – The information on emotional anxiety may be unreliable because it was based on self-report.
- **E** – The findings may not be true for non-violent crimes. Halford *et al.* found that victims of violent crimes were more accurate in their recall of crime scene information than victims of non-violent crimes.
- **L** – This challenges the generalisability of these findings to all EWT.

COULD know ...

Third study: Deffenbacher *et al.*

How?
Deffenbacher *et al.* conducted a meta-analysis, analysing 18 studies of anxiety and the accuracy of EWT.

In total this covered almost 2,000 participants.

Showed?
High anxiety conditions generally led to reduced accuracy in recall.

There are individual differences, e.g. adult witnesses were less accurate when anxious but the same was not true for children.

However, some studies showed that anxiety was not associated with reduced accuracy.

We can explain the apparent contradiction ...

... in studies that find positive or negative effects.

- **E** – It may be that there isn't a simple linear relationship between anxiety and accuracy (correlations can be linear, i.e. in a line, or in a curve).
- **E** – The *Yerkes–Dodson model* proposes a U-shaped relationship: both low and high levels of anxiety produce poor performance; moderate levels of anxiety produce good performance.
- **L** – Such models explain why anxiety is not always linked to poor recall.

FILL IN THE BLANKS

Johnson and Scott conducted a study on the effects of anxiety on EWT. Participants were sat in a waiting room when they (1) .... There were (2) .... conditions in this study. The low anxiety group of participants (condition 1) saw a man running through the room with a (3) .... The other group of participants (condition 2) saw a man holding (4) .... This was the (5) .... anxiety condition. Participants were later asked to identify the man's face. In the low anxiety condition they were (6) .... accurate and in the high anxiety condition they were (7) .... accurate. This shows that high anxiety (8) .... accuracy. High anxiety may focus attention on a (9) .... instead of the perpetrator's face. This is called the (10) .... effect.

Answers on page 189

A MARKING EXERCISE

Read the student answer to the following exam question:

Outline one study that has investigated the effect of anxiety on eyewitness testimony. *(6 marks)*

Christianson and Hubinette did a study looking at a real-life bank robbery. They interviewed people that were threatened and those who were not directly threatened to see if anxiety affected eyewitness testimony. Those who are directly threatened will be more anxious than those not directly threatened.

This answer was awarded 2 out of 6 marks. Why do you think it got this mark?

Suggest **two** pieces of information that could be added to improve this answer:

1 ....
....

2 ....
....

Answers on page 189

FILL IN THE BOXES

Finish the sentences in columns 2 and 3.

Anxiety reduces accuracy of EWT.	One piece of evidence for this is …	This suggests that …
Anxiety enhances accuracy of EWT.	One piece of evidence for this is …	This suggests that …
Anxiety may sometimes reduce and sometimes enhance the accuracy of EWT.	One explanation for this contradiction is …	This suggests that …

Answers on page 189

JUMBLED SENTENCES

Here are three criticisms linked to the Must and Should studies on the facing page. However, the sentences making up these criticisms have been jumbled up. Sort them into order, using the information on the facing page to help you. The first one has been done for you.

Criticism 1

2	**1** This shows that raised anxiety may indeed reduce accuracy information from eyewitnesses.
	2 There is research that supports the weapon focus effect.
	3 This would reduce their accuracy.
	4 Studies show that eyewitnesses do look more at a weapon than at other features of the crime scene.
	5 For example, Loftus *et al.* used eye-tracking to examine eyewitnesses' eye movements.

Criticism 2

	6 Rinolo *et al.* considered the EWT of survivors of the *Titanic*, who were in a state of considerable anxiety, nevertheless their reports were accurate.
	7 There is evidence that challenges the view that anxiety reduces accuracy of EWT.
	8 This supports the view that anxiety does not necessarily result in inaccurate recall.
	9 At the time of the sinking 75% of the survivors reported that the ship broke in two when it sank. When the wreck was found the survivors were proved right.

Criticism 3

	10 Christiansen and Hubinette's study was flawed in certain respects.
	11 The findings may not be true for non-violent crimes.
	12 The information on emotional stress may be unreliable because it was based on self-report.
	13 This challenges the generalisability of these findings to all EWT.
	14 Halford *et al.* found that victims of violent crimes to be more accurate than victims of non-violent crimes.

Answers on page 189

Possible essay question …

Outline and evaluate research into the effects of age of witness on the accuracy of eyewitness testimony. *(12 marks)*

Other possible exam questions …

+ Outline how psychologists have investigated the effects of age of witness on the accuracy of eyewitness testimony. *(4 marks)*

+ Outline what research has shown about the effects of age of witness on the accuracy of eyewitness testimony. *(4 marks)*

+ Outline **one** research study on the effects of age of witness on the accuracy of eyewitness testimony. *(6 marks)*

+ Apply this knowledge to … *(6 marks)*

MUST know …

Key study: Yarmey

How?

The study was conducted in various public places.

A young woman stopped 651 adults and spoke to them for 15 seconds.

Two minutes later the adults were unexpectedly asked to recall the physical characteristics of the young woman.

Showed?

Three age groups were considered: young adults (aged 18–29), middle-aged (30–44) and older (45–65).

Recall was best in the younger adults and worst in the older adults.

Young and middle-aged adults were significantly more confident about their recall.

There were significant correlations between confidence and accuracy of recall.

 The findings may not be generalisable …

… because the 'victim' was a young woman.

- ***E*** – Research has found that people are more accurate when recalling the details of someone of the same age group (the 'own-age bias').

 There may be extraneous variables …

… such as confidence.

- ***L*** – The reason the younger participants were more accurate might be because they were also more confident.

SHOULD know …

Second study: Parker and Carranza

How?

48 primary school children and 48 college students were shown a slide sequence of a mock crime.

This was followed by target-present or target-absent photo identification with a no-choice option, central and peripheral questions related to the crime, and a second photo identification.

Showed?

Child witnesses had a higher rate of making selections than adult witnesses, suggesting that children are more willing to respond.

This was further supported in the questioning task where adults made significantly more 'don't know' choices.

Child witnesses were less accurate in line-ups when the 'target' was absent, but there were no differences between age groups in the line-ups when the 'target' was present.

- ***E*** – Anastasi and Rhodes found that each age group (young, middle-aged and old) was most accurate when identifying photographs of people from their own age group.
- ***L*** – This bias might explain why the young adults did best in Parker and Carranza's study – because they were recalling the details of a young woman.

- ***E*** – This would mean that younger participants might just be more willing to take a chance and say whatever was in their mind, whereas the older participants were less forthcoming with information.
- ***L*** – Their enhanced accuracy would be due to confidence rather than age differences.

 Parker and Carranza's findings have …

… been supported by other research studies.

- ***E*** – For example, Goodman and Reed found that children (aged 6–8) were not less accurate than older participants but were more suggestible.
- ***E*** – 'Suggestibility' means the tendency to accept the suggestions made by others.
- ***L*** – These findings mean that it is especially important to avoid misleading information when questioning children to ensure accuracy.

COULD know …

Third study: Memon *et al.*

How?

Young adults (aged 16–33) and older adults (60–82) were tested on ability to identify the perpetrator.

Participants viewed two videotaped incidents, one with a young perpetrator and one with an older perpetrator.

Showed?

When the test delay was short (35 minutes), there was no difference in the accuracy of the two age groups.

However, when test delay was long (one week), the older witnesses were significantly less accurate.

 One explanation for this might be …

… the source-recollection hypothesis.

- ***E*** – Research has shown that older adults have increased difficulty remembering specific details of a crime (e.g. Johnson *et al.*).
- ***E*** – Such impairments increase over time.
- ***L*** – This would explain why older adults' accuracy declines over time.

KEY PHRASES

Select key phrases to help you remember the key study by Yarmey.

A few have been done for you.

How?	Showed?
Public	Younger best
15 seconds	

On a separate piece of paper, use your key words to answer the following exam questions:

• Outline how psychologists have investigated the effects of age on eyewitness testimony. *(4 marks)*
• Outline what research has shown about the effects of age on eyewitness testimony. *(4 marks)*

A MARKING EXERCISE

Read the student answer to the following exam question:

Outline and evaluate research into the effects of age on eyewitness testimony. *(8 marks)*

A study was undertaken where participants on the street were asked to describe a young woman who had just walked past. Each participant had to recall the woman and the youngest adults did best, therefore showing that age affected immediate recall. Although this study was a natural experiment participants may have been aware when being asked to describe a woman as this isn't an everyday task therefore it lacks ecological validity. It also has low ecological validity because it was difficult to control the extraneous variables so it would be difficult to replicate. Throughout many studies a factor called own-age bias was discovered. This would affect recall on eyewitness testimony because if the witness was 17 then they are more likely to recognise a criminal of age 17 due to own-age bias. Again if a 75 year old saw a criminal age 75 they would be more likely to identify them accurately than a 17 year old due to own-age bias. In another study participants watched a video of a car accident and were told to come back a week later. They recalled information accurately. This study lacked ecological validity because the participants watched a video and therefore weren't emotionally involved. Also it didn't take into account individual differences.

Task 1: This student has not separated the essay into paragraphs. Insert stars to indicate where new paragraphs could start.

Task 2: Colour in the sentences that are evaluation.

Task 3: What mark would you give this answer?

A01 = ... out of 4

A02 = ... out of 4

Answers on pages 189 and 190

You can read the marking guidelines on pages 10 and 12.

APPLYING YOUR KNOWLEDGE

The police were called to a corner shop where there had been a robbery. There was one eyewitness, an older woman aged about 50. She told the police the robber was a young lad aged about 20.

Explain how the age of the witness might have affected the accuracy of the eyewitness testimony for this event. Refer to psychological research in your answer. *(4 marks)*

Outline an explanation of how the witness' recall might be affected by her age in the context of this robbery	Link to psychological research
Explanation 1 …	This is supported by research …
Explanation 2 …	This is supported by research …

Answers on page 190

DRAWING CONCLUSIONS

The table on the right shows the findings from the own-age bias study by Anastasi and Rhodes.

State **two** findings and for each one draw a conclusion (state what the finding shows):

Finding 1:
Conclusion 1: This shows that …
Finding 2:
Conclusion 2: This shows that …

Table showing % correct recognition

	Young photographs	Middle-aged photographs	Older photographs
Young participants	90	87	85
Middle-aged participants	85	93	87
Older participants	56	62	66

Answers on page 190

KEY WORDS

- Cognitive interview (CI)
- Standard interview

Possible essay question ...
Outline and evaluate the cognitive interview. *(12 marks)*

Other possible exam questions ...

+ Outline **one** technique used in the cognitive interview. *(3 marks)*
+ Outline the cognitive interview. *(6 marks)*
+ Evaluate the cognitive interview. *(6 marks)*
+ Apply this knowledge to ... *(6 marks)*

MUST know ...

Fisher and Gieselman developed the following techniques based on psychological research related to effective memory recall techniques.

1 Report everything

Witnesses are encouraged to include every single detail of the event, even though it may seem irrelevant.

2 Mental reinstatement of context

The witness should imagine the environment and people from the original incident.

3 Changing the order

Events should be recalled from the final point back to the beginning, or from the middle to the beginning.

4 Changing the perspective

Witnesses should recall the incident as it would have appeared to other witnesses or the perpetrator present at the time.

 The CI has proved effective ...

... as shown in research studies.

- **E** – Köhnken *et al.* conducted a meta-analysis of 53 studies and found a 34% increase in the amount of correct information recalled using CI compared with using a standard interview technique.

 The CI may be particularly effective ...

... with older witnesses.

- **E** – Older witnesses are overcautious about reporting what they saw.

 There are problems in doing research ...

... because many different versions of the CI are used.

- **E** – The Thames Valley Police Force don't include 'changing perspectives'.

SHOULD know ...

Techniques 1 and 2 aim to increase the consistency between the actual event and the recreated situation.

This should lead to an increased likeliness that witnesses will recall more details, and be more accurate in their recall.

Techniques 3 and 4 aim to vary the route through memory in order to increase accuracy of recall.

This is successful because such methods of recall remove the effects of 'scripts' (a person's memory for routine activities – once a 'script' is triggered elements of a scene are filled in without thinking).

- **E** – Milne and Bull found that using only one of the techniques didn't produce better results but using both techniques 1 and 2 gave better recall.
- **L** – This suggests that the success of the CI technique relies on using at least two of the techniques at any time.

- **E** – Mello and Fisher found greater improvements using the CI with older rather than younger participants, but there were no differences when using the standard interview.
- **L** – This means the CI should be prioritised with older witnesses but is less important with younger witnesses.

- **E** – Other forces just use 'report everything' and 'reinstate context' (Kebbell and Wagstaff).
- **L** – This makes it difficult to demonstrate effectiveness because each police force uses their own version.

COULD know ...

The enhanced CI

The enhanced CI was developed more recently.

It includes more focus on the social dynamics of the interaction, e.g. knowing when to establish and relinquish eye contact.

It also includes techniques for improving information output, e.g. starting with open-ended questions and moving on to more direct ones based on previous answers.

Focused imagery is also included where witnesses are encouraged to repeatedly probe their mental images.

 Police are reluctant to use the CI ...

... because it takes much more time than a standard interview.

- **E** – Kebbel and Wagstaff found that police officers prefer to use strategies that limit the amount of information collected.
- **E** – The enhanced CI places even greater demands on the interviewer and training is often inadequate.
- **L** – This means that police tend to fall back on standard techniques.

FILL IN THE BLANKS

Select **two** techniques used in the cognitive interview and fill in the boxes below in relation to your chosen techniques.

Technique	Brief outline	For example …

CIRCLE TRUE OR FALSE

T or F There are greater improvements in recall with older participants when using the CI.

T or F Generally police forces use all four techniques of the CI.

T or F Fisher and Gieselman first developed the CI technique.

T or F Police tend to prefer to use the standard interview because the CI takes more time.

T or F Using the CI means that the influence of 'scripts' will be enhanced.

T or F Milne and Bull found that using just one technique produced the best recall.

T or F The CI aims to increase accuracy of recall by increasing the amount that is recalled.

T or F The enhanced CI focuses on improving the quality of communication between interviewer and witness.

T or F There is only one version of the CI.

Answers on page 190

DRAWING CONCLUSIONS

Select **one** evaluation point from the facing page and write it out in your own words below.

Underline key words to help you remember the point.

S	
E	
E	
L	

See page 14 for an explanation of how to S E E L.

APPLYING YOUR KNOWLEDGE

Briefly outline a technique	During one psychology lesson a man burst into the classroom and demanded to speak to the teacher. He told her that he was very angry about the way she had treated his son and continued shouting until the teacher managed to get him to leave.	Explain how it could be used with the students
	Afterwards the teacher asked her students to write down a description of everything they remembered.	
	Suggest how the teacher might use some of the techniques of the cognitive interview to question her students.	

Answers on page 190

KEY WORDS

- Acronyms
- Acrostics
- Chunking
- Keyword method
- Method of loci
- Mind maps

Possible essay question ...

Outline and evaluate strategies for memory improvement.
(12 marks)

Other possible exam questions ...

+ Outline **one** strategy for memory improvement.
  (3 marks)

+ Apply this knowledge to ...
  (6 marks)

MUST know ...

Method of loci

The learner associates material to be learned with different locations (such as places in their house or places along a familiar route).

Then the learner mentally retraces their steps to recall the items.

Mind maps

The main topic is placed in the centre and then branching links are made producing a unique visual appearance.

Imposes organisation of facts to be remembered.

Distinctiveness (e.g. different colours) aids recall.

Chunking

Capacity of memory increased by grouping items, as discussed on page 30. This is a form of organisation.

For example, phone numbers and post codes.

 Memory strategies are effective ...

... in studies of real-world application.

- **E** – For example, Down syndrome children who received training in memory improvement techniques (rehearsal and organisation) had significantly improved memory skills compared with a control group (Broadly and David).

Method of loci / mind maps are effective ...

... because they involve elaboration of the material to be remembered.

- **E** – Craik and Tulving's research showed that elaboration leads to more enduring memories.

There are limitations with this research ...

... because studies of memory strategies are often conducted in lab conditions.

- **E** – The materials in lab studies are not always the same as the kind of thing people have to actually remember, such as using word lists instead of names of students in your class.

SHOULD know ...

Acronyms and acrostics

Acronyms involve constructing a word(s) to represent the first letter of each word to be remembered, e.g. ROY G. BIV for the colours of the rainbow: Red, Orange, Yellow, Green, Blue, Indigo, Violet.

An acrostic is where a new sentence is constructed out of each of the first letters, e.g. My Very Easy Method Just Speeds Up Naming Planets is used to remember the order of the planets: Mercury, Venus, Earth, Mars, Jupiter, Saturn, Uranus, Neptune, Pluto.

Rhymes

Encoding information with a tune enhances recall – thinking of the tune brings the words into memory.

For example, the tune of *Twinkle Twinkle Little Star* is used to remember the letters of the alphabet.

- **E** – O'Hara *et al.* found that training in the use of mnemonic techniques (e.g. method of loci) has long-term memory benefits for older adults.
- **L** – Such research supports the effectiveness of memory strategies in improving memory.

- **E** – Craik and Tulving showed that words that were elaborated (deep processing, e.g. asking whether a word fitted in a sentence) were remembered better than words that were not elaborated (shallow processing, e.g. asking whether a word was printed in capital letters).
- **L** – This means that the success of such techniques could be due to the deeper processing they create.

- **E** – This is supported by Slavin, who found memory techniques that work in lab conditions don't work in 'real' contexts, e.g. in speaking foreign languages better.
- **L** – Therefore, the results of the studies may not apply to everyday life.

COULD know ...

Keyword method

This method is used when trying to associate two pieces of information.

For example, when learning a foreign language and wanting to remember a foreign word and its English equivalent.

You think of an image to link the two words: the Spanish word for 'horse' is 'caballo' ('cob-eye-yo'). The keyword could be 'eye', so you visualise a horse with a large eye riding on its back. Conjuring up the visual image should trigger the recall of the Spanish word.

 There is supporting evidence ...

... in a study of people using keywords.

- **E** – Atkinson found that participants using keywords learned significantly more Russian vocabulary than a control group not using the method.
- **E** – However, the long-term advantage of the keyword technique is less well supported.
- **L** – This might explain the fact that the keyword method has not been widely adopted.

A MARKING EXERCISE

Exam question:

Psychology students study strategies for memory improvement as part of their A level course. Explain how a student might use **one or more** of these strategies to revise effectively for exams. (4 marks)

Read the following student answer to this exam question:

A student could use the method of loci which is a memory improvement strategy. This involves the student placing the item they are trying to remember in an object they are familiar with or in the room with them. This method places a visual image with the item, making it easier for the student to remember.

The students could also do levels of processing devised by Craik and Lockhart. This involves reading about items they want to remember then making notes, they would then elaborate on these notes before going through it again.

Has this student displayed knowledge of strategies for memory improvement? **YES / NO**

Has this student applied this knowledge to the stem? **YES/ NO**

MARK

.... out of 4

Answers on page 190

JUMBLED SENTENCES

You need to rearrange the sentences below into an order that makes sense, based on the information provided on the facing page. The first one has been done for you.

6	**1**	Capacity of memory increased by grouping items. This is a form of organisation.
	2	A fifth strategy is acrostics.
	3	A third strategy is chunking.
	4	Then the learner mentally retraces their steps to recall the items.
	5	A second strategy is mind maps.
	6	The first strategy for memory improvement is the method of loci.
	7	For example, My Very Easy Method Just Speeds Up Naming Planets is used to remember the order of the planets: Mercury, Venus, Earth, Mars, Jupiter, Saturn, Uranus, Neptune, Pluto.
	8	For example, ROYGBIV for the colours of the rainbow: Red, Orange, Yellow, Green, Blue, Indigo, Violet.
	9	This imposes organisation of facts to be remembered.
	10	The main topic is placed in the centre.
	11	A fourth strategy is acronyms.
	12	You construct a word(s) to represent first letter of each word to be remembered.
	13	Branching links are made producing a unique visual appearance.
	14	A new sentence is constructed out of each of the first letters.
	15	For example, phone numbers and post codes.
	16	The learner associates material to be learned with different locations.

Answers on page 190

APPLYING YOUR KNOWLEDGE

Mary has volunteered to present a school assembly. She plans to tell the students about an interesting psychological study. She is not allowed to use any prompts or written notes during her talk, so she is going to identify key words to be remembered.

Explain how Mary might use **one** memory strategy to revise effectively for exams. *(4 marks)*

Identify **one** memory strategy:

What is the material to be remembered?

With reference to the material to be remembered, explain how Mary would use the identified memory strategy:

Answers on page 190

DRAWING CONCLUSIONS

You can read about standard deviation on page 90.

A psychologist decides to conduct a study comparing different strategies for memory improvement. The participants in the study are children from a local school. One group of students use strategy A and a second group use strategy B. The results are shown below.

	Mean score of correct answers	Standard deviation
Strategy A	12	1.9
Strategy B	14	3.8

State **two** findings and for each one draw a conclusion (state what the finding shows):

Finding 1:

Conclusion 1: This shows that …

Finding 2:

Conclusion 2: This shows that …

Answers on page 190

MUST — Peterson and Peterson

HOW?
24 students
8 trials
consonant syllable
3 digit number
Counted backwards for between 3–18 secs, then tried to recall syllable

SHOWED?
Participants were, on average ...

after 3 secs ... 90% correct	after 9 secs ... 20% correct	after 18 secs ... 2% correct

∴ STM has very short duration

SHOULD — Bahrick et al.

CLASS of '75

HOW?
400 people 17–74
Tested on their memory of classmates in a yearbook

Photo recognition task → **SHOWED?** → Free recall test

90% accurate within 15 yrs of graduation
70% after 48 years

60% within 15 yrs
30% after 48 yrs

COULD — Nairne et al.

HOW?
Table   village   errand
    child   horse
Retention interval 0–96 secs
Errand   child   horse
    village   table

correct order

SHOWED?
Items could still be recalled in the correct order after 96 secs.
Information remains in STM provided no interference from other items.

EVALUATION

Study lacks ecological validity

Remembering consonant syllables doesn't reflect everyday memory activities.
However ...

This means that ...

Displacement not decay

Counting numbers in STM displaced syllables.
Reitman used tones ...

This suggests that ...

Bahrick's results may be due to rehearsal

Some participants may have looked at their yearbooks regularly.
In this case ...

This means that ...

Words rather than syllables
People may remember words more easily than nonsense syllables.

TOPIC 2 — *The capacity of memory*

MUST — Miller

HOW?

Made everyday observations.
Reviewed studies on the span of STM.

SHOWED?
Participants accurate for 7 dots/words, less so more than that. People can recall 5 words as well as they could 5 letters (chunking).

SHOULD — Jacobs

HOW?
42793

Er...42 7....

SHOWED?
Mean digit span — 9.3 for digits / 7.3 for letters
Improves with age — 6.6 digits at age 8 / 8.6 digits at 19
Better strategies with age (e.g. chunking).

COULD — Simon

HOW?
Dog
Dogma
Dogmatism
Tested recall of one, two and three syllable nouns.
Also ... familiar phrases.

SHOWED?
Shorter span for three syllables than one or two syllables.
Shorter span for longer phrases than shorter phrases.

EVALUATION

Miller overestimated STM capacity

Cowan reviewed research on STM and concluded it was 4 chunks not 7. *IT'S 4*

This finding was further supported ...

This means that ...

There are real-world applications
Baddeley used research on chunking to make recommendations for UK postcodes.

He found that ...

This shows that ...

Jacob's study is very old
It was conducted in **1897** so lacked the formal control found in modern research studies.

The instructions might have differed.

This might explain ...

Study may lack generalisability

GENERAL LISA BILITY

TOPIC 3 — Encoding in memory

MUST **Baddeley**

| ACOUSTICALLY SIMILAR | ACOUSTICALLY DISSIMILAR | SEMANTICALLY SIMILAR | SEMATICALLY DISSIMILAR |

HOW? Four groups heard five words. Then shown 10 words to select their five in correct order.

SHOWED?
STM – Acoustically similar lowest recall
LTM – Semantically similar lowest recall
Suggests STM acoustic encoding and LTM semantic.

SHOULD Brandimote et al.

HOW?

SHOWED?

COULD Frost

15 mins

HOW?

SHOWED?

EVALUATION

A limitation is the stimuli used in this study

CAUTION — ARTIFICIAL STIMULI USED

For example ...

This means that ...

LTM task not really <u>long term</u>

20 mins ≠ LONG-TERM MEMORY

It is possible that ...

However ...

Brandimote et al.'s study is supported by research

STM may use semantic code

WICKENS et al
FROST

LTM also uses visual coding

Therefore ...

Speed of response important

Requirement of quick decision affects the kind of information recalled.

TOPIC 4 — The multi-store model

MUST

SM → STM → LTM

Duration: MILLISECONDS
Capacity: VERY LARGE
Encoding: AUDITORY/VISUAL

Duration: LESS THAN 18 SECS
Capacity: LIMITED (7±2)
Encoding: MAINLY ACOUSTIC

Duration: POTENTIALLY FOREVER
Capacity: VERY LARGE
Encoding: MAINLY SEMANTIC

SHOULD

Rehearsal — Attention

COULD

NEW IMPROVED MSM NOW WITH ELABORATIVE REHEARSAL

EVALUATION

Research support for MSM

Prefrontal cortex

STM TASK   LTM TASK

Beardsley – prefrontal cortex active in STM task but not in LTM task.

Squire et al. found ...

This shows that ...

Case of HM supports MSM

After removal of his hippocampi ... HM could not transfer material from STM to LTM.
HM was still able to ...

HM'S HIPPOCAMPUS

This shows ...

MSM is too simplified

 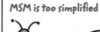
VERBAL, EPISODIC, VISUAL, SEMANTIC

STM and RTM can be further subdivided into verbal and visual (STM) and episodic, semantic, etc. (LTM).

However ...

Research support for elaboration

Craik and Tulving gave tasks requiring shallow or deep processing.

MUST

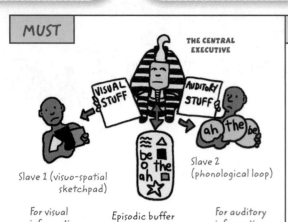

THE CENTRAL EXECUTIVE

VISUAL STUFF

AUDITORY STUFF

ah the be

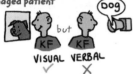

Slave 1 (visuo-spatial sketchpad)

Slave 2 (phonological loop)

For visual information

Episodic buffer (integrates information)

For auditory information

SHOULD

DUAL-TASK PERFORMANCE

PHONOLOGICAL LOOP DIVIDED — Phonological store / Articulatory process

VISUO-SPATIAL SKETCHPAD DIVIDED — Visual cache / Inner scribe

COULD Episodic buffer

Integrates information

be the ah

EVALUATION

Research support from brain damaged patient

Dog

but

KF ✓ KF ✗
VISUAL VERBAL

Shallice + Warrington study of KF
This suggests that …

However …

Research support from Baddeley et al.

'LENGTHY MORPHEMES ARE DIFFICULT TO REMEMBER'
'SHORT WORDS ARE EASY TO RECALL'

Baddeley et al. word-length effect.
This occurs because …

This effect disappears if …

Components not well defined

WORKING MEMORY
6/10
UNSATISFACTORY SEE ME

Description of central executive described as 'unsatisfactory'.

Needs to be more clearly specified …

There may be more than one …

Doesn't offer a full account

What about …

However …

MUST Loftus and Palmer

HOW?

45 US students shown film clips of car accident

You were doing over 40 when you smashed into me

Er no. When I contacted you I was doing about 30 mph

Asked a critical question about how fast the cars were going with 'action' verb changed in each

SHOWED?

Group with verb 'smashed' gave highest estimate at 40.8 mph.

Group with verb 'contacted' gave lowest estimate at 31.8 mph.

SHOULD Loftus and Palmer

HOW?

Did you see any broken glass …?

SHOWED

COULD

HOW?

DISNEYLAND
NO WASCALLY WABBITS!

SHOWED

EVALUATION

Lacks ecological validity

That's just a film. How about showing us some real accidents?

Oh good grief

Participants may not take it seriously because it was not a real accident.

This was supported by …

This suggests that …

Real-world application

It's N° 5

Wells and Olsen: EWT the single largest factor in convicting innocent people.
Loftus and Palmer's research was important …

This suggests that …

Further research support

STOP YIELD

Participants shown pictures and then asked questions consistent or inconsistent with the pictures.
Loftus et al. found that …

This shows that …

This supports Loftus and Palmer's research

WARNING. This Ad. may alter your memory

MUST Johnson and Scott

THE PEN IS MIGHTIER THAN THE SWORD
more memorable / knife

HOW? Participants hear an argument in the adjoining room then see either:
man with pen covered in grease
or man with knife covered in blood.

SHOWED? Mean accuracy 49% for pen, 33% for knife.

Shows high anxiety reduces accuracy.
Suggests a 'weapon focus' which reduces recall of other details.

SHOULD Christiansen and Hubinette

HOW?

VICTIM   BYSTANDER

SHOWED

COULD

DEFFENBACHER
Study 1 / META ANALYSER / Study 8

HOW?

SHOWED

EVALUATION

Research supports the weapon focus effect

Eyewitnesses look more at a weapon than other features.
For example …

This shows that …

Evidence challenges anxiety/EWT relationship

ANXIOUS SURVIVORS

Titanic sinking gave accurate eyewitness accounts (Rinolo et al.).
They found …

This supports the view that …

C&H'S study is flawed
Recall accuracy for
E.g. **VIOLENT VS. NON-VIOLENT** crimes

Findings may not be true for non-violent crimes. May be unreliable because of reliance on self-report.
Halford et al. …

This challenges …

Explaining the contradiction

HIGH / ACCURACY / LOW
ANXIETY   HIGH

The Yerkes-Dodson model

MUST Yarmey

HOW?

Hello   Hello   Hello
15 secs   15 secs   15 secs

651 participants

Then, 2 minutes later …
Asked to recall her physical details.

SHOWED? Recall best in younger adults and worst in oldest adults.
Young and middle aged more confident about recall. Significant correlation between confidence and recall.

SHOULD Parker and Carranza

HOW?

WHODUNNIT?

SHOWED

COULD Memon et al.

HOW?

16–33
60–82

SHOWED

EVALUATION

Findings not generalisable

The own-age bias …

… because people are more accurate recalling their own age group.
Anastasi and Rhodes found …

This bias might explain …

Confidence and accuracy
Younger participants possibly more accurate because more confident.
This would mean …

Their enhanced accuracy would be due to …

P&C supported by research
Goodman and Reed found 6–8 yr olds more suggestible to misleading information but not less accurate.
Suggestibility means …

These findings mean …

Explained by the source-recollection hypothesis

I remember that it happened It's just where, who and when I'm having problems with

MUST

Tell me everything you remember. Imagine yourself back in the bank. Start at the end and tell me what led up to that point. What would the cashier have seen?

1. REPORT EVERYTHING — even if it seems irrelevant.
2. REINSTATE CONTEXT — imagine original situation.
3. CHANGE ORDER — recall from middle or end.
4. CHANGE PERSPECTIVE — how would others see it?

SHOULD

Techniques 1 & 2

Aim to ...

This should lead to ...

Techniques 3 & 4

Aim to ...

Successful because ...

COULD

Police reluctant to use the CI

NEW ENHANCED CI

EVALUATION

The CI has proved effective

34% BETTER!

Köhnken *et al.* meta analysis — CI achieved 34% increase in recall compared to standard interview. Milne and Bull ...

This suggests that ...

Particularly effective with older witnesses

I don't know I can't remember much   Maybe I didn't see anything, I can't be sure ...

Older witnesses are overly cautious about reporting what they saw. Mello and Ashen found ...

This means that ...

Problems with doing research

MERSEYSIDE CI
1. Report everything
2. Reinstate Context
3. Change orders
4. Change perspective

THAMES VALLEY CI
1. Report everything
2. Reinstate Context
3. Change orders
4. Change perspective

Different versions of CI are used, e.g. Thames Valley Police do not use 'change perspective'. Other forces ...

This makes it difficult ...

The enhanced CI

We are reluctant to use the CI because ...

MUST	Method of loci, mind maps, chunking	SHOULD	Acronyms, acrostics and rhymes	COULD	Keywords

METHOD OF LOCI

Material associated with different locations along a route.

Learner mentally retraces route to recall items.

MIND MAPS

Main topic in centre with branching links.

Imposes visual organisation on material.

CHUNKING

Capacity of memory increased by grouping items.

Organising phone numbers, etc. to make them memorable.

0116 254 9568
LE1 7DR
25 12 2013

ROYGBIV

Twinkle, twinkle little star

MVEMJSUNP

Caballo = 'Cob-eye-yo'

EVALUATION

Memory strategies effective

Broadly and David found memory improvements in Down syndrome children. O'Hara et al. — with older adults.

Such research supports …

Elaboration makes mind maps/ method of loci effective

Both techniques involve elaboration, leads to more enduring memories.

Craik and Tulving found …

This means that …

Limitations with research

Studies of memory strategies are carried out in lab conditions which do not reflect real life.

This is supported by …

Therefore …

There is supporting evidence

Здравствуйте!

KEY WORDS

- Attachment
- Classical conditioning
- Conditioned response (CR)
- Conditioned stimulus (CS)
- Learning theory
- Modelling
- Neutral stimulus (NS)
- Operant conditioning
- Primary reinforcer
- Reinforcement
- Secondary reinforcer
- Social learning theory
- Unconditioned response (UCR)
- Unconditioned stimulus (UCS)
- Vicarious reinforcement

Possible essay question ...

Outline and evaluate the learning theory of attachment. *(12 marks)*

Other possible exam questions ...

+ Outline the learning theory of attachment. *(4 marks)*
+ Outline research findings that challenge the learning theory of attachment. *(4 marks)*
+ Apply this knowledge to ... *(6 marks)*

MUST know ...

Classical conditioning

An attachment may be formed as a result of association.

Before conditioning
Unconditioned stimulus (UCS) produces an unconditioned response (UCR).

Food (UCS) produces a sense of pleasure (UCR).

During conditioning
The person who feeds the infant is a neutral stimulus (NS), i.e. that person has no 'value' or 'meaning'.

Food (UCS) and person (NS) are paired because they occur together a number of times. The NS gradually becomes a conditioned stimulus (CS).

After conditioning
Conditioned stimulus (CS) produces a conditioned response (CR).

Person who feeds the infant (CS) produces pleasure (now a CR).

 One limitation of this explanation is that ...

... research shows that feeding is not the main factor in the formation of attachments.

- **E** – Infants are more likely to become attached to the person who offers contact comfort rather than the person who feeds them.

 Human studies also challenge ...

... the importance of food in attachment formation.

- **E** – Schaffer and Emerson investigated attachment through an observational study of 60 babies in their own homes for a period of about a year.

One strength of this explanation is ...

... that learning theory can be used to explain attachment formation.

- **E** – Food is not a reinforcer but other things may be reinforcers, e.g. attention and responsiveness, i.e. these are experienced as rewards for the infant.

SHOULD know ...

Operant conditioning

An attachment may be formed as a result of reinforcement (Dollard and Miller).

Primary reinforcer
A hungry infant feels uncomfortable.

This creates a drive to reduce discomfort.

When the infant is fed, the drive is reduced.

This produces a feeling of pleasure (which is rewarding/reinforcing).

Thus food is a primary reinforcer.

Secondary reinforcer
The person who supplies the food is associated with relieving discomfort.

This person becomes a secondary reinforcer.

Attachment occurs because the child seeks the person who can supply the same response of pleasure.

- **E** – This limitation was demonstrated in a study by Harlow. Infant monkeys preferred a wire mother who offered contact comfort (cloth-covered) rather than the one with a feeding bottle.
- **L** – This shows that attachment cannot be explained in terms of feeding alone.

- **E** – Schaffer and Emerson found that babies were most attached to the person who was most responsive to them and who interacted with them the most.
- **L** – This provides support for Harlow's findings and again undermines the suggestion that attachment is related to feeding.

- **E** – Support for this comes from Schaffer and Emerson's study which found that babies were most attached to the person who was most responsive to them.
- **L** – This means that learning theory may not be wrong, however 'food' as the basis of conditioning is wrong.

COULD know ...

Social learning theory (Hay and Vespo)

An attachment may be formed through the process of indirect reinforcement and direct instruction.

Infants learn attachment behaviours by observing how other people relate to each other. Infants then imitate this behaviour (called 'modelling') if it has been indirectly reinforced (vicarious reinforcement).

Infants also receive direct instruction from parents about how to behave and are encouraged to show love towards their parents/carers and thus form attachments.

 There are real world-applications ...

... of the social learning explanation of attachment.

- **E** – Parents should be aware that their behaviour is being observed and modelled by their infants.
- **E** – For example, if parents argue with each other and are not responsive to their infants, these behaviours may be imitated later in life, leading to poor attachments.
- **L** – This means that it is important for parents to act as positive role models.

MATCH THEM UP

On the facing page there is an explanation of how attachments can develop through classical conditioning.

Match up the terms below.

1	Conditioned stimulus	**A**	Pleasure
2	Unconditioned stimulus	**B**	Mother
3	Conditioned response	**C**	Food

Answers on page 190

SPOT THE MISTAKES

Read the text below. There are six mistakes, draw a circle round each.

An infant may develop an attachment through operant conditioning. In this case food is a secondary reinforcer. Food increases the infant's sense of discomfort. One criticism of this explanation comes from Barlow's research with cats. In this study he showed that the animals spent most time with the wire mother with a feeding bottle. Another study with human babies also showed that food matters in attachment. The babies were observed in their own home.

Answers on page 190

DRAWING CONCLUSIONS

The graph below shows the results from Harlow's study of monkeys.

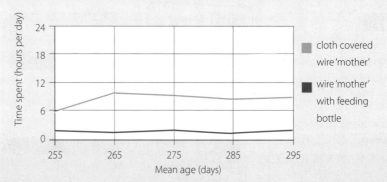

State **two** findings and for each one draw a conclusion (state what the finding shows):

Finding 1:

Conclusion 1: This shows that …

Finding 2:

Conclusion 2: This shows that …

Answers on page 190

> Marking guidelines can be found on pages 10 and 14.

A MARKING EXERCISE

Read the student answer to the following exam question:

Outline and evaluate learning theory as an explanation of attachment. *(8 marks)*

The learning theory consists of classical and operant conditioning. Both of these involve the association of responses and stimuli. For example, classical conditioning is when you associate something new with something already associated. This could explain attachment because the caregiver might give a baby food and then the baby associates the caregiver with food. This creates a bond because the baby associates the caregiver with food and pleasure too. Operant conditioning is where a reward is given. For example, when a baby is hungry it will feel discomfort. If the caregiver gives the baby food this will take away the discomfort. The baby will feel rewarded and will want more of this reward from the caregiver, which is why an attachment is formed. However, this goes against what Harry Harlow found out. He found that contact comfort was more important to babies than food. This shows that babies don't need the association with food to create a bond.

(158 words)

AO1 mark for an outline of learning theory

Has material been appropriately selected? YES / NO

Is the material accurate? YES / NO

Is the material REASONABLY DETAILED / LESS DETAILED / BASIC / VERY BRIEF

What mark would this answer get for AO1? _____ marks out of 4

AO2 mark for an outline of learning theory

The evaluation is (select one phrase):

A RANGE IN GREATER DEPTH

A RANGE OF POINTS IN REASONABLE DEPTH

A RESTRICTED RANGE

RUDIMENTARY

What mark would this answer get for AO2? _____ marks out of 4

Answers on page 190

KEY WORDS

- Adaptive
- Continuity hypothesis
- Critical period
- Insecure attachment
- Innate
- Internal working model
- Monotropy
- Primary attachment figure
- Secondary attachment figure
- Secure attachment
- Sensitive period
- Social releasers
- Temperament hypothesis

Possible essay question ...

Outline and evaluate Bowlby's theory of attachment.
(12 marks)

Other possible exam questions ...

+ Outline Bowlby's theory of attachment. *(6 marks)*
+ Evaluate Bowlby's theory of attachment. *(4 marks)*
+ Apply this knowledge to ... *(6 marks)*

MUST know ...

Attachment is adaptive

Forming an attachment with an adult makes it more likely that an infant will survive because, for example, in the distant past this made them safe from predators.

Innate characteristics

Since attachment is adaptive, it is therefore governed by the genes we inherit – the tendency to become attached is innate.

Infants are born with certain characteristics that ensure they receive care from others. For example, an infant's large eyes and little nose are 'cute' and elicit caregiving. These characteristics are called social releasers.

Sensitive period

Innate (biological) behaviours usually have a special time period when they develop. This is called a critical or sensitive period.

Bowlby suggested that infants are most sensitive to becoming attached around 6–9 months.

 There is research support ...

... for the innate basis for attachment.

- **E** – Lorenz found that goslings had an innate tendency to follow and stay close to the first moving object they saw (either their natural mother or him). This is called imprinting.

 There is further research support ...

... for the innate basis for attachment.

- **E** – Tronick *et al.* studied Africans with different cultural practices to our own (e.g. infants were breastfed by several women). Nevertheless, infants formed a primary attachment to one person (monotropy).

SHOULD know ...

Monotropy and internal working model

Infants have one special emotional bond (monotropy) with their primary attachment figure (usually their mother).

Infants have many secondary attachments that are important for healthy emotional and social development.

The relationship between primary attachment figure and infant creates expectations about what all relationships will be like, leading to an internal working model of relationships.

The continuity hypothesis

Individuals who are securely attached in infancy *continue* to be securely attached in later childhood and adulthood. This means they are likely to be socially and emotionally more competent, and form secure attachments with adult partners.

Insecurely attached children have more social and emotional difficulties in childhood and also in adulthood.

- **E** – The fact that the goslings became 'attached' to Lorenz demonstrates an innate process that has survival value.
- **L** – This suggests that a similar innate process evolved in humans to promote survival.

- **E** – If a behaviour is innate, then we would expect people from different cultures to display the same kind of behaviour, i.e. we would expect attachment to be universal.
- **L** – This shows that attachment is innate rather than being culturally determined.

 There are problems with ...

... the concept of monotropy.

- **E** – Rutter argued that all attachment figures are equally important to the child.
- **E** – For healthy emotional development it may actually be preferable to have a number of primary attachments.
- **L** – This suggests that the internal working model is based on several relationships rather than one special one.

COULD know ...

Caregiver sensitivity

Bowlby argued that the key feature of the primary attachment relationship was the responsiveness and sensitivity of the caregiver.

It is the quality of the infant–adult relationship that matters, rather than the time spent together.

According to Bowlby, a parent who deals with their infant by being accepting, cooperative and accessible is more likely to form a secure attachment.

 There is an alternative view ...

... described by the temperament hypothesis (Kagan).

- **E** – It could be that an infant's temperament (emotional type) is as important as caregiver sensitivity in determining the quality of attachment.
- **E** – This is supported by research that found that infants who are irritable from birth are more likely to develop insecure attachments (Belsky and Rovine).
- **L** – This suggests that attachment is not just explained by parent behaviour.

CONSTRUCTING AN ANSWER

Fill in the boxes below to help prepare an answer to the exam question 'Outline Bowlby's theory of attachment'. *(6 marks)*

In the left-hand column we have written key elements of Bowlby's theory. On the right-hand side you should explain the element identified. The first one has been done for you.

Key element	Further elaboration
Innate	Infants are born with a predisposition to become attached and this increases their chances of survival.
Social releasers	
Sensitive period	
Monotropy	
Internal working model	
Continuity hypothesis	

CIRCLE TRUE OR FALSE

T or F Big eyes are an example of a social releaser.

T or F Monotropy refers to having multiple attachment figures.

T or F Bowlby's theory includes classical conditioning.

T or F Rutter suggested that all attachment figures are equally important.

T or F Cross-cultural evidence is used to consider whether any behaviour is universal.

T or F When children are breastfed by more than one woman they don't form one special emotional bond.

T or F Children who were securely attached as infants tend to be more socially competent.

T or F Goslings became imprinted on Lorenz when he was the first moving thing they saw.

Answers on page 190

See page 20 for an explanation of the 'two-pronged attack' needed to answer 'applying your knowledge' questions.

FILL IN THE BLANKS

The text below relates to some of the criticisms given on the facing page.

Bowlby claimed that attachment is innate. Two studies that support this were by (1) .... and

(2) .... The study of goslings showed that animals will imprint on the first thing they see that (3)

.... This means that they have an innate predisposition to acquire this attachment. The other study was conducted in Africa. Despite (4) .... differences between the Africans and people in the UK, the infants still formed one (5) .... attachment.

Rutter argued that all attachment figures are equally important, which challenges the concept of (6) ....

Answers on page 190

APPLYING YOUR KNOWLEDGE

The manager of a day care centre for babies aged 1–2 years old found out about Bowlby's theory when studying A Level psychology. The manager decided she would try to apply some of the ideas to the way she and her staff looked after the children in the day care centre.

Explain what new strategies they might try. Relate your ideas to Bowlby's theory. *(4 marks)*

New strategies	Link to Bowlby's theory

Answers on page 190

KEY WORDS

- Attachment type
- Secure attachment
- Separation anxiety
- Strange Situation (SS)
- Stranger anxiety

Possible essay question ...

Outline and evaluate the use of the Strange Situation to assess attachment. *(12 marks)*

Other possible exam questions ...

+ Outline the Strange Situation as a means to assess attachment. *(6 marks)*
+ Explain **one** criticism of using the Strange Situation to assess attachment. *(3 marks)*
+ Apply this knowledge to ... *(6 marks)*

! Think

There is a further criticism you might think about:

How ethical is it to put infants in a situation that might cause them distress?

MUST know ...

The Strange Situation (SS) is a research technique used to measure the kind of attachment between an infant (aged 9–18 months) and a parent.

It is conducted in a lab environment with a 9×9 foot square marked off in 16 squares to help record the infant's movements.

There are eight episodes, each lasting about three minutes:

1 Parent and infant play.
2 Parent sits while infant plays.
3 Stranger enters and talks to parent.
4 Parent leaves, infant plays, stranger offers comfort if necessary.
5 Parent returns, greets infant, offers comfort if needed, stranger leaves.
6 Parent leaves, infant is alone.
7 Stranger enters and offers comfort.
8 Parent returns, greets infant, offers comfort.

 One strength of the SS is ...

... its usefulness.

- **E** – Most research on attachment requires a means of assessing the quality of the attachment bond between an infant and parent. The SS was developed by Ainsworth in order to do this.

 One criticism of the SS is ...

... it may not be a valid measurement of attachment.

- **E** – The SS only measures attachment in the context of one particular relationship – so it assesses the quality of that relationship rather than telling us about the 'attachment type' of the individual.

 Another criticism of the SS is ...

... it may not apply to every culture.

- **E** – The SS was developed in the US (by Mary Ainsworth) and is based on certain assumptions. For example, the assumption that a securely attached child should only be mildly distressed when separated from their parent.

SHOULD know ...

Attachment type is assessed in the SS by creating situations of mild anxiety:

The room is strange to the infant
This creates some anxiety, though it may also encourage the infant to explore. Secure attachment is associated with more willingness to explore (using parent as a secure base).

Stranger present, creates stranger anxiety
Some infants are more distressed than others in the presence of a stranger and especially when left alone with a stranger.

Being left alone, creates separation anxiety
Some infants become very distressed when their parent leaves, others are only mildly distressed and easily comforted.

Reunion behaviour
The returning parent may be greeted enthusiastically or ignored. An infant who ignores their parent has a weak (insecure) attachment.

- **E** – The method was tested extensively by Ainsworth (see next spread). Without the SS technique it would not be possible to investigate the causes and effects of attachment.
- **L** – This shows that it is an essential tool for conducting research on attachment.

- **E** – However, research has found that attachment type is mainly influenced by the mother (Main and Weston).
- **L** – This means it may well be justified to measure the attachment type of an individual infant by just testing their relationship with that one person (their mother) in the SS.

- **E** – In some other cultures, such as Japan, dependence rather than independence is valued. Therefore, well-attached children show much greater signs of distress on separation – but in the SS this would be seen as a sign of poor attachment.
- **L** – This means that different measures of attachment are needed in different cultures.

COULD know ...

Data collection in the Strange Situation

The SS involves a group of observers recording what the infant is doing every 15 seconds.

Each observer records intensity of behaviour on a scale of 1 to 7.

The behavioural categories are: (1) proximity and contact-seeking behaviours; (2) contact-maintaining behaviours; (3) proximity and interaction-avoiding behaviours; (4) contact and interaction-resisting behaviours; (5) search behaviours.

 There can be problems with ...

... observational research.

- **E** – For example, an observer may be unsure how to code particular behaviours. This would mean that different observers have quite different records of what happened.
- **E** – Ainsworth checked inter-observer reliability and found it was excellent (a correlation of +.94 between observers).
- **L** – This suggests that the behavioural categories in the SS can be relied on.

FILL IN THE TABLE

Who is in the room? In the table below place a tick for each step of the Strange Situation indicating who is in the room at each stage.

	1	2	3	4	5	6	7	8
Parent								
Stranger								

Answers on page 191

APPLYING YOUR KNOWLEDGE

Ella is studying A Level psychology and has a one-year-old baby called Omar. When she learned about the Strange Situation she decided to try it out with her son and his father.

Explain how Ella could investigate Omar's attachment type using the Strange Situation. *(3 marks)*

(Note: you would not need to list all the stages in a question worth 4 marks. Instead select key aspects of the Strange Situation.)

Element of Strange Situation	How it would be used

Answers on page 191

ETHICAL ISSUES

One criticism that is made about the Strange Situation relates to whether the procedure is ethically acceptable. There is no right answer to this issue – it's up to you to decide whether the technique is unethical because of the anxiety that was created. Read about ethical issues on page 92 and then develop your own critical point.

S	One criticism of the Strange Situation relates to ethics.
E	Some people suggest the technique is not ethical because the children were exposed to situations that might distress them.
E	
L	

Find out more about SEEL on page 14.

JUMBLED SENTENCES

The eight stages of the Strange Situation are listed below, but not in the right order. Place the number for each sentence in the correct square. The first one has been done for you.

(Note that the words used are slightly different from on the facing page.)

5	**1**	The stranger returns and offers comfort.
	2	A stranger enters and talks to the parent. This is the first time the infant has met the stranger.
	3	The parent leaves again and the infant is alone.
	4	The parent returns for the second time, greets infant and offers comfort.
	5	At the beginning the parent and infant are playing.
	6	The parent leaves the infant alone with the stranger. The stranger offers comfort if necessary.
	7	The parent returns and greets the infant, the stranger leaves.
	8	The infant gets used to the situation and plays, with its parent nearby.

Answers on page 191

A MARKING EXERCISE

Evaluate the Strange Situation as a method for investigating types of attachment. *(4 marks)*

Answer: One criticism of the Strange Situation is that it lacks validity as it only studies one particular relationship. Psychologists have found that an infant with two parents changes behaviour between the two of the parents. This suggests that the Strange Situation cannot determine an attachment type just by investigating the behaviour of one relationship of an infant.

Explain why this answer would only receive 3 out of 4 marks?

Explain **two** ways that this answer could have been improved.

Answers on page 191

KEY WORDS

- Disinhibited attachment
- Disorganised attachment
- Insecure-avoidant attachment
- Insecure-resistant attachment
- Maternal reflexive thinking
- Secure attachment
- Strange Situation (SS)

Possible essay question ...

Outline and evaluate research related to types of attachment. *(12 marks)*

Other possible exam questions ...

+ Explain what is meant by secure attachment. *(2 marks)*
+ Explain the difference between insecure-resistant attachment and insecure-avoidant attachment. *(4 marks)*
+ Outline how psychologists have investigated types of attachment. *(6 marks)* [The answer to this question would be using the Strange Situation, on the previous spread.]
+ Apply this knowledge to ... *(6 marks)*

MUST know ...

Ainsworth used the Strange Situation technique (see previous spread) to assess infant behaviour. She found three main types:

1. Secure attachment

Greets parent enthusiastically on return.

Willing to explore, some stranger anxiety, some separation anxiety.

2. Insecure-avoidant attachment

Avoids or ignores parent on their return, a kind of indifference.

Willing to explore, avoids or ignores stranger (low stranger anxiety), indifferent to separation (low separation anxiety).

3. Insecure-resistant attachment

Resists or rejects parent on their return.

Less willing to explore, high stranger anxiety, high separation anxiety.

 One criticism of the three types is ...

... that attachment behaviours may not be consistent.

- **E** – Main and Solomon re-analysed over 200 video recordings of Strange Situation studies and proposed a fourth attachment type – disorganised attachment.

 It might be inaccurate to suggest ...

... that children have just one attachment type.

- **E** – Ainsworth suggested attachment type was consistent within one situation and also consistent across time. However, children may display a different attachment type in different situations and with different people.

 There are real-world applications ...

... of the concept of type of attachment.

- **E** – When infants are classed as insecurely attached, intervention strategies may be used to improve the parent–infant bond. For example, the 'Circle of Security' project aims to do this (Cooper *et al.*).

SHOULD know ...

For each attachment type, we can consider why that type might develop and the eventual consequences of that attachment type.

Secure attachment

Secure attachment is related to the sensitivity the mother shows when responding to their child's needs.

Secure attachment is related to later healthy social, emotional and cognitive development.

Insecure attachment

Insecure attachment is related to a lack of sensitive responsiveness from the parent.

Insecure-avoidant children generally avoid intimacy with others.

Insecure-resistant children alternate between seeking and rejecting intimacy. The parent's behaviour may also involve seeking and rejecting.

- **E** – Main and Solomon's disorganised type is characterised by a lack of *consistent* patterns of social behaviour – one minute a child shows higher stranger anxiety, the next minute the child displays low stranger anxiety.
- **L** – This means that Ainsworth's idea of consistent behaviour patterns may be mistaken.

- **E** – For example, a child may be securely attached when with his father but insecurely attached when with his mother (Main and Weston).
- **L** – This means that the child doesn't have just one attachment type and therefore we can't draw links between attachment type and later developmental consequences.

- **E** – The 'Circle of Security' project teaches parents to understand their infants' signals and respond more sensitively. The outcome has been a decrease in insecure attachment and increase in secure attachment.
- **L** – This suggests that the concept of attachment types (and their descriptions) may assist in identifying problems and provide ways to improve parent–child communications.

COULD know ...

The disinhibited attachment type

Infants who have failed to form attachments during their early life show a pattern of attachment called 'disinhibited'.

Such children tend be indiscriminate and superficial in their attachments, being overfriendly and displaying inappropriate affection towards strangers. They may also be attention seeking.

Parental sensitivity may not ...

... be the cause of secure attachment

- **E** – Some studies have found low correlations between maternal sensitivity and strength of attachment (Raval *et al.*).
- **E** – Slade *et al.* found a greater role for maternal reflective functioning – the ability to understand what someone else is thinking.
- **L** – They suggest that high maternal reflective thinking may lead to secure attachment.

MATCH THEM UP

Attachment types are listed on the left and attachment behaviours on the right. Decide which type goes with which behaviours.

1	Secure attachment	**A**	Willing to explore, high stranger anxiety.
2	Insecure-resistant attachment	**B**	Willing to explore, low stranger anxiety.
3	Insecure-avoidant attachment	**C**	No consistent pattern of behaviour.
4	Disorganised attachment	**D**	Less willing to explore, high stranger anxiety.

Answers on page 191

 DRAWING CONCLUSIONS

The data from a study by Van IJzendoorn *et al.* are shown below. The percentages show the distribution of attachment types across a sample of about 6,000 infants.

Secure attachment	Insecure-avoidant	Insecure-resistant	Disorganised
62%	15%	8%	15%

State **two** findings and for each finding draw a conclusion (state what the finding shows):

Finding 1:

Conclusion 1: This shows that …

Finding 2:

Conclusion 2: This shows that …

Answers on page 191

 KEY PHRASES

On the facing page, there are four critical points. Select three of these for the activity below.
For each of your critical points select **three** key words/phrases. Suggestions are made for the first one.

Criticism 1	Inconsistent	Main and Solomon	Disorganised
Criticism 2			
Criticism 3			

 A MARKING EXERCISE

Attachment types are tested in the Strange Situation. Explain how the behaviour of a child showing insecure-avoidant attachment type would be different from the behaviour of a child showing insecure-resistant attachment type in the Strange Situation. *(4 marks)*

There are three exam answers to this question shown below. What marks would you give them? One got 2 out of 4 marks, one got 3 out of 4 marks and one got full marks. But which do you think got each mark?

Tanya's answer

In the Strange Situation, when the mother leaves both children would cry but they would both settle down. However, when she comes back the insecure-resistant child would not seek proximity from the mother even though the child had cried and been upset. The insecure-avoidant child would seek comfort from their mother but reject it when it is given.

MARK
.... out of 4

Bethany's answer

A child with an insecure-avoidant attachment would not show any distress if the mother left the room and equally would not show much interest on her return. However, a child with an insecure-resistant attachment would show distress at the mother leaving the room, but upon her return the child would be unable to be comforted by her and would still be crying and showing signs of distress.

MARK
.... out of 4

Corey's answer

An insecure-avoidant child in the Strange Situation would not worry when the mother left, they would continue to play. However, when the mother returns the child will be angry and avoid any contact or intimacy with the caregiver and push them away if they try contact. An insecure-resistant child would cry when the mother left and cry when she returned.

MARK
.... out of 4

Answers on page 191

KEY WORDS

- Culture
- Indigenous theory
- Strange Situation (SS)

Possible essay question ...

Discuss research on cultural variations in attachment.
(12 marks)

Other possible exam questions ...

+ Outline how psychologists have investigated cultural variations in attachment.
(4 marks)

+ Outline what research has shown about cultural variations in attachment.
(4 marks)

+ Explain **one** criticism of using the Strange Situation to assess attachment.
(3 marks)

+ Apply this knowledge to ...
(6 marks)

⭐ Exam tip

When considering cultural variations you can also refer to Ainsworth's study of American infants because it relates to one cultural group. The results of this study found that 66% of infants were securely attached, 22% were insecure-avoidant and 12% were insecure-resistant.

MUST know ...

Key study: van IJzendoorn and Kroonenberg

How?
A meta-analysis of 32 studies conducted in eight different countries.

The studies selected all used the Strange Situation to assess attachment type between infants and mothers.

The researchers excluded any study that looked at special groups of participants, such as Down's syndrome or twins, and excluded those involving fewer than 35 infants.

Showed?
Secure attachment was the most common classification in every country.

Insecure-avoidant was the next most common, except in Israel and Japan which both had particularly high rates of insecure-resistant attachment.

The variation within countries was 1.5 times greater than between countries.

 One criticism of this research is ...

... the Strange Situation (SS) may not be a valid measure of attachment in all cultures.

- **E** – The SS was developed in the US and is based on certain assumptions. For example, the assumption that a well-attached child should only be mildly distressed when separated from their parent.

The meta-analysis looked at 'countries' ...

... which is not the same as 'cultures'.

- **E** – Within any country there are a number of cultures, which means it may be meaningless to compare attachment rates in different countries.

Not all studies have found ...

... that there are cultural differences.

- **E** – For example, Tronick *et al.* studied people in the Democratic Republic of Congo (Africa) who had different cultural practices to Western ones but nevertheless the infants formed a primary attachment to one person.

SHOULD know ...

Second study: Grossmann *et al.*

How?
Two samples of mothers and their infants were studied: one from northern and one from southern Germany.

Attachment type was assessed in infancy using the Strange Situation.

The children were assessed again at age 11.

Showed?
In southern Germany the distribution of attachment types was similar to Ainsworth's US sample (two-thirds secure attachment).

In northern Germany two-thirds were insecurely attached, the rest were securely attached.

High levels of insecure attachment were attributed to an emphasis on self-reliance and emotional independence by parents in northern Germany.

The same infants at age 11 had poorer peer relationships and showed greater dependence than the southern sample.

- **E** – Takahasi suggests that the high rates of insecure attachment in Japanese infants may be because they are not used to being left alone and therefore were highly distressed.
- **L** – This means that, in some cultures, high levels of distress on separation are not because of insecure attachment but because of a lack of experience of separation.

- **E** – van IJzendoorn and Sagi found an over-representation of insecure-resistant infants in a rural Japanese sample whereas rates in urban Tokyo were more like the US rates.
- **L** – This means that it really only makes sense to compare cultural groups rather than pooling data within different countries.

- **E** – This is further supported by the Japanese study (above) which found similarities between Japanese urban samples and the US data on distribution of attachment types.
- **L** – This suggests that, despite cultural differences, elements of the attachment process are the same around the world.

COULD know ...

Third study: Ainsworth

How?
Ainsworth carried out an observational study in Uganda before conducting her main study in the US.
This Ugandan study involved 26 mothers and their infants.

Showed?
She observed that mothers who showed more sensitivity to their infants' needs had more securely attached infants (they cried less and explored more).

 The issue of culture bias ...

... is important in attachment research.

- **E** – Rothbaum *et al.* argue that attachment theory has a Western bias.
- **E** – Attachment theory assumes that independence is important for secure attachment, however in some non-Western cultures dependence is more important.
- **L** – This suggests that psychologists should seek to develop indigenous theories of attachment – explanations of attachment rooted in different cultures.

CIRCLE TRUE OR FALSE

T or F van IJzendoorn and Kroonenberg found that variation between countries was greater than within countries.

T or F A total of 32 different countries were included in this meta-analysis.

T or F Israeli children had higher rates of insecure attachment than most other countries.

T or F Grossmann *et al.* found that the infants in southern Germany showed similar levels of secure attachment to US infants.

T or F Infants in northern Germany were more likely to be insecurely attached.

T or F In the German study, insecure attachment was associated with poor social development.

T or F Takahashi suggested that Japanese appeared insecure because they were not used to separation.

T or F The study by Tronick *et al.* supported the notion of cultural differences in attachment.

Answers on page 191

SPOT THE MISTAKES

Read the text below. There are five mistakes, draw a circle round each.

The Special Situation (SS) may not be a valid measure of attachment in all cultures. It was developed in the UK and therefore may not apply to other cultures. In some cultures, such as Japan, infants are rarely separated from their mothers and therefore show little distress in the Strange Situation. Another criticism of the research on cultural variations is that it often assumes that 'country' is the same as 'culture'. The study by van IJzendoorn and Kroonenberg showed that different cultural groups in Japan differed in terms of attachment type. In rural Japan there were more securely attached infants than in urban cities.

Answers on page 191

An idea
On a separate piece of paper, draw a mind map relating to cultural variations in attachment and include material on the Strange Situation and attachment types – as these are all inter-related.

APPLYING YOUR KNOWLEDGE

Identify the psychology		Link to Yuna's behaviour
	Yuna comes from a Japanese family. Her parents wish to raise her following Japanese traditions. Yuna took part in a research project where her attachment type was assessed in the Strange Situation.	
	Use your knowledge about cultural variations in attachment to explain how Yuna may have reacted in the Strange Situation. *(4 marks)*	

Answers on page 191

KEY WORDS

- Disruption of attachment
- Separation
- Strange Situation (SS)

Possible essay question ...

Outline and evaluate research related to the disruption of attachment. *(12 marks)*

Other possible exam questions ...

+ Explain what is meant by the disruption of attachment. *(2 marks)*
+ Outline **one** study of the effects of disruption of attachments. *(6 marks)*
+ Give **one** criticism of research on the effects of disruption of attachments. *(6 marks)*
+ Apply this knowledge to ... *(6 marks)*

MUST know ...

Key study: Robertson and Robertson

How?

The Robertsons filmed young children while they were separated from their mothers.

John was in a residential nursery for two weeks, separated from his mother. He experienced both emotional and physical separation because the nurses did not have time to look after him.

Jane, Lucy, Thomas and Kate experienced only physical separation from their mothers because their emotional needs were met by the Robertsons who cared for them.

Showed?

John initially coped well but became depressed and withdrawn, refused to eat and cried a lot.

The other children coped well and returned to their families happily.

This shows that physical disruption alone did not have a negative outcome but emotional disruption did.

There are individual differences ...

... because not all children are affected by emotional disruption in the same way.

- **E** – Bowlby *et al.* supported this in their study of children who had prolonged stays in hospital, away from their families. Some children were less affected than others.

There are real-world applications ...

... to the care of children in hospital.

- **E** – It is possible to minimise the effects of both physical and emotional disruption by allowing parents 24-hour access to their children in hospital as well as providing good substitute emotional care.

Disruption may not always have ...

... long-term negative effects.

- **E** – Bifulco *et al.* proposed that early experiences of disruption can create a vulnerability that is only triggered in some individuals later in life.

SHOULD know ...

Second study: Hart *et al.*

How?

There were 64 participants recruited from a maternity unit for a longitudinal study.

At 12 months the mothers were assessed using a depression questionnaire, and divided into two groups: depressed and non-depressed.

The mothers and their infants were observed while playing with toys, and infant and mother behaviours recorded by two observers.

Showed?

At 12 months, infants whose mothers were classified as depressed showed less separation anxiety, less proximity to their mothers and greater proximity to a stranger than the non-depressed group.

All of these are signs of insecure attachment.

Depressed mothers are more emotionally distant so this suggests that emotional disruption has negative effects on an infant's attachment type.

- **E** – When the children were later assessed, some showed no ill social or cognitive effects. Bowlby suggested that infants who are securely attached may be less affected by separation (physical and/or emotional).
- **L** – This suggests that some children may be more resilient and the reason may be because they are securely attached.

- **E** – In the 1950s, when the Robertsons did their research, 12% of hospitals prohibited any visiting by families, today parents are encouraged to stay overnight and have 24-hour access.
- **L** – This suggests that research had a benefit in terms of the way hospitals care for children.

- **E** – Bifulco *et al.* found that disruption of attachment (through divorce or death) before the age of 17 was associated with increased depressive or anxiety disorders in adulthood.
- **L** – This suggests that early disruptions may not necessarily cause long-term negative effects but they are a risk factor.

COULD know ...

Third study: Robertson and Bowlby

How?

The responses of children to being left in hospital were recorded.

Showed?

There was a consistent pattern of response called the PDD model:

1. **Protest:** on initial separation (disruption) the child is very distressed. This may last a few hours or days.
2. **Despair:** the initial anger turns into apathy. Children often comfort themselves by rocking or sucking their thumb.
3. **Detachment:** the child appears to be coping but this masks inner turmoil. The child may be indifferent to the caregiver's return.

The PDD model may be ...

... over simplified

- **E** – Barrett examined the original films of the children and claimed that the initial response was more often a determined effort to cope rather than protest.
- **E** – It may be true that an insecure child would be plunged into protest and despair more immediately.
- **L** – This suggests that the model should be adapted to reflect individual differences.

FILL IN THE BLANKS

The text below relates to studies and criticisms on the facing page.

The Robertsons studied children who experienced disruption of

attachment. John was in a (1) ....

for (2) .... weeks. During this time John gradually became

withdrawn. By contrast, the Robertsons looked after (3) ....

other children who were also separated from their mothers but

experienced no negative effects. This may be because they only

experienced (4) .... and not

(5) .... disruption. This finding was supported

in another study of depressed women by (6) .... *et al.*

who found more signs of (7) .... attachment in

the children of depressed women. This research has had real-world

applications when considering the effects of disruption on children

in (8) ....

Answers on page 191

WRITE YOUR EVALUATION POINT

Select one evaluation point from the facing page and write it out in your own words below.

Underline key words to help you remember the AO2 point.

S	
E	
E	
L	

See page 14 for an explanation of how to SEEL.

APPLYING YOUR KNOWLEDGE

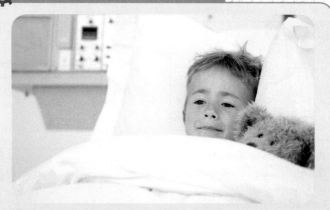

Sally's one-year-old son Max has to go into hospital for a minor operation and stay there for a week. She is worried what effect this may on him, especially as she has to go to work during the day so cannot be with him.

Suggest what Sally might do to ensure Max's emotional well-being. Use psychological research to support your answer. *(4 marks)*

Suggestion for Sally:
Link to psychological research:

Suggestion for Sally:
Link to psychological research:

Answers on page 191

FILL IN THE BOXES

List five behaviours that a child might show as a result of disruption of attachment.

1.
2.
3.
4.
5.

Answers on page 191

KEY WORDS

- Attrition
- Disinhibited attachment
- Institutional care
- Privation
- Sociability

Possible essay questions ...

Outline and evaluate research into the effects of failure to form attachments (privation). *(12 marks)*

Outline and evaluate research on the effects of institutional care on attachment. *(12 marks)*

Other possible exam questions ...

+ Explain what is meant by the terms 'institutional care' and 'privation'. Use examples in your answer. *(2 marks + 2 marks)*

+ Outline the effects of institutional care on the development of attachment. *(6 marks)*

+ Explain how psychologists have investigated the effects of failure to form attachment (privation). *(4 marks)*

+ Apply this knowledge to ... *(6 marks)*

MUST know ...

Key study: Hodges and Tizard

How?

Longitudinal study of 65 UK children placed in institutional care under four months old (they were too young to have formed attachments).

Attachment was assessed at age four years, at which time some were 'restored' to their own homes and some had been adopted.

They were assessed again aged eight and 16 years and teachers and parents answered questions about their social behaviour.

There was a control group of home-reared children.

Showed?

At age four years all children showed signs of disinhibited attachment.

At ages eight and 16 years the adopted children had close attachments with their families (shows that recovery is possible).

All ex-institutional children had poor peer relationships (e.g. less liked) and sought more attention from adults (shows that privation leads to difficulties in relationships).

 Attrition is a problem ...

... in longitudinal studies.

- **E** – Hodges and Tizard's original sample of 65 children was reduced to 51 children by age eight and 49 by age 16. It was intended to study the children again in adulthood but a sufficiently large sample could not be assembled.

 Privation may be only one factor ...

... in explaining long-term negative effects.

- **E** – Children who experience early emotional privation also often experience other negative experiences, such as cognitive privation. This may explain the ultimate negative effects.

There are individual differences ...

... in the ability to cope with early privation.

- **E** – In all studies of privation some of the children recover well, even those adopted after six months (see study by Rutter *et al.*).

SHOULD know ...

Second study: Rutter *et al.*

How?

A longitudinal study of a random sample of 165 Romanian orphans adopted by UK families who had spent their early lives in institutional care in Romania.

The children were assessed at ages four, six, 11 and 15 on their social, psychological and cognitive abilities.

A control group of 52 UK-adopted children were also studied.

Showed?

Those children who were adopted by British families before the age of six months showed 'normal' emotional development (compared with a control group).

One-third of those adopted after six months showed signs of disinhibited attachments and had problems with peer relationships.

This suggests that a lack of attachment after six months is associated with long-term social and emotional difficulties.

- **E** – The problem with attrition is that the individuals who 'disappear' may be the ones who are different in some way, e.g. they may be the more troubled participants.
- **L** – This means that the remaining sample is biased, which challenges the validity of the results.

- **E** – Children who suffer early emotional privation also often continue to have negative life experiences, e.g. depression.
- **L** – This, means that we cannot conclude that early emotional privation is the sole cause of later emotional and cognitive difficulties.

- **E** – It may be that those children who are less sociable and outgoing are the ones who don't get adopted early.
- **L** – Their eventual relationship difficulties may be due to innate social/emotional issues (they are individuals with less sociable personalities).

COULD know ...

Third study: Rutter and Quinton

How?

A sample of 94 ex-institutional women were compared to 51 women from the general population (control group).

Home observations of the women (in their 20s) and their children.

Showed?

More of the ex-institutional women had children who had spent time in care. The women were rated as lacking in warmth when interacting with their children. This creates a cycle of privation.

 One problem with the conclusions ...

... is that early privation may not have long-term effects.

- **E** – Hodges and Tizard suggested that ex-institutional children may have social problems because of developmental delays.
- **E** – Their early experiences may not have harmed their social development but just meant that it would take longer than in normal children.
- **L** – However, Rutter and Quinton's study seems to show that there are enduring long-term effects.

CIRCLE TRUE OR FALSE

T or F Attrition refers to the loss of participants over time.

T or F Longitudinal studies involve testing behaviour on many occasions over time.

T or F Hodges and Tizard stopped the children forming attachments.

T or F Rutter *et al.* studied Russian orphans.

T or F Rutter *et al.* found that children coped well as long as adoption took place before eight months of age.

Answers on page 191

 **APPLYING YOUR KNOWLEDGE**

The Government has sought advice from psychologists on the psychological effects of adoption.

Based on your knowledge of psychological research, what recommendations would you make regarding adoption?

Identify the psychology	Recommendations

Answers on page 191

 CONSTRUCTING AN ANSWER

Fill in the boxes below to help prepare an answer to the exam question:

What is the difference between disruption and failure to form attachment (privation)?

You may use examples to help explain the difference.

Difference	Example of disruption	Example of failure to form attachment

Answers on page 191

 A MARKING EXERCISE

Two answers to the following exam question are shown below. Decide on your own mark.

Outline **and** evaluate research into the effects of failure to form attachment (privation). *(6 marks)*

Mario's answer

One study that looks at the effects of privation is by Hodges and Tizard. They carried out a longitudinal observation of children living in institutions. The children were under four months old and were not able to form attachments in their institutions. When they were four years old many were adopted or they were restored back to their original families. Children who were adopted were found to have better attachments to mothers than restored children. However, both lacked peer relationships. One criticism of this study is that people may drop out which would leave a biased sample. The children with bad attachments may drop out leaving children with good attachments. This would mean that the results are not valid as the sample is biased with children who are good at forming relationships.

Radu's answer

Rutter *et al.* investigated whether the age of babies who were in Romanian orphanages made a difference to attachment. They found that the babies put in as soon as they were born went on to be securely attached but the babies put in at six months old were insecurely attached. This supports Bowlby's idea of a sensitive period in attachment because he said attachments had to be formed early or else there would be difficulty and then the child would be insecurely attached. This investigation has low ecological validity as it cannot be generalised to the rest of the world as it was just done in Romania. But it was done in a natural environment and is a real situation.

Mario's mark	
AO1 = _____ out of 3	AO2 = _____ out of 3

Radu's mark	
AO1 = _____ out of 3	AO2 = _____ out of 3

Answers on page 191

You can read marking guidelines on pages 10 and 12.

KEY WORDS

- Day care
- EPPE
- NICHD

Possible essay questions ...

Outline and evaluate the impact of day care on aggression. *(12 marks)*

Outline and evaluate research into the effect of day care on children's social development (e.g. aggression, peer relations). *(12 marks)*

Other possible exam questions ...

+ Name **two** forms of day care. *(2 marks)*
+ Describe **one or more** studies of the effect of day care on aggression. *(6 marks)*
+ Outline what research has shown about the effects of day care on aggression. *(4 marks)*
+ Apply this knowledge to ... *(6 marks)*

MUST know ...

Key study: NICHD study

How?

A study that has been conducted in the US of over 1,300 children from diverse families and locations.

The children have been studied from infancy to age 15, assessing social and cognitive development regularly.

Children in different forms of day care were studied as well as those home-cared.

Showed?

At age five, children who had been in day care of any kind were rated as more assertive, disobedient and aggressive.

Children in full-time day care were about three times more likely to show behaviour problems (e.g. arguing, hitting) compared to those cared for by their mothers at home.

Children who averaged more than 30 hours per week in day care were more likely to show problem behaviours when they went to school.

 The strength of both these studies ...

... lies in the strong design.

- **E** – Both studies involve a wide spread of children and families and day care providers. Both studies also controlled for background factors such as parental occupation.

 One problem with these studies is that ...

... they are natural experiments or correlations.

- **E** – In natural experiments, the independent variable is day care versus home care, but the children are not randomly allocated to these groups and therefore it is not reasonable to draw causal conclusions.

There are some contradictory results ...

... which suggest that day care is *not* associated with aggression.

- **E** – The NICHD study found that 83% of the children attending day care between 10 and 30 hours per week did *not* show higher levels of aggression.

SHOULD know ...

Second study: EPPE study

How?

A study conducted in the UK of over 3,000 children from the age of three to 11.

The children attended a wide range of day care providers (e.g. attached to a school or not, low and high quality) and were compared with home-cared children.

Cognitive and social development were assessed and teacher ratings were used.

Showed?

Children who spent longer in day care showed more evidence of aggression (as rated by their teachers).

Starting day care at an early age was associated with increased aggression but by age 10 this was no longer apparent.

The quality of care was important – low-quality care was associated with increased aggressiveness.

- **E** – This means that some extraneous factors can be ruled out. For example, it might be that children who attend day care come from homes where both parents work and this might explain negative effects when compared with home-cared children.
- **L** – Such strong design suggests that the observed effects can be attributed to day care rather than other factors, i.e. are valid.

- **E** – The association between increased time spent in day care and increased levels of aggression is a correlation, which again doesn't demonstrate a cause.
- **L** – This means that assumptions should not be made about day care *causing* aggression.

- **E** – In fact, maternal sensitivity, maternal education and family income were better predictors of aggressiveness than time spent in day care.
- **L** – Such findings suggest that the role of day care in increasing aggression has been exaggerated.

COULD know ...

Third study: Vandell and Corsanti

How?

A longitudinal study of 20 middle-class children in good-quality and poor-quality day care.

Maternal and observer ratings were taken at four and eight years.

Showed?

Children who attended poorer-quality day care were rated as more unfriendly and less socially competent.

From the ages of four to eight years the children's behaviour didn't change, suggesting that any causes of behaviour (e.g. aggression) may precede the day care experience (starting age four).

 Even if day care does cause some increase ...

... in aggressiveness this is counterbalanced by positive effects.

- **E** – The EPPE study concluded that pre-school experience, compared to none, enhances children's development.
- **E** – There are benefits for both cognitive and social development (see next spread). Furthermore, negative effects are less likely in high-quality care.
- **L** – This means that any negative effects can be counteracted by improving the quality of day care.

JUMBLED SENTENCES

On the facing page there are three criticisms related to the 'Must' and 'Should' studies. Similar sentences are presented below in a jumbled order. Place the number for each sentence in the correct square. The first one has been done for you.

Criticism 1

[4] **1** This means that some extraneous factors can be ruled out.

[ ] **2** Both studies controlled for background factors such as parental occupation.

[ ] **3** Such strong design suggests that the findings can be relied on.

[ ] **4** The strength of the NICHD and EPPE studies lies in their strong design.

Criticism 2

[ ] **5** Therefore, it is not reasonable to draw causal conclusions.

[ ] **6** One problem with these studies is that they are natural experiments.

[ ] **7** The independent variable is day care versus home care, but the children were not randomly allocated to these groups.

[ ] **8** This means that the assumptions should not be made about day care *causing* aggression.

Criticism 3

[ ] **9** There were some contradictory results.

[ ] **10** In addition to maternal sensitivity, maternal education and family income were better predictors of aggressiveness than time spent in day care.

[ ] **11** The actual evidence was that 83% of the children attending day care between 10 and 30 hours per week did *not* show higher levels of aggression.

[ ] **12** The NICHD study found evidence that showed that day care is *not* associated with aggression.

[ ] **13** Such findings suggest that the role of day care in increased aggression has been exaggerated.

Answers on page 191

 ## SPOT THE MISTAKES

Read the description of the EPPE study below.
There are five mistakes, draw a circle round each.

The EPPE study was conducted in the US and involved over 3,000 children from the age of 5 to 11. There were two groups of children: those in day care and those home-cared. Cognitive and social development was assessed and teacher ratings were used. The results showed that the longer time children spent in day care the less aggressive they were. It was also found that starting pre-school at an early age was associated with increased aggression. This effect had increased by age 10. The quality of care was important – high-quality care was associated with increased aggressiveness.

Answers on page 192

KEY PHRASES

Select key phrases to help you remember the key study by NICHD.
Some have been done for you.

How?	Showed?
US study	More assertive
1300+	

On a separate piece of paper, use your key phrases to answer the following exam question:

Outline **one** study of the effect of day care on aggression. *(6 marks)*

DRAWING CONCLUSIONS

The graph below shows the data from a study on the relationship between day care and levels of aggression. Observers recorded levels of aggression in four year olds at a day care centre and asked the day care centre to report how many hours a week the children had spent in day care. The results of this study are shown in the graph below.

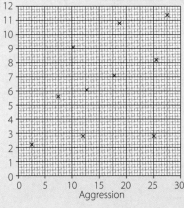

State **two** findings and for each one draw a conclusion (state what the finding shows):

Finding 1:
Conclusion 1: This shows that …
Finding 2:
Conclusion 2: This shows that …

Answers on page 191

KEY WORDS

- Day care
- EPPE
- Peer relations
- Sociability

Possible essay question ...

Outline and evaluate the impact of day care on peer relations.
(12 marks)

Other possible exam questions ...

+ Explain what is meant by 'peer relations'. *(2 marks)*
+ Outline how psychologists have investigated the effects of day care on peer relations. *(4 marks)*
+ What have studies shown us about the effects of day care on peer relations? *(4 marks)*
+ Apply this knowledge to ... *(6 marks)*

MUST know ...

Key study: EPPE study

How?

A study conducted in the UK of over 3,000 children from the age of three to 11.

The children attended a wide range of day care providers (e.g. attached to a school or not, low and high quality) and were compared with home-cared children.

Cognitive and social development were assessed using tests and teacher ratings.

Showed?

Pre-school day care improves all aspects of social behaviour, e.g. independence, cooperation and peer relationships.

Starting day care at an early age was associated with increased sociability.

Children with limited or no day care experience had poorer sociability.

There was no difference between children in full- and part-time attendance.

 There are individual differences ...

... in the way children respond to day care.

- *E* – Some children feel more uncomfortable or distressed to be in the day care situation, away from home and with many other children.

 There are some contradictory results ...

... that suggest that day care is *not* associated with improved peer relations.

- *E* – Belsky and Rovine found that more than 20 hours per week of day care was associated with increased insecure attachment which, in turn, is associated with decreased popularity and lower social competence.

SHOULD know ...

Second study: Clarke-Stewart *et al.*

How?

Two samples were compared: a total of 150 children aged between two and four years either in day care centres or home care (with mother or carer).

The children came from a range of different home backgrounds in Chicago, USA.

Many aspects of social and cognitive development were assessed.

Showed?

Day care children were better at negotiating with peers and settling disputes (both important for good peer relations).

Day care children were more self-confident, outgoing and verbally expressive, and less distressed and timid in new situations.

Children who played with a greater number of children were rated as more sociable.

This suggests that day care provides opportunities to practise social skills.

- *E* – For example, shy children may find day care overwhelming (Pennebaker *et al.*) and insecurely attached children may be more distressed (NICHD).
- *L* – This means that day care may not promote peer relations for all children.

- *E* – However, Belsky and Rovine's association may be due to other reasons (e.g. working mothers are more likely to have insecurely attached children) and other research has found that insecurely attached children actually benefit most from day care (Egeland and Hiester).
- *L* – This suggests that day care may actually have a negative effect on peer relations, at least for some children.

 Clarke-Stewart et al. did suggest that ...

... day care may sometimes have negative effects on peer relations.

- *E* – They found that when there were too many children (more than 20) the effects could be harmful.
- *E* – Children in large classes spent more time being aggressive and less time socialising.
- *L* – This shows that interacting with peers is not always beneficial to peer relations.

COULD know ...

Third study: Creps and Vernon-Feagans

How?

Compared 41 US children who started day care either before six months old or between six and 12 months old.

The children were observed at three years.

Family background, temperament and hours spent per week in day care were controlled.

Showed?

Children who started day care before six months old engaged in less solitary play and more positive peer behaviours.

 It is difficult to disentangle ...

... cause and effect.

- *E* – For example, in the study above it could be that parents who are more outgoing and confident send their infants to day care early.
- *E* – The parents' personality might be the cause of their child's increased sociability rather than the day care experience.
- *L* – This could explain why early day care attendance is associated with higher sociability.

CONSTRUCTING AN ANSWER

This is a possible exam question:

What have studies shown us about the effects of day care on peer relations? *(4 marks)*

Fill in the boxes below to help you construct and answer.

Effect	Research support
Positive effects	
Negative effects	

Answers on page 192

 **MATCH THEM UP**

Identify which finding goes with which researcher.

1	Pennebaker *et al.*	A	Day care children learn negotiating skills.
2	EPPE study	B	Insecure children may benefit most from day care.
3	Egeland and Hiester	C	The earlier in day care the better.
4	Clarke-Stewart *et al.*	D	Shy children distressed in day care.
5	Belsky and Rovine	E	Day care associated with increased insecure attachment.

Answers on page 192

 APPLYING YOUR KNOWLEDGE

Mark and his wife are considering placing their one-year-old daughter in day care but are concerned about all the negative reports they have read about in the newspapers.

Outline some possible benefits of day care for Mark's daughter. Refer to psychological research in your answer. *(4 marks)*

Benefits for Mark's daughter	Link to research

Answers on page 192

 A MARKING EXERCISE

Two answers to the following exam question are shown below. Decide on your own mark.

Describe **one or more** studies of the effects of day care on peer relations. *(4 marks)*

Bill's answer

One study on day care had two different groups of children. One group were in day care and the other group were looked after at home. They studied how the children behaved with each other by observing them when they were playing. They found that the children in day care had better peer relations than the other group. They also were more aggressive but this may be related to the quality of their care.

Betsy's answer

A number of psychologists have conducted research on the effects of day care on peer relations. One such study was by Clarke-Stewart that suggested children who attend day care have greater confidence and sociability, these would help them develop better peer relations in the future, like secondary schools and when they go to work. However, other research has contradicted this and found that day care increases aggression.

Consider which of the following applies to the answers on the left:

- No creditworthy material *(0 marks)*
- Brief *(1 mark)*
- Basic, some relevance *(2 marks)*
- Less detailed, relevant *(3 marks)*
- Reasonably detailed *(4 marks)*

(Note: this is an AO1 question only.)

Bill's answer _____ out of 4

Betsy's answer _____ out of 4

Answers on page 192

71

KEY WORDS

- Attachment disorder
- Child care
- Disinhibited attachment
- Disruption of attachment
- Primary attachment
- Secondary attachment
- Secure attachment

Possible essay question ...

Discuss the influence of research into attachment on child care practices. *(12 marks)*

Other possible exam questions ...

+ Explain how child care practices have been influenced by findings of research into attachment. *(4 marks)*

+ Apply this knowledge to ... *(6 marks)*

 Exam tip

On this spread we have provided description and evaluation in order to compose an answer to an essay question. However, if an exam question is just description (AO1) you can use the research evidence as part of your description.

MUST know ...

Improving day care

Children who attend day care spend many hours apart from their primary attachment figures.

This is a physical and emotional disruption of attachment.

The effects of emotional disruption can be compensated for by the provision of alternative attachment figures.

For example, the Soho Family Centre in London bases its day care programme on an understanding of the importance of secondary attachment figures.

Each carer is assigned special responsibility for a maximum of three children and is paired with another carer who can step in if need be.

 There is research support for ...

... the effects of disruption of attachment.

- *E* – The Robertsons (see page 64) showed that children who experience disruption of attachment, without good substitute *emotional* care, experience negative effects.

 There is theoretical support for ...

... the value of substitute emotional care.

- *E* – Bowlby (see page 56) proposed that primary attachments are important for healthy social and emotional development.

SHOULD know ...

Improving hospital care

When children are in hospital they may also experience physical and emotional disruption of attachment.

Parents should be allowed unrestricted visiting to avoid possible emotional disruption of attachment.

Staff should be aware of the need to provide good substitute emotional care.

Improving adoption

The first six months of an infant's life are important in the development of attachment, based on Bowlby's research.

Children who fail to form attachments by that age may later experience attachment disorder (e.g. Rutter *et al.*).

Therefore adoptions should ideally take place before the age of six months.

- *E* – In the Robertsons' study, John lacked substitute emotional care and became depressed and withdrawn, whereas the children cared for by the Robertsons didn't appear to experience any negative effects.
- *L* – This shows that substitute emotional care is important when disruption of attachment occurs.

- *E* – Bowlby also proposed that secondary attachments provide an important emotional safety net when the primary attachment figure is not present.
- *L* – This means that special emotional relationships with substitute carers are important, especially when there is long-term child care as in the day care situation.

 COULD know ...

Improving the quality of parenting

Parents who have had poor attachment experiences themselves may find it more difficult to provide the sensitive responsiveness necessary to form secure attachments with their own children.

Parenting advice and classes may help teach parents the important skills to be able to provide good emotional care for their own children and form secure attachments.

 This is supported by theory and research ...

... related to attachment.

- *E* – Rutter and Quinton (see page 66) found that mothers who were insecurely attached as infants were more likely to have insecurely attached infants.
- *E* – Bowlby's continuity hypothesis suggests that children who are insecurely attached in infancy will later experience more difficulties in their relationships, for example with their own children.
- *L* – This suggests that it is important to offer help to break the cycle of privation.

Research shows that six months ...

... is a critical age in attachment development.

- *E* – Rutter *et al.*'s study of Romanian orphans (see page 66) found that children adopted before the age of six months were normal in their development, whereas this was less true of children adopted after the age of six months.
- *E* – The children adopted after the age of six months displayed signs of disinhibited attachment and attachment disorder.
- *L* – This suggests that six months is a critical age in the development of attachment.

FILL IN THE BLANKS

Children who attend day care are both physically and

(1) .... separated from their

(2) .... attachment figure. Such separation

can be compensated by providing (3) ....

.... attachment figures. At the Soho Family

Centre in London each carer is assigned special responsibility

for a maximum of (4) .... children. Children in

hospital may experience disruption of attachment. The potential

negative effects can be dealt with by allowing parents unrestricted

(5) .... and ensuring that staff provide good

substitute (6) .... care.

Answers on page 192

 CONSTRUCTING AN ANSWER

Explain how child care has been influenced by research into attachment. *(4 marks)*

On the facing page there are suggestions, based on attachment research, for improving child care. Select **two** and for each write one sentence explaining the link between attachment research and your suggestion.

Suggestion	Link to attachment research

Answers on page 192

 DRAWING CONCLUSIONS

A research study on adoption compared secure versus insecure attachment in children adopted before or after the age of six months. The findings are shown in the graph below.

State **two** findings and for each one draw a conclusion (state what the finding shows):

Finding 1:

Conclusion 1: This shows that …

Finding 2:

Conclusion 2: This shows that …

Answers on page 192

RESEARCH ISSUES

Throughout this chapter we have looked at research on attachment and on the problems that occur when attachments fail or are disrupted. Many of the criticisms of the research are related to *validity*.

Write down a definition for validity and identify **one** argument suggesting that the validity of attachment research is high and **one** counter-argument.

Definition of validity:	
Argument suggesting that the validity of attachment research is high:	Support for this argument:
Argument suggesting that the validity of attachment research is low:	Support for this argument:

Answers on page 192

KEY WORDS

- Day care
- Disruption of attachment
- EPPE
- NICHD
- Sociability

Possible essay question ...

Discuss the influence of research into attachment on child care practices. *(12 marks)*

Other possible exam questions ...

+ Explain how child care practices have been influenced by research into attachment. *(4 marks)*

+ Apply this knowledge to ... *(6 marks)*

 Exam tip

On this spread we have provided description and evaluation in order to compose an answer to an essay question. However, if an exam question is just description (AO1) you can use the research evidence as part of your description.

MUST know ...

In order to provide high-quality child care, research on day care suggests that the following characteristics are important:

Good staff-to-child ratios

The NICHD study found that day care staff could only provide sensitive care if the ratios were as low as one adult to three children.

Minimal staff turnover

When staff are employed only for short periods of time children may fail to form attachments to the staff.

Or, if they have formed an attachment with a staff member, the children will experience the anxiety associated with disruption of attachment when the staff member leaves.

Qualified and experienced day care staff

Sylva *et al.* found that the higher the qualifications of day care staff, the better the children's social development.

 Quality of care is important ...

... because it is related to positive effects.

- *E* – A study by Field found that the greatest benefits of day care on peer relations were for those children in high-quality care.

 The importance of staff–child ratio is ...

... that it is related to sensitive care.

- *E* – For example, the NICHD study found that day care staff could only provide sensitive care if the ratios were as good as one member of staff to three children.

 One problem with day care studies is ...

... they are natural experiments or correlations.

- *E* – In natural experiments the independent variable is day care versus home care, but the children are not randomly allocated to these groups and therefore it is not reasonable to draw causal conclusions.

SHOULD know ...

Day care research has also identified other characteristics that are important for child care practices:

Number of years in day care

Research has found that the number of years spent in day care is associated with increased aggression (EPPE).

On the other hand, the EPPE study also found that the younger children are when they begin day care, the more sociability was improved by day care.

Number of hours per week

Research has found that 30+ hours per week spent in day care is associated with increased aggression (NICHD).

Large class sizes

Day care generally enhances peer relationships, but this is not the case if class sizes are too big (Clarke-Stewart *et al.*).

- *E* – Poor-quality day care has been linked to negative outcomes (Vandell and Corsanti).
- *L* – Therefore, if we wish to maximise these positive effects we need to maximise the *quality* of care.

- *E* – Sensitive care is also related to attachment. Research has demonstrated the importance of such responsiveness in maintaining secure attachment (Cooper *et al.*).
- *L* – This suggests that, where day care staff have special responsibility for more than three children, the quality of care will suffer.

- *E* – The association between increased time spent in day care and increased levels of aggression is a correlation, which again doesn't demonstrate a cause.
- *L* – This means that assumptions should not be made about day care *causing* aggression.

COULD know ...

Individual differences

Shy children may feel more uncomfortable or distressed to be in the day care situation with many other children and away from home (Pennebaker *et al.*).

Insecurely attached children may be more distressed by day care experiences (NICHD) but may actually benefit most from day care (Egeland and Hiester).

 The overall conclusion from day care research ...

... is that children benefit from day care.

- *E* – For example, the EPPE study found cognitive and social development were both enhanced.
- *E* – However, the EPPE study also noted that quality of care was important – low-quality care was associated with increased aggressiveness.
- *L* – This shows that quality of care is the issue, not whether or not day care is harmful to children.

APPLYING YOUR KNOWLEDGE

Jenny plans to become a child minder and look after children in her own home.

What advice would a psychologist give to Jenny? Make reference to psychological research on day care in your answer. *(4 marks)*

Use the table below to plan an answer.

Advice	Reference to psychological research

Answers on page 192

CHOOSE THE RIGHT ANSWER

Tick three items in the following list that might lead to low-quality day care:

A	Regular changes of staff	☐
B	A good staff-to-child ratio	☐
C	Untrained staff	☐
D	Large class sizes	☐
E	Insecurely attached children	☐

Answers on page 192

A MARKING EXERCISE

Three answers to the following exam question are shown below:

Outline **one** characteristic of high-quality day care for nine-month-old children. *(2 marks)*

One of the answers got 0 marks, one got 1 mark and one got 2 marks. Which is which?

Answer A The children are not left alone for long periods and are accompanied suitably.

Answer B Attentive carers who can provide the infants with comfort if necessary.

Answer C The care given was one to one so the child could form an attachment.

0 marks	=	answer _____
1 mark	=	answer _____
2 marks	=	answer _____

Answers on page 192

An idea

You could draw a mind map, on a separate piece of paper, relating to this spread and the previous one.

Your mind map should show:
1 A piece of attachment research or day care research, linked to . . .
2 An application of this research to a form of child care.

PRACTICE ELABORATION

In the marking exercise above the key factor in gaining 2 marks instead of 1 mark is elaboration.

In the activity below, write two characteristics of high-quality day care in the left-hand column and write detailed explanations of the characteristics on the right (i.e. explain what is involved with that characteristic).

Characteristic of high-quality day care	Elaboration

Answers on page 192

TOPIC 11 — Learning theory and attachment

MUST — Classical conditioning

Attachment formed through association. Food (UCS) produces pleasure (UCR). Person who feeds infant (CS) eventually produces same pleasure response (CR) because of their association with food.

SHOULD — Operant conditioning

Hungry and uncomfortable

Pleasure

Primary Reinforcer

Secondary Reinforcer — BELCH

COULD — Social learning theory

I love you Dale
I love you too Jo Ellen
Be a nice little boy

Modelling

Direct Instruction

EVALUATION

Food not the main factor

Infants more likely to develop attachment with the person who provides comfort rather than food.
This was demonstrated by …

This shows that …

Human studies also challenge the importance of food

Shaffer and Emerson — babies most attached to person who was most responsive rather than one with food.
This study involved …

This provides support …

A strength of this account

MY REINFORCERS

Learning theory can explain attachment formation. Food is not the reinforcer, but attention and responsiveness are.
Support comes from …

This means that …

Real-world applications

Parents act as role models.

TOPIC 12 — Bowlby's theory of attachment

MUST

Safe — INNATE CHARACTERISTICS

Adaptive

CUTE   NOT SO CUTE

6 months SENSITIVE PERIOD

Adaptive — attachments make it more likely an infant will survive.
Innate — certain characteristics (social releasers) elicit caregiving.
Sensitive period — develops around six months; difficult after that.

SHOULD

INTERNAL WORKING MODEL — Mummy

Monotropy

Continuity hypothesis

COULD

WANTED
Mummy for secure attachment — Must be accepting cooperative and accessible please

---

EVALUATION

Support for innate basis

Lorenz found that goslings imprinted on first moving object.
The goslings attaching to Lorenz …

This supports the idea …

Cross-cultural studies

Different Child rearing Practices

If attachment is innate, it should be universal.
Tronick et al. …

This shows that …

Problems with monotropy

Rutter argues that all attachment figures equally important.
It may be preferable …

This suggests that …

There is an alternative view

The Temperament Hypothesis

MUST — Episodes of the Strange Situation

EPISODE 6 EPISODE 7

uh?

mum leaves   stranger enters

Research technique to measure attachment between infant and a parent.

Conducted in a lab environment.

Eight episodes, each lasting about three minutes, involving infant, parent and a stranger.

SHOULD — Situations of mild anxiety

This place is strange

I'm ignoring you

MUM RETURNS

COULD

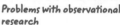

① Proximity seeking
② Contact maintaining
③ Proximity avoiding
④ Contact resisting
⑤ Search behaviour

INTENSITY

EVALUATION

Useful measure of attachment type

STRANGE ... but USEFUL

As a means of assessing the quality of an attachment bond between infant and parent.

The method was tested by ...

This shows that ...

Not a valid measurement

Only measures attachment in the context of one particular relationship.

∴ it is about the quality of <u>that</u> relationship rather than attachment 'type'.

However, research has found that ...

This means ...

May not apply to all cultures

SS developed in US — assumptions of securely attached child may not be true in all cultures.

In some other cultures ...

This means that ...

Problems with observational research

Erm?

Mum leaves

Uncertainty of coding

MUST

THE STRANGE SITUATION

Secure Infants   Insecure Infants

SECURE: greet parent enthusiastically on return.
Willing to explore, high stranger anxiety, some separation anxiety.
INSECURE-AVOIDANT: indifferent to parent.
Willing to explore, low stranger anxiety, low separation anxiety.
INSECURE-RESISTANT: resists or rejects parent.
Less willing to explore, high stranger anxiety, high separation anxiety.

SHOULD

Sensitivity of mother

Lack of sensitive responding from parent

SECURE   INSECURE

Later healthy social, emotional and cognitive development

Later problems with intimate relationships

COULD

BUS STOP

Disinhibited attachment type

EVALUATION

Attachment behaviours not consistent

Main and Solomon identified fourth type — disorganised attachment.
This is characterised by ...

This means that ...

Display more than one type

Children may display a different attachment type with different people and different situations.
For example ...

This means that ...

Real-world application

Circle of Security project — used to improve parent—infant bond in insecurely attached children.
The project teaches parents to ...

This suggests that ...

Sensitivity may not be because of secure attachment

MATERNAL SENSITIVITY ≠ SECURE ATTACHMENT

(necessarily)

TOPIC 15 — Cultural variations in attachment

MUST — van IJzendoorn and Kroonenberg

HOW?

Meta analysis of 32 studies in 8 countries. Studies used Strange Situation to assess attachment types. Excluded studies with special groups or fewer than 35 infants.

SHOWED? Secure attachment most common type in every country.

Insecure-avoidant second most common except in Israel and Japan (insecure-resistant). Variation within countries 1.5 times higher than variation between countries.

SHOULD — Grossman et al.

Longitudinal studies in N + S Germany

HOW?

SHOWED?

COULD — Ainsworth

Observational study in Uganda

HOW?

SHOWED?

Uganda

EVALUATION

Strange Situation not valid in all cultures

Developed in US and based on US assumptions about secure attachment.

Takahasi suggests ...

This means that ...

Countries not the same as cultures

COUNTRIES ≠ CULTURES

There are many cultures in each country, making it meaningless to compare attachment between countries.

van IJzendoorn and Sagi ...

This means that ...

Not all studies find cultural differences

CULTURAL SIMILARITIES in primary attachment formation (Tronick et al) In Democratic Republic of Congo

This is further supported by ...

This means that ...

Cultural bias in attachment research

Independent kids are secure kids / Dependence is best / WEST / EAST

TOPIC 16 — Disruption of attachment

MUST — Robertson and Robertson

HOW?

Nurse busy with other children

Filmed young children separated from their mother.
John, two weeks in a residential nursery, experienced emotional and physical separation.
Other children experienced only physical separation.

SHOWED?

John became increasingly depressed and withdrawn and cried a lot. Jane etc. coped well and remained happy. Physical disruption alone did not have negative outcomes but emotional disruption did.

SHOULD — Hart et al.

Maternity Unit 64 Participants 12 months

Mothers assessed on depression questionnaire

OBSERVED PLAYING

HOW?

SHOWED?

COULD — Robertson and Bowlby

HOW?

SHOWED?

EVALUATION

Individual differences

children's ward / secure attachment is the best medicine

Some children less affected by hospital stays than others (Bowlby et al.).

Bowlby suggested ...

This suggests that ...

Real-world applications

Effects of disruption can be minimised by 24hr parental access or good substitute emotional care.

In the 1950s ...

This suggests that ...

Doesn't always have long-term negative effects

Early disruption makes individuals more vulnerable to disruption of attachments in later life.

Bifulco et al. found ...

This suggests that ...

PDD model oversimplified

Protesting or coping?

TOPIC 17 — Failure to form attachment (privation) and institutional care

MUST	Hodges and Tizard

HOW?

65 CHILDREN AGED 4 MONTHS — Age 4 → RESTORED TO OWN HOMES → Age 8 → Age 16

ADOPTED → Age 8 → Age 18

Longitudinal study of children in institutional care either restored to own homes or adopted at age 4.

SHOWED?   Assessed again at 8 + 16 and compared to control group of home-reared children.

At 4 years all children showed disinhibited attachment. At 8 and 16 years adopted children had close attachments. All ex-institutional children had poor peer relationships and sought more adult attention.

SHOULD	Rutter et al.

HOW?

SHOWED?

COULD	Rutter and Quinton

HOW?

94   51

SHOWED?

EVALUATION

The problem of attrition

4 Months 65 | 8 Years 51 | 16 Years 49

Hodges and Tizard's sample was reduced over the course of the study from 65 to 51 to 49.

The problem with attrition ...

This means that ...

Privation only one factor

Emotional Privation
Social Privation   Cognitive Privation

Children who experience emotional privation also tend to experience other forms of privation.

Children who suffer ...

This means that ...

Individual differences in coping

Securely attached children are less affected by emotional disruption.

Bowlby suggested ...

This suggests that ...

Privation may not have long-term effects

VULNERABLE   DIVORCE

TOPIC 18 — Day care and aggression

MUST	NICHD study

HOW?   US study of 1,300 children across the USA. Studied from infancy to age 15. Assessed for social and cognitive development.

SHOWED?   At age five day care children more disobedient + aggressive.

Children in full-time day care three times more likely to show behaviour problems. More than 30 hours per week day care — more behaviour problems.

SHOULD	EPPE study

HOW?

3,000 children aged 3–11

SHOWED?

COULD	Vandell and Corsanti

HOW?

Age 4   Age 8

SHOWED?

EVALUATION

Studies have a strong design

WIDESPREAD | GOOD CONTROL
STRONG | DESIGN

Widespread of children, families and day care providers. Good control of background factors.

This means that ...

Such strong design suggests that ...

Studies are natural experiments/ correlations

CORRELATION ≠ CAUSALITY
NATURAL EXPERIMENT ≠ RANDOM ALLOCATION

Not reasonable to draw causal conclusions from natural experiments or correlations.

This means that ...

Some contradictory results

NICHD study — 83% of children attending day care 10–30 hrs/week had no increase in aggression.

In fact ...

Such findings suggest ...

Negative effects counter-balanced by positive

HIGH-QUALITY DAY CARE CENTRE
Positive Effects Here | As Recommended by EPPE

MUST — EPPE study

HOW?

High Quality
Home Based
School Based
Low Quality

3,000 children 3–11 yrs. Wide variety of day care providers compared to home-reared children. Cognitive and social development assessed.

SHOWED? Pre-school day care improves all aspects of social behaviour.
Starting day care early = increased sociability. Limited/no day care = poorer sociability.
Part-time of full-time attendance = no difference.

SHOULD — Clarke-Stewart et al.

HOW?

CHICAGO

SHOWED?

COULD — Creps and Vernon-Feagans

<6 months ..... 6–12 months ..... → 3 Years

HOW?

SHOWED?

EVALUATION

Individual differences in responses to day care

Distressed → Insecurely attached

Overwhelmed → Shy

Some children feel more uncomfortable.
For example ...

This means that ...

Some contradictory results

20+ hours = INCREASED INSECURE ATTACHMENT = POOR PEER RELATIONS

Belsky and Rovine: 20+ hrs day care per week associated with insecure attachment = decreased popularity and lower social competence.
However ...

This suggests that ...

Day care — negative effects

>20 children = Potentially harmful effects

Clarke-Stewart et al. found too many children can have negative effects on peer relations.
Children in large classes ...

This shows that ...

Difficult to disentangle cause and effect

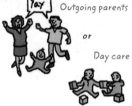

Yay → Outgoing parents
or
Day care

MUST — Improving day care

Soho Family Centre

Effects of emotional disruption can be overcome by alternative attachment figures. E.g. Soho family centre based on understanding of this. Each carer max of 3 children and paired with a 'substitute' carer.

SHOULD — Improving hospital care and adoption

SUBSTITUTE EMOTIONAL CARE

Adoption checkout 6 months or less

ADOPTION <6 MONTHS

COULD — Improving parenting quality

INSECURE CHILD → INSECURE ADULT → PARENTING CLASSES

EVALUATION

Research support for disruption of attachment

Nurse busy with other children

Robertsons showed how disruption of attachment without substitute emotional care has negative effects.
Bowlby proposed ...

This shows that ...

Theoretical support for substitute emotional care

Primary attachments are important. Secondary attachments are also important

Primary attachments important for healthy social/emotional development.
Bowlby proposed ...

This means that ...

Six months is a critical age

6 months

Rutter's study of orphanages: children adopted <6 months had normal development.
Children adopted after 6 months ...

This suggests that ...

Supported by theory/research

Insecure as a child

More likely to have insecure children

MUST	Research has shown that high-quality day care requires:	SHOULD	Other important characteristics are:	COULD	Individual differences

MUST — Research has shown that high-quality day care requires:

Good staff to child ratio — e.g. 1 adult to 3 children

Minimal staff turnover

"How long will you be staying?"

Qualified and experienced day care staff

SHOULD — Other important characteristics are:

Number of years in day care	More years =	Increased aggression but also increased sociability (EPPE)
Number of hours per week	30+ per week =	Increased aggression but also increased sociability (EPPE)
Large class sizes		Make development of peer relationships more difficult.

EVALUATION

Quality of care is important

Confident, happy, well adjusted

"So I'm guessing he goes to a high-quality day care"

High-quality day care is related to positive effects, e.g. peer relationships.

Poor quality day care linked to ...

Therefore ...

Staff–child ratio related to sensitive care

NICHD found **1 to 3** maximum

Sensitive care related to ...

This suggests that ...

Day care studies are natural experiments/correlations

CORRELATION ≠ CAUSALITY
NATURAL ≠ RANDOM
EXPERIMENT ≠ ALLOCATION

Not reasonable to draw causal conclusions from natural experiments or correlations.

The association between increase time in day care ...

This means that ...

Overall conclusion is that children benefit

CHILDREN BENEFIT! Supported by EPPE study

KEY WORDS

- Aim
- Demand characteristics
- Dependent variable (DV)
- Directional hypothesis
- Experiment
- Experimenter (investigator) effect
- Extraneous variable (EV)
- Hypothesis
- Independent variable (IV)
- Laboratory experiment
- Mundane realism
- Non-directional hypothesis
- Operationalise
- Replication
- Validity

Possible exam questions (these are generally paired with a 'stem' describing a study) ...

+ Identify the operationalised independent variable (IV) in this study. *(2 marks)*
+ Write an appropriate non-directional hypothesis for this experiment. *(2 marks)*
+ Explain **one** strength of a laboratory experiment. *(2 marks)*
+ Identify **one** possible extraneous variable in this experiment. *(1 mark)*
+ Describe possible demand characteristics in this research. *(3 marks)*

 Important

In this chapter we have not always followed the S E E L rule (see page 14) for AO2 because many of the evaluation questions are only worth 2 marks (see the possible questions above).

MUST know ...

An experiment

A form of research where cause-and-effect relationships can be studied by comparing the effects of an independent variable (IV) on a dependent variable (DV).

The IV is an event that is directly manipulated by the experimenter in order to observe its effects on the DV.

The DV depends in some way on the IV.

The DV is the variable that is measured at the end.

Laboratory experiment

Some experiments are conducted in a laboratory, a special environment where variables can be investigated under controlled conditions.

(Note that some studies are conducted in a laboratory but are not laboratory experiments.)

Aims and hypotheses

The aim of any study is a statement of what the researcher intends to investigate.

A hypothesis is a precise and testable statement about the expected relationship between variables.

 One strength of a lab experiment is ...

... that researchers can minimise extraneous variables.

- **E** – This means that we can be more certain that the IV did cause the change in the DV instead of another variable causing the change.

 One limitation of a lab experiment is ...

... that the setting is contrived (it is said to lack 'mundane realism').

- **E** – This means that participants may not behave as they would in everyday life and then the results cannot be generalised to everyday life situations.

SHOULD know ...

Extraneous variables (EVs)

Any variable, other than the IV, which may potentially affect the DV and thereby confound ('confuse') the findings, affecting validity.

For example, if some participants are tested in the morning and some in the evening then time of day may act as an EV because the participants are tired, which may affect their performance.

Operationalisation

Variables must be operationalised, i.e. defined in a way that they can easily be measured or tested.

For example, instead of saying that the DV is 'educational attainment' an experimenter must specify a way to measure this, such as GCSE grades.

Hypotheses

A directional hypothesis states the direction of the difference between two conditions or two groups of participants (e.g. group A is better than Group B).

A non-directional hypothesis states there is a difference without identifying the direction (e.g. there is a difference between group A and group B).

 A second limitation is ...

... that the level of control makes it easier to replicate the study.

- **E** – Replication means that you can demonstrate the validity of the results because they happen again when the study is repeated.

A second limitation is ...

... that experimenter effects may influence the results.

- **E** – For example, an experimenter may expect boys to do better than girls and this means that the experimenter subtly encourages boys to try harder.
- **E** – In the end the boys do better because of the subtle encouragement not because they are actually superior.

COULD know ...

Demand characteristics

A cue that makes participants aware of the aims of a study. This may affect a participant's behaviour.

For example, participants may be given one memory test in the morning and one in the afternoon. Participants might guess that the study is comparing the effect of time of day on performance and this makes the participants try harder in the afternoon.

These demand characteristics act as an EV and this reduces the validity of the results.

 One strength of all experiments is ...

... that causal conclusions can be drawn.

- **E** – The deliberate manipulation of the IV in a lab experiment means that we can claim that any observed changes in the DV were caused by the IV. (Field and natural experiments are described on page 86.)
- **E** – For example, if you manipulate the time of day when people are tested and they do better in the morning than in the afternoon, this suggests that time of day *causes* differences in performance.
- **L** – This is especially true in a lab experiment where EVs have been controlled.

FILL IN THE BLANKS

In an experiment, the experimenter controls the

(1) .... variable. The experimenter then

measures the (2) .... variable. If the IV has

caused a change in the DV the experimenter can then conclude that

there is a causal relationship – unless there were

(3) .... variables. Such variables may

(4) .... the results of the study, affecting the

(5) .... of the conclusions.

Answers on page 192

CIRCLE TRUE OR FALSE

T or F This is a directional hypothesis: 'People who are hot are more aggressive than people who are cold'.

T or F This is a hypothesis: 'To investigate the effect of temperature on aggression'.

T or F This is a non-directional hypothesis: 'Men and woman are different in terms of their aggression scores'.

T or F This is a hypothesis: 'Drinking through a straw is better than not drinking through a straw'.

T or F Operationalisation makes it clear how you can measure a variable.

Answers on page 192

A MARKING EXERCISE

Student answers to the following question are given below:

An experiment was conducted where participants completed a test in a very hot room or a cool room to demonstrate the effect of temperature on aggression levels. Aggressiveness was assessed by a researcher and each participant was given an aggression score.

Identify the operationalised independent variable and the operationalised dependent variable in this study. *(2 marks + 2 marks)*

Kerry's answer

The operationalised independent variable is room temperature and the operationalised dependent variable is aggression.

Megan's answer

The operationalised independent variable is temperature and the operationalised dependent variable is the difference in aggression between the participants.

Rohan's answer

The operationalised independent variable is the room temperature (hot or cool) and the operationalised dependent variable is the aggression score.

For each answer there are 2 marks available. Write the marks you would give each answer in the table below.

	Mark for IV out of 2	Mark for DV out of 2
Kerry		
Megan		
Rohan		

Answers on page 192

APPLYING YOUR KNOWLEDGE

A researcher becomes interested in the effects of simple rewards on children's ability to do well on school tests. The researcher intends to conduct a laboratory experiment to investigate this. He invites 30 children to his laboratory and gives them a general knowledge test. Beforehand he tells half of the children that he will give them a £1 as a reward for doing the test. Afterwards he compares the children's scores on the test.

Answer the following questions:

(a) What is the aim of this study? *(2 marks)*

(b) Identify the operationalised independent variable **and** the operationalised dependent variable in this study. *(2 marks + 2 marks)*

(c) Write a hypothesis for this study. *(2 marks)*

(d) Is your hypothesis directional or non-directional? *(1 mark)*

(e) Identify **one** possible extraneous variable in this study. Explain how this extraneous variable could have affected the results of this experiment. *(1 mark + 3 marks)*

(f) Describe possible demand characteristics in this research. *(3 marks)*

(g) With reference to this study, explain **one** strength and **one** limitation of lab experiments. *(2 marks + 2 marks)*

Answers on page 192

KEY WORDS

- Boredom effect
- Counterbalance
- Double blind
- Experimental condition
- Extraneous variable
- Independent groups design
- Matched pairs design
- Order effects
- Participant variables
- Practice effect
- Random allocation
- Repeated measures design
- Single blind

Possible exam questions (these are generally paired with a 'stem' describing a study) …

+ What experimental design was used in this study? *(1 mark)*

+ Explain why the researcher used an independent groups design for this experiment. *(2 marks)*

+ Explain **one** strength of using an independent groups design for this experiment. *(2 marks)*

 Exam tip

Questions on research methods appear through the exam paper – there are 24 marks' worth on PSYA1 and 12 marks' worth on PSYA2.

MUST know …

Experimental design

A set of procedures used to control the influence of certain extraneous variables.

Repeated measures design: Same participants in every experimental condition. For example, each person is tested in a cold room (condition 1) and their aggression measured. Then they are tested in a hot room (condition 2) and their aggression measured.

Independent groups design: Participants are allocated to two (or more) groups representing different experimental conditions. For example, some participants are tested in the cool room (group 1 gets condition 1) and some participants are tested in the hot room (group 2 gets condition 2). The scores of group 1 and group 2 are compared.

Matched pairs design: Pairs of participants are matched on key participant variables (e.g. intelligence and age). One member of each pair is placed in group 1 and the other member in group 2.

 One limitation of repeated measures is …

… participants perform better on the second task because of an order effect.

- **E** – If participants repeat a task twice they are likely to improve through practice – or they may do worse (because of becoming tired or bored).

 One limitation of independent groups is …

… the lack of control of participant variables.

- **E** – The participants in the two groups may differ (e.g. one group may be more intelligent) and this acts as an extraneous variable.
- **E** – Random allocation should eliminate this issue but sometimes random allocation is not possible.

 One limitation of matched pairs is …

… it is very time consuming to match participants on key variables.

- **E** – It is necessary to start with a very large group of participants in order to obtain pairs of sufficiently matched participants.

SHOULD know …

Order effects

In repeated measures, each participant repeats the task, e.g. takes the test in a cool room and then takes the test in a hot room.

The order of these tests is important because participants may inevitably do better on the second task because they are more practised (practice effect).

Alternatively they may do less well because they are bored (boredom effect).

Random allocation

In an independent groups design one way to try to make the two groups equivalent (eliminate bias) is to use a random technique to put participants in groups, such as drawing names from a hat.

Participant variables

Participant variables are a potential extraneous variable. If participants in one group are more experienced, intelligent, etc. at a task then this may explain why that group does better than the other group.

 A second limitation of repeated measures is …

… participants may guess the aims of the study after doing the task the first time.

- **E** – This may alter their behaviour and reduce the validity of the results.

 A second limitation of independent groups is …

… more participants are needed than in repeated measures.

- **E** – If an independent groups design is used, then twice as many participants are needed.
- **E** – Therefore repeated measures is easier to do as fewer people need to be recruited.

 A second limitation of matched pairs is …

… this can't control all participant variables because the potential list is too long.

- **E** – This means that some participant variables may still act as extraneous variables.

COULD know …

Counterbalance

Counterbalancing can be used to deal with order effects by ensuring that each condition is tested first or second in equal amounts.

There are two ways to do this:

- Some participants receive condition A then condition B, others receive B then A.
- An ABBA design can be used where all participants are tested four times – all participants receive A B then B A.

Single and double blind

Single blind design means that participants are 'blind' to the aims of the study. They may be given a 'cover' story to stop them guessing the true aims and be affected by this knowledge.

Double blind design means both the participants and the person conducting the experiment are 'blind' to the aims of the study. This reduces the possibility of experimenter effects.

CHOOSE THE RIGHT ANSWER

Experimental design is a strategy used in planning experiments. One kind of experimental design is called repeated measures. Tick three statements below that apply to repeated measures design.

A	All participants are tested twice.	☐
B	Participants are allocated to separate groups.	☐
C	Participants are matched on key characteristics.	☐
D	Participants may guess the aims of the study.	☐
E	This design may lead to order effects.	☐
F	Participant effects are not controlled.	☐

Answers on page 192

 MATCH THEM UP

1	Participant variable	**A**	Same participants in both conditions.
2	Repeated measures	**B**	Two groups, unpaired participants.
3	Independent groups	**C**	Used in independent groups design.
4	Order effect	**D**	Two groups where participants are paired.
5	Matched pairs	**E**	A problem in independent groups design.
6	Random allocation	**F**	A problem in repeated measures design.

Answers on page 192

 JUMBLED SENTENCES

On the facing page there are six criticisms. Similar sentences are presented below in a jumbled order. Place the number for each sentence in the correct square.

Some of them have been done for you.

Box	No.	Sentence
4	**1**	Random allocation should eliminate this issue but sometimes random allocation is not possible.
	2	This practice effect is an example of an order effect.
	3	One limitation of independent groups is the lack of control of participant variables.
	4	One limitation of repeated measures is that participants perform better on the second task because of practice.
3	**5**	One limitation of matched pairs is it is very time consuming to match participants on key variables.
	6	The participants in the two groups may differ (e.g. one group may be more intelligent) and this acts as an extraneous variable.
	7	This can be dealt with by counterbalancing conditions.
5	**8**	You probably have to start with a very large group of participants in order to obtain pairs of sufficiently matched participants.
	9	A practice effect occurs when participants repeat a task twice and then they are likely to improve.

Answers on page 192

 APPLYING YOUR KNOWLEDGE 1

A researcher wants to conduct an experiment to investigate differences between people who are left- and right-handed. One area of interest is creativity. The researcher intends to assess creativity using a test.

Answer the following questions:

(a) Explain why this is an independent groups design. *(2 marks)*

(b) Explain why a repeated measures design would be unsuitable to use in this experiment. *(3 marks)*

(c) Explain **one** strength and **one** limitation of using an independent groups design. *(2 marks + 2 marks)*

(d) Write a non-directional hypothesis for this experiment. *(2 marks)*

Answers on page 192

APPLYING YOUR KNOWLEDGE 2

A study investigates the effect of coffee on reaction time by testing each participant twice – at the start of the experiment and again after they have drunk a cup of coffee.

Explain **two** reasons why it was more appropriate to use a repeated measures design than an independent groups design. *(2 marks + 2 marks)*

Answers on page 193

KEY WORDS

- Debrief
- Dependent variable (DV)
- Ecological validity
- Experimenter effect
- External validity
- Extraneous variables
- Field experiment
- Independent variable (IV)
- Informed consent
- Internal validity
- Laboratory experiment
- Mundane realism
- Natural experiment
- Reliability
- Replication
- Validity

Possible exam questions (these are generally paired with a 'stem' describing a study) ...

+ What is a field experiment? *(2 marks)*
+ Explain **one** limitation of a field experiment. *(2 marks)*
+ Explain why this study is an example of a natural experiment. *(2 marks)*
+ Identify **one** limitation of this study and explain how you would correct it. *(2 marks)*
+ Suggest **one** reason why the researchers decided to use a field experiment rather than a laboratory experiment. *(2 marks)*

MUST know ...

Three types of experiment

The three types of experiment are: laboratory, field and natural. They all have one thing in common: an IV and a DV.

Field experiment

The experimenter directly controls the IV and observes its effect on the DV (as in a lab experiment).

The DV is assessed in an environment that is more like everyday life (more 'natural') and therefore likely to be less controlled.

Natural experiment

In a natural experiment, the experimenter does not manipulate the IV but uses an IV that would vary even if the experimenter wasn't around.

The DV may be tested in a laboratory.

It is necessary because some IVs cannot be controlled for ethical or practical reasons, e.g. whether someone is adopted or not.

 One strength of a field experiment is ...

... it is conducted in a more everyday environment.

- *E* – Therefore field experiments have greater ecological validity which means the findings may tells us more about the 'real' world.

 One limitation of a field experiment is ...

... there is less control of extraneous variables.

- *E* – This reduces the internal validity of the study as changes in the DV may not be caused by the IV.

 One strength of a natural experiment is ...

... it allows research to be carried out where an IV can't be manipulated for ethical or practical reasons.

- *E* – This enables researchers to study aspects of behaviour that could not otherwise be studied.

 One limitation of a natural experiment is ...

... the IV is not directly manipulated by the experimenter.

- *E* – Therefore we cannot claim that the IV has caused any observed change in the DV.

SHOULD know ...

Which kind of experiment is more 'valid'?

Internal validity

The degree to which an observed effect was due to experimental manipulation rather than factors such as extraneous variables.

* Internal validity is usually highest in a lab experiment.

Ecological (external) validity

The extent to which research environment can be generalised to other environments.

The findings from a research environment that has mundane realism can be generalised to everyday life.

* Field and natural experiments tend to have higher ecological validity than lab experiments (but not always).

* A lab experiment can have ecological validity if the materials that are used are less contrived and more like what we experience in everyday life (i.e. have mundane realism).

 A second strength of a field experiment ...

... participants tend not to be aware of being studied.

- *E* – This increases mundane realism because participants behave more naturally as they are not affected by experimenter effects.

 A second limitation of a field experiment is ...

... it tends to raise more ethical issues than a lab experiment.

- *E* – Usually participants are not asked for informed consent beforehand and they often cannot be debriefed afterwards.

 A second strength of a natural experiment is ...

... it enables psychologists to study 'real' problems.

- *E* – For example, the effects of a disaster on health. This increases the ecological validity of the approach.

 A second limitation of a natural experiment is ...

... there is less control of extraneous variables.

- *E* – This reduces the internal validity of the study.

COULD know ...

Reliability

Reliability refers to consistency. In an experiment there are two aspects of this:

1 How consistent are the results? If we repeat an experiment using the same conditions and similar participants (replication), do we get the same results? If so, the results are reliable.

Low reliability also threatens the validity of the study.

2 The way the IV and DV are measured may lack consistency, i.e. if you measured a person's reaction time twice in a row, would the outcome be the same? If not, the method of measurement lacks reliability.

The reliability of the method of measurement also affects the validity of the study.

FILL IN THE BLANKS

One strength of a field experiment is that the

(1) .... variable is measured in a natural

environment whereas in a natural experiment it may be measured in

a (2) .... One strength of a natural experiment

is that it means researchers can study behaviours that could not

be controlled for ethical or (3) .... reasons.

A limitation of a field experiment is that it tends to be low in

(4) .... validity but tends to be high in

(5) .... validity. The opposite tends to be

true for a (6) .... experiment.

Answers on page 193

CIRCLE TRUE OR FALSE

T or F Lab experiments tend to have high internal validity.

T or F Field experiments tend to have high internal validity.

T or F Natural experiments tend to have higher internal validity than lab experiments.

T or F Lab experiments tend to have lower ecological validity than field experiments.

T or F Field experiments tend to have high ecological validity.

T or F Natural experiments tend to have high ecological validity.

T or F Lab experiments can have ecological validity if the materials used are similar to everyday events.

Answers on page 193

FILL IN THE BOXES

We have covered three types of experiment, which are listed below. They share some features in common but for each kind of experiment there is something that is unique (special) to that type.

What is unique about a lab experiment?	
What is unique about a field experiment?	
What is unique about a natural experiment?	
What do all types of experiment have in common?	

Answers on page 193

APPLYING YOUR KNOWLEDGE

Some students thought they would assess strategies for memory in an everyday situation. They did this by identifying two memory strategies – strategy A and strategy B. One group of students were asked to use strategy A and the other group were asked to use strategy B. Both groups were asked to prepare for a class test using their strategy.

Answer the following questions:

(a) Explain why you think this is an example of a field experiment. *(2 marks)*

(b) Outline **one** strength of conducting memory research outside a laboratory setting. *(2 marks)*

(c) Identify the experimental design used in this study and explain **one** limitation of this design. *(1 mark + 2 marks)*

(d) Identify **one** other limitation of this study and explain how you would correct it. *(1 mark + 2 marks)*

(e) How could you conduct a similar study as a natural experiment? *(2 marks)*

(f) Explain how the students could find out whether the results of their study are reliable. *(2 marks)*

Answers on page 193

KEY WORDS

- Ecological validity
- Opportunity sample
- Quota sample
- Random sample
- Random technique
- Representative
- Sampling
- Stratified sample
- Target population
- Volunteer bias
- Volunteer sample

Possible exam questions (these are generally paired with a 'stem' describing a study) ...

+ Explain **one** strength of using an opportunity sample to select participants. *(2 marks)*

+ Suggest **one** way in which a sample could be obtained in this study. *(2 marks)*

+ Identify the sampling technique used in this study. Evaluate the choice of technique. *(1 mark + 3 marks)*

MUST know ...

Opportunity sample

A sample of participants produced by selecting people who are most easily available at the time of the study.

How? Ask people in the street, i.e. select those who are available.

Volunteer sample

A sample of participants produced by asking for volunteers.

How? Advertise in a newspaper or on a noticeboard.

Random sample

A sample of participants is produced using a random technique such that every member of the target population has an equal chance of being selected.

How? Using a random technique such as placing all names in a hat and drawing out the required number.

 One strength of an opportunity sample is ...

... the easiest method.

- **E** – You just use the participants who are most easily available to you.
- **E** – This means it takes less time to locate your sample than if using one of the other techniques.

 One strength of a volunteer sample is ...

... it can give access to a variety of participants.

- **E** – For example, all the people who read a newspaper can be a wider sample than just stopping people in the street in your hometown.

 One strength of a random sample is ...

... it is unbiased.

- **E** – All members of the target population have an equal chance of selection.

SHOULD know ...

Target population

The group of people that the researcher is interested in.

The group of people from whom a sample is drawn.

The group of people about whom generalisations can be made following the study.

Sampling

The process of taking a sample.

The sampling techniques on the left aim to produce a representative selection of the target population.

Ecological (external) validity

The representativeness of the sample affects the ability to generalise the findings to other people (in the target population) and situations.

The less representative the sample, the lower the ecological validity.

 One limitation of an opportunity sample is ...

... this is inevitably biased/lacks representativeness.

- **E** – The sample is drawn from a small part of the target population, for example using students from one school would not represent the UK school population.

 One limitation of a volunteer sample is ...

... participants are likely to be more highly motivated and/or with extra time on their hands (volunteer bias).

- **E** – This means, for example, that participants may be especially willing and thus more susceptible to experimenter (investigator) effects.

 One limitation of a random sample is ...

... it takes more time and effort than the other methods.

- **E** – You need to obtain a list of all the members of the target population, select your sample and contact them.

COULD know ...

Stratified and quota samples

Groups of participants are selected according to their frequency in the population.

How? Subgroups (or strata) within a population are identified (e.g. boys and girls, or age groups: 10–12 years, 13–15, etc.).

Participants are obtained from each of the strata in proportion to their occurrence in the target population. Selection is done randomly (stratified sample) or by another method such as opportunity sampling (quota sample).

 One strength of these methods is ...

... that they provide a good representation of the target population because there is equal representation of subgroups.

- **E** – Although the sample represents subgroups, each quota taken may be biased in other ways.
- **E** – For example, if opportunity sampling is used, the researcher only has access to certain sections of the target population.

CHOOSE THE RIGHT ANSWER

The table below lists the three main methods used to select participants.

Underneath the table are descriptions of the sampling methods used in various studies. Place the letters A–F next to the appropriate sampling method.

Sampling method	Matching description
Opportunity sample	
Volunteer sample	
Random sample	

A A study is conduced in a primary school. Only ten participants are needed. All the names in the school are put in a hat and ten names are drawn out.

B Some psychology students advertise for participants by putting a notice on the school noticeboard.

C A psychology class do an experiment in class and the participants are the class members.

D Opinions on smoking are collected by interviewing people in a town centre.

E People fill in a questionnaire in a magazine and the data is used in a psychology study.

F Participants for a child health study are selected by using a random technique to pick 100 names from a list of the babies born in the UK in the week beginning 1 January 2013.

Answers on page 193

 A MARKING EXERCISE

Student answers to the following question are given below:

A study used opportunity sampling. Evaluate the choice of this sampling technique. *(3 marks)*

What marks would you give the following answers?

Dylan's answer

Opportunity sampling can create a bias as the types of people who are available will vary depending on the time and place. However, opportunity sampling is often good because it doesn't involve a long process or special criteria for how to choose participants.

MARK

.... out of 3

Carrie's answer

Opportunity sampling allows you to take advantage of whoever is available to the researcher at the time. This means there is a high chance of bias and low population validity therefore this may not be representative data.

MARK

.... out of 3

Charlotte's answer

Opportunity sampling is a good technique because everyone has an equal chance of being in the research. However, it may be biased and participants may not be aware that they are being studied.

MARK

.... out of 3

Answers on page 193

 SPOT THE MISTAKES

Read the text below.

There are four mistakes, draw a circle round each.

Psychologists need to select participants for their research studies. One way to do this is by using a voluntary sample. This means you ask people if they want to take part. Such a sample is likely to be unbiased. Another technique that can be used is the random sample. To do this you identify your main population and then put all the names in a machine like they use for the lottery and randomly select the number you require. A third method is the opportunity sample. The people who are chosen are the ones most willing.

Answers on page 193

APPLYING YOUR KNOWLEDGE

A psychologist plans to study the use of mobile phones by adults. The psychologist selects 30 participants for the study and divides them into two groups: heavy users (more than three calls per day) and light users (three calls or less per day). All participants are rated for friendliness to test the hypothesis that heavy users are more friendly than light users.

Answer the following questions:

(a) Identify a suitable method to use for selecting your sample and explain how this sample would be obtained. *(1 mark + 2 marks)*

(b) Identify **one** strength of using this sampling technique in this study. *(2 marks)*

(c) Identify the experimental design. *(1 mark)*

(d) Identify the operationalised independent variable (IV) in this study. *(2 marks)*

(e) Explain why this is a natural experiment. *(2 marks)*

Answers on page 193

KEY WORDS

- Bar chart
- Graph
- Line graph
- Mean
- Measures of central tendency
- Measures of dispersion
- Median
- Mode
- Qualitative data
- Quantitative data
- Range
- Scattergram
- Standard deviation

Possible exam questions (these are generally paired with a 'stem' describing a study) ...

+ Explain what is meant by qualitative data. *(2 marks)*
+ Sketch and label a bar chart to illustrate the data. *(4 marks)*
+ Identify a suitable measure of central tendency that could be used with these data. Justify your answer. *(2 marks)*
+ Name **one** measure of dispersion that the researcher could have used to describe the data. *(1 mark)*

MUST know ...

Quantitative data

Represent how much, how long, or how many, etc. there are of something.

Data that can be counted.

Presentation of quantitative data: In tables or graphs (bar chart, line graph, scattergram).

Qualitative data

Express the 'quality' of things.

This includes descriptions, words, meanings, pictures, texts and so on.

Such data can be turned into quantitative data by placing items in categories and counting how many are in each category.

Presentation of qualitative data: Group similar items into categories, summarise data by giving some examples of content within each category.

 One strength of quantitative data is ...

... it is easier to analyse than qualitative data.

- *E* – Numerical data can be summarised using graphs and measures of central tendency and dispersion. This generally makes it easier to draw conclusions.

 One limitation of quantitative data is ...

... it tends to oversimplify reality and human experience.

- *L* – It suggests that there are simple descriptions of human behaviour that can be expressed in numbers.

 One strength of qualitative data is ...

... it can represent the true complexities of human behaviour.

- *E* – It illustrates people's thoughts and feelings that may not be illustrated using quantitative methods.

 One limitation of qualitative data is ...

... summarising such data can be affected by personal expectations and beliefs.

- *E* – However, quantitative methods are also affected by bias; they may simply appear to be more objective.

SHOULD know ...

Measures of central tendency

Central (or middle) values in a data set, i.e. the average.

Mean Calculated by adding up all the numbers and dividing by how many numbers there are.

Median The middle value in a list of numbers in order from highest to lowest.

Mode The value that occurs most often in a set of data.

Measures of dispersion

The spread of the data set.

Range The difference between the highest and lowest score in a data set.

Standard deviation Shows the amount of variation in a data set and assesses the spread of the data around the mean.

 One strength of the mean is ...

... it makes use of the values of all the data in the final analysis.

 One limitation of the mean is ...

... it can be misrepresentative of the data as a whole if there are extreme values.

 One strength of the median is ...

... it is not affected by extreme scores.

 One limitation of the median is ...

... it is not not always as 'sensitive' as the mean because not all values are reflected.

 One strength of the mode is ...

... it is useful when the data are in categories, i.e. qualitative data.

 One limitation of the mode is ...

... it isn't a useful way of describing data when there are several modes.

 One strength of the range is ...

... it is easy to calculate.

 One limitation of the range is ...

... it is affected by extreme values.

 One strength of standard deviation is ...

... it is a more precise measure of dispersion because all the values of the data are used in the calculation.

 One limitation of standard deviation is ...

... it may hide some characteristics of the data, e.g. extreme values.

COULD know ...

Quantitative versus qualitative

It is sometimes said that qualitative data concern 'thoughts and feelings' – but you can also have *quantitative* data about thoughts and feelings.

For example, a researcher could ask participants to rate their feelings about a film on a scale of 1 to 5.

The difference between quantitative and qualitative research runs deeper than 'thoughts and feelings'.

MATCH THEM UP

1	Quantitative	**A**	Spread of data around the mean.
2	Qualitative	**B**	A 'typical' value that makes use of all the values of the data.
3	Central tendency	**C**	Data that is numerical.
4	Mean	**D**	Middle value of an ordered list.
5	Median	**E**	Difference between highest and lowest.
6	Mode	**F**	The most frequent.
7	Dispersion	**G**	Data that expresses meanings.
8	Range	**H**	A general name for all kinds of average.
9	Standard deviation	**I**	General name for spread of data.

Answers on page 193

KEY PHRASES

For each definition select two key words to help you remember the meaning. The first one has been done for you.

Quantitative	Numbers	How much
Qualitative		
Mean		
Median		
Mode		
Range		
Standard deviation		

FILL IN THE BLANKS

For each of the following data sets, state what measure of central tendency would be most suitable and why.

Data set 1: 1, 2, 5, 7, 8, 9, 11, 14, 17, 18, 20, 28

The .... would be most

suitable because ....

....

Data set 2: budgie, cat, dog, cat, hamster, dog, cat

The .... would be most

suitable because ....

....

Answers on page 193

DRAWING CONCLUSIONS 1

A psychologist conducted a study about working memory. The participants in Group A were asked to carry out two visual tasks at the same time. Group B participants were asked to carry out a visual task and a verbal task at the same time. The results are shown in the graph below.

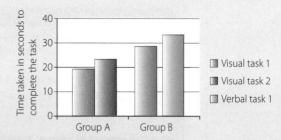

What does the graph show about working memory?

One finding:
Draw a conclusion: This suggests that …
Second finding:
Draw a conclusion: This suggests that …

Answers on page 193

DRAWING CONCLUSIONS 2

A day care study followed children over a period of ten years, testing each child's social development every two years. The mean social development scores for children in day care and home care are shown in the graph below.

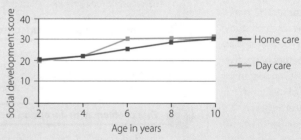

What does the graph show about the effects of day care on social development?

One finding:
Draw a conclusion: This suggests that …
Second finding:
Draw a conclusion: This suggests that …

Answers on page 193

KEY WORDS

- Anonymity
- BPS Code of Ethics
- Confidentiality
- Debriefing
- Deception
- Ethical guidelines
- Informed consent
- Presumptive consent
- Privacy
- Protection from harm
- Right to withdraw

Possible exam questions (these are generally paired with a 'stem' describing a study) ...

+ Describe **two** ethical issues that arose in Milgram's research. *(4 marks)*

+ Identify **one** ethical issue a researcher would need to consider in a study on attachment type. Suggest how the researcher could deal with this ethical issue. *(3 marks)*

+ Explain **one** problem that arises when giving participants the right to informed consent. *(2 marks)*

+ Identify **one** research study with which you are familiar. Discuss whether or not the psychologist showed an awareness of the British Psychological Society (BPS) Code of Ethics when recruiting participants for this experiment. *(3 marks)*

MUST know ...

Informed consent

The British Psychological Society (BPS) Code of Ethics sets out ethical standards for psychological research.

Participants must be given comprehensive information concerning the nature and purpose of a study, their role in it and any risks of participation.

Deception

Deception should be avoided. This occurs when a participant is not told the true aims of a study (e.g. what participation will involve). Thus, participants cannot give truly informed consent.

Protection from harm

During a research study, participants should not experience negative physical or psychological effects, e.g. bruising, embarrassment.

Confidentiality

A participant's right to have personal information protected.

Privacy

A person's right to control the flow of information about themselves (public places may be an exception).

Right to withdraw

Participants should have the right to withdraw from a study if they feel uncomfortable.

 One problem with informed consent is ...

... it can reduce the meaningfulness of the research.

- *E* – Such information will reveal the study's aims and this is likely to affect participants' behaviour.

 One problem with deception is ...

... it may be a necessary part of valid research.

- *E* – Participants knowing the true aims may affect their behaviour and reduce the validity of a study.

 One problem with protection from harm is ...

... it may not be possible to estimate harm before conducting a study.

- *E* – However, any study should be stopped as soon as harm is apparent.

 One problem with privacy is ...

... some behaviour in public is still private.

- *E* – For example, in a public toilet or confiding secrets to a friend in a restaurant.

SHOULD know ...

Dealing with ethical issues

Ethical guidelines: Professional advice on how to deal with ethical issues. Psychologists who do not follow guidelines may be barred from the BPS.

Specific techniques:

Debriefing: A post-research interview designed to inform participants about the true nature of a study. This aims to restore participants to the state they were in at the start of the study.

Providing informed consent: A means of dealing with many ethical issues. In the case of child participants, parents are asked to give consent.

Right to withhold data: Offered to participants at the end of a study, e.g. as a means of compensating for lack of informed consent.

Right to withdraw: A means of dealing with harm experienced during a study.

Anonymity: A means of protecting privacy and confidentiality by withholding identity of participants.

 One problem with ethical guidelines is ...

... they may discourage researchers from thinking about ethical issues for themselves.

- *E* – Researchers may assume that, as long as they are obeying guidelines, what they do is acceptable.

One problem with debriefing is ...

... it may not remove any anxiety or distress.

- *E* – Participants may still experience psychological harm from their experience.

COULD know ...

Presumptive consent

A method of dealing with lack of informed consent or deception.

Asking a group of people who are similar to the participants whether they would in principle agree to take part in a study.

If this group of people agree to the procedures in the proposed study, it is presumed that the real participants would agree as well.

One problem with presumed consent is ...

... what people think is different from the actual experience.

- *E* – People may think they would be willing to take part in a study but, if they were actually involved, might feel quite different.

SIMPLE SELECTION

Ethical issues are described below. Place the correct letter in the table that follows.

A Being able to stop participating in a study if you feel uncomfortable.

B Information about the nature and purpose of a study.

C Not making someone feel embarrassed or anxious.

D Invading a person's personal space.

E Withholding key information about a study.

Informed consent	
Deception	
Protection from harm	
Lack of privacy	
Right to withdraw	

Answers on page 193

FILL IN THE BLANKS

For each ethical issue suggest a suitable method of dealing with that issue (S) and explain this (E).

Issue	Way to deal with the issue
Lack of informed consent	(S) (E)
Deception (aims not revealed)	(S) (E)
Protection from harm	(S) (E)
Confidentiality	(S) (E)
Lack of privacy	(S) (E)

Answers on page 193

APPLYING YOUR KNOWLEDGE

A researcher plans to study age and eyewitness testimony. She plans to show participants a recording of a robbery. She asks them to report back a week later for a further study but doesn't tell them she is going to test their recall. At this second session she shows participants some photographs and asks them to identify the robber and one of the victims. There will be two groups of participants: children aged 6–10 years old and adults aged 30–40 years old.

Answer the following questions on a separate piece of paper.

(a) Explain why this study is a laboratory experiment. *(2 marks)*

(b) Explain why the researcher used an independent groups design in this study. *(3 marks)*

(c) Identify **two** ethical issues associated with this study. Suggest how psychologists could deal with each of these issues. *(1 mark + 1 mark + 3 marks + 3 marks)*

(d) Aside from ethical issues, explain **one** problem with conducting research with children. *(2 marks)*

(e) Explain the purpose of the BPS Code of Ethics. *(3 marks)*

The results of the study are displayed in the table below.

	Mean number of correct identifications	Standard deviation
Children	0.83	0.57
Adults	1.23	0.81

(f) Explain what is meant by the mean. *(2 marks)*

(g) What do the data in the table show about the relationship between age and eyewitness testimony? *(2 marks)*

Answers on page 193

A MARKING EXERCISE

Student answers to the following question are given below:

Identify **one** ethical issue. Explain how a psychologist could deal with this issues. *(1 mark + 3 marks)*

What mark would you give each answer?

Ahmed's answer

One issue is confidentiality. Don't identify the participants. Don't use photographs or names in published research. Names of people and/or places should be changed.

> **MARK**
> 1 mark + ... out of 3

Christian's answer

One issue is confidentiality. The researcher used 100 adults. To fix confidentiality the research could use fake names in the data. The researcher could also just use numbers or statistics.

> **MARK**
> 1 mark + ... out of 3

Answers on page 194

TOPIC 28 — *Studies using correlational analysis*

KEY WORDS

- Continuous variable
- Correlation coefficient
- Correlational analysis
- Co-variable
- Curvilinear correlation
- Directional hypothesis
- Hypothesis
- Intervening variable
- Linear correlation
- Negative correlation
- Non-directional hypothesis
- Observation
- Pilot study
- Positive correlation
- Rating scale
- Reliability
- Scattergram
- Self-report
- Standardised instructions
- Standardised procedures
- Validity
- Zero correlation

Possible exam questions (these are generally paired with a 'stem' describing a study) ...

+ What kind of correlation is this research showing? *(2 marks)*

+ Write a suitable directional hypothesis for this correlational analysis. *(2 marks)*

+ Outline **one** strength and **one** limitation of using correlations in stress research. *(4 marks)*

+ Explain why a psychologist might want to carry out a pilot study before the main research study. *(2 marks)*

MUST know ...

Correlational analysis

A correlational analysis is a way of measuring the relationship between two co-variables.

These variables must be continuous.

Zero correlation – co-variables not linked.

Positive correlation – co-variables increase together. Dots on scattergram go from bottom left to top right.

Negative correlation – as one co-variable increases, the other decreases. Dots on scattergram go from top left to bottom right.

Hypotheses for a correlational analysis

Directional hypothesis:

- There is a positive correlation between variable 1 and variable 2.
- There is a negative correlation between variable 1 and variable 2.
- Variable 1 and 2 increase together.

Non-directional hypothesis:

- There is a correlation between variable 1 and variable 2.

 One strength of correlational analysis is ...

... it may suggest whether or not there is a causal relationship between two variables.

- **E** – If there is no correlation between co-variables then there can't be a causal relationship.
- **E** – If the correlation is strong then further investigation is justified because there may be a causal link.

 One limitation of correlational analysis is ...

... it cannot show a causal relationship.

- **E** – People often misinterpret correlations and assume that a causal relationship has been demonstrated.
- **E** – Stories are frequently presented in the media implying that a cause has been found when there was only a correlation.

SHOULD know ...

Strength of correlation

Correlation coefficient is a number between −1 and +1 that tells us how closely the co-variables in a correlational analysis are related.

Weak correlation – dots widely distributed in scattergram. Correlation coefficient is low (between 0 and about .20).

Strong correlation – dots close together and in a diagonal line. Correlation coefficient is high (between about .50 and 1.0).

Weak positive

Strong negative

Pilot study

Pilot studies are used in all research. The intention is to try out standardised procedures with a small group of people. This permits changes to be made before conducting the full-scale study.

There might be some simple problems (e.g. the standardised instructions are unclear) or some more fundamental changes are needed (e.g. if one variable lacks reliability).

 A second strength of correlational analysis is ...

... it can be used when it would not be ethical or practical to conduct an experiment.

- **E** – Correlational analysis involves no manipulation of variables.
- **E** – It just involves measurement of behaviour such as intelligence or number of children in a family.

 A second limitation of correlational analysis is ...

... there may be intervening variables that explain the correlation but are overlooked.

- **E** – For example, research has shown a positive correlation between day care and sociability.
- **E** – This relationship may be due to the fact that working mothers have more confident, sociable children – so the intervening variable is working mothers.

COULD know ...

Validity and reliability

The **validity** ('trueness') of correlations is related to the assessment of each co-variable. For example, if one co-variable is memory, we need to consider how this has been assessed and the validity of that assessment.

Reliability is related to how variables are measured and the consistency of this measurement. Measurement may involve observation or self-report (e.g. rating scale).

 One problem with correlational analysis is ...

... it may appear to be a weak correlation but isn't.

- **E** – This is because only a linear correlation is considered, but the relationship can be curvilinear.
- **E** – In a curvilinear correlation the curve may be U-shaped. This doesn't produce a significant correlation coefficient and appears to be a zero correlation.
- **L** – Nevertheless, there is an important relationship between the co-variables, just not a linear one.

MATCH THEM UP

Match the terms on the left with their descriptions on the right.

1	Positive correlation	**A**	Bottom left to top right.
2	Negative correlation	**B**	A number that expresses the strength of a correlation.
3	Zero correlation	**C**	All dots closely together in a line.
4	Correlation coefficient	**D**	Random scatter.
5	Scattergram	**E**	Top left to bottom right.
6	Strong correlation	**F**	Graph showing a correlational analysis.

Answers on page 194

 WRITE YOUR OWN EVALUATION POINT

Exam questions asking about the strength or limitation of particular research methods tend to be worth 2 marks. Occasionally they are worth more and include the phrase 'in this study'. In such cases you need to include context as a way of elaborating your critical point.

Try this out for the study described below right (applying your knowledge).

Explain **one** limitation of using a correlation in this study. *(3 marks)*

S	
E	
E or L	

 RESEARCH ISSUES

In the study described on the right, the researcher was not sure whether to conduct a pilot study.

Explain why it would be appropriate for a researcher to use a pilot study. In your answer you must refer to details of the study given on the right. *(4 marks)*

Answer on page 194

 DRAWING CONCLUSIONS

A study looked at the behaviour of twins to see how similar they are. Each twin was rated for aggressiveness on a scale of 1 to 10. The results are displayed in the table below.

Twin 1	8	6	4	5	2	8	9	6	7
Twin 2	6	5	8	6	5	4	8	5	7

(a) How many people were tested in this study? ☐

(b) Draw an appropriate scattergram to display this data. Correctly label the scattergram.

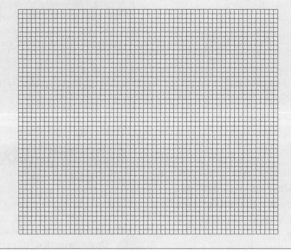

(c) What does this graph show about the twins in terms of their aggression? *(2 marks)*

Answers on page 194

 APPLYING YOUR KNOWLEDGE

A research study looks at the relationship between hours spent in day care per week and aggressiveness. The study finds a positive correlation.

Answer the following questions:

(a) Suggest how you might operationalise aggressiveness. *(2 marks)*

(b) Write an appropriate non-directional hypothesis for this study. *(2 marks)*

(c) One newspaper claimed that the results showed time in day care caused aggressiveness. Explain why this claim may be untrue. *(3 marks)*

Answers on page 194

KEY WORDS

- Behaviour checklist
- Behavioural categories
- Coding system
- Content analysis
- Controlled observation
- Covert observation
- Ethical issues
- Event sampling
- Inter-observer reliability
- Naturalistic observation
- Observational techniques
- Observer bias
- Overt observation
- Reliability
- Sampling
- Time sampling
- Validity

Possible exam questions (these are generally paired with a 'stem' describing a study) ...

+ Suggest **two** operationalised behavioural categories a researcher could use to record behaviour. *(2 marks + 2 marks)*

+ Give **one** strength of using observation in psychological research. *(2 marks)*

+ Explain how a researcher could use content analysis to analyse data. *(4 marks)*

 Exam tip

Observational techniques are used in many different studies, e.g. in an experiment as a means of measuring the DV. The term 'observational studies' refers to a study where the main method is the use of observational techniques.

MUST know ...

Observational techniques

Unstructured methods involve watching or listening and recording information. This may be done as a way to develop behavioural categories.

Structured methods include behavioural categories and sampling procedures.

Behavioural categories (coding system)

Behavioural categories aim to operationalise target behaviour(s) by identifying component behaviours.

For example, the component behaviours of 'aggressiveness' include talking loudly, hitting, pushing. Categories must include all possibilities.

A behaviour checklist is drawn up. The categories can be ticked each time they are observed and an overall score calculated.

Sampling procedures

Event sampling – counting the number of times a certain behaviour (event) occurs in a target individual.

Time sampling – recording behaviours at regular intervals, e.g. every 30 seconds.

 One strength of observational techniques is ...

... being able to see (or hear) what people actually do rather than what they think they do.

- **E** – People often don't know or don't realise what they actually do.

 One limitation of observational techniques is ...

... they may lack reliability.

- **E** – Observers should be reasonably consistent in their observations (inter-observer reliability).
- **E** – Low reliability may be due to not having behavioural categories that are clear or that do not cover all possibilities.

 A second limitation of observational techniques is ...

... that observers may be biased (observer bias).

- **E** – Expectations affect observations, e.g. an observer who expects girls to be less aggressive may unconsciously interpret girls' behaviours as less aggressive.

SHOULD know ...

Types of observational study:

Naturalistic observation

Environment is unstructured, everything left as normal, all variables are free to vary.

Controlled observation

In addition to using structured observational techniques, the *environment* is structured, i.e. the researcher determines the elements of the environment are.

For example, certain toys are made available to see how boys and girls respond differently.

Content analysis

Indirect observation of behaviour based on written or verbal material such as interviews or TV.

The process involved is similar to any observational study: the researcher has to make design decisions about behavioural categories and also about sampling. A behaviour checklist is used and categories are ticked.

 One strength of naturalistic observation is ...

... it provides a realistic picture of natural, spontaneous behaviour.

- **E** – This means observations tend to have high ecological validity.

 One strength of controlled observations is ...

... they allow focus on particular aspects of behaviour, e.g. playing with certain toys.

- **E** – The controlled environment may mean that participants' behaviour is unnatural (observations lack validity).

 One strength of content analysis is ...

... it avoids ethical and practical issues.

- **E** – It makes use of existing data (in books or other media) and tends to have high ecological validity because it is based on observations of what people actually do – real communications.

COULD know ...

Overt and covert observations

Participants who are aware of being observed (overt observation) may alter their behaviour, so validity is reduced.

Many observational studies are therefore covert – made without a participant's prior knowledge – such as using one-way mirrors or conducting a study in a public place without informing participants.

 A strength of covert observations is ...

... participants behave more naturally because they are not aware of being observed.

- **E** – This means informed consent cannot be gained, although participants can be debriefed.
- **E** – This cannot always be done, e.g. in public places when participants cannot be contacted.

FILL IN THE BLANKS

When observations are conducted using a systematic method this is called a (1) .... observation. One technique that is used is behavioural categories – when each category is given a code – is called a (2) .... system. The behavioural categories are put in a list called a behaviour (3) .... Another systematic system that is used is a method of deciding *when* to make observations. This can either be done at regular time intervals and is called (4) .... sampling. Or you can count the number of times a certain behaviour occurs in a target individual, this is called (5) .... sampling.

Answers on page 194

 APPLYING YOUR KNOWLEDGE 1

A psychologist observed ten infants using the Strange Situation technique.

Answer the following questions:

(a) Identify **two** behavioural categories used in this technique. *(2 marks)*

(b) Identify **one** limitation of using observational techniques. *(2 marks)*

(c) Give **one** strength of conducting an observational study in a laboratory setting. *(2 marks)*

Answers on page 194

 RESEARCH ISSUES

A researcher is interested in what young people talk about. He sits in a pub and records the conversations he hears.

Identify **one** ethical issue the researcher would need to consider in this research. Suggest how the researcher could deal with this ethical issue. *(3 marks)*

Answers on page 194

 A MARKING EXERCISE

Decide on a mark for the answers to the following exam question:

A researcher analysed children's TV programmes over a period of a week to see what kinds of programmes were available.

Explain how the researcher could have used content analysis to analyse the data he collected. *(4 marks)*

Robbie's answer

The researcher could create a coding system where he wrote the different kinds of programme and then mark these off. This would give the results he wants.

> **MARK**
> .... out of 4

Anne's answer

The researcher could have predicted certain categories e.g. comedy, cartoons, etc. and then ticked these off on a behaviour checklist.

> **MARK**
> .... out of 4

Pierre's answer

He could use content analysis to compare what different children watched and then decide what was the most common programme they watched. The categories are for each child.

> **MARK**
> .... out of 4

Answers on page 194

 APPLYING YOUR KNOWLEDGE 2

A research team investigated peer relations in children. They planned to observe children in their day care environment and assess their social development. To conduct the observations they selected behavioural categories, one of which was 'argues with other children'.

Answer the following questions:

(a) Suggest **one other** relevant behavioural category the psychologist could select. *(1 mark)*

(b) Explain how a content analysis could be carried out on the data collected. *(3 marks)*

(c) Explain **one or more** possible limitations of this investigation. *(4 marks)*

Answers on page 194

KEY WORDS

- Closed question
- Interview
- Interviewer bias
- Investigator effect
- Leading question
- Open question
- Qualitative data
- Quantitative data
- Questionnaire
- Reliability
- Semi-structured interview
- Social desirability bias
- Structured interview
- Test–retest method
- Unstructured interview
- Validity

Possible exam questions (these are generally paired with a 'stem' describing a study) ...

+ Give **one** limitation of using questionnaires in this research. *(2 marks)*
+ Explain **one** strength and **one** limitation of using a questionnaire rather than an interview. *(4 marks)*
+ Write **one** suitable question that could be used in the interviews to produce qualitative data. *(2 marks)*

MUST know ...

The most obvious way to find out what a person feels, thinks or does is to ask them.

Questionnaire

Respondents record their own answers. The questions are predetermined (i.e. structured).

Interview

In a structured interview predetermined questions are used (i.e. like a questionnaire), delivered in real-time (e.g. over the telephone or face to face).

In a semi-structured or unstructured interview some or all of the questions are developed during the interview. The interviewer creates additional questions in response to the respondent's answers.

 One strength of a questionnaire is ...

... it can be exactly and easily repeated.

- **E** – This means that data can be collected from large numbers of people relatively cheaply and quickly (more so than in an interview).

 One strength of an interview is ...

... in an unstructured interview more detailed information can be obtained from each respondent than in a structured interview.

- **E** – This is because the questions can be specially shaped to the participant.

 One limitation of self-report methods is ...

... answers may not be truthful (lack validity).

- **E** – For example, people want to make themselves 'look good' (social desirability bias).

 A limitation of a questionnaire is ...

... respondents may misunderstand questions or not take the task seriously.

- **E** – This means the answers lack validity.

 A limitation of an interview is ...

... it is affected by interviewer bias.

- **E** – An interviewer may ask leading questions and this may affect the validity of the answer.

SHOULD know ...

Good questions

A 'good question' should be clear and unambiguous. It should not be biased (i.e. not a leading question).

Closed questions have a range of answers from which respondents select one. They produce quantitative data which is easier to analyse. However, respondents may be forced to select answers that don't represent their real thoughts.

Open questions invite respondents to provide their own answers (rather than select one provided by the researcher). They tend to produce qualitative data that can provide unexpected answers, allowing researchers to gain new insights. However, it is more difficult to draw conclusions because there may be a wide variety of responses.

 A second strength of a questionnaire is ...

... respondents may feel more willing to reveal confidential and/or truthful information in a questionnaire than in an interview.

- **E** – This increases validity.

 A second strength of an interview is ...

... the interviewer can explain questions.

- **E** – This may make it easier for the respondent to provide meaningful answers because they understand the questions more fully.

 A second limitation of self-report methods is ...

... the sample may be biased because only certain kinds of people are willing to take part.

- **E** – Questionnaires can only be filled in by people who can read and write.
- **E** – Self-report methods depend on people being willing to spend time doing them.

 A third limitation of self-report methods is ...

... people don't know what they think or do.

- **E** – In Milgram's study, participants predicted that only 4% would continue to 300 volts whereas, in fact, 100% did.
- **L** – This suggests that self-report techniques may not provide us with valid information.

COULD know ...

Assessing reliability

The test–retest method can be used to evaluate reliability of a measurement.

The same questionnaire or interview is given to the same person on two occasions.

If the answers are reliable then the scores or responses on both occasions should be very similar.

 One problem with test–retest is ...

... getting the interval right.

- **E** – The interval between test and retest must be long enough so that the participant can't remember their previous answers.
- **E** – But not too long because then their thoughts or feelings may have changed and we would expect their score to be different.

CIRCLE TRUE OR FALSE

T or F In a structured interview one problem may be interviewer bias.

T or F Qualitative data is not produced in a questionnaire.

T or F Social desirability bias is a problem in both questionnaires and interviews.

T or F It is easier to summarise data collected by closed questions compared to open questions.

T or F Interviewer bias is an example of an investigator effect.

T or F Open questions are only used in interviews.

T or F People might be more truthful in an interview than in a questionnaire.

Answers on page 194

SIMPLE SELECTION

The list below gives strengths and limitations for questionnaires and interviews. Place the correct letters in the appropriate box at the bottom of the list.

A They can be exactly and easily repeated.

B Questions can be explained to the respondent.

C It is affected by interviewer bias.

D The sample may be biased because only people who can read and write can answer the questions.

E Questions can be specially shaped to the participant.

F Respondents may feel more willing to reveal confidential information

Questionnaire	
Interview	

Answers on page 194

RESEARCH ISSUES

Explain **two** possible ethical issues that might arise when using questionnaires in research on failure to form attachment. *(4 marks)*

Answers on page 194

APPLYING YOUR KNOWLEDGE

A psychologist conducted a study of day care experiences, using a questionnaire with children aged 10–18 who had attended day care.

Answer the following questions:

(a) Explain why the psychologist might want to carry out a pilot study before the main study. *(2 marks)*

(b) Write **one** suitable question that could be used in the questionnaire to produce quantitative data. *(2 marks)*

(c) Write **one** suitable question that could be used in the questionnaire to produce qualitative data. *(2 marks)*

(d) For this study, explain **one** strength of collecting information using a questionnaire. *(3 marks)*

(e) The researcher wonders if it might be better to use an interview instead of a questionnaire. Explain why an interview might be better. *(3 marks)*

Answers on page 194

DRAWING CONCLUSIONS

A research study explored the number of attachments that teenage children had. The children were asked the following question: 'If you were seriously injured and in hospital, who would you most like to be there to comfort you? You are allowed to identify more than one person'.

The percentage for each kind of answer is shown below.

Identified three or more people	33%
Identified two people	26%
Identified one person	41%

What does this table show about teenagers' attachments?

Finding:
Conclusion: This shows that …

Answers on page 194

KEY WORDS

- Case study
- Cohort effect
- Controlled observation
- Cross-sectional study
- Interview
- Longitudinal study
- Meta-analysis
- Psychological test
- Qualitative data
- Quantitative data
- Questionnaire
- Role play
- Scientific method

Possible exam questions (these are generally paired with a 'stem' describing a study) ...

+ What is meant by a case study? *(2 marks)*
+ Outline **one** strength and **one** limitation of conducting a case study. *(2 marks + 2 marks)*
+ How could a psychologist maintain confidentiality when reporting a case study? *(2 marks)*
+ Psychologists use a range of techniques to gather information in case studies. Outline **one** technique that the psychologist could use in this case study. *(2 marks)*

MUST know ...

What is it?
A case study is a detailed study of one case – but the case could be one person (e.g. a gambler), one group of people (e.g. a family or a football team) or one event (e.g. a riot).

A case study may be about unusual events, such as a person with brain damage, or may be about 'normal' events, such as a day in the life of a typical teenager.

How a case study is conducted
A case study may be conducted within a short space of time (one day) or over many years.

The key feature is that a lot of information is collected about the case and this is likely to involve a variety of research techniques – interviews, psychological tests (e.g. a personality test), observations and even experiments to test what an individual can do.

The information might be collected from the case being studied or from other people, such as family and friends. It is likely to be based on qualitative data but may include quantitative data too.

 One strength of a case study is ...

... it provides rich, in-depth data.

- **E** – Therefore information that might be overlooked using other research methods can be identified.
- **E** – It also means that the complex interaction of many factors can be studied.

 One limitation of a case study is ...

... it is difficult to generalise from individual cases to other people.

- **E** – This is because each case has unique characteristics.
- **L** – Therefore any conclusions may only apply to the case study.

SHOULD know ...

Some other research methods

Longitudinal study Observation of the same items over a long period of time. Such studies usually aim to compare the same individuals at different ages, in which case the IV is age. A longitudinal study might also observe a school over a long period of time.

Cross-sectional study One group of participants representing one section of society (e.g. young people or working-class people) are compared with participants from another group (e.g. old people or middle-class people).

Meta-analysis A researcher looks at the findings from a number of different studies in order to reach a general conclusion about a particular hypothesis.

Role play A controlled observation in which participants are asked to imagine how they would behave in certain situations, and then asked to act out the part. This method has the advantage of permitting the study of certain behaviours that might be unethical or difficult to find in the real world.

 A second strength of a case study is ...

... it can be used to investigate instances of behaviour that are rare.

- **E** – For example, studying cases of the effects of brain damage (such as HM).
- **L** – Therefore a case study may be the only way to study some aspects of human behaviour and experience.

 A second limitation of a case study is ...

... it often involves the recollection of past events.

- **E** – Such recall is unreliable because, for example, it is influenced by subsequent information (see Loftus and Palmer's research on page 38, relating to the effect of misleading information).

 One limitation of longitudinal and cross-sectional studies is ...

... cohort effects.

- **E** – These can affect cross-sectional studies because one group is not comparable with another.
- **E** – And can affect longitudinal studies because the group studied is not typical.

COULD know ...

Scientific method

- Scientists start by observing natural phenomena.
- They then develop explanations and hypotheses.
- These are tested using systematic and objective research methods.
- Results are collected.
- Conclusions are drawn, and lead to revision of the explanation and new hypotheses can be developed and tested ...

A lab experiment is an ideal scientific method because it lends itself to being objective, highly controlled and replicable, but other methods (such as observations and interviews) can also be objective, replicable and controlled.

 One strength of the scientific method is ...

... it provides a means of establishing the truth.

- **E** – It encourages repeated testings of hypotheses against reality.
- **E** – In this way we get closer and closer to what is true.
- **L** – Science is superior to belief.

MATCH THEM UP

Match the terms on the left with their definitions on the right.

1	Lab experiment	**A**	The relationship between continuous variables are analysed.
2	Field experiment	**B**	A study where the researcher does not interfere in any way.
3	Natural experiment	**C**	Experiment conducted in an everyday setting where the experimenter controls the IV.
4	Study using correlational analysis	**D**	Using observations of behaviour made indirectly.
5	Observation	**E**	Study with IV and DV, in contrived environment with high level of control.
6	Naturalistic observation	**F**	A study where behaviour is recorded by watching or listening to what people do.
7	Controlled observation	**G**	A self-report technique with a pre-determined set of questions in written form.
8	Content analysis	**H**	A detailed study of one individual, group or event.
9	Questionnaire	**I**	Study with an IV and DV, researcher makes use of an IV that is not controlled by the researcher but as a consequence of some other action.
10	Interview	**J**	A self-report technique where questions are delivered by another person who may respond if needed.
11	Case study	**K**	A study using observational techniques where the researcher controls some aspects of the environment.

Answers on page 194

RESEARCH ISSUES

A psychologist plans to conduct research on the effects of adoption. To do this he is going to do a case study of a woman who was adopted as a child.

> How could the psychologist maintain confidentiality when reporting this case study? *(3 marks)*

Answers on page 194

APPLYING YOUR KNOWLEDGE 1

A university psychology department is asked to conduct a case study of the 2011 riots in London.

Answer the following questions:

(a) Psychologists use a range of techniques to gather information in case studies. Outline **one** technique that the psychologist could use in this case study. *(2 marks)*

(b) Apart from ethical issues, explain **one or more** limitations that may be a problem in this case study. *(4 marks)*

(c) Explain **one** strength of studying this behaviour by using a case study. *(2 marks)*

Answers on page 194

APPLYING YOUR KNOWLEDGE 2

The effects of privation were investigated by looking at one institution in Eastern Europe where orphaned children were looked after.

Answer the following questions:

(a) Aside from interviewing the staff at the institution, describe **one** other technique that might be used as part of this case study. *(2 marks)*

(b) In order to conduct this study the researchers had to select just one institution in Eastern Europe. Describe a sampling method they might have been used to select this institution. *(2 marks)*

Answers on page 194

An idea
The study of research methods involves learning an extensive vocabulary. Your memory for this vocabulary might be improved by trying to produce a mind map of these terms. Think about how you are going to link them all!

MUST

By manipulating the IV, we can study the cause & effect relationship between it and the DV

EXPERIMENT
IV → DV
(cause) (effect)

Laboratory experiments — variables can be investigated under controlled conditions.

Aims — what the researcher intends to investigate.

Hypothesis — testable statements of relationships between variables.

SHOULD

Extraneous variables e.g. tested in daytime or evening

Operationalisation e.g. educational attainment = GCSE grades

Hypotheses
Directional =

Non-directional =

COULD

Demand characteristics

EVALUATION

A strength of lab experiments

Researchers can minimise extraneous variables.

This means that ...

A second strength

The level of control makes it easier to replicate study.

Replication means that ...

A limitation of lab experiments

The setting is contrived (it lacks mundane realism). This means that ...

A second limitation of lab experiments

Experimenter effects may influence the results.

For example ...

Boys, you shouldn't have any problem with this task.

Girls, just do your best

A strength of all experiments is that ...

CAUSAL

CONCLUSIONS CAN BE DRAWN

MUST

An experimental design is a way of controlling the influence of extraneous variables

A repeated measures design uses the same participants in every experimental condition

What's an experimental design?

In an independent groups design, participants are allocated to different experimental conditions

So they are in different groups

A matched pairs design matches participants on key variables

Like IQ, age, got it!

SHOULD

Order effects =

Random allocation =

Participant variables =

COULD | Counterbalancing

Used to deal with order effects

A → B or B → A
Half participants / Other half

A B B A
All participants

EVALUATION

Limitation of repeated measures

CONDITION 1 — CONDITION 2

Any difference may be due to order effects (e.g. practice or boredom).

Second limitation is

Participants may guess the aims of study after first condition. This may alter their behaviour.

Limitation of independent groups

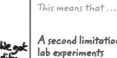 

IQ

GROUP 1 — GROUP 2

Lack of control of participant variables, e.g. IQ differences.

Second limitation is

More participants are needed (twice as many as in repeated measures design).

Limitation of matched pairs

It is time consuming to match participants on all key variables and requires starting with large group.

Second limitation is

The potential list of participant variables is too long for effective matching, leading to some still acting as extraneous variables.

Single and double blind

I don't know the aims — SINGLE

I don't know the aims — DOUBLE

TOPIC 24 — Field and natural experiments

MUST

FIELD EXPERIMENT
Experimenter controls the IV and observes its effect on a DV. DV is assessed in a more natural environment.

NATURAL EXPERIMENT
Experiment uses an IV that varies naturally. Necessary when IVs cannot be controlled for practical or ethical reasons.

SHOULD Experiments and validity

INTERNAL VALIDITY
Highest in lab experiment.

ECOLOGICAL (EXTERNAL) VALIDITY
Usually higher in field + natural experiments.

COULD Reliability

EVALUATION

Strength of field experiments They are conducted in more everyday environments. *Therefore …*	**Second strength of field experiments** Participants are generally not aware of being studied. *Therefore …*	**Strength of natural experiments** Allows research to be carried out when the IV can't be manipulated. *This enables researchers to …*	**Second strength of natural experiments** They enable researchers to study 'real' problems in their natural environment. *For example …*
Limitation of field experiments There is less control over extraneous variables. *This reduces …*	**A second limitation of field experiments** Tends to raise more ethical issues than lab experiments. *For example …*	**Limitation of natural experiments** IV is not directly manipulated by the experimenter. *Therefore …*	**Second limitation of natural experiments** There is less control of extraneous variables. *This reduces …*

Measurement consistency

TOPIC 25 — Selection of participants

MUST Sampling techniques

OPPORTUNITY SAMPLE
People who are most easily available, e.g. ask people in street.

VOLUNTEER SAMPLE
Produced by asking for volunteers, e.g. advert or noticeboard.

RANDOM SAMPLE
Every member of target population has equal chance of selection, e.g. names in a hat.

SHOULD

TARGET POPULATION
E.g. 16–18 yr olds in Somerset.

SAMPLING
Produces representative sample.

ECOLOGICAL (EXTERNAL) VALIDITY
Affects ability to generalise findings.

COULD Stratified and quota samples

Identifying the subgroups within a population defines the sample.

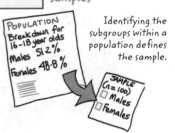

EVALUATION

Strength of opportunity samples The easiest method as just uses most easily available participants. *This means that …*	**Strength of volunteer samples** Can give access to a variety of participants. *For example …*	**Strength of random samples** They are unbiased. *This is because …*	**Strength of stratified and quota samples** They provide a good representation of the target population … *Because …*
Limitation of opportunity samples They are inevitably biased or lacking in representativeness. *This is because …*	**Limitation of volunteer samples** Participants highly motivated or with more time (volunteer bias). *This means that …*	**Limitation of random samples** They take more time and effort than other methods. *This is because …*	*However …* *For example …*

MUST

QUANTITATIVE DATA

How much, how long, how many, etc. Data in numbers or quantities. Presentation in tables or graphs.

QUALITATIVE DATA

Descriptions, meanings, pictures, texts, etc. Cannot be quantified but can be grouped in categories. Presentation through categories/examples.

Reaction to Horror Films

P1. They terrify me I can't sleep afterwards

P2. I'm not bothered by them

SHOULD

MEASURES OF CENTRAL TENDENCY

Mean: $5+7+6 = 18 \div 3 = 6$

Median: 5, 5, 6, (6), 6, 7, 7 = 6

Mode: 4, 4, $\boxed{5, 5, 5,}$ 6, 7, 8 = 5

MEASURES OF DISPERSON

Range: e.g. 4, 4, 5, 5, 5, 6, 7, 8 = 8 − 4 = 4

Standard deviation: shows amount of variation in data set and their spread around the mean.

COULD — Quant. versus qual.

How did the film make you feel? QUAL

How frightened were you on a scale of 1–10? QUANT

EVALUATION

Strength of quantitative data — It is easier to analyse. Numerical data can be summarised to make it easier to draw conclusions.	**Strength of qualitative data** — Represents the true complexities of human behaviour. Illustrates thoughts and feelings – not possible with quantitative. I'm complex I am · NIRVANA	**Strength of the mean** — Makes use of all the data.	**Limitation of the mean** — Misrepresentative if there are extreme values.
		Strength of the median — Not affected by extreme scores.	**Limitation of the median** — Not always sensitive as not all values reflected.
		Strength of the mode — Useful when data in categories.	**Limitation of the mode** — Not a useful way of describing data if several modes.
Limitation of quantitative data — It oversimplifies reality and human experience. Suggests that there are simple answers that can be expressed in numbers.	**Limitation of qualitative data** — Subjective analysis can be affected by expectations and beliefs. However, quantitative methods are also affected by bias – just appear objective.	**Strength of the range** — It is easy to calculate	**Limitation of the range** — It is affected by extreme values.
		Strength of standard deviation — More precise as all values used.	**Limitation of standard deviation** — May hide some characteristics of the data.

MUST — BPS Code of Ethics

Idiot Donkeys Party

Crazy Pink Rabbits

Informed consent
Deception
Protection from harm

Confidentiality
Privacy
Right to withdraw

SHOULD — Dealing with ethical issues

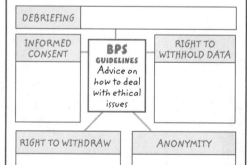

DEBRIEFING

INFORMED CONSENT — **BPS GUIDELINES** Advice on how to deal with ethical issues — RIGHT TO WITHHOLD DATA

RIGHT TO WITHDRAW

ANONYMITY

COULD — Presumptive consent

Would you still agree to take part in a study if you knew X was going to happen?

Before study

I don't need to talk to them about X as I have presumptive consent

Real participants

EVALUATION

A problem with informed consent
It may reduce the meaningfulness of the research.
Information might reveal ...

A problem with deception
It isn't always an ethical issue.
For example ...

A problem with protection from harm
May not be possible to estimate harm prior to conducting a study.
However ...

A problem with privacy
Some behaviour in public is still private.
For example ...

A problem with ethical guidelines
May discourage researchers from thinking about ethical issues themselves.
Researchers may assume ...

A problem with debriefing
It doesn't remove anxiety or distress.
Participants may still experience ...

A problem with presumptive consent
What people might 'think' is different from the actual experience.
For example ...

TOPIC 28 — Studies using correlational analysis

MUST — Correlational analysis

A way of measuring relationships between two continuous variables.

MPH + MPG

Negative correlation

↓

Related to lower MPG

MPH + DISTANCE COVERED

Positive correlation

→

Driving _faster_ covers _more_ distance

MPH + SEX APPEAL OF DRIVER
Zero correlation!

SHOULD — Strength of correlation

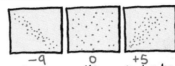

−9
Strong Negative

0
No Correlation

+5
Moderate Correlation

Pilot study
Used as a way of trying out procedures prior to the main study. Permits changes to be made. May uncover simple problems or where fundamental changes are needed.

COULD — Validity and reliability

VALIDITY =

RELIABILITY =

EVALUATION

Strength of correlational analysis

It may suggest the possibility (or not) of a causal relationship.

If no correlation there can't be a causal relationship.

If a strong correlation then further investigation is justified (there may be a causal relationship).

Limitation of correlational analysis

It can't show a causal relationship.

But correlations can be misinterpreted as such.

This leads to confusion when media gets this wrong.

COMPUTER GAMES CAUSE AGRESSION

Second strength of correlational analysis

Can be used when unethical or impractical to conduct an experiment.

This is because …

It just involves …

Second limitation of correlational analysis

Other overlooked variables may explain the correlation.

For example …

This may be due to …

A problem with correlational analysis

EWT ACCURACY / AROUSAL

Not linear but curvilinear.

TOPIC 29 — Observational techniques

MUST — Observational techniques

Unstructured — watching, listening, recording.
Structured — e.g. behavioural categories and sampling procedures.

BEHAVIOURAL CATEGORIES
Identify component behaviours and record when they are observed.

SAMPLING PROCEDURES
Event sampling — counting number of times a certain behaviour occurs.
Time sampling — recording behaviours at regular intervals.

AGGRESSIVENESS
Talking Loudly ✓✓
Hitting ✓
Pushing ✓✓✓
Overall Score 6

SHOULD — Types of observational study

NATURALISTIC OBSERVATION.
Environment unstructured. Everything left as normal.

CONTROLLED OBSERVATION.
Structured observational techniques, e.g. time and event sampling. Context of behaviour also structured.

CONTENT ANALYSIS.
Indirect observation of behaviour. Based on e.g. interviews, letters, TV.

COULD — Overt and covert observations

Overt — participants aware, may alter their behaviour so validity reduced.
Covert — participants not aware, behaviour more natural.

EVALUATION

Strength of observational techniques
Enables a researcher to see how people behave rather than how they think they behave.
Important because sometimes people are unaware of this.

Limitation of observational techniques
They may lack inter-observer reliability.
This may be due to unclear or limited behaviour categories.

Second limitation of observational techniques
The possibility of observer bias.
Observer's 'expectations' may influence what they record.

Strength of covert observations
Participants behave more naturally because they aren't aware they are being observed.
This means …

This cannot always be done …

Strength of naturalistic observation
Provides a realistic picture of natural behaviour.
This means …

Strength of controlled observations
Allow focus on particular aspects of behaviour.
This may mean …

Strength of content analysis
Avoids ethical and practical issues.
This is because …

MUST — Questionnaires and interviews

QUESTIONNAIRE
Respondents record their own answers to predetermined questions.

INTERVIEW
Structured — face to face using predetermined questions.
Semi-structured or unstructured — some questions developed during interview in response to respondent's answers.

SHOULD — Good questions

Closed questions:

Open questions:

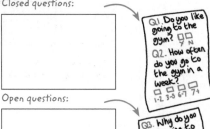

COULD — Assessing reliability

TEST

RE-TEST

EVALUATION

Strength of questionnaires
They can be easily and exactly replicated.
This means that ...

Strength of interviews
More detailed information possible in unstructured than structured interviews.
This is because ...

Limitation of questionnaires
Respondents may misunderstand questions or not take them seriously.
This means ...

Limitation of interviews
They can be affected by interviewer bias.
For example ...

Limitation of all self-report methods
Answers may not be truthful.
For example ...

Second strength of questionnaires
Respondents may be more willing to reveal confidential information in questionnaire than interview.
This increases validity ...

Second strength of interviews
Interviewer can explain questions if necessary.
This makes it easier ...

A problem is getting the interval right i.e. ...

Second limitation of all self-report methods
Sample may be biased because only certain people are willing to take part.
For example ...

Third limitation of all self-report methods
People may not be fully aware of how they actually behave.
This suggests ...

MUST — Case study

Detailed study of one 'case' (e.g. one person, one group of people or one event). Can be about unusual or normal events.

How is a case study conducted?

Interviews

'Case'

Observations

Psychological tests

Family and friends

SHOULD — Other research methods

LONGITUDINAL STUDY:

(e.g. following children from birth—18)

CROSS-SECTIONAL STUDY:

(e.g. comparing people from different age groups)

META-ANALYSIS:

(e.g. meta-analysis of EWT studies)

ROLE PLAY:

(e.g. role play in attachment scenarios)

COULD — Scientific method

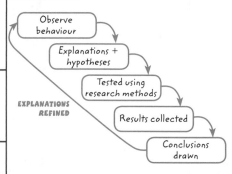

Observe behaviour

Explanations + hypotheses

Tested using research methods

Results collected

Conclusions drawn

EXPLANATIONS REFINED

Lab experiment is the ideal scientific method because …

EVALUATION

Strength of case studies

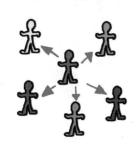

"I'm just misunderstood"

"After reviewing all the evidence we conclude he's just lazy …"

They are a way of getting rich and in-depth data.

Material that might otherwise be overlooked can be identified.

It also means the complex interaction of many factors can be studied.

Limitation of case studies

Difficult to generalise from individual cases.

Because each case has unique characteristics.

Therefore conclusions valid for single rather than general case.

Second strength of case studies

Can be used to investigate rare instances of a behaviour.

For example …

Therefore …

Second limitation of case studies

It often involves the recollection of past events.

Such evidence may be …

This is supported by …

Strength of the scientific method

THE TRUTH IS OUT THERE

Limitation of longitudinal/cross-sectional studies

Cohort effects — people born at same time have similar experiences.

This can affect …

Can also affect …

KEY WORDS

- Adrenal cortex
- Adrenal medulla
- Adrenaline
- Adrenocorticotrophic hormone (ACTH)
- Corticotrophin-releasing factor (CRF)
- Cortisol
- Fight or flight
- Hypothalamus
- Parasympathetic nervous system (PNS)
- Pituitary-adrenal system
- Pituitary gland
- Stress
- Sympathetic nervous system (SNS)
- Sympathomedullary pathway

Possible essay question …

Discuss how the body responds to stress. *(12 marks)*

Other possible exam questions …

+ Outline **two** ways in which the body responds to stress. *(3 marks + 3 marks)*
+ Outline **one** way in which the body responds to stress and give one criticism of this bodily response. *(6 marks)*
+ Apply this knowledge to … *(6 marks)*

MUST know …

The sympathomedullary pathway

- Sympathetic nervous system (SNS) prepares the body for action in conditions of immediate (acute) stress.
- SNS causes changes such as an increase in heart rate and blood pressure.
- SNS causes the adrenal medulla to release adrenaline into the bloodstream.
- Parasympathetic nervous system (PNS) restores body to resting state after stressor has passed.

The pituitary-adrenal system

- Activated under conditions of ongoing (chronic) stress.
- Activation of hypothalamus leads to release of CRF into the bloodstream.
- CRF causes pituitary gland to release ACTH – transported to adrenal cortex.
- Activation of adrenal cortex leads to release of the hormone cortisol.
- Cortisol has effects throughout the body, some positive, some negative.

 The stress response can lead to cardiovascular problems …

… because repeated activation of the stress response can affect the heart and blood vessels.

- *E* – For example, increased blood pressure associated with SNS activation can cause damage to the lining of blood vessels.

 This can lead to immune system problems …

… because too much cortisol suppresses the immune system.

- *E* – This causes the process that fights infection to shut down, increasing the likelihood that the person will become ill.

 There are individual differences …

… in how males and females display bodily responses to stress.

- *E* – Males tend to have a fight or flight response, whereas females often have a 'tend and befriend' response, regulated by the hormone oxytocin.

SHOULD know …

The sympathomedullary pathway

- Fight or flight – the rapid action necessary when an animal is under threat.
- SNS also leads to metabolic changes, such as the mobilisation of fat and glucose in the bloodstream.
- Adrenaline boosts the supply of oxygen to the brain and suppresses non-emergency bodily processes.
- PNS slows down heartbeat and reduces blood pressure.

The pituitary-adrenal system

- The hypothalamus is activated when stressors are perceived by higher brain centres.
- ACTH = adrenocorticotrophic hormone, transported via the bloodstream.
- Prolonged release of ACTH causes the adrenal cortex to increase in size to cope with increased cortisol production.
- Positive effects, e.g. lower sensitivity to pain. Negative, e.g. lowered immune response.

- *E* – Research (e.g. Orth-Gomér *et al.*) found that exposure to ongoing stressors, such as marital conflict, was associated with an increased likelihood of heart attack.
- *L* – This suggests that, although these bodily changes evolved as an adaptive response to stress among our distant ancestors, they may be unsuited to many modern stressors.

- *E* – Kiecolt-Glaser *et al.* found that exposure to short-term stressors such as an examination caused a decrease in immune system functioning among medical students.
- *L* – This suggests that if short-term stressors can lead to suppression of the immune system, longer-term stressors would have even more adverse effects.

- *E* – Taylor *et al.* found that females have higher levels of oxytocin, which is associated with reduced cortisol responses to stress and faster recovery.
- *L* – This means that men are more vulnerable to the adverse effects of stress whereas the tend and befriend system may protect women against stress.

COULD know …

Feedback and the pituitary-adrenal system

The system is very efficient at regulating itself.

The hypothalamus and pituitary gland have special receptors that monitor circulating cortisol levels.

If cortisol levels rise above normal levels, this initiates a reduction in CRF and ACTH levels, which then brings cortisol levels back to normal.

This limits the potentially damaging effects of cortisol on the body.

 However …

… this system does not always work.

- *E* – Some researchers believe that this feedback system may break down when individuals are exposed to long-term stress.
- *E* – Research has found that the longer an individual is exposed to stress, the more adverse the effects are.
- *L* – This would explain why individuals in stressful jobs or stressful relationships are more likely to suffer stress-related illness.

FILL IN THE BLANKS

The (1) .... nervous system (SNS) prepares the body for

activity in conditions of (2) .... stress. The SNS leads to

changes such as (3) .... in heart rate and blood pressure.

The SNS causes the (4) .... to release

(5) .... which boosts the supply of (6) ....

and glucose to the brain and suppresses non-emergency bodily processes. The

(7) .... restores the body to a resting state

after the stressor has passed, slowing down the heartbeat and

(8) .... blood pressure.

Answers on page 195

MATCH THEM UP

1	ACTH	A	Slows down heart rate and decreases blood pressure.
2	Adrenaline	B	Causes pituitary gland to release ACTH.
3	Cortisol	C	Boosts the supply of oxygen and glucose to the brain.
4	CRF	D	Associated with the 'tend and befriend' response to stress.
5	PNS	E	Has both positive and negative effects in the body.
6	Oxytocin	F	Activates adrenal cortex to release cortisol.

Answers on page 195

APPLYING YOUR KNOWLEDGE

Identify the psychology

Ian doesn't enjoy scary films. When he gets to a really scary bit his heart pounds, his hands feel clammy and he feels generally uncomfortable.

Using your knowledge of the body's response to stress, explain why Ian is likely to have experienced these changes. *(4 marks)*

Using your knowledge of psychology, describe the likely bodily response Ian is experiencing. *(3 marks)*

Link to Ian's response

Answers on page 195

A MARKING EXERCISE

Read the student answers to the following exam question:

Outline **one** way in which the body responds to stress. *(3 marks)*

Thomas' answer

When a stressor is experienced, the hypothalamus causes the release of CRF. This causes the release of ACTH from the pituitary gland, which is carried in the bloodstream to the adrenal cortex. Activation of the adrenal cortex leads to release of the hormone cortisol, which has various effects, including lowering the body's immune response.

Ellie's answer

The pituitary-adrenal system is one way in which the body responds to stress. This involves the pituitary gland, which releases a hormone called the adrenocorticotrophic hormone and the adrenal gland, which releases a stress hormone called cortisol. Cortisol helps the body respond to the stressful situation.

What mark do you think each answer would get?

Your comments on Thomas' answer:

....

....

....

Thomas would get _____ out of 3 marks

Your comments on Ellie's answer:

....

....

....

Ellie would get _____ out of 3 marks

Answers on page 195

You can read the marking guidelines on page 10.

KEY WORDS

- Cortisol
- Immune system
- Meta-analysis
- Natural experiment

Possible essay questions ...

Outline and evaluate research into stress-related illness. *(12 marks)*

Discuss research into the relationship between stress and the immune system. *(12 marks)*

Other possible exam questions ...

+ Explain how researchers have studied the relationship between stress and the immune system. *(4 marks)*

+ Describe what research has shown about the relationship between stress and the immune system. *(6 marks)*

+ Apply this knowledge to ... *(6 marks)*

MUST know ...

Key study: Kiecolt-Glaser *et al.* (1984)

How?

This was a natural experiment using medical students about to take an important exam.

Researchers assessed immune system functioning (in terms of natural killer (NK) cell activity) one month before the exam and during the exam period itself.

Students completed a questionnaire to measure other life stressors being experienced at the time, e.g. financial or relationship problems.

Showed?

NK cell activity was significantly reduced during the exam period compared to one month before the exam period.

Also found that students reporting the highest level of loneliness had lowest immune system functioning.

Participants with higher levels of loneliness also had the highest levels of cortisol.

 There is research support ...

... from Segerstrom and Miller.

Meta-analysis of 293 studies conducted over a 30-year period found that short-term stressors could boost the immune system whereas long-term stressors suppressed it.

 Not a simple relationship ...

... because it is difficult to establish a causal relationship between stress and the immune system.

Health is affected by many different factors (e.g. genetics, lifestyle), so it is difficult to disentangle the specific effects that could be attributed to stress.

SHOULD know ...

Second study: Kiecolt-Glaser *et al.* (2005)

How?

Studied the effects of unhappy relationships on immune system functioning.

Involved a volunteer sample of married couples aged between 22 and 77 years.

Showed?

They found that blister wounds healed more slowly on couples that showed high levels of hostile behaviour toward each other.

These healed at 60% of the rate of wounds of couples that showed low levels of hostility.

 There are individual differences ...

... in immune system changes due to stress.

- **E** – Kiecolt-Glaser *et al.* found that women show more adverse immune system changes in how they react to long-term stressors, e.g. marital conflict.
- **L** – Older couples also showed more adverse immune system changes in response to marital conflict than did younger couples.

- **E** – Short-term stressors prompted the immune system to deal with potential challenges to the body. The most chronic long-term stressors led to the most global suppression of immune system functioning.
- **L** – This suggests that the more long-lasting the stressor, the more damaging the effect on immune system functioning.

- **E** – Health is fairly stable and slow to change, therefore it is difficult to demonstrate that exposure to particular stressors has caused a change in immune system functioning.
- **L** – As a result, demonstrating a link over the long-term is extremely difficult. Therefore, researchers have concentrated only on the impact of relatively short-term stressors.

COULD know ...

Third study: Malarkey *et al.*

How?

Researchers studied 90 newlywed couples over a 24-hour period in a laboratory.

The couples were asked to discuss marital issues likely to cause conflict between them (e.g. finances).

Showed?

Marital conflict produced significant changes in adrenaline and noradrenaline levels.

These changes were associated with lower levels of immune system functioning.

 There are problems with validity ...

... because this study took place in a laboratory.

- **E** – As a result, the study can be criticised as lacking validity due to the artificial nature of the laboratory environment compared to real-life situations.
- **L** – However, researchers believe that marital conflict would be even more negative in the couple's home environment.
- **L** – Therefore, it is likely that in more natural situations, the adverse effects on immune system functioning would be even greater.

JUMBLED SENTENCES

On the facing page there are three criticisms related to the key study. The same sentences are presented below in a jumbled order. Number them correctly.

3	**1**	Immune system activity was significantly reduced during the exam period compared to one month before.
	2	Researchers also assessed immune system functioning during the exam period itself.
	3	A natural experiment using medical students about to take an important exam.
	4	Participants with higher levels of loneliness also had the highest levels of cortisol.
	5	Questionnaire completed to measure other life stressors being experienced at the time.
	6	Also found that students reporting the highest level of loneliness had lowest immune system functioning.
	7	Researchers assessed immune system functioning one month before the exam.

Answers on page 195

✔✗ CIRCLE TRUE OR FALSE

T or F Kiecolt-Glaser *et al.* found the lowest levels of immune system functioning one month before the exam.

T or F Kiecolt-Glaser *et al.* found participants with higher levels of loneliness had the lowest levels of cortisol.

T or F Kiecolt-Glaser *et al.* found that blister wounds healed more quickly on couples that showed high levels of hostile behaviour toward each other.

T or F Research has shown that short-term stressors can enhance immune system functioning.

T or F Men tend to show more adverse immune system responses than women to marital conflict.

T or F Older couples show more adverse immune system responses to marital conflict than younger couples.

Answers on page 195

APPLYING YOUR KNOWLEDGE

Laura is a manager in a busy mobile phone call centre. Her staff are constantly under high levels of stress from heavy workloads, long hours and lots of abuse from dissatisfied customers. She notices that staff often suffer from colds and flu-like symptoms and absence due to illness is at an all-time high.

Use your knowledge of the relationship between stress and the immune system to explain the high levels of absence among Laura's staff. *(4 marks)*

See page 20 for an explanation of the 'two-pronged attack' needed to answer 'applying your knowledge' questions.

Identify the psychology	Link to Laura's staff absences

Answers on page 195

KEY PHRASES

Outline what **one** study has shown about the relationship between stress and the immune system. *(4 marks)*

On the facing page there are three findings from the key study by Kiecolt-Glaser *et al.*

For each one select **three** key words or phrases and enter them in the grid below plus an appropriate conclusion. The first one has been done for you.

Finding 1	Immune system	Reduced	Exam
Finding 2			
Finding 3			
Conclusion			

Now try to write an answer to the exam question on the left using your key words. Your answer should be about 100 words in length.

KEY WORDS

- Life change units (LCU)
- Life changes
- Schedule of Recent Experiences (SRE)
- Social Readjustment Rating Scale (SRRS)

Possible essay question …

Outline and evaluate research related to life changes and stress. *(12 marks)*

Other possible exam questions …

+ Give **one** example of a life change and explain why this might cause stress. *(3 marks)*
+ Outline **one** study that has investigated the relationship between life changes and stress. *(6 marks)*
+ Outline how researchers have investigated the relationship between life changes and stress. *(4 marks)*
+ Outline what research has shown about the relationship between life changes and stress. *(6 marks)*
+ Apply this knowledge to … *(6 marks)*

MUST know …

Key study: Rahe *et al.*

How?

Involved a male sample of 2,664 sailors of various ranks from three US Navy ships.

Sailors completed the SRE (a military version of the SRRS), which measured life events experienced over the two years prior to a six-month tour of duty.

A record was kept of any illnesses experienced during their six months at sea.

Showed?

Found a small but positive correlation between scores on the SRE and reported levels of illness while at sea.

Sailors who scored low on the SRE had low levels of illness, sailors with high scores on the SRE tended to report high levels of illness.

The relationship between life events (as measured by the SRE) and illness was more evident in married rather than single sailors.

 There are individual differences …

… in the impact of life events.

- *E* – Life change questionnaires such as the SRE and SRRS ignore the fact that the impact of life changes such as divorce or retirement.

 One limitation of life changes as a source of stress …

… is that they may be less important than daily hassles.

- *E* – Life-changing events are relatively rare in the lives of most people, whereas minor stressors such as a family argument or a missed bus (i.e. hassles) are commonplace.

Research does not show a causal relationship …

… as studies such as Rahe *et al.* have yielded only correlational data.

- *E* – It is possible that a third variable, such as anxiety, may affect both the life-changing event *and* any resulting stress-related illness.

SHOULD know …

Second study: Holmes and Rahe – the SRRS

The SRRS was developed to test the idea that life changes are related to stress-related illnesses such as anxiety and depression.

The SRRS is based on 43 life events taken from an analysis of over 5,000 patient records.

Enlisted 400 participants who rated each event in terms of the amount of readjustment that would be required by an average person.

Marriage was given a 'readjustment' score (or 'life change unit' – LCU) of 50.

Events requiring more readjustment than marriage were given a LCU higher than 50.

Those that required less readjustment than marriage were given a LCU lower than 50.

The highest LCU for a life event was for 'death of a spouse' (LCU of 100).

- *E* – For example, Sherbourne *et al.* found that the impact of bereavement was greater for younger individuals than for older individuals.
- *L* – Although questionnaires may provide a quantitative measure of life changes, they may not reflect the actual amount of stress resulting from specific life events for different individuals.

- *E* – DeLongis *et al.* found no relationship between life events and health in a sample of married couples but did find a significant positive correlation between hassles and next-day health problems.
- *L* – This suggests that daily hassles may be more significant as a source of stress in their own right, or alternatively may amplify the stress caused by major life events.

- *E* – Brown claims that people with high levels of anxiety would be more likely to report experience of negative life events *and* also be more prone to illness.
- *L* – This means that, although there may well be a relationship between life changes and stress-related illness, most research has failed to establish a *causal* relationship between the two.

COULD know …

Third study: Michael and Ben-Zur

How?

A natural experiment involving 130 recently divorced or bereaved men and women.

Inventories assessed their current well-being and adjustment, as well as life satisfaction before and after the separation or loss.

Showed?

For the bereaved group, levels of life satisfaction were higher *before* and lower *after* bereavement.

For the divorced group it was the other way around, with higher levels of life satisfaction after the divorce than before.

 This difference can be explained …

… because divorced participants were better able to turn their life change into a positive experience.

- *E* – For example, researchers found that current well-being was related positively to dating or living with a new partner.
- *E* – However, the *negative* impact of loss was more obvious for members of the bereaved group and their current level of well-being was much lower.
- *L* – This was because they were unable to balance out their loss with the positive effect of being in a new relationship.

FILL IN THE BLANKS

The SRRS was developed by (1) .... to test

the idea that life changes are related to (2) ....

.... such as anxiety and depression. The SRRS

lists (3) .... life events taken from an analysis of over 5,000

patient records. Each event was rated in terms of the amount of

(4) .... that would be required by an

average person to cope with that life event. This was referred to as

the LCU, which stands for (5) ....

Marriage was given a LCU score of (6) .... Events that were

potentially more stressful than marriage were given a higher LCU,

those requiring less readjustment a lower LCU. The highest LCU for

a life event was for (7) .... , which was

given a LCU of (8) ....

Answers on page 195

DRAWING CONCLUSIONS

The graph below shows findings from a study on gender and age differences on the impact of different life events.

Gender and age differences in the impact of life events

State **two** findings and for each one draw a conclusion (state what the finding shows).

Finding 1:
Conclusion 1: This shows that …
Finding 2:
Conclusion 2: This shows that …

APPLYING YOUR KNOWLEDGE

Identify the psychology		Link to David's illness

David tries to keep fit and stay healthy. He married 12 months ago and his wife has just given birth to his first child. Because he has been promoted to a senior post at work he has taken on a very large mortgage. However, he has also experienced more frequent bouts of illness over the last year.

Using your knowledge of psychology, describe why David is experiencing more frequent bouts of illness. *(4 marks)*

Answers on page 195

WRITE YOUR OWN EVALUATION POINT

Using the material on the facing page, write out one of the evaluative points in your own words, underlining the key words.

S	
E	
E	
L	

See page 14 for an explanation of how to SEEL.

KEY PHRASES

Select key phrases to help you remember the Rahe *et al.* study. Some have been done for you.

How?	Showed?
2,664 US sailors	Small positive correlation

Use your key phrases to answer the following exam question:

Outline **one** study that has investigated the relationship between life changes and stress. *(6 marks)*

KEY WORDS

- Daily hassles
- Daily uplifts
- Depression

Possible essay question ...

Outline and evaluate research relating to daily hassles and stress. *(12 marks)*

Other possible exam questions ...

+ Give **one** example of a daily hassle and explain why this might cause stress. *(3 marks)*

+ Outline **one** study that has investigated the relationship between daily hassles and stress. *(6 marks)*

+ Outline what research has shown about the relationship between daily hassles and stress. *(6 marks)*

+ Apply this knowledge to ... *(6 marks)*

MUST know ...

Key study: Bouteyre *et al.*

How?

Studied French psychology students making the transition from school to university.

Sample was 207 females and 26 males. The mean age of the sample was 20.48 years. Students completed the *Beck Depression Inventory*, the *Social Support Questionnaire* and the *Daily Hassles Scale*.

Showed?

Results showed that 41% of those surveyed suffered from depressive symptoms.

There was a positive correlation of .33 between these depressive symptoms and scores on the daily hassles scale.

Students with good social support, even when faced with overwhelming daily hassles, were less likely to develop depression.

 One limitation of this approach ...

... concerns problems with retrospective recall, because participants have to rate hassles experienced over the previous month.

- **E** – The accuracy of such memories tends to vary according to the time interval involved, with longer intervals being associated with less accurate memories.

 A second limitation of this approach ...

... is that studies such as the Bouteyre *et al.* study only produce correlational data.

- **E** – This means that we can't draw causal relationships between daily hassles and our physical and psychological well-being.

There are real-world applications ...

... of research into daily hassles

- **E** – For example, research has shown that an accumulation of daily hassles can mean that some people are more likely to experience road rage during their commute home.

SHOULD know ...

Second study: Gervais

How?

Gervais asked nurses to keep diaries for a month, recording all the daily hassles (e.g. continual interruptions) and uplifts (such as helping a patient recover) experienced while at work.

The nurses were also asked to rate their performance at work (e.g. how well they were getting things done) and to note any physical symptoms of strain.

Showed?

After one month, it was clear that daily hassles increased job strain and decreased job performance.

From nurses' diary entries, daily uplifts appeared to counteract the stressful impact of the daily hassles.

Nurses also reported that uplifts improved their job performance.

- **E** – For example, Rubin and Baddeley refer to the phenomenon of 'telescoping' where events that occurred prior to a reference period (e.g. the previous month) intrude into memory and are recalled as being more recent than they actually were.
- **L** – However, this problem can be overcome by using a diary method, where stressors and feelings are recorded daily.

- **E** – The Bouteyre *et al.* research does not demonstrate that depression was directly attributable to hassles, as a third variable (e.g. finances) may have been the cause of both.
- **L** – However, correlations do suggest that hassles have the *potential* to have adverse effects on well-being.

- **E** – Gulian *et al.* found that participants who reported a difficult day at work tended to report higher levels of stress on their drive home.
- **L** – This shows that unresolved hassles during the day can be carried forward so that the behaviour of others are more likely to be interpreted negatively by the stressed driver.

COULD know ...

Third study: Flett *et al.*

How?

Students read a scenario describing someone who had experienced either major life events or daily hassles.

They then rated the amount of emotional and practical support that person would be likely to receive and would seek from others.

Showed?

Major life events such as divorce and bereavement differed from daily hassles in the extent that people would seek and receive social support.

People experiencing life events were seen as more likely to seek and receive social support than those experiencing daily hassles.

 This suggests that ...

... daily hassles may be stressful because of the reduced level of social support from others.

- **E** – This has therapeutic implications for people who experience multiple hassles as part of their everyday life.
- **E** – Because the negative effects of these daily hassles tend not to be relieved by emotional and practical support from others, their stressful impact is increased.
- **L** – This suggests that the provision of support for such people can prevent the development of stress-related illnesses such as depression.

JUMBLED SENTENCES

Below is a description of the key study from the facing page. The sentences are presented in a jumbled order. Number them correctly.

3	**1**	Results showed that 41% of those surveyed suffered from depressive symptoms.
	2	There was a positive correlation of .33 between depressive symptoms and scores on the hassles scale.
	3	Bouteyre *et al.* carried out a study using correlational data.
	4	Students with good social support were less likely to develop depression when faced with daily hassles.
	5	Studied students in the first year of a psychology degree course at a French university.
	6	Sample was mostly female (n=207) with 26 males. Mean age was 20.48 years.
	7	Students completed *Beck Depression Inventory*, *Daily Hassles Scale* and *Social Support Questionnaire*.

Answers on page 195

CIRCLE TRUE OR FALSE

T or F Bouteyre *et al.* found that social support made no difference to the impact of daily hassles among a student sample.

T or F In Gervais' study of nurses, the stressful effect of daily hassles was relieved to some extent by daily uplifts.

T or F Telescoping refers to memories being recalled as more recent than they actually are.

T or F An advantage of correlational data is that it enables researchers to infer a causal relationship between hassles and stress.

T or F Absence of hassles during the day made people more vulnerable to road rage on the drive home.

T or F People are more likely to receive support from others when experiencing daily hassles than when experiencing life changes.

Answers on page 195

KEY PHRASES

Outline what **one** study has shown about the relationship between daily hassles and stress. *(4 marks)*

On the facing pages there are three findings from the key study by Bouteyre *et al.*

For each one select **three** key words or phrases and enter them in the grid below plus an appropriate conclusion. The first one has been done for you.

Finding 1	41%	Sample	Depressive symptoms
Finding 2			
Finding 3			
Conclusion			

Now try to write an answer to the exam question on the left using your key phrases. Your answer should be about 100 words in length.

A MARKING EXERCISE

Read the student answer to the following exam question:

Outline how research has investigated the relationship between daily hassles and stress. *(4 marks)*

Devon's answer

Bouteyre et al. studied psychology students at a French university. The students filled in a depression inventory and a hassles scale. The researchers found that about 40% of the students showed depressive symptoms and there was a positive correlation between the level of daily hassles experienced and the severity of depressive symptoms. A second study was carried out on nurses, who were asked to keep a diary of daily hassles and uplifts experienced over one month. The study found that nurses who had lots of daily hassles experienced the highest levels of job strain and the lowest levels of job performance. Experiencing daily uplifts, however, decreased the adverse effects of the hassles.

Your comments on Devon's answer:

....
....
....
....
....
....
....

What mark do you think her answer would get?

Devon would get _____ out of 4 marks

Answers on page 195

KEY WORDS

- Adrenaline
- Burnout
- Coronary heart disease (CHD)
- Job control
- Job strain
- Workload
- Workplace stressors

Possible essay question …

Discuss the effects of workload as a source of workplace stress. *(12 marks)*

Other possible exam questions …

+ Outline what research has shown about the effects of workload as a workplace stressor. *(6 marks)*
+ Outline how researchers have investigated the effects of workload as a source of workplace stress. *(4 marks)*
+ Apply this knowledge to … *(6 marks)*

MUST know …

Key study: Johansson *et al.*

How?
Group of sawmill 'finishers' performed repetitive jobs that required high levels of attention and responsibility (i.e. high levels of workload).

Workers who carried out maintenance at the mill or were cleaners were used as a control group.

Adrenaline was measured several times a day, at home and at work, and participants rated themselves on well-being and efficiency.

Showed?
This 'high risk' group (i.e. the finishers) had higher illness rates and higher levels of adrenaline than a 'low risk' group within the sawmill.

Finishers' adrenaline levels were over twice as high at work than at home.

In the control group, adrenaline levels were less than 1.5 times higher at work than at home.

Finishers were more irritable, had lower feelings of well-being and higher absence rates than workers in the control group.

 There is research support …

… from Kivimäki *et al.*

Their meta-analysis of 14 studies found that employees with high levels of job strain (i.e. high workload, low levels of control) were 50% more likely to develop coronary heart disease (CHD) than those with low levels of job strain.

 However, other research disagrees …

… that workload is a significant source of stress.

A study of civil servants (Marmot *et al.*) did not find that workload was a contributory factor in stress-related illness.

 Work underload is also stressful …

… although research tends only to focus on work *over*load.

Work underload occurs where people are employed in jobs that are beneath their capacities or which lack creativity or stimulation.

SHOULD know …

Second study: Naylor and Malcomson

How?
The study involved 644 secondary English teachers in Canada.

Teachers completed a survey on their levels of workload and stress.

They were asked to identify the most significant aspects of stress in their professional lives.

Showed?
Teachers worked in excess of 53 hours a week during term time. Meetings and administration added to their workload.

They reported widespread symptoms of stress and varying abilities to cope.

Female and younger teachers reported the worst impact and least coping ability.

More than 85% reported that their work resulted in significant levels of fatigue and more than one-third reported health problems related to their work life.

- **E** – Choi *et al.* argue that Kivimäki examined the impact of only one work stressor (job strain) yet several other stressors (long working hours, poor social support, job insecurity) are associated with CHD, independent of job strain.
- **L** – This suggests that tackling job strain alone without other risk factors may not dramatically reduce levels of CHD.

- **E** – Marmot *et al.*'s study found that it was job control rather than workload that was the main contributory factor in the development of coronary heart disease (CHD).
- **L** – This suggests that although 'job strain' appears to be a determinant of stress-related illness, control appears to be more influential than workload.

- **E** – Shultz *et al.* found that employees reporting work overload had the highest levels of stress-related illness but those who reported work underload also experienced significant levels of stress-related illness.
- **L** – This suggests that work stress may be determined by having too *little* work to do as well as having too *much* work.

COULD know …

Workload can lead to burnout

The term 'burnout' describes workers' reactions, e.g. emotional exhaustion, to the chronic stress common in various occupations, particularly those involving direct interaction with people.

Burnout becomes more likely when workers must deal with a high workload, high levels of job stress and high job expectations.

 This is supported by research evidence by…

… for example, Van Bogaert *et al.*

- **E** – They found a positive correlation between workload and burnout in nurses working in psychiatric hospitals in Belgium.
- **E** – This was particularly evident among female nurses.
- **L** – They suggest that burnout may be a particular problem for women, who must juggle multiple roles, not only at work but also those related to the home and family, for which they may have sole or major responsibility.

PRACTICE ELABORATION

On the facing page, there are a number of evaluative points for the effects of workload as a source of stress. After reading these points (and without looking back at them), try to expand the three points included in the table below.

State the point	Evidence	Elaboration	Conclusion (link back)
There is research support …			
Other research disagrees …			
Work underload can also be stressful …			

APPLYING YOUR KNOWLEDGE

Identify the psychology	Jackie is feeling very stressed. There never seems to be enough hours in the day to get through the work her boss expects her to do, and she always feels under pressure. Using your knowledge of psychology, suggest why Jackie feels so stressed. *(4 marks)* 	Link to Jackie's stress

Answers on page 195

 ## A MARKING EXERCISE

Read the student answer to the following exam question:

Outline what research has shown about the effect of workload as a source of stress in the workplace. *(4 marks)*

Parveen's answer

Johansson *et al.*'s study found that sawmill workers with high workload levels suffered higher stress levels. They had significantly higher levels of adrenaline while at work than home. This was not the case for a control group with lower levels of workload. They also had lower levels of well-being. A study of teachers found that a high proportion claimed health problems that were directly linked to their workload levels. A problem for this type of research is that it only concentrates on work overload whereas some research has found that work underload can also be stressful. Shultz *et al.* found that, although work overload was the main source of stress, work underload was also linked to stress-related illness.

Your comments on Parveen's answer:

....
....
....
....
....
....
....

What mark do you think her answer would get?

Parveen would get _____ out of 4 marks

Answers on page 195

KEY WORDS

- Coronary heart disease (CHD)
- Job control
- Longitudinal study
- Workplace stressors

Possible essay question ...

Discuss the effects of control as a source of workplace stress. *(12 marks)*

Other possible exam questions ...

+ Outline what research has shown about the effects of control as a workplace stressor. *(6 marks)*
+ Outline how researchers have investigated the effects of control as a workplace stressor. *(4 marks)*
+ Apply this knowledge to ... *(6 marks)*

MUST know ...

Key study: Marmot *et al.*

How?

Longitudinal study of 10,308 civil servants aged 35–55 (67% men and 33% women).

Participants completed a questionnaire on job control, workload and level of social support.

Independent check made of participants' job specification and role responsibilities.

Researchers checked for any symptoms of CHD in participants.

Showed?

After five years, those who reported low levels of job control were more likely to have developed CHD than those with high levels of job control.

This association was independent of other risk factors, e.g. smoking or physical activity, or employment grade.

Workload and social support at work were not related to risk of CHD.

There are individual differences ...

... in how workers respond to lack of control.

- *E* – Research into the impact of workplace stressors misses the point that there are wide individual differences in how people react to, and cope with, individual stressors such as lack of control.

Lack of control can be harmful ...

... in that it can have adverse effects on mental health.

- *E* – High levels of stress at work, such as that caused by lack of control, combined with other stressors (such as problems at home or daily hassles) can make illnesses, such as depression, more likely.

Lack of control may have indirect effects ...

... for example the development of diabetes as a consequence of stress.

- *E* – Smith *et al.* found that low levels of job control were associated with an increased risk of diabetes among women, but not among men.

SHOULD know ...

Second study: McCarthy *et al.*

How?

McCarthy *et al.* studied 227 men who had experienced a first-time coronary event (heart attack or unstable angina).

Each man was matched with a man of similar age and background.

This was in order to study the relationship between the coronary event and their job characteristics (e.g. level of job control).

Showed?

A significant factor in the likelihood of a coronary event was low job control.

Older workers (over 50) reported significantly lower levels of job control than did younger workers (under 50) and were also more susceptible to coronary events.

Higher job control was seen as a potential protective factor for heart disease and this was particularly the case in older workers.

- *E* – Schaubroeck *et al.* found that some workers respond differently to lack of control – they are *less* stressed by having no control or responsibility in their work. They also had higher immune responses in low rather than high-control situations.
- *L* – This suggests that lack of control may only be experienced as stressful by some individuals.

- *E* – Melchior found that work stress, in particular low levels of job control, can precipitate depression and anxiety in previously healthy young workers.
- *L* – This suggests that helping workers cope with work stress or reducing work stress levels could prevent the occurrence of mental health problems.

- *E* – Smith *et al.* claim that men and women react differently to stress. Women are more likely than men to turn to unhealthy habits, e.g. eating comfort foods containing fat and sugar.
- *L* – As a result, this makes women more vulnerable than men to developing diabetes when faced with a lack of control.

COULD know ...

Third study: Bond and Bunce

How?

Carried out a one-year intervention study in three business sites in the UK (known as X, Y and Z regions).

They raised levels of job control in X, Y and Z regions compared to a control group (C region), where they stayed the same.

Showed?

Any benefits seen in general mental health, motivation levels and absenteeism rates were mainly due to increases in job control.

For example, there was a significant reduction in mental health problems in the groups with increased job control, but not in the control group.

There are additional benefits ...

... to increasing job control.

- *E* – Because in the three business sites studied, employee absence cost each organisation, on average, £574 per year per absent individual.
- *E* – This figure dropped to £442 after increasing job control, compared to similar businesses where there was no increase in job control. In these businesses, the amount spent per absent individual rose to £706.
- *L* – This shows that the benefits of increased job control are not restricted to the individual, but also to employers.

WRITE YOUR OWN EVALUATION POINT

Using the material on the facing page, write out one of the evaluative points in your own words, underlining the key words.

S	
E	
E	
L	

See page 14 for an explanation of how to SEEL.

✓✗ CIRCLE TRUE OR FALSE

T or F A longitudinal study of 10,308 male civil servants aged 35–55.

T or F Independent checks were made of participants' job specification and role responsibilities.

T or F Participants with greater workload levels were more at risk of coronary heart disease.

T or F Participants with high levels of job control were less likely to have developed coronary heart disease.

T or F Lack of social support at work was a significant risk factor for the development of coronary heart disease.

T or F Participants in higher employment grades were more likely to have developed coronary heart disease.

Answers on page 195

⚙ APPLYING YOUR KNOWLEDGE

Rick has recently started a new job on a daily newspaper. Although Rick is a media studies graduate, he has to work at a basic grade within the company. As a result he plays no part in deciding what goes into the newspaper, nor how the news is collected. He finds this difficult, and is particularly irritated by the fact that others tell him what to do all the time.

Use your knowledge of the relationship between job control and stress to explain why Rick feels the way he does. *(4 marks)*

Identify the psychology	Link to Rick's feelings of stress

Answers on page 195

An idea 👍

Draw a mind map relating to the effects of control as a source of workplace stress. Try linking together the main research findings and the points of evaluation.
You might need to do this on a separate piece of paper.

(Job control)

✎ FILL IN THE BLANKS

The text below is an answer to the following exam question:

Outline what research has shown about the effects of control as a workplace stressor. *(6 marks)*

Marmot *et al.* found that civil servants who reported

(1) .... levels of job control were more likely to have

developed (2) .... than those with (3) ....

levels. This association was independent of risk factors such as

(4) ...., physical activity or employment grade. McCarthy

et al. found that low job control was a significant factor that increased the

likelihood of a (5) .... event. Older workers reported

significantly (6) .... levels of job control than younger

workers. This made them (7) .... susceptible to heart attacks

or unstable (8) .... A higher level of job control was

found to be a (9) .... factor for heart disease. This was

particularly true for (10) .... workers.

Answers on page 195

KEY WORDS

- Cardiovascular problems
- Coronary heart disease (CHD)
- Cortisol
- Prospective study
- Type D behaviour

Type A behaviour pattern

- Characterised by time-urgency, competitiveness and impatience.
- Believed to increase the risk of coronary heart disease (CHD).

Type B behaviour pattern

- Characterised by a patient, relaxed and easy-going approach to life.
- Believed to decrease the risk of CHD.

Possible essay questions ...

Discuss the relationship between Type A behaviour and stress. *(12 marks)*

Discuss the relationship between personality factors and stress. *(12 marks)*

Other possible exam questions ...

+ Outline what psychologists have found out about the relationship between Type A behaviour and stress. *(6 marks)*
+ Outline how psychologists have investigated the relationship between Type A behaviour and stress. *(4 marks)*
+ Apply this knowledge to ... *(6 marks)*

MUST know ...

Key study: Friedman and Rosenman

How?
Researchers studied approximately 3,000 men aged 39–59, living in California.

Men were examined for signs of CHD (to exclude any that were already ill).

Interviewed and observed to see how they responded to everyday pressures (e.g. having to wait in a long queue).

Men were classified as either Type A or Type B.

Showed?
After eight years twice as many Type A men had died of cardiovascular problems than Type B men.

Over 12% of the Type A men had experienced a heart attack compared to 6% of the Type B men.

The Type A men also had higher blood pressure and higher levels of cholesterol.

Type A men were more likely to smoke and have a family history of coronary heart disease.

 One criticism of this study ...

... comes from a research review by Bunker *et al.*

- **E** – They found no strong or consistent evidence for a causal relationship between Type A behaviour patterns and the development of CHD.

 There are real-life implications ...

... to help people with extreme Type A behaviour patterns change them to more of a Type B style.

- **E** – For example, the *Recurrent Coronary Prevention Project*, which was conducted in the 1980s in San Francisco.

 Type D is more important than Type A ...

... in predicting adverse health outcomes.

- **E** – Type D individuals have increased levels of anxiety and depression. They overreact to stressful situations but conceal their feelings from others out of fear of rejection. Type Ds respond differently to stress, having raised levels of cortisol, which leads to an increased risk of CHD.

SHOULD know ...

Second study: Myrtek

How?
Meta-analysis covering all prospective studies carried out up to 1998.

Correlated the relationship between Type A behaviour and development of CHD.

Also looked specifically at whether there was a relationship between hostility (one component of Type A) and CHD.

Showed?
The relationship between the Type A behaviour pattern and CHD was not significant.

There *was* a significant relationship between hostility and CHD.

However, this was so low that it was considered to have no practical meaning for the prediction and prevention of CHD.

- **E** – Bunker *et al.* carried out a review of research studies. Although they found a relationship between some factors and development of CHD, Type A behaviour was no more significant than other risk factors such as smoking.
- **L** – This suggests that although Type A behaviour is a risk factor, it has no *causal* relationship with CHD.

- **E** – Follow-up studies of this project found that changes were achieved in many people. Heart attack rates were reduced in those who received the Type A reduction efforts (Thoreson and Powell).
- **L** – However, intervention is difficult because the Type A behavioural style has many rewarding features for people who are motivated by career advancement.

- **E** – Denollet *et al.* studied 300 heart patients in a cardiac rehabilitation programme and found that 27% of those classified as Type D died within eight years, compared to 7% of non-Type Ds.
- **L** – Unlike Type As who tend to vent their anger and impatience, Type Ds have no outlet for their stress, which makes it so harmful for them and CHD is more likely.

COULD know ...

TABP can impact on driving behaviour

Because of the nature of the Type A behaviour pattern (TABP) (e.g. time urgency, competitiveness and impatience) it is likely that people with this type of behaviour pattern will experience more stress when driving and display a more aggressive form of driving behaviour.

As a result they are likely to experience more traffic accidents than those displaying the Type B behaviour pattern.

This is supported by research evidence ...

... of driving behaviour.

- **E** – For example, in a study of bus drivers in the USA and India (Evans *et al.*) it was found that drivers characterised as having the TABP experienced more stress.
- **E** – They showed more impatience in their driving behaviour and had higher traffic accident rates than those with Type B.
- **L** – This shows that people with the Type A behaviour pattern (e.g. time urgency and impatience) consequently show a more aggressive form of driving behaviour.

DRAWING CONCLUSIONS

The table below contains some of the observational data of Evans *et al.*'s study of bus drivers in the US and India (see facing page for a summary of this study).

	Indian sample		US sample	
	Type A	Type B	Type A	Type B
Braking per 100 mins	146	108	115	120
Horn blowing per 100 mins.	502	320	3	2

State **two** findings and for each one draw a conclusion (state what the findings show).

Finding 1:

Conclusion 1: This shows that …

Finding 2:

Conclusion 2: This shows that …

Answers on page 195

 CIRCLE TRUE OR FALSE

T or F Type B behaviour is defined by an impatient, competitive and time urgent approach to life.

T or F Research suggests that people with a Type D behaviour pattern may be more prone to CHD.

T or F Friedman and Rosenman found no difference in incidence of heart attacks between Type A and Type B men.

T or F Heart attack rates can be reduced by Type A behaviour reduction programmes.

T or F Hostility is an important predictor of CHD.

T or F Research has failed to demonstrate a causal relationship between Type A behaviour and CHD.

T or F Type B men were more likely to have a family history of heart disease.

T or F The recurrent Coronary Prevention Project was designed to help people with extreme Type A behaviour.

Answers on page 195

 KEY PHRASES

Outline what **one** study has shown about the relationship between Type A behaviour and stress. *(6 marks)*

On the facing page there are four findings from the key study by Friedman and Rosenman.

For each one select **three** key words or phrases and enter them in the grid below plus an appropriate conclusion. The first one has been done for you.

Finding 1	Twice as many	Type A	Died
Finding 2			
Finding 3			
Finding 4			

Now try to write an answer to the exam question on the left using your key phrases. Your answer should be about 100 words in length.

 APPLYING YOUR KNOWLEDGE

Karl always meets deadlines when he is working. He is always looking for things to do while at work. Max has a more relaxed approach to work although he tries to meet deadlines, he is not worried if he misses some of them.

a) Is Karl or Max more likely to have a Type A behaviour pattern? *(1 mark)*

b) Suggest **two** other ways you would expect these two men to differ if one was Type A and the other Type B. *(2 marks)*

Answers on page 195

 CHOOSE THE RIGHT ANSWER

Tick **two** of the boxes below to indicate which of the following are features of Type A behaviour.

A Push themselves with deadlines and hate delays ☐

B Don't mind losing when faced with competition ☐

C Patient and even-tempered ☐

D High-achieving 'workaholics' ☐

Answers on page 195

TOPIC 39   *Personality factors: hardiness*

KEY WORDS
- Hardiness
- Hardiness training
- Negative affectivity (NA)

The components of hardiness
- **Control** – being in control of one's life rather than being controlled by external forces.
- **Commitment** – being involved with the world around oneself and having a strong sense of purpose.
- **Challenge** – seeing life challenges as problems to be overcome and as an opportunity for development rather than as threats or stressors.

Possible essay questions ...
Outline and evaluate the relationship between the hardy personality and stress. *(12 marks)*

Outline and evaluate the relationship between personality factors and stress. *(12 marks)*

Other possible exam questions ...
+ Outline what research has shown about the relationship between the hardy personality and stress. *(6 marks)*
+ Explain how researchers have investigated the relationship between the hardy personality and stress. *(4 marks)*
+ Apply this knowledge to ... *(6 marks)*

MUST know ...

Key study: Kobasa *et al.*
How?
Gathered data from a sample of 259 business executives in a large utility company.

Questionnaires used to assess stressful life events and illness symptoms over a two-year period.

Researchers also assessed constitutional predisposition (e.g. family history of illness).

Separate scales measured the three components of hardiness (control, commitment and challenge).

Showed?
All three factors (stressful life events, constitutional predisposition, hardiness) had an effect on illness.

Of the three, hardiness had the largest influence.

The presence of a constitutional predisposition in someone experiencing stressful life events increased the likelihood of them becoming ill.

Scoring high on the three hardiness components appeared to decrease this likelihood.

 There is research support ...

... from the study of soldiers undergoing the stress of military deployment.
- **E** – In the 1990's Gulf War, the higher the hardiness level, the less likely soldiers were to experience negative health consequences.

 There is a real-world application ...

... of hardiness research in the development of hardiness training programmes.
- **E** – It should be possible to increase hardiness in individuals and make them more resistant to stress. In hardiness training programmes, individuals are coached in an attempt to strengthen hardy attitudes.

One criticism of Kobasa's study ...

... comes from the concept of negative affectivity (NA).
- **E** – Individuals high in NA dwell more on their failures and on negative aspects of themselves and are more likely to report dissatisfaction and distress. This suggests hardy individuals are simply low in NA.

SHOULD know ...

Second study: Maddi *et al.*
How?
Natural experiment over a 12-year period from 1975 to 1987 at Illinois Bell Telephone (IBT).

Company was reducing workforce dramatically over that period, particularly during 1981–1982.

Each year data was collected from a sample of 450 male and female supervisors.

Showed?
Two-thirds of the sample suffered stress-related illness.

One-third showed no evidence of stress-related illness and appeared to thrive.

Those who thrived scored significantly higher in the three components of hardiness.

These hardy employees were more likely to face stressful circumstances rather than deny them and attempted to turn potential disasters into opportunities.

- **E** – Bartone studied US army soldiers on combat and peacekeeping missions. He found evidence that lower levels of hardiness were associated with a greater likelihood of mental breakdown or post-traumatic stress disorder (PTSD).
- **L** – As a result, hardiness training has become widespread in the US military.

- **E** – Maddi *et al.* used a hardiness training programme to help stressed-out employees. Those that took part reduced their anxiety and other signs of strain, while increasing their job satisfaction.
- **L** – This shows that hardiness is important not only for coping with stressful conditions but also for thriving in those conditions.

- **E** – This is challenged by studies that do not involve self-reports of health or performance. For example, Maddi found that hardiness levels were higher among employees whose blood pressure was normal compared to those with high blood pressure.
- **L** – This would be difficult to explain using the concept of NA as this is a physiological measure.

COULD know ...

Third study: Lifton *et al.*
How?
In a longitudinal study, researchers measured hardiness in 1,432 first-year students at five US universities to find its association with ability to cope with stresses of academic life.

Showed?
Found that students scoring low on hardiness were disproportionately more likely to drop out of university, and those scoring high were more likely to complete their degree.

 There are problems with the concept of hardiness ...

... as not all components may be important.
- **E** – Sheard examined whether all components of hardiness equally predicted university success.
- **E** – Female students significantly outperformed males in their dissertation marks and final degree grade and also reported a significantly higher score on *commitment* compared to males (but not on the other components).
- **L** – Therefore *commitment* was found to be the most significant positive correlate of academic achievement.

DRAWING CONCLUSIONS AND RESEARCH ISSUES

A psychology class decides to test which class members and teachers have a hardy personality and which do not.

They use a hardiness questionnaire with students in their class and also with some teachers.

The bar chart shows the mean scores for male and female students and for male and female teachers.

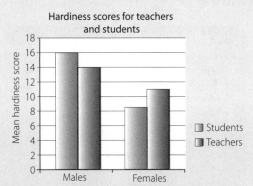

Hardiness scores for teachers and students

(a) Suggest **two** conclusions that might be drawn from this bar chart. *(4 marks)*

Conclusion 1

Conclusion 2

(b) A questionnaire was used to assess hardiness. Outline **one** problem with using questionnaires in studies such as this. *(2 marks)*

Answers on page 195

 APPLYING YOUR KNOWLEDGE

Kenzi and Cynthia are well-qualified and experienced teachers. Kenzi is exhausted at the end of every week, frequently complains about the amount of work she has to do and admits to her friends that with another reorganisation due next year, she may just give up teaching. Cynthia, on the other hand, finds teaching very stimulating, her enthusiasm for the job is obvious and she welcomes any reorganisation as an opportunity to develop her role within the school.

Use your knowledge of the relationship between stress and hardiness to explain the different responses of Kenzi and Cynthia to the stresses of teaching. *(4 marks)*

Identify the psychology	Identify the psychology
Link to Kenzi's response	Link to Cynthia's response

Answers on page 196

 A MARKING EXERCISE

Read the student answers to the following exam question:

Outline how psychologists have studied the relationship between the hardy personality and stress. *(4 marks)*

Jon's answer

Kobasa *et al.* studied whether hardiness was an important factor in determining absence due to illness among business executives. They used questionnaires to assess experience of stressful life events, illness levels and family history of illness. They used three scales to measure control, commitment and challenge independently. Maddi *et al.* carried out a natural experiment in a US company. They collected data from 450 supervisors when the company was reducing its workforce. Their reactions to these events were then related to their hardiness scores.

Sam's answer

Psychologists have used a variety of different techniques to study the hardy personality and stress. They have used questionnaires to measure hardiness. Hardiness has three components, control, challenge and commitment. People who are high in all three of these components are described as having a hardy personality. Questionnaires therefore need to measure how high people are in all three. Stress can then be measured using a stress questionnaire in order to see if lower hardiness scores means higher stress levels.

Your comments on Jon's answer:

What mark do you think his answer would get? _____ out of 4 marks

Your comments on Sam's answer:

What mark do you think his answer would get? _____ out of 4 marks

Answers on page 196

KEY WORDS

- Hardiness training
- Maladaptive behaviour
- Stress inoculation training (SIT)
- Systematic desensitisation
- Terrorism

Possible essay question ...

Outline and evaluate stress inoculation training as a method of stress management. *(12 marks)*

Other possible exam questions ...

+ Outline stress inoculation training as a method of stress management. *(6 marks)*
+ Outline what is involved in stress inoculation training as a method of stress management. *(6 marks)*
+ **(a)** Outline **one** psychological method of stress management. *(3 marks)*
  (b) Outline **one** strength of this psychological method of stress management. *(3 marks)*
+ Apply this knowledge to ... *(6 marks)*

 Exam tip

SIT is *required* but hardiness training is only necessary if you are asked for two methods. Take care not to muddle the hardy *personality* with hardiness *training*.

MUST know ...

Stress inoculation training (SIT)

SIT helps people to cope with the aftermath of exposure to stressful events and to 'inoculate' themselves against a stressor before it arises.

The aim of SIT is to enhance individuals' coping repertoires and enable them to use their already existing coping skills.

Three phases of stress inoculation training are:

- *Conceptualisation* – clients are taught to think differently about a stressor, and how to break down major stressors into specific short-term, intermediate and long-term coping goals.
- *Skills acquisition* – coping skills taught then rehearsed in real life. These include problem-solving and using social support systems.
- *Application* – learned coping skills are applied in increasingly stressful situations. Relapse prevention procedures and booster sessions are built into SIT.

SIT usually consists of between 8–15 one-hour sessions, plus booster and follow-up sessions, conducted over a 3–12-month period.

 There is research support ...

... for the effectiveness of SIT.

- *E* – Meichenbaum used SIT to effectively help individuals deal with the stress associated with their snake phobia.

 Another area of research support ...

... is that SIT also works with non-clinical populations such as students.

- *E* – SIT has been shown to be effective for students when dealing with the stresses of academic life.

 One problem with SIT is ...

... that it is time consuming and requires high levels of motivation.

- *E* – As a result, this may limit its usefulness as a method of stress management because people are reluctant to invest sufficient time and effort.

SHOULD know ...

Hardiness training

People can be trained in hardiness, to help them manage stress better by becoming more resistant to its potentially harmful effects.

Involves three stages: focusing, reliving stress encounters, self-improvement.

- *Focusing* – on the sources and signs of stress.
- *Reliving stress encounters* – the client is given an insight into their current coping strategies.
- *Self-improvement* – learning new techniques, e.g. stressors seen as challenges not problems.

 There are limitations of hardiness training ...

... because of learned coping habits.

It must first address learned habits of coping that are difficult to modify.

- *E* – For example, Lindquist *et al.* found men tended to use more 'maladaptive' coping strategies, e.g. alcohol abuse, or interpersonal withdrawal.
- *L* – This means that hardiness training cannot be seen as a rapid solution to stress management.

- *E* – Both SIT and systematic desensitisation were effective in reducing snake phobia, but SIT also helped clients deal effectively with a different (untreated) phobia.
- *L* – This shows that SIT not only deals with the stress of current problems but also inoculates against future stressors.

- *E* – Sheehy and Horan found that law students who received SIT displayed lower levels of anxiety and stress over time, and improved academic performance.
- *L* – Demonstrates that, although academic stress may be unavoidable, the use of SIT can minimise its adverse effects.

- *E* – However, Meichenbaum demonstrated the effectiveness of brief periods of therapy, e.g. for victims of sexual assault or for preparing patients for surgery.
- *L* – This shows the effectiveness of SIT is not necessarily reduced when the time available for therapy is limited.

COULD know ...

SIT in the community

Meichenbaum suggests that it is sometimes necessary to go beyond individual and group interventions and to adopt a community-based focus for SIT.

Stress does not affect individuals alone, but also others who are the secondary victims of trauma, e.g. people stressed in the aftermath of terrorist attacks.

It should be possible, therefore, to use stress inoculation training in situations where communities are exposed to extreme forms of stress on a regular basis.

There is supporting evidence ...

... for the effectiveness of SIT in this context.

- *E* – Ayalon used a SIT approach to prepare Israeli children to cope with the fears associated with terrorist attacks.
- *E* – Other studies have shown that exposure to trauma can itself be an effective form of stress inoculation effect, because individuals have gained experience in successfully mastering traumatic events (Ursano *et al.*).
- *L* – This supports Meichenbaum's assertion that whole communities can be prepared to deal with future stressors before they arise.

SPOT THE MISTAKES

Read this student answer to the following exam question:

Outline what is involved in stress inoculation training as a method of stress management. *(6 marks)*

There are four mistakes, draw a circle round each.

Stress inoculation training aims to raise individuals' hardiness levels to make them more resistant to stress. The main phases of SIT are conceptualisation, focusing and application. In the first phase individuals are taught how to think differently about stressors, and to break these down into what they might achieve in the short, medium and long-term. In the second phase individuals are taught a range of coping skills, including problem solving and avoidance. In the final phase, application, these skills are put to the test in real-world situations. SIT usually consists of somewhere between 8 and 15 one-hour sessions. After treatment, clients are expected to practise their newly acquired coping skills without further input from the SIT therapist. This is because relapse prevention skills are built into the initial SIT sessions.

Answers on page 196

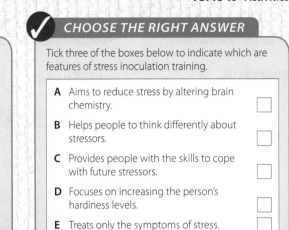 **CHOOSE THE RIGHT ANSWER**

Tick three of the boxes below to indicate which are features of stress inoculation training.

A Aims to reduce stress by altering brain chemistry. ☐

B Helps people to think differently about stressors. ☐

C Provides people with the skills to cope with future stressors. ☐

D Focuses on increasing the person's hardiness levels. ☐

E Treats only the symptoms of stress. ☐

F Effective with secondary victims of trauma (e.g. terrorist attacks). ☐

Answers on page 196

 APPLYING YOUR KNOWLEDGE

Kelda has recently been promoted at work but is worried that she may not be up to the demands of her new role. She finds it hard to switch off when not working and constantly worries that everything will get too much for her and she will have a breakdown. A colleague suggests that she might try stress inoculation training to help her cope with her stress.

Explain how a therapist might use stress inoculation training with Kelda. *(6 marks)*

Identify the psychology	Link to Kelda

Answers on page 196

 PRACTICE ELABORATION

Using the material on the facing page, complete the table below to prepare an answer to the following exam question:

Evaluate stress inoculation training as a method of stress management. *(6 marks)*

State the point	Evidence	Elaboration	Conclusion (link back)
One strength of SIT is …			
Another strength of SIT is …			
A limitation of SIT is …			

Key Words

- Adrenaline
- Anxiety
- Benzodiazepines (BZs)
- Beta-blockers (BBs)
- Central nervous system (CNS)
- Depression
- GABA
- Noradrenaline
- Placebo
- Sympathomedullary
- Tolerance
- Withdrawal symptoms

Possible essay question …

Outline and evaluate drug therapy as a method of stress management. *(12 marks)*

Other possible exam questions …

+ Outline drug therapy as a method of stress management. *(6 marks)*
+ Outline what is involved in drug therapy as a method of stress management. *(6 marks)*
+ (a) Outline **one** biological method of stress management. *(3 marks)*
  (b) Outline **one** limitation of this biological method of stress management. *(3 marks)*
+ Apply this knowledge to … *(6 marks)*

MUST know …

Drug therapies: benzodiazepines (BZs)

BZs are a class of drugs used to treat anxiety that is a consequence of stress.

They slow down activity in the central nervous system by enhancing the action of GABA.

This slows down activity in the central nervous system (CNS), making the person feel more relaxed.

Drug therapies: beta-blockers (BBs)

BBs reduce the effects of adrenaline and noradrenaline in response to stress, and so reduce anxiety levels.

They bind to cells of the heart and other parts of the body that are usually stimulated during arousal, blocking their activity.

The heart beats slower and with less force, blood pressure falls and the person feels calmer.

 One strength of drug therapies …

… is that drugs are effective in combating the effects of stress.

- **E** – For example, Kahn *et al.* found that BZs were superior to a placebo in reducing the effects of patients' stress over an eight-week period.

 A second strength of drug therapies …

… is that drugs are easy to use compared to other forms of treatment.

- **E** – Drug treatments require little effort from the patient compared to the significant investment in time and motivation required in psychological methods, e.g. stress inoculation.

 One limitation of drug therapies …

… is that drugs can be addictive and can lead to withdrawal symptoms.

- **E** – These occur when patients stop taking BZs, indicating psychological dependence.

 A second limitation of drug therapies …

… is that drugs can have unpleasant side effects.

- **E** – With BZs these include drowsiness, confusion and memory impairment.

SHOULD know …

Benzodiazepines (BZs)

GABA causes chemical changes within neurons of the CNS, making it harder for them to be stimulated.

By binding to special sites on the GABA receptor, BZs increase this inhibitory effect within the neuron.

This makes the neuron even more resistant to excitation, making the person feel even more relaxed.

Beta-blockers (BBs)

Adrenaline and noradrenaline form part of the body's sympathomedullary response to stress.

By blocking beta-receptors on the surface of the heart, BBs cause the reverse effect of adrenaline and noradrenaline.

For example, blood vessels do not contract so easily, which results in a fall in blood pressure and less strain on the heart.

- **E** – BBs were also effective in reducing performance anxiety among musicians who felt less stressed when performing and performed better (Lockwood).
- **L** – This shows that reducing the anxiety associated with stressful situations is an effective form of stress management.

- **E** – Patients need only remember to take the drug, whereas stress inoculation involves a lengthy therapeutic process and a great deal of input from the client.
- **L** – The relative ease of use of drug treatments means that people are more likely to continue with treatment, increasing the effectiveness of their stress management.

- **E** – With regular use the body comes to depend on BZs for normal function. Tolerance develops so larger doses are needed to produce the same effects (Ashton).
- **L** – This means that the use of BZs tends to be limited to short-term treatment of stress only.

- **E** – By contrast, there are no side effects associated with psychological methods of stress management, such as stress inoculation.
- **L** – Side effects make patients less likely to continue with the treatment, thus decreasing its effectiveness.

COULD know …

Reducing stress-related illness

Pariante *et al.* identified a protein (SGK1) that prolongs the detrimental effects of stress hormones, which may lead to stress-related illnesses such as depression.

The researchers developed a drug compound to block this effect, and ultimately increase the number of new brain cells, avoiding the development of depression.

There is a major issue with drug treatments …

… because they focus only on the symptoms of stress.

- **E** – A problem with any sort of drug treatment of stress is that when treatment ends, the symptoms, such as anxiety or high blood pressure, are likely to return
- **E** – This because the underlying problem that caused the stress is not addressed with drug treatments.
- **L** – It is more effective in the long term to use a treatment that focuses on the problem itself (e.g. stress inoculation therapy).

SPOT THE MISTAKES

Read this student answer to the following exam question:

Outline what is involved in stress inoculation training as a method of stress management. *(6 marks)*

There are five mistakes, draw a circle round each.

> Benzodiazepines (BZs) combat the symptoms of stress by reducing the actions of noradrenaline. This slows down action in the CNS, making it harder for neurons to be stimulated and consequently making the person feel more relaxed. Beta-blockers (BBs) work by increasing the effects of adrenaline in the brain, which reduces anxiety levels and makes the person feel calmer. BBs stimulate special receptors on the surface of the heart, increasing their activity. This makes the heart beat faster and makes it harder for blood vessels to contract. This causes blood pressure to fall, which makes the person feel calmer.

Answers on page 196

WRITE YOUR OWN EVALUATION POINT

Using the material on the facing page, find an evaluative point relevant to biological methods of stress management and write it in your own words below, underling the key words.

S	
E	
E	
L	

See page 14 for an explanation of how to S E E L.

APPLYING YOUR KNOWLEDGE

Kelda has recently been promoted at work but is worried that she may not be up to the demands of her new role. She finds it hard to switch off when not working and constantly worries that everything will get too much for her and she will have a breakdown. A colleague suggests that she might try drug therapy to help her cope with her stress.

Explain why drug therapy might help Kelda cope with her stress. *(6 marks)*

Identify the psychology	Link to Kelda's use of drug therapy

Answers on page 196

★ **Exam tip**

When responding to specific demands in questions, remember that 'drug therapy' (BZs and BBs together) can count as *one* form of biological treatment. Alternatively, BZs and BBs can count as *two* forms of treatment if explicitly introduced as such.

A MARKING EXERCISE

Read the student answer to the following question:

Outline **one** strength and **one** limitation of drug therapies as a method of stress management. *(6 marks)*

Cleo's answer

A strength of drug therapies is that they help people to deal more effectively with the anxiety they feel as a result of being exposed to a stressor (e.g. an examination). As a result they feel calmer and better able to deal with the stressor in question.

A limitation is that drug therapies only tackle the symptoms of stress. For example, someone taking an examination may feel anxious. Drug therapies cannot help them deal with the examination, just feel a bit less nervous about it.

TASK 1

What mark do you think this answer would get? _____ out of 6 marks

TASK 2 Your turn

Write an improved answer here:

Answers on page 196

TOPIC 32 — The body's response to stress

MUST | Two responses

SYMPATHOMEDULLARY PATHWAY
(Acute stress)

1. SNS increases heart rate and blood pressure
2. Adrenal medulla releases adrenaline
3. PNS restores body to resting state

PITUITARY–ADRENAL SYSTEM
(Chronic stress)

1. Hypothalamus releases CRF
2. Pituitary releases ACTH
3. Adrenal cortex releases cortisol

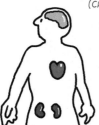

SHOULD | A bit more detail

SYMPATHOMEDULLARY PATHWAY
Fight or flight ...
Metabolic changes ...
Adrenaline ...
PNS ...
PITUITARY-ADRENAL SYSTEM
Hypothalamus activated ...
ACTH =
ACTH causes ...
Positive effects ...
Negative effects ...

COULD | Feedback and the pituitary-adrenal system

Send a message to the hypothalamus to reduce CRF production

CORTISOL LEVEL
TOO HIGH
NORMAL

EVALUATION

Cardiovascular consequences

I'm stressed at work | He's got high blood pressure

Repeated activation affects heart and blood vessels, e.g. raised blood pressure damages lining of blood vessels.

Research found ...

This suggests that ...

Immune system consequences

Too much cortisol suppresses immune system, leading to illness..

I can't come in today. My cortisol levels are up....

E.g. Kiecolt-Glaser et al. ...

This suggests that ...

Individual differences

STRESS

Fight or Flight | Tend and befriend

OXYTOCIN

Males and females have a different response to stress.

Taylor et al. found ...

This means that ...

However, the feedback system doesn't always work

LONG-TERM STRESS

FEED BACK SYSTEM

TOPIC 33 — Stress-related illness and the immune system

MUST | Kiecolt-Glaser et al. (1984)

HOW?

Medical students
OHIO

NK cell activity measured
One month later
EXAM

NK activity and life stressors questionnaire

SHOWED?

NK cell activity	Loneliness	Cortisol
Lower during exam period than one month before.	Those with highest levels had lowest immune system functioning.	Higher levels in those with highest levels of loneliness.

SHOULD | Kiecolt-Glaser et al. (2005)

HOW?

SHOWED?

COULD | Malarkey et al.

HOW?

FINANCES! | BAD HABITS

SHOWED?

EVALUATION

There is research support

1960 | 1963 | 1973 | 1989 | 2001

Segerstrom and Miller — meta analysis of 293 studies. Found short-term stressors could boost immune system; long-term stressors suppressed it.

The most chronic ...

This suggests that ...

It isn't a simple relationship

Health is affected by many factors, so it is difficult to disentangle specific effects that are attributable to stress.

This is because ...

As a result ...

Individual differences ...

Conflict in immune system changes in response to stress.

Kiecolt-Glaser et al. found ...

Older couples also showed ...

Problems with validity

It was only a lab study | erm

Malarky

TOPIC 34 — Life changes

MUST — Rahe et al.

Recorded illness while at sea.

SHOWED?

Found a positive correlation of +.118 between SRE scores and illness.

Higher the SRE score, more illness while at sea.

Completed SRE prior to 6 months tour of duty.

HOW? 2,700 sailors in 3 US Navy ships.

SHOULD

HOLMES and RAHE → using life changes to measure stress

COULD

MICHAEL and BEN-ZUR
Widowhood and divorce

EVALUATION

Individual differences
SRRS ignores fact that life events have different effects on different people.

For example ...

This suggests ...

yippee! oh no
KIDS LEAVING HOME

Spurious relationship
Most research yields correlational data only, i.e. doesn't show causal relationship.

There may be a third variable ...

For example ...

I'm stressed
HIGHLY ANXIOUS PERSON

Life changes and daily hassles
Minor daily hassles more significant as a source of stress.

DAILY HASSLES
↓
HEALTH PROBLEMS

Evidence from ...

This suggests that ...

Positive and negative events
Does the quality of the event make a difference?

TOPIC 35 — Daily hassles

MUST — Bouteyre et al.

SHOWED
41% showed depressive symptoms + correlation between hassles scores and depression scores

HOW? 120 first year Ψ students completed Daily Hassles scale and Beck Depression Inventory to determine stress of transition.

SHOULD

GERVAIS → Hassles and uplifts

Dear diary...

Nurses

COULD

FLETT et al. → Daily hassles versus life changes

Life event?
Hassle?

= Support from others?

EVALUATION

Problems of restrospective recall
Participants usually have to rate hassles experienced over previous month.

This creates a problem ...

This can be overcome by ...

Correlation is not the same as causality
Therefore they cannot tell us that daily hassles **caused** changes in psychological well-being.

However ...

As a result ...

HASSLES
= ?
WELL-BEING CHANGES

Real-world application

Grrrr

Accumulation of daily hassles can explain road rage on commute home.

Evidence from Gulian et al. ...

This suggests that ...

The amplification effect
Chronic stress makes people more vulnerable to daily hassles.

MUST — Johansson et al.

HOW? Sawmill 'finishers' had high levels of workload.
Control group of cleaners and maintenance workers. Adrenaline levels checked and workers rated themselves on well-being and efficiency.

SAWMILL

SHOWED? 'Finishers' had higher illness rates than controls. Adrenaline levels 3 times as high at work (than home) for finishers, 1.5 times for controls. Finishers also more irritable and higher absence rates.

SHOULD — Naylor and Malcomson

HOW?

Secondary teachers in Canada

SHOWED?

COULD — Burnout

EVALUATION

There is research support
Kivimäki et al.'s meta analysis found employees with high workloads 50% more likely to develop heart disease.
However, Choi et al. argues ...

This suggests that ...

Other research disagrees
Marmot et al. found no evidence that workload was a major contributory factor in development of stress-related illness.
They found that ...

This suggests that ...

Work underload also stressful

Bored Bored Bored Bored
Occurs where people are employed in jobs that lack stimulation or are beneath their capabilities.

Schultz et al. found ...

This suggests that ...

Burnout supported by research evidence

CLINIQUE PSYCHIATRIQUE

MUST — Marmot et al.

HOW?

10,000 CIVIL SERVANTS
+ +
Independent check of job specification and role responsibilities.

SHOWED?

Low job control → more heart disease → than higher job control
AFTER 5 YEARS

Association independent of other risk factors. Workload and social support not linked to heart disease.

SHOULD — McCarthy et al.

HOW?

LOW JOB CONTROL   HIGH JOB CONTROL

SHOWED?

COULD — Bond and Bunce

HOW?

Control group
Y
X Z
Raised level of job control
SHOWED?

EVALUATION

Individual difference

No control Yippee

No control Boo Hoo
Workers respond differently to lack of control (Lazarus).

Schaubroeck et al. ...

This suggests that ...

Lack of control harmful
Lack of control at work combined with home stressors makes illnesses such as depression more likely.
Melchior found ...

This suggests that ...

Lack of control has indirect effects

Stress   Comfort eating   Diabetes

Smith et al. claim ...

As a result ...

Increasing job control has additional benefits
INCREASED JOB CONTROL
 SAVES £

MUST — Friedman and Rosenman

HOW?

3,000 men aged 39–59

CHD check

Interview and observation

Classified as TYPE A or TYPE B

SHOWED?

After 8 years

	TYPE A	TYPE B
HEART ATTACK RATE	12%	6%

TYPE A
- Higher blood pressure
- Higher levels of cholesterol
- More likely to smoke
- Family history of CHD

SHOULD — Myrtek

HOW?

Meta-analysis of prospective studies.

SHOWED?

Type A inc. Hostility → CHD

COULD — TABP and driving behaviour

TABP
- stress while driving
- more traffic accidents
- aggressive driving

EVALUATION

Lack of causal relationship

The Medical Journal of Australia. STRESS AND CORONARY HEART DISEASE. Stephen J Bunker et al...

No strong or consistent causal relationship between Type A behaviour and CHD (Bunker et al.).

Type A behaviour no more significant ...

This suggests that ...

Real-life implications

RECURRENT CORONARY PREVENTION PROJECT

Helps change extreme Type A behaviour into more Type B.
Follow-up studies found ...

Intervention is difficult because ...

Type D more important

Type Ds overreact to stressful situations. They have raised levels of cortisol and greater risk of CHD. Denollet et al. ...

Unlike Type As ...

Supported by research

TABP

MUST — Kobasa et al.

HOW?

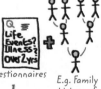

259 execs + Questionnaires **1** + E.g. Family history of illness **2** + Hardiness scales **3**

Q: Life Events? Illness? Over 2 yrs

Commitment / Control / Challenge

SHOWED?

Factors 1, 2 & 3 all influenced illness rates.
Hardiness had the largest influence.
Constitutional predisposition (e.g. family history PLUS stressful life events = illness).

SHOULD — Maddi et al.

HOW?

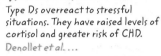

ILLINOIS BELL Telephone Co. 1975 → 1987. 450 Ss

Natural experiment on company reducing workforce over 12-year period.
Data collected each year from 450 supervisors.

SHOWED?

COULD — Lifton et al.

HOW?

Ithaca USA → HARDINESS QQQ

1,432 first-year students at five US universities.

SHOWED?

EVALUATION

There is research support

Soldiers on military deployment are less likely to suffer negative health consequences if high on hardiness.

Bartone found ...

As a result ...

Real-world application

Hardiness training is used to increase hardiness in individuals and make them more resistant to stress.
Maddi et al.

This shows that ...

May just be negative affectivity (NA)

NEGATIVITY AFFECTIVITY

Hardy individuals ↓

Individuals who dwell on failures ↑

Individuals high in NA focus more on negative aspects of themselves. Hardy people just low on NA?
This is challenged by ...
This would be difficult to ...

Problems with concept of hardiness

Q Which component of hardiness predicts academic success?

A It's commitment

Sheard found ...

Therefore ...

MUST — Stress inoculation training (SIT)

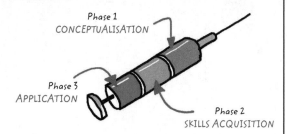

Phase 1
CONCEPTUALISATION

Phase 3
APPLICATION

Phase 2
SKILLS ACQUISITION

To enhance individuals' coping skills.

Conceptualisation — breaking down major stressors into short-term, intermediate and long-term coping goals.

Skills acquisition — coping skills taught and rehearsed in real life.

Application — in increasingly stressful situations.

SHOULD — Hardiness training

Client helped to focus on sources and signs of stress.

Given an insight into current coping strategies.

Focussing

Relieving Stress Encounters

Self Improvement

Learning new techniques to cope with stressors.

Hardiness training helps people become more resistant to harmful effects of stress.

COULD — SIT in the community

TERRORISM

SIT used with secondary victims of trauma.

EVALUATION

Research supports the effectiveness of SIT

Meichenbaum used SIT to treat snake phobia.
SIT also ...

This shows that ...

Works with non-clinical populations

I need a bit of SIT

Revision Money Worries v Exams Deadlines Travel

SIT has been shown to be effective for students dealing with stresses of academic life.
Sheehy and Horan found ...

Demonstrates that ...

A problem with SIT

TIME CONSUMING

HIGH MOTIVATION

Usefulness of SIT limited because people reluctant to invest time and effort.
However ...

This shows ...

Limitations of hardiness training

Learned coping habits

Must first address learned coping habits that are difficult to modify.
Lindquist et al. found ...

This means that ...

Supporting evidence

Skills acquisition conceptionalisation

Ayalon — SIT with Israeli children.

MUST Drug therapies	SHOULD	COULD Reducing stress-related illness with drugs

MUST Drug therapies

BENZODIAZEPINES (BZs)

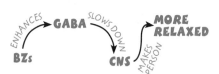

ENHANCES → **GABA** SLOWS DOWN → **CNS** MAKES PERSON → **MORE RELAXED**

BZs

BETA-BLOCKERS

ah

BB BB BB BB BB

Reduce action of adrenaline and noradrenaline in response to stress by binding to beta-receptors.

SHOULD

GABA

Makes it harder for neurons to be stimulated.

GABA + BZS

Makes it even harder for neurons to be stimulated!

Adrenaline

BB

Noradrenaline

Receptor

For example:

Blood vessels do not contract so easily.

=

Fall in blood pressure and less strain on the heart.

COULD Reducing stress-related illness with drugs

Blocks effect

SGK1

GSK 650394

Prolongs action of stress hormones

EVALUATION

A strength of drug therapies

They are effective in reducing effects of stress. Kahn et al. — BZs superior to placebo.
BBs also effective …

This shows that …

A second strength of drug therapies

Drugs are easy to use compared to other treatments. Require little effort compared to stress inoculation, for example.
For example, patients need only …

This means that …

A major issue with drug treatments

AFTER TREATMENT

BZ SYMPTOMS   SYMPTOMS

DURING TREATMENT

A limitation of drug therapies

Drugs can have side effects (e.g. confusion and tiredness) which are unpleasant.
In contrast …

This makes it less likely …

A second limitation of drug therapies

Drugs can be addictive and lead to withdrawal symptoms indicating dependence.
Tolerance develops …

This means that …

KEY WORDS

- Collectivism
- Confederate
- Conformity
- Individualism
- Majority influence
- McCarthyism

Compliance

- Going along with others to gain their approval or avoid their disapproval.
- No change in the person's underlying attitude, only their public behaviour.

Internalisation

- Going along with others because of an acceptance of their point of view.
- Leads to an acceptance of the group's view, both in public and in private.

Possible essay question ...

Outline and evaluate research into conformity. *(12 marks)*

Other possible exam questions ...

+ Explain what is meant by 'internalisation' and 'compliance' in the context of conformity. *(2 + 2 marks)*
+ Outline how psychologists have investigated conformity. *(6 marks)*
+ Outline what research has shown about conformity. *(3 marks)*
+ Apply this knowledge to ... *(6 marks)*

MUST know ...

Study showing compliance (Asch, 1956)

How?

Laboratory study of 123 male US students who had volunteered for a study to 'test their vision'.

All the other participants were confederates.

Each had to say which of three comparison lines was the same length as a standard line.

The real participant always answered last or second to last.

On 12 of 18 trials, confederates were instructed to give the same wrong answer.

Showed?

On the 12 'critical' trials, 36.8% of the responses given by real participants were also incorrect.

Only 25% of the real participants never conformed in any of the critical trials.

Without confederates giving the same wrong answers, participants were correct in their judgements 99% of the time.

One issue with this study ...

... is that it took place in a particular period of US history when conformity was high.

- *E* – In 1956, the USA was in the grip of McCarthyism, a strong anti-Communist period when people were scared to go against the majority and so more likely to conform.

One criticism of this study ...

... is that the confederates were unconvincing, which would cast doubts on the validity of Asch's findings.

- *E* – The confederates would have found it difficult to act convincingly in their role when giving the wrong answer in a simple task.

Asch's study shows more evidence of independent behaviour ...

... rather than conformity.

- *E* – Participants showed more evidence of independence of judgement during the critical trials than they did evidence of conformity.

SHOULD know ...

Extensions to Asch's study

When the task was made more difficult, the level of conformity increased.

It also increased with the size of majority but only up to three, after which it made little difference.

Unanimity in confederates was vital, otherwise conformity dropped away almost completely.

Study showing internalisation (Vartanian and Hopkinson)

How?

Female students (n=300), mean age 18.8 years.

Questionnaires on their tendency to conform; internalisation of societal attitudes of physical attractiveness; and body image concerns.

Showed?

Students' tendency to conform was positively correlated to the degree of their internalisation of societal attitudes.

Internalisation of these attitudes also predicted body image concerns and the likelihood of dieting behaviours.

- *E* – Perrin and Spencer found no evidence of conformity in 1980 using UK students. After manipulating relationship between participant and majority to make the costs of not conforming appear high, conformity levels rose close to Asch's.
- *L* – Conformity was more likely if the perceived costs of non-conformity are high.

- *E* – Mori and Arai overcame this problem by using filters, which altered what each participant actually saw, removing the need for real confederates. Levels of conformity were similar to those obtained by Asch.
- *E* – This suggests that Asch's participants *had* acted convincingly and that the findings remain valid.

- *E* – Although one-third produced a conforming response, on *two-thirds* of the trials where the majority unanimously gave the same wrong answer, participants stuck to their original opinion.
- *L* – This suggests that we are not overly conformist, but capable of independent behaviour even in the face of an overwhelming majority.

COULD know ...

Culture and conformity (Bond and Smith)

In individualist cultures, social behaviour is more determined by personal rather than group goals.

In collectivist cultures, social behaviour is determined more by goals shared with other members of the group or collective.

In collectivist cultures, individuals should be more likely to conform to the majority position, because of the higher value given to group relations.

There is supporting evidence for ...

... cultural differences in conformity.

- *E* – For example, Bond and Smith carried out a meta-analysis of studies of conformity across 17 cultures.
- *E* – They established that collectivist cultures showed higher levels of conformity than individualist cultures, in line with the prediction.
- *L* – However, not everyone in a culture shares the same values, therefore drawing conclusions based on differences *between* cultures is an oversimplification.

CHOOSE THE RIGHT ANSWER

The following statements are all related to conformity.

A Doing what the group does because we have no other choice.

B Going along with the group, even if we do not really agree with what they are doing.

C Going along with the group because we admire what they are doing.

D Doing what the group does because we accept their beliefs and attitudes into our own cognitions.

In the table below, write which statement, **A**, **B**, **C** or **D**, describes each type of conformity.

Type of conformity	Statement
Internalisation	
Compliance	

Answers on page 196

WRITE YOUR EVALUATION POINT

Using the material on the facing page, write an evaluative point in your own words, underlining the key words.

S	
E	
E	
L	

See page 14 for an explanation of how to SEEL.

KEY PHRASES

Exam question:

Describe what **one** study has shown about conformity. *(4 marks)*

On the facing page there several findings from the study by Asch.

For each one select **three** key words or phrases. The first one has been done for you:

Finding 1	Critical trials	36.8%	Conformity
Finding 1			
Finding 1			
Conclusion			

Now try to write an answer to the exam question using your key words. Your answer should be about 100 words in length.

DRAWING CONCLUSIONS

A researcher decided to investigate conformity by putting marbles in a jar and then asking children to guess how many there were.

The participants were asked to write down their estimates on a special form, which also showed what previous participants had estimated (although these were actually made up by the researcher).

For one group of participants, the previous estimates were high (more than 80), whereas for the other group, the estimates on their form were low (less than 50). The results are shown in the table below.

Table showing mean estimates for each group

	Group with high estimates (>80)	Group with low estimates (<50)
Boys	95	42
Girls	81	56

What can you conclude about conformity from the results of this study? *(4 marks)*

Conclusion 1:

Conclusion 2:

Answers on page 196

135

KEY WORDS

- Compliance
- Conformity
- Group norm
- Informational social influence
- Internalisation
- Normative social influence
- Reference group

Possible essay question ...

Outline and evaluate **two** explanations of why people conform. *(12 marks)*

Other possible exam questions ...

+ Outline **two** explanations of why people conform. *(3 marks + 3 marks)*

+ Outline **one** explanation of why people conform and explain **one** criticism of this explanation. *(3 marks + 3 marks)*

+ Apply this knowledge to ... *(6 marks)*

MUST know ...

Normative social influence

An individual conforms because of a desire to be liked and accepted by a reference group, i.e. motivation to conform to group norms.

As a result, the person conforms in action alone without needing to *accept* the group's view, i.e. compliance rather than internalisation.

Informational social influence

An individual conforms because they believe the majority to be right, i.e. they have more information about an issue than the individual.

As a result, the person conforms in both behaviour *and* attitude, i.e. internalisation rather than compliance.

 There is research support ...

... for the power of normative influence.

- **E** – US research has shown the relationship between people's normative beliefs and the likelihood of them smoking.

There are real-world applications of ...

... in changing people's attitudes towards conservation of resources.

- **E** – It is possible to use normative influence to manipulate people into behaving more responsibly.

 There is research support ...

... for the claim that informational social influence shapes opinion.

- **E** – Research has supported the important role that informational social influence plays in shaping political opinion.

Informational influence helps to explain ...

... the development of social stereotypes.

- **E** – Research has shown that exposure to other people's beliefs has an important influence on the development of social stereotypes.

SHOULD know ...

Normative social influence

Because humans are a social species, they have a strong desire to be accepted and a fear of rejection.

This makes it difficult for them to deviate from the majority, because of the risk of rejection.

Informational social influence

Informational influence is more likely when:

- The situation is ambiguous, i.e. the right course of action is not clear.
- Situation is a crisis, i.e. rapid action required.
- We believe others to be experts, i.e. they are more likely to know what to do.

- **E** – Linkenbach and Perkins found that adolescents who were exposed to the message that the majority of their age peers didn't smoke were subsequently less likely to take up smoking.
- **L** – This supports the claim that people shape their behaviour to fit in with their reference group.

- **E** – Schultz *et al.* found that hotel guests exposed to the normative message that 75% of guests reused their towels each day were then more likely to reuse their own towels.
- **L** – This shows that normative influence can be used to change people's behaviour in positive ways.

- **E** – Fein *et al.* showed how judgements of candidate performance in US presidential debates were influenced by knowledge of the reactions of the majority.
- **L** – This supports the view that we are influenced by the majority view if we are uncertain as to the right course of action.

- **E** – People exposed to negative information about black Americans (represented as the 'view of the majority') then reported more negative beliefs about a black individual (Wittenbrink and Henly).
- **L** – This supports the view that we are influenced when we believe others know more about an issue than we do.

COULD know ...

Normative social influence may not be detected

Directly witnessing the actions of others has a powerful effect on the behaviour of the individual.

However, research has shown that *direct* observation of others is not required for normative influence to have an effect.

Researchers have now speculated whether individuals do actually recognise the real or imagined behaviour of others as a causal factor in their own behaviour.

 There is supporting evidence for this ...

... from a study by Nolan *et al.*

- **E** – Investigated whether people detected the influence of social norms on their own energy conservation behaviour.
- **E** – Participants believed the behaviour of neighbours had the least impact on *their* energy conservation (compared to other factors), yet results showed that it had the *strongest* impact.
- **L** – This suggests that people rely on beliefs about what *should* motivate their behaviour, and so under-detect the impact of normative influence.

CIRCLE TRUE OR FALSE

T or F *Compliance* results in a change in private attitude but not in public behaviour.

T or F *Internalisation* follows a close examination of the group's position.

T or F *Compliance* is motivated by the desire to avoid the group's disapproval.

T or F *Internalisation* results in a change in public behaviour but not in private attitude.

T or F *Compliance* is associated with normative social influence.

T or F *Internalisation* is associated with informational social influence.

Answers on page 196

APPLYING YOUR KNOWLEDGE

(a) It is Matt's first day in a new job and he spends a lot of time watching to see what his colleagues are doing so that he will fit in with them and be liked. Explain Matt's behaviour in terms of compliance. *(2 marks)*

(b) After a few weeks in the job, Matt's girlfriend comments that his old work-shy student self seems to have disappeared and he has become an ambitious workaholic like the people he works with. Explain Matt's behaviour in terms of internalisation. *(2 marks)*

Answers on page 196

A MARKING EXERCISE

Read the student answers to the following exam question:

Outline **one** explanation of why people conform. *(3 marks)*

Wesley's answer

People conform because they want to fit in and be liked by other members of the group. This is called normative social influence and is based on the need to fit in to the group. However, sometimes people conform because they want to be right, and so they conform because of informational social influence.

Lucy's answer

Because humans have a fear of being rejected by the group, they are motivated to sometimes conform just to be accepted. As their motivation is a desire to be accepted by the group, this leads to conformity in actions alone, with private attitudes remaining the same.

You can read marking guidelines on page 10.

Your comments on Wesley's answer:

....

....

....

....

What mark do you think his answer would get? _____ out of 4 marks

Your comments on Lucy's answer:

....

....

....

....

What mark do you think his answer would get? _____ out of 4 marks

Answers on page 196

PRACTICE ELABORATION

Using the material on the facing page, complete the table below to help prepare an answer to following exam question:

Outline **two** explanations of why people conform. *(3 marks + 3 marks)*

Normative social influence		
Point 1	Point 2	Example of normative influence

Informational social influence		
Point 1	Point 2	Example of informational influence

- Confederate
- Deception
- External validity
- Holocaust
- Informed consent
- Internal validity
- Obedience
- Protection from harm

Possible essay questions ...

Outline and evaluate research into obedience. *(12 marks)*

Outline and evaluate Milgram's research into obedience. *(12 marks)*

Other possible exam questions ...

+ Outline what research has shown about obedience. *(6 marks)*

+ Outline what Milgram's research has shown about obedience. *(6 marks)*

+ Explain **two** criticisms of Milgram's study of obedience. *(3 marks + 3 marks)*

+ Apply this knowledge to ... *(6 marks)*

MUST know ...

Key study: Milgram

How?

Forty male volunteers were told this was a study of how punishment affects learning.

After drawing lots, the real participant was always the 'teacher', the confederate always the 'learner'.

The teacher's job was to administer a learning task and to deliver shocks (in 15 volt increments up to max of 450V) when learner made a mistake. No real shocks were given.

In the 'remote condition', the learner was in a different room to the teacher.

Showed?

All participants went to at least 300V in the 'remote condition'.

Only 12.5% of participants refused to continue giving shocks when they reached 300V level.

In this condition, 65% of participants continued to obey the authority figure all the way to the maximum shock level (450V).

These results were contradictory to predictions made prior to the study that only 4% would go as far as 300V.

Milgram's study lacks internal validity ...

... because participants may not have been taken in by the deception.

- **E** – Orne and Holland claim that participants must have known they were not giving real shocks because the experimenter appeared unconcerned over the learner's distress.

There are ethical problems ...

... associated with Milgram's research.

- **E** – These include deception, lack of any opportunity for informed consent and a failure to protect participants from the possibility of psychological harm as a result of participation.

SHOULD know ...

Milgram's variations

How?

Studied different situational pressures to see which had the greatest effect on obedience, e.g. bringing the learner closer to the teacher.

Showed?

Proximity of the learner – in the same room as teacher, obedience rates dropped to 40% and to 30% in the 'touch proximity' condition.

Proximity of authority figure – when the authority figure left the room and gave orders over the phone, obedience dropped to 21%.

Presence of allies – when two confederates refused to continue, obedience rates dropped to 10%.

Milgram's study may lack external validity ...

... because it does not explain real-life obedience.

- **E** – Mandel claims that Milgram's variations do not adequately explain actual Holocaust events.
- **E** – Mandel found little similarity when comparing results in these variations to similar situations involving Reserve Police Battalion 101.
- **L** – This suggests that Milgram's conclusions may not be borne out by real-life events.

- **E** – Orne and Holland suggest that participants have learned to distrust experimenters in psychology because they know that the real purpose of the experiment is likely to be disguised.
- **L** – However, Milgram challenged this claim, pointing out that in post-experimental interviews, the vast majority stated they *had* believed they were giving real shocks.

- **E** – For example, participants were misled about the true purpose of the study as they had been told the study was about the effects of punishment rather than its true purpose (obedience to authority).
- **L** – As a result, participants were effectively denied the right to informed consent, although Milgram claimed post-experimental interviews found no evidence of psychological harm.

COULD know ...

Second study: Hofling *et al.*

How?

Hofling *et al.* conducted a study in a hospital. Nurses were ordered to carry out an action that contravened hospital regulations (accepting order over the phone from an unknown doctor to give over the maximum drug dose allowed).

Showed?

Of the 22 nurses involved in the study, 21 of them obeyed the order they were given.

This conclusion is challenged ...

... in a study by Rank and Jacobsen.

- **E** – They repeated the study but with a familiar drug and nurses were allowed to consult colleagues.
- **E** – Under these more realistic conditions, most of the nurses (16 out of 18) *refused* to obey the order.
- **L** – This suggests that the unquestioning obedience found in Hofling's study may not be relevant to real life.

KEY PHRASES

Select key phrases to help you remember the key study by Milgram. The first few have been done for you.

How?	Showed?
40 male volunteers	65%
Teacher and leaner	

On a separate piece of paper, use your key phrases to answer the following exam question:

Outline Milgram's study of obedience. *(6 marks)*

DRAWING CONCLUSIONS

The graph below shows findings from Milgram's study.

Maximum shock level administered

Location moved to run down office	48%
Teacher in same room as learner	40%
Teacher presses learner's hand on shock plate	30%
Experimenter gives orders over the phone	21%
Another 'teacher' refuses to give shocks	10%

State **two** findings and for each one draw a conclusion (state what the finding shows).

Finding 1:

Conclusion 1: This shows that …

Finding 2:

Conclusion 2: This shows that …

Answers on page 196

PRACTICE ELABORATION

On the facing page, there are a number of evaluative points for Milgram's research on obedience to authority. After reading these points (and without looking back at them), try to expand the three points included in the table below.

State the point	Evidence	Elaboration	Conclusion (link back)
Milgram's study may lack external validity …			
Milgram's study lacks internal validity …			
There are ethical problems …			

MATCH THEM UP

Match up the numbers on the left with the description on right.

1	4	A	This % of participants went to the maximum shock level in the remote condition.
2	12.5	B	All participants went to this shock level in the remote condition.
3	15	C	This % of participants went to the maximum shock level when the learner was in the same room.
4	30	D	The maximum shock level.
5	40	E	The size of the incremental increase between shock levels (in volts).
6	65	F	The % of participants who went to the maximum shock level in touch proximity condition.
7	300	G	Prediction was that only this % of participants would go to 300V.
8	450	H	The % of participants who refused to obey beyond 300V.

Answers on page 197

CIRCLE TRUE OR FALSE

T or F Participants in Milgram's study were given the opportunity for informed consent.

T or F The study involved an all male volunteer sample of 40 participants.

T or F One factor that reduced obedience was when the learner was in a different room from the teacher.

T or F One factor that increased obedience was when the authority figure was in the room with the teacher.

T or F 65% of participants went to the maximum 450 volts.

T or F Milgram carried out post-experimental interviews with participants.

Answers on page 197

KEY WORDS

- Agentic shift
- Agentic state
- Autonomous state
- Buffers
- Gradual commitment
- Holocaust

Possible essay question ...

Outline and evaluate **two or more** explanations of why people obey. *(12 marks)*

Other possible exam questions ...

+ Outline **two** explanations of why people obey. (2 marks + 2 marks)
+ Explain **one** or more reasons why people obey authority. *(6 marks)*
+ Apply this knowledge to ... *(6 marks)*

 Exam tip

In an exam question you might also be asked about obedience in more everyday settings, e.g. 'Why are we more likely to obey someone in uniform?'

Any of the explanations on this spread could be used to address this sort of question, although you could also describe the importance of socialisation for obedience.

Learning to obey adult authority is an important part of the socialisation process in childhood, and a uniform is seen as a symbol of authority.

MUST know ...

1. Gradual commitment

Milgram's participants had already committed themselves to giving lower-level shocks.

As a result, it was harder to resist the order to give shocks at a higher level (known as the 'foot in the door' technique).

2. Agentic shift

When receiving an order from someone in authority, people move into an agentic state.

They see themselves as acting as the agent of the authority figure and so more likely to obey.

3. The role of buffers

In Milgram's study the teacher and learner were in separate rooms (i.e. a physical buffer).

As a result they did not have to witness the consequences of giving shocks to the learner so were more likely to obey.

 The gradual commitment explanation is supported by real-life events ...

... where individuals have carried out their actions because of a gradual escalation in the demands being made.

- *E* – For example, Lifton's study of Nazi doctors working in the death camps during World War II.

 The agentic shift claim is challenged by...

... the fact there are differences between the laboratory and real-life obedience.

- *E* – There are distinctions between obedience in the lab and obedience in real life, which would challenge the claim that agentic shift is responsible for both types of obedience.

 The role of buffers in obedience is supported by ...

... situational variations in Milgram's research.

- *E* – Milgram found that the teacher was less likely to obey the authority figure when the learner was in the same room, i.e. where the visual buffer was removed and they were able to witness the consequences of their actions.

SHOULD know ...

1. Gradual commitment

As the transition from lower to higher shocks is very gradual, it is difficult for participants to change their minds about continuing and go against the authority figure.

2. Agentic shift

Milgram argued that people shift back and forth from an autonomous state, where they take responsibility for their own actions to agentic state, where they do not.

3. The role of buffers

Buffers protect the individual from the distress they would experience when they carry out actions that harm another person, therefore are an important factor in obedience.

- *E* – The demands made on these Nazi doctors gradually increased from orders to sterilise mental defectives, through having to conduct cruel medical experiments and eventually consenting to murder.
- *L* – Their obedience to these orders was made possible because of the gradual escalation of demands made on them.

- *E* – For example, Milgram's participants were in a situation where they were not sure what to do for less than an hour, whereas Holocaust perpetrators acted as they did over a period of months or even years.
- *L* – This suggests that a simple agentic shift explanation is not sufficient to explain obedience in real-life situations.

- *E* – However, analysis of the actions of Reserve Police Battalion 101 at Josefow showed that close physical proximity to their victims made no difference to these men's willingness to obey orders to kill.
- *L* – This shows that, although buffers may reduce some of the distress associated with harmful obedience, they may not always reduce obedience in real-life situations.

COULD know ...

A fourth explanation: justifying obedience

Many examples of harmful obedience directed against others are justified on the basis of an underlying ideology.

These include the importance of science or revenge for a previous transgression by the target group.

For example, in Milgram's study, participants who tried to extricate themselves from their role were told they must continue 'because the experiment requires it'.

 There is evidence for this in real-life obedience ...

... during the Holocaust.

- *E* – During the Holocaust, the Nazi propaganda machine had portrayed the Jews as a danger to all Germans.
- *E* – For many Germans, this gave them the justification to obey orders to carry out harmful acts against Jews.
- *L* – This suggests people are willing to sacrifice freedom of action in the belief they are serving a justifiable cause.

CHOOSE THE RIGHT ANSWER

Three of the following statements are related to explanations of obedience. Identify the correct statements and place the letters corresponding to those statements in the table that follows.

A Obeying because we think the person giving the order knows more about the situation than we do.

B Obeying because of our prior obedience to smaller requests.

C Obeying because we want to be liked by other group members.

D Obeying because we see ourselves as no longer responsible for our actions.

E Obeying because we cannot see or hear the consequences of our obedient actions.

F Obeying because we are in an autonomous state.

Gradual commitment	
Agentic shift	
The role of buffers	

Answers on page 197

 RESEARCH ISSUES

A researcher is interested in why people obey and under what circumstances. She stops people in a shopping centre, beginning with a small request (helping her with directions to a shop), a medium request (taking her to the shop) and a large request (asking them to help carry her bags from the shop). She then interviews each participant to see what motivated them to comply (or not) with her requests.

> Identify **one** ethical issue the researcher would need to consider in this research. Suggest how the researcher could deal with this ethical issue. *(3 marks)*

Answers on page 197

 FILL IN THE BOXES

In each box below write one sentence describing each explanation of why people obey in about 25 words

Gradual commitment:
Agentic shift:
The role of buffers:

In each box below expand the content on the left, writing about another 25 words for each.

Another aspect of gradual commitment is …
Another aspect of agentic shift is …
Another aspect of the role of buffers is …

 APPLYING YOUR KNOWLEDGE

Interviews with bomber pilots serving in World War II revealed insights into why they felt able to obey orders that harmed other people. In this extract, a pilot talks about his experiences.

Pilot: To start with we used to drop our bombs from altitude. That wasn't too bad. We knew what we were doing but somehow it didn't bother us. Then the orders changed and we were forced into low level bombing, so low we could see people running for shelter beneath us … that really brought home to us what we doing, it was truly awful.

Pilot: I know people think we were monsters for what we did, but it wasn't personal. We didn't make the plans or decide who to drop our bombs on, we just did what we were told. They should blame the people who are in charge, not people like me who were just doing their duty.

Use your knowledge of explanations of why people obey to explain these insights. *(4 marks)*

Identify the psychology	Link to pilot's experiences

Answers on page 197

See page 20 for an explanation of the 'two-pronged attack' needed to answer 'applying your knowledge' questions.

CIRCLE TRUE OR FALSE

T or F An agentic state is where people take responsibility for their own actions.

T or F Obedience is more likely if the steps taken toward the target action are gradual.

T or F The presence of buffers decreases any distress connected to a person's obedience.

T or F People are more likely to obey when in an agentic state.

T or F Lifton's study of Nazi doctors illustrates gradual commitment in the real world

T or F In Milgram's study, the presence of a physical buffer made participants less likely to obey.

Answers on page 197

KEY WORDS

- Heroic imagination
- Independent behaviour
- Moral dilemma
- Morality
- Social support

Possible essay question ...

Outline and evaluate **two or more** explanations of how people resist pressures to conform. *(12 marks)*

Other possible exam questions ...

+ Outline **two** explanations of how people might resist pressures to conform. *(6 marks)*
+ Explain why some people might resist pressures to conform. *(4 marks)*
+ Apply this knowledge to ... *(6 marks)*

MUST know ...

Social support and the role of allies

People are better able to resist pressure to conform if they have the support of others.

Asch found that the presence of social support enabled an individual to resist majority pressure.

Introducing an ally who resisted the majority caused conformity levels to drop sharply.

Presence of an ally makes an individual feel more confident and better able to stand up to the majority.

The role of morality

People are better able to resist pressure to conform if their decision has a moral dimension.

For Asch's participants, the costs of conforming were not particularly great given the insignificance of the task.

However, if the behaviour is judged as immoral (e.g. joining others in cheating) there is less evidence of conformity as the costs (e.g. guilt) are judged to be greater (Hornsey *et al.*).

 One problem with social support ...

... is that it may not be enough in opinion-type tasks.

- *E* – Asch's study found that if an ally gave the correct response in a visual task, conformity reduced dramatically. However, other research has found that the ally needs to have the *same* opinion as the participant in opinion-type tasks.

 There is research support ...

... for the importance of morality in resisting conformity.

- *E* – For example, Hornsey *et al.*'s study of the relationship between the strength of a person's moral views, and their conformity to a majority position concerning the rights of gay couples.

 Immoral acts may appear less immoral...

... because other people's actions may make these acts seem more acceptable.

- *E* – Kundu and Cummins found that morally impermissible actions were judged to be more permissible if confederates judged them so.

SHOULD know ...

Social support and the role of allies

The presence of a fellow dissenter from the majority position provides the individual with support for their point of view.

Valid (e.g. expert) and invalid (e.g. inexpert) support reduces conformity, although valid support has more impact on conformity levels.

The most important aspect of social support is that it breaks the unanimous position of the majority.

The role of morality

An over-reliance on social conformity in guiding behaviour is indicative of a less mature level of moral development (Kohlberg).

Kohlberg found that individuals who are able to resist pressure to conform and make judgements based on their own moral values tend to be more morally advanced.

- *E* – Allen and Levine argue that the presence of an ally with the *same* opinion as the participant is necessary in order to resist the group position. An extreme dissenter (with an even more incorrect opinion than the group) would have no effect.
- *L* – This suggests the nature of the task determines the effectiveness of social support.

- *E* – Participants with a weak moral basis for their attitude shifted toward the group norm (i.e. conformed) whereas those who had a strong moral basis for their attitude resisted the group norm (i.e. resisted conformity).
- *L* – Among those with strong moral attitudes, motivation to resist the group norm was even stronger in the face of perceived opposition.

- *E* – Kundu and Cummins used the Asch experimental set-up, with participants making decisions about moral dilemmas either alone or in a group of confederates who acted as peers.
- *L* – The results suggest that although morality may sometimes cause individuals to resist the majority position, the urge to conform may be stronger.

COULD know ...

A third explanation: the heroic imagination

This is a way of thinking that makes it more likely that a person will be able to resist pressure to conform to anti-social norms when the occasion arises.

They will also understand when independence should take precedence over conformity despite the possibility of social rejection.

 This has been shown to be effective ...

... in helping people resist inappropriate conformity.

- *E* – Heroic imagination training has been used to help students gain an increased awareness of their automatic tendencies to conform (Zimbardo *et al.*).
- *E* – This resulted in a decreased tendency to conform to group norms when the consequences of doing so might be harmful.
- *L* – This allowed them to replace their unwanted conforming tendencies with independent behaviours using strategies suggested from psychological research.

MATCH THEM UP

Complete the statement on the left with the correct text on right.

1	Presence of an ally who also resisted the majority	**A**	Is a way of thinking that guides behaviour.
2	Tasks that have a moral dimension	**B**	Has more impact on conformity levels.
3	Independence may often be more appropriate	**C**	Means the costs of conforming seen as greater.
4	The heroic imagination	**D**	Tended to be more morally advanced.
5	Kohlberg found those who resisted conformity	**E**	Made the participant more confident to resist.
6	Valid (expert) social support	**F**	Despite the possibility of social rejection.

Answers on page 197

APPLYING YOUR KNOWLEDGE

Sophie and Jasmine are best friends. Both are bright and popular students who have done well at school and are soon to leave for university. There is one noticeable difference between them, and that is the degree to which they follow the crowd. Unlike Sophie, Jasmine finds herself just agreeing with whatever everyone wants to do, even if she doesn't want to act in that way. When Sophie is with her she is able to say no but without her best friend it is a different story.

Using your knowledge of psychology, explain why Sophie and Jasmine might differ in their ability to resist pressures to conform. *(4 marks)*

Answers on page 197

A MARKING EXERCISE

Read Romeo's answer below to the following exam question:

Describe **two** ways in which people might resist conformity. *(3 marks + 3 marks)*

One way in which the person might resist conformity is for the person to get the support of another person. Another person makes the participant more able to resist conformity because together they can take on the majority. A second way is for the person to improve their morality because there is evidence that people with a higher level of morality are less likely to conform.

TASK 1

What mark do you think Romeo would get? AO1 _____ AO2 _____

See page 197 for our suggested mark.

TASK 2 Your turn

Write an improved answer here

WRITE YOUR EVALUATION POINT

Using the material on the facing page, write out one of the evaluative points in your own words, underlining the key words.

S	
E	
E	
L	

See page 14 for an explanation of how to SEEL.

AN IDEA

On a separate piece of paper draw a mind map linking each of the following points (with some elaboration). Try to make it as visual as possible to help you with your revision.

- Social support and the role of allies
- Elaboration of social support and the role of allies
- The role of morality
- Elaboration of the role of morality
- Social support may not be enough
- Elaboration of this evaluative point
- Research support for the importance of morality
- Elaboration of this evaluative point
- Morality may lead to greater conformity
- Elaboration of this evaluative point
- The heroic imagination ... and its effectiveness

KEY WORDS

- Demand characteristics
- Independent behaviour
- Legitimate authority
- Monitoring/challenging

Possible essay questions ...

Outline and evaluate **two or more** explanations of how people might resist obedience. *(12 marks)*

Outline and evaluate **two or more** explanations of independent behaviour. *(12 marks)*

Other possible exam questions ...

+ Outline **two** explanations of how people might resist obedience. *(6 marks)*

+ Explain why some people might resist pressures to obey. *(4 marks)*

+ Apply this knowledge to ... *(6 marks)*

MUST know ...

The role of disobedient allies

Individuals can resist obedience if they have an ally who also opposes the authority figure.

In Milgram's study, when two confederates refused to continue giving shocks, only 10% of participants continued to the 450V shock level.

Milgram claims that the presence of allies who resist an authority figure makes individuals more confident in their ability to do the same.

Questioning legitimacy

Human beings have a tendency to obey anyone who projects a commanding presence, either by their status or their context.

By questioning the legitimacy of an order, or the person's right to give it, people are more able to resist obedience.

When Milgram's study was moved from Yale University to a run-down office, more people felt able to resist the commands of the authority figure.

 EVALUATION   *The role of disobedient allies has been demonstrated ...*

... in a real-life example of resistance to authority.

- *E* – In the Rosentrasse protest in 1943, German women refused an order to disperse while protesting against the arrest of their Jewish husbands.

 EVALUATION   *Real-world application of questioning legitimacy ...*

... and its role in preventing air crashes.

- *E* – Research suggests that a significant proportion of air crashes due to flight crew error can be attributed to inadequate levels of monitoring and challenging of the authority figure (the flight captain).

 EVALUATION   *There are individual differences ...*

... in people's ability to resist authority.

- *E* – Milgram found that a person's educational level and their religious background made a difference when it came to being able to resist the commands of the experimenter.

SHOULD know ...

The role of disobedient allies

The obedient behaviour of others makes a harmful action appear acceptable whereas their disobedience changes that perception.

Individuals are then able to use the defiance of peers as an opportunity to extricate themselves from causing any further harm to a victim.

Peers therefore act as role models on which the individual can model their own behaviour.

Questioning legitimacy

Morelli argues people don't distinguish between someone who *is* an authority (i.e. with expert knowledge) and someone who is *in* authority.

By questioning whether the authority figure actually has appropriate expert knowledge, we can avoid making the wrong decision.

For example, one of Milgram's participants was an electrical engineer, challenging the claim that the shocks caused no permanent damage.

- *E* – Many women felt afraid to disobey, but in the presence of others who were also prepared to defy the authority of the Gestapo, they felt more confident about their own ability to do so.
- *L* – This demonstrates that the role of disobedient allies in resisting obedience is not simply a laboratory phenomenon but an important factor in real-life social protest.

- *E* – Tarnow has proposed the introduction of monitoring and challenging scenarios as part of the training of senior flight crews.
- *L* – This technique means that the first officer is given the opportunity to detect and challenge errors made by the flight captain during flight simulations, and so avoid potentially catastrophic obedience in the future.

- *E* – Less-educated participants were less able to resist and Roman Catholics were also more likely to obey the experimenter than were Protestants or Jews.
- *L* – This research suggests that our ability to resist pressures to obey may be due to personal as well as situational factors.

COULD know ...

A third explanation: the role of morality

Some people base decisions to act in a particular way on their moral principles rather than the need to be obedient.

Kohlberg found that individuals who reasoned at a more advanced moral level were more likely to defy the experimenter in an obedience study than were individuals who reasoned at a more restricted moral level.

 EVALUATION   ### A suspension of personal morality may not be the reason ...

... why so many of Milgram's participants failed to resist.

- *E* – A question in Milgram's study is why the desire not to harm another person did not overturn demands to continue giving shocks.
- *E* – Kaposi argues that the total lack of any *learner* response to the protests of the teacher that he did not wish to continue, would have convinced the teacher that the shocks he was giving were not real.
- *L* – This suggests that the relative low resistance rates found in Milgram's study were more a consequence of 'demand characteristics' than an abandonment of personal morality.

MATCH THEM UP

Complete the statements on the left below with the correct part on the right.

1	Presence of an ally who resists obedience	**A**	Caused obedience levels to drop to just 10%.
2	When Milgram's study was moved to a less 'legitimate' location	**B**	Helps us to avoid making the wrong decision.
3	Some people base their decisions to act on their moral principles	**C**	Were less likely to engage in harmful acts of obedience.
4	Questioning the legitimacy of an order	**D**	Rather than on a need to obey.
5	Milgram found the presence of two disobedient peers	**E**	This led to lower rates of obedience.
6	Kohlberg found people at higher levels of morality	**F**	Serves as a role model for the individual.

Answers on page 197

APPLYING YOUR KNOWLEDGE

Jason is used to taking orders after 12 years in the Royal Marines. However, when he is out with his friends he finds himself less willing to do as he is told by people such as nightclub doormen or anybody else that he feels has not earned his respect or obedience.

Use your knowledge of how people resist obedience to explain Jason's behaviour. *(4 marks)*

Identify the psychology:

Link to Jason's behaviour:

Answers on page 197

RESEARCH ISSUES

A researcher wanted to investigate some of the factors that might affect whether a person obeyed or resisted a request from another person.

The table below shows the percentages of people who obeyed a simple request from a confederate who was either smartly dressed or casually dressed.

Request	Smartly dressed confederate	Casually dressed confederate
Pick up some litter	80%	61%
Post a letter found near a post box	61%	40%
Carry a heavy box up some stairs	30%	30%

Outline **two** findings and **two** conclusions that you might draw from this table.

Finding 1:

Conclusion 1: This shows that …

Finding 2:

Conclusion 2: This shows that …

Answers on page 197

WRITE YOUR EVALUATION POINT

Using the material on the facing page, find an evaluative point relevant to Milgram's study of obedience and write it in your own words below, underlining the key words.

S	
E	
E	
L	

CIRCLE TRUE OR FALSE

T or F The presence of obedient allies causes obedience levels to drop.

T or F The obedient behaviour of peers makes an action appear less harmful.

T or F The Rosenstrasse protest was a real-life example of questioning legitimacy.

T or F Human beings are more likely to obey in high-status contexts than in low-status contexts.

T or F Questioning the legitimacy of an authority is now a feature of flight crew training.

T or F Roman Catholics were less likely to obey an authority figure than were Protestants.

Answers on page 197

KEY WORDS

- Collectivist
- Externality
- Independent behaviour
- Individualist
- Internality
- Learned helplessness
- Locus of control

Possible essay questions …

Outline and evaluate the relationship between locus of control and independent behaviour. *(12 marks)*

Discuss one or more explanations of independent behaviour. *(12 marks)*

Other possible exam questions …

+ Explain what is meant by locus of control. *(4 marks)*
+ Explain how locus of control influences independent behaviour. *(4 marks)*
+ Apply this knowledge to … *(6 marks)*

MUST know …

Locus of control

Internals

A strong internal locus of control is associated with that belief that an individual can control events in their life.

What happens to them is seen as a consequence of their own ability and effort.

People high in internality rely less on the opinions of others, which means they are better able to resist social influence.

They take more responsibility for what they do and are more likely to display independent behaviour.

Externals

A strong external locus of control is associated with the belief that what happens to an individual is determined by external factors.

These external factors include the actions of others or luck.

People with an external locus of control approach events with a more passive and fatalistic attitude.

As a result, they take less responsibility for their actions and are less likely to display independent behaviour.

 Research has found gender differences …

… in locus of control.

- **E** – Semykina and Linz found that males are more likely to have an internal locus of control, whereas females are more likely to exhibit an external locus of control.

Research has found cultural differences …

… in locus of control.

- **E** – People from different cultures may also vary in terms of their locus of control, with people living in Western cultures tending to be more internal than people in non-Western cultures.

SHOULD know …

Research: Twenge *et al.*

How?

Twenge *et al.* carried out two meta-analyses of locus of control studies of young Americans.

Data included 97 samples of college students and 41 samples of children aged between nine and 14 years.

Showed?

They found that locus of control scores had become increasingly more external between 1960 and 2002.

Participants increasingly believed that their fate was determined more by luck and powerful others rather than their own actions.

 This finding has both positive and negative consequences …

… for adolescents' lives.

- **E** – The positive is that they are more tolerant of others regardless of background (believing that situational factors shape *everybody's* life).
- **E** – The negative is that high levels of externality are associated with increasing feelings of helplessness.
- **L** – This shows that young people increasingly feel that outside forces control their lives.

- **E** – Gender differences in locus of control and independent behaviour are usually attributed to differences in the opportunities perceived as being available to males and females in those cultures.
- **L** – Sherman *et al.* suggest that although females tend to be more external than males, research has also shown that both males *and* females are becoming more external.

- **E** – For example, Kongsonpong and Leithner found that, compared to people in individualist cultures, those in collectivist cultures show a greater reliance on external factors (such as group norms) in their consumer behaviour.
- **L** – This suggests that locus of control may be passed on as part of a culture's tradition, explaining cultural differences in dependent and independent behaviour.

COULD know …

Locus of control and well-being

Seligman found that people with an external locus of control are more likely to develop learned helplessness than are those with an internal locus of control.

Learned helplessness is a condition in which someone behaves as if they were helpless in a particular situation, even if they have the power to change their circumstances.

This can contribute to poor health when people neglect diet and exercise, falsely believing they have no power to change.

Internality is not necessarily healthy …

… for an individual.

- **E** – April *et al.* found that people generally felt happier and healthier with a combination of internal *and* external locus of control.
- **E** – This involves a recognition of their own ability to control their life, but also that certain aspects may be uncontrollable or impacted by external factors.
- **L** – This emphasises that extremities of control are not conducive to optimal well-being.

FILL IN THE BLANKS

People with a strong internal locus of control believe that they can (1).............................

events in their life. What happens to them is seen as a consequence of their own

(2).............................. and (3)................................. Such people rely

(4)............................... on the opinions of others, meaning they are better able to

resist social influence and more likely to display (5)...................................

behaviour. People with a strong external locus of control believe that what happens to

them is determined by (6)...............................factors. These include the actions of

others or (7)................................ Such people approach events with a more

(8)............................ and fatalistic attitude, meaning they take

(9)............................ responsibility for their actions and so are less likely to display

(10)............................ behaviour.

Answers on page 197

SPOT THE MISTAKES

Read the following student answer to this exam question:

Explain how locus of control influences independent behaviour. *(4 marks)*

There are four mistakes, draw a circle round each.

People who have an internal locus of control tend to see themselves as responsible for whatever happens to them. This is seen as a product of their ability or their good luck. People who are high in internality are more likely to rely on the opinions of others to determine how they behave. They are also more likely to take responsibility for their behaviour. Externals, on the other hand, believe that whatever happens to them is a product of their own effort or the effort of others. People who are high in externality are more likely to display independent behaviour. They are also less likely to take responsibility for their behaviour.

Answers on page 197

APPLYING YOUR KNOWLEDGE

Two students, Jack and Leanne, have just started at university. Jack is a confident student who puts himself forward for the student council because he 'wants to make a difference'. He tries to convince other students they should vote for him because he will fight against the cuts to student funding being proposed by the university. Leanne also put her name forward but confides to Jack that she probably wouldn't be much good as a student representative because she doesn't feel confident around authority. As a result, she doesn't bother trying to convince other students to vote for her, instead she just trys her luck.

(a) What type of locus of control does Jack's behaviour show?

(b) What type of locus of control does Leanne's behaviour show?

(c) Which **one** of these two students is most likely to show independent behaviour?

Use your knowledge of psychology to explain your choice. *(4 marks)*

Answers on page 197

PRACTICE ELABORATION

Using the material on the facing page, complete the **AO2 evaluation** part of the following exam question:

Outline and **evaluate** the role of locus of control in independent behaviour. *(12 marks)*

State the point	Evidence	Elaboration	Conclusion (link back)
Twenge's research has positive and negative consequences …			
Research has found gender differences in locus of control …			
Research has found cultural differences in locus of control …			

KEY WORDS

- Majority influence
- Meta-analysis
- Minority influence
- Social change
- Suffragettes
- Terrorism

Possible essay questions ...

Discuss how social influence research helps us to understand social change. *(12 marks)*

Discuss the role of minority influence in social change. *(12 marks)*

Other possible exam questions ...

+ Explain how social influence research helps us to understand social change. *(6 marks)*

+ Explain how a minority can bring about social change. *(4 marks)*

+ Apply this knowledge to ... *(6 marks)*

MUST know ...

Minority influence and social change

If an individual is exposed to a persuasive argument under certain conditions, they may change their views to match those of the minority.

1. Drawing attention to an issue
Minorities can bring about social change by drawing attention to a particular social issue.

2. Creating a conflict
This causes a conflict in the minds of the majority, between what they currently believe and the position advocated by the minority.

3. Consistent with each other and over time
Social change is more likely when the minority is consistent in their position.

4. The augmentation principle
If a minority appears willing to suffer for their views, they are taken more seriously.

5. The snowball effect
Minority influence initially has a relatively small effect but this then spreads more widely until it eventually leads to large-scale social change.

 One problem with minority influence and social change ...

... is that social change due to minority influence is very gradual.

- *E* – History challenges the claim that groups such as the suffragettes can bring about social change quickly.

 A second problem is ...

... is that minorities are seen as deviant, which limits their influence.

- *E* – The influence of minorities such as the suffragettes is often decreased because they are seen as 'deviant' in the eyes of the majority.

There is research evidence supporting ...

... the influence of minorities in changing the ways in which majorities think about issues.

- *E* – A meta-analysis of studies of minority and majority influence (Wood et al) found that on private measures of change, minorities had equal or greater influence than majorities.

SHOULD know ...

An example: the suffragettes

The suffragettes used educational, political and militant tactics to **draw attention** to the fact that women were denied the same voting rights as men.

They **created a conflict** in the mind of majority group members between the majority position and the positions advocated by the suffragettes. Some dealt with this conflict by accepting the suffragettes' arguments.

The suffragettes were **consistent** in their views, regardless of the attitudes of those around them. Protests and political lobbying continued for years.

Because the suffragettes were willing to risk imprisonment or even death from hunger strike, their influence became more powerful (i.e. was **augmented**).

Several years after the actions of the suffragettes, women were finally given the vote. At this point, the idea had finally spread to the majority of people (an example of the **snowball effect**).

- *E* – Because there is a strong tendency for human beings to conform to the majority position, groups are more likely to maintain the status quo rather than engage in social change.
- *L* – This explains why social change happens so slowly and why the suffragettes fought for their views for 15 years before social change was achieved.

- *E* – Members of the majority may avoid agreeing with the minorities such as the suffragettes because they do not want to be seen as being deviant themselves.
- *L* – As a result, the real influence of minorities is that they create the *potential* for social change rather than direct social change.

- *E* – Minorities that were especially consistent had greater influence than less consistent sources.
- *L* – However, in public, minority sources generated less change than majorities, which suggests that although minorities can change the way people *think*, they are still concerned about not doing or saying anything in public that might alienate them from the majority.

COULD know ...

Second example: terrorism

Kruglanski claims that terrorism may be usefully explained as a form of minority influence.

For example, terrorists can draw attention to an issue through innovative ways of spreading terror.

This creates a conflict in the minds of the target group with the choice of either acceding to terrorist demands and saving further life, or resisting them forcefully.

Persistent suicide bombings demonstrates consistency and their apparent willingness to lay down their life for a cause means that others take them more seriously (augmentation).

 There is real value in minority influence research ...

... for increasing our understanding of terrorism.

- *E* – Kruglanski argues that, based on similarities in how minorities generally and terrorists specifically exert their influence, minority influence research is a powerful tool for increasing our understanding of terrorism.
- *E* – However, the observation of society's reactions to terrorism as well as the limitations of terrorism as a social influence tactic can also teach us more about minority influence.
- *L* – Although minority influence has usually been associated with the actions of non-violent minorities, it can also be a tactic used by violent minorities to bring about social change.

MATCH THEM UP

Match the different aspects of minority influence with the examples of suffragette actions in the table below.

1	Drawing attention to an issue	**A**	Continued to protest and lobby politicians for many years until social change was achieved.
2	Creating a conflict	**B**	After several years the acceptance of women being able to vote had spread to the majority of people.
3	Consistency with each other and over time	**C**	Used militant tactics such as chaining themselves to railings or disrupting Parliament.
4	The augmentation principle	**D**	Made members of the majority re-examine what they previously held to be true after learning about the views of the minority.
5	The snowball effect	**E**	Showed willingness to risk imprisonment and even death to express their views.

Answers on page 197

 DRAWING CONCLUSIONS

The graph below is a summary of the percentage of violent and non-violent minorities that were successful in overthrowing regimes and bringing about social change in the years 1940–2006 (Chenoweth).

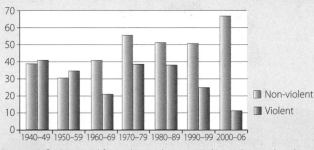

State **two** findings and for each one draw a conclusion (state what the finding shows).

Finding 1:
Conclusion 1: This shows that …
Finding 2:
Conclusion 2: This shows that …

Answers on page 197

 APPLYING YOUR KNOWLEDGE 1

Identify the psychology	Recent years have seen a rapid increase in obesity rates in the UK and illnesses linked to unhealthy eating. Campaigns by vegetarian groups and by celebrity chefs have highlighted the need for a change in people's attitudes toward what they eat. This is now beginning to have an effect, producing a widespread change in our attitudes to healthy eating. Using your knowledge of minority influence, explain how this social change might have occurred. *(6 marks)*	Link to changing eating habits

Answers on page 198

APPLYING YOUR KNOWLEDGE 2

Using the five aspects of minority influence described on the facing page, think up another example of social change through minority influence and break it down into these five sections in the table below.

Drawing attention	
Creating a conflict	
Consistency over time	
Augmentation	
Snowball effect	

 CIRCLE TRUE OR FALSE

T or F The quickest route to social change is through minority influence.

T or F The influence of the suffragettes decreased because of their use of hunger strikes.

T or F Social change is more likely when minority group members are consistent with each other.

T or F Minorities who are seen to suffer for their view are taken more seriously.

T or F In public, minority sources generate less change than majorities.

T or F Minority influence tends to be latent rather than direct.

Answers on page 198

MUST — Asch

HOW?

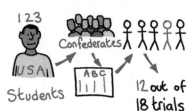

123
Confederates
ABC
USA
Students
12 out of 18 trials

SHOWED?

On 12 critical trials 36.8% of responses were correct. 25% of participants never conformed. Without confederates, participants were correct 99% of the time.

SHOULD — Extensions to Asch

Task more difficult — conformity increased
Increased majority size — only up to 3
Unanimity among confederates — vital!

Vartanian and Hopkinson

HOW?

Tendency to Conform
Likelihood of dieting
Internalisation of Societal standards of attractiveness

SHOWED? Tendency to conform positively correlated to internalisation of standards which predicted likelihood of dieting.

COULD — Bond and Smith

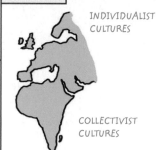

INDIVIDUALIST CULTURES

COLLECTIVIST CULTURES

EVALUATION

An issue with this study

It took place in an era of US history when pressures to conform were high.
Perrin and Spencer found ...

They concluded that ...

A criticism of Asch's study

The confederates might have been unconvincing, casting doubt on the validity of findings.
Mori and Arai ...

This suggests that ...

More evidence of independent behaviour

Trials with conformity response $\frac{1}{3}$

Trials with independent response $\frac{2}{3}$

Participants showed more evidence of independence of judgement than of conformity.

This suggests that ...

Evidence for cultural differences

META-ANALYSIS 17 CULTURES

Bond and Smith established ...

However ...

MUST — Normative and informational social influence

NORMATIVE

I don't have to accept their views
I want to fit in and be liked
I suppose I could conform in action alone
It's OK. I'm complying, not internalising

SHOULD — Humans are a social species

This means we have a strong sense of rejection.

I wonder if they'd laugh at me if I pulled these up?

COULD

NEWS The majority of students listen to opera
LEADS TO
Nessun Dorma Nessun Dorma
CONFORMITY BUS

INFORMATIONAL

They must be right because they know more than I do
I should go along with them and I should change my attitude
My people!

HELP!
What's going on? Looks like a crisis. They look like they're experts ...

HELP!

EVALUATION

Research support for normative influence

MONTANA SOCIAL NORMS PROJECT
MOST OF US (76%) Are Tobacco Free

Relationship between normative influence and intention to smoke.
Linkenbach & Perkins found ...

This supports ...

Real-world applications

It is possible to influence people's conservation behaviour using normative influence.

75% choose to re-use their towels every day

Schulz et al. found ...

This suggests ...

Research support for informational influence

He can't be any good then
YES NO

Informational influence can shape political opinion.
Fein et al. ...

This supports the view ...

Explains social stereotypes

Exposure to views of majority influences the development of social stereotypes.
Wittenbrink & Henly found ...

This supports the view that ...

Supporting evidence for indirect influence

Study by Nolan et al.

HOW ARE MOST SAN MARCOS RESIDENTS CONSERVING THIS SUMMER? BY USING FANS INSTEAD OF A/C!

TOPIC 44 — Obedience

MUST Milgram

HOW?

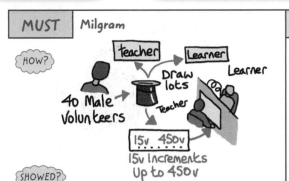

40 Male Volunteers

Draw lots — teacher / Learner

15v — 450v
15v increments
Up to 450v

SHOWED?

All participants delivered 300 volts. Only 12.5% refused to go further. 65% gave max 450 volts. Predictions — only 4% would go to 300 volts.

SHOULD Milgram's variations

HOW?

Studied effect of different situational pressures on obedience rates.

proximity of learner
proximity of authority figure
presence of allies

SHOWED?

Learner and teacher same room dropped to 40%
'Touch proximity' condition dropped to 30%
Authority figure left room dropped to 21%
Two confederates disobey dropped to 10%

COULD Hofling et al.

HOW?

This is Dr Smith 20mg to Mr Jones

SHOWED?

21 obeyed   **1** didn't

EVALUATION

Ethical problems with study

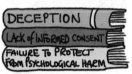

DECEPTION
LACK OF INFORMED CONSENT
FAILURE TO PROTECT FROM PSYCHOLOGICAL HARM

For example …

As a result …

Lacks internal validity

uncconcerned   These can't be real shocks

Participants not taken in by deception because experimenter appeared unconcerned over learner's distress.
Orne and Holland suggest …

However …

May lack external validity

Milgram's research ≠ Holocaust

Mandel — Milgram's variations do not explain real-life obedience.
Mandel found …

This suggests that …

Conclusions challenged

Three times the max dose? What should I do?

Rank and Jacobson

TOPIC 45 — Explanations of why people obey

MUST

GRADUAL COMMITMENT

15 30 45 → Makes it harder to resist later on

AGENTIC SHIFT

DO AS I SAY — Agentic state — I must obey

ROLE OF BUFFERS

Everything Seems Fine

SHOULD

The gradual transition …

People shift from an autonomous state …

Buffers protect …

COULD Justifying obedience

UNDERLYING IDEOLOGIES   REVENGE   SCIENCE IS IMPORTANT

Harmful obedience justified on basis of underlying ideology.

EVALUATION

Gradual commitment supported by real-life events

nazi Doctors

Lifton's study of doctors working in Nazi death camps.
Lifton found …

Their obedience was because …

Agentic shift challenged

Agentic shift
LABORATORY obedience   HOLOCAUST obedience

There are important distinctions between the two that challenge its relevance to both types.
For example …

This suggests …

Role of buffers supported

SEE
BUFFERS REMOVED → LESS OBEDIENCE
HEAR

Milgram found that removal of buffers meant witnessing consequences of actions and lower obedience.
However …

This shows that …

Evidence to support this

Evidence from Holocaust propaganda.

nazi Jude propaganda

MUST — Social support and the role of allies

Confederate

 Participant

Others resist majority

More confident

- ✦ Asch – social support helps individuals to resist majority pressure
- ✦ Introduction of ally – conformity decreases

SHOULD — Why does it work?

Fellow dissenter provides support for individual's point of view.

Valid support more impact than invalid.

Most important factor is breaking unanimous position of majority.

COULD — The heroic imagination

Resisting conformity through heroic imagination

The role of morality

People better able to resist pressure to conform if there is moral dimension.

ASCH
Line judgement
No moral dimension

HORNSEY ET AL.
Cheating
Moral dimension

High ——————————————→ Low
Conformity levels

Less mature morally

Morally advanced

Over-reliance on social conformity

More able to resist pressure to conform

KOHLBERG'S RESEARCH

EVALUATION

Social support not enough

Presence of ally works in visual tasks even with a different response. Not so in opinion task.

Allen and Levine …

This suggests …

Research support for the importance of morality

Hornsey et al. found relationship between strength of moral beliefs and resisting conformity.

They found …

The motivation to resist …

Making the impermissable permissable

Kundu and Cummins – morally impermissible actions judged less so if majority judged them as permissible.

They used the Asch set-up …

The results suggest …

Need to act morally

Need to Conform

Effective in resisting inappropriate conformity

HEROIC IMAGINATION TRAINING

Heroic imagination training used to help students.

MUST

Role of disobedient allies

Individuals better able to resist authority in the presence of allies.

Makes individual more confident in their ability to do the same.

"We aren't giving any more shocks" / "I'm more confident"

Questioning legitimacy

Questioning legitimacy of an order or person's right to give it …

Reducing the status of an authority figure …

Increases an individual's ability to reduce obedience.

SHOULD

Disobedience of others changes perception that harmful actions are acceptable.

Their defiance used by individual as an opportunity to extricate themselves.

Role model

Distinction between someone 'in' authority or who 'is' authority.

Questioning whether someone has expert knowledge ('is' an authority) or not allows individual to resist inappropriate obedience.

"What gives you the right?"

COULD — Role of morality

"I won't obey as it would be morally wrong"

Reasoning at postconventional level of morality

EVALUATION

Disobedient allies in real life

Rosenstraße

Rosenstrasse protest when German women defied orders to disperse.

In the presence of others …

This demonstrates …

Real-life application

Some aircraft crashes are due to inadequate monitoring and challenging of authority.

Tarnow proposes …

This technique means …

"You sure this is right?" / "Yes, it's fine"

Individual differences

OBEY ME! / NO I've got education and religion to back me up …

Religion and education made a difference to ability to resist.

Milgram found that …

This research shows …

Morality not the reason

"Why doesn't he say something?"

Kaposi – lack of learner response created doubts.

TOPIC 48 — Locus of control

MUST — Internals and externals

Events caused by ability and effort

What happens determined by external factors

Belief in control over personal events

Many things happen by luck

Rely less on opinions of others

Approach life with passive attitude

HIGH INTERNAL

HIGH EXTERNAL

Take more responsibility for their own behaviour

Take less responsibility for their own behaviour

SHOULD — Twenge et al.

 HOW? Two meta-analyses of locus of control studies of young Americans.

Included 97 samples of college students and 41 samples of children aged 9–14.

SHOWED? 1960 → Increase in externality → 2002

Increasing belief that events were determined by luck and powerful others rather than their own actions.

COULD — Locus of control and well-being

EXTERNAL LOCUS OF CONTROL → LEARNED HELPLESSNESS

NEGLECT DIET AND EXERCISE → POOR HEALTH

EVALUATION

Gender differences

Internal ← → external

Semykina and Linz — males are more likely to have internal and females an external locus of control.

These are attributed to ...

Research has also shown ...

Cultural differences

More internal / More external

People in Western cultures more internal than in non-Western cultures.

Kongsonpong and Leithner ...

This suggests that ...

Twenge's study has positive and negative consequences

＋ Adolescents more tolerant of others, believing that situational factors shape everybody's life.

－ High levels of externality associated with increasing feelings of helplessness.

This shows that ...

Internality is not necessarily healthy

APRIL et al
Internality & externality
Now with increased health and happiness!

TOPIC 49 — Social change

MUST — Minority influence

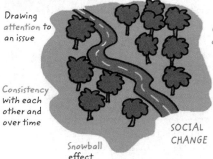

Drawing attention to an issue

Creating a conflict

Augmentation principle

Consistency with each other and over time

Snowball effect

SOCIAL CHANGE

SHOULD — An example: the suffragettes

Drawing attention ...

Creating conflict ...

Consistency ...

Augmentation ...

Snowball effect ...

VOTES FOR WOMEN

COULD — Second example

TERRORISM

Create attention ...

Create conflict ...

Consistency ...

Augmentation ...

EVALUATION

Research support for minority influence

THE META-ANALYSER
Minority influence more powerful on private measures
CONSISTENCY IS THE KEY

Wood et al. meta-analysis 97 studies.

Minorities that were consistent ...

However ...

Minorities seen as deviant

Deviants!

NO NO NO

Influence decreased because seen as deviant by majority.

This means that ...

As a result ...

Social change is very gradual

ANTI

SOCIAL CHANGE

History challenges claim that minorities can bring about social change quickly.

This is because ...

This explains why ...

Minority influence research increases understanding of terrorism

TERRORISM
MINORITY INFLUENCE

Each teaches us about the other.

KEY WORDS

- Abnormality
- Cultural relativism
- Deviation from ideal mental health
- Deviation from social norms
- Failure to function adequately

Possible essay question ...

Outline and evaluate **two or more** definitions of abnormality. *(12 marks)*

Other possible exam questions ...

+ Outline the deviation from social norms definition of abnormality. *(3 marks)*
+ Outline and evaluate the failure to function adequately definition of abnormality. *(6 marks)*
+ Outline **two** limitations of the deviation from ideal mental health definition of abnormality. *(4 marks)*
+ Identify **one** definition of abnormality and explain **one** limitation associated with this definition. *(3 marks + 3 marks)*
+ Apply this knowledge to ... *(6 marks)*

MUST know ...

Deviation from social norms

Standards of acceptable behaviour, for example standards of normal politeness or appropriate sexual behaviour exist in any society.

Abnormality is defined in terms of behaviours that break these social norms.

Deviation is related to context and degree ...

- **E** – Judgements of deviation are dependent on the context of behaviour.
- **E** – Some behaviours are acceptable in one context but not in another.
- **L** – Also, there is no clear line between what is abnormal and what is harmless eccentricity.

Failure to function adequately

Mentally healthy people are judged as being able to operate within certain acceptable limits.

If behaviour interferes with this functioning (e.g. feeling excessive anxiety or having depressive symptoms) then it is labelled as 'abnormal'.

EVALUATION
Abnormal behaviours can also help us ...

- **E** – Behaviours that appear dysfunctional can also lead to helpful intervention from others.
- **E** – For example, depression may lead to extra attention, helping the person deal with stress in their life.
- **L** – This suggests that behaviours that appear abnormal may be adaptive for an individual.

Deviation from ideal mental health

Abnormality is seen as deviating from an ideal of positive mental health, defined in terms of Jahoda's criteria of ideal mental health.

Absence of the criteria for positive mental health indicates abnormality and a possible disorder.

EVALUATION
Few people can achieve all the criteria ...

- **E** – According to this definition, all of us would be described as abnormal to some degree.
- **E** – It would be unusual to find people that satisfy all of the criteria all of the time.
- **L** – We need to ask how many criteria need to be absent before someone is judged as abnormal.

SHOULD know ...

Deviation from social norms

These standards are not formally stated but are implicit rules concerning what people expect in the behaviour of other members of society.

Behaviours that break these unwritten rules are considered undesirable and so are 'abnormal'.

This explanation is limited because ...

- **E** – Defining behaviour as abnormal is pointless without also considering cultural context.
- **E** – What is considered a diagnosable disorder in one culture may be considered normal in another.
- **L** – This means there are no universal standards for labelling behaviour as abnormal.

Failure to function adequately

From an individual's point of view, abnormality is judged in terms of 'not being able to cope'.

When people experience this feeling, they may label their own behaviour as being abnormal and seek treatment.

This explanation is limited because ...

- **E** – Definitions of adequate functioning are related to cultural ideals of how life should be lived.
- **E** – This is likely to produce different diagnoses when applied to people from different cultures.
- **L** – Explains cultural differences in diagnosis of abnormality, as lifestyle differences can be mis-interpreted as failure to function adequately.

Deviation from ideal mental health

Jahoda identified six characteristics of ideal mental health, including:

- *Self-attitudes* – positive self-esteem and a strong sense of identity.
- *Integration* – being able to deal with stressful events.

This explanation is limited because ...

- **E** – Most criteria of ideal mental health apply mainly to individuals living in Western cultures.
- **E** – Applying them to members of non-Western cultures would, therefore, be inappropriate.
- **L** – This would lead to an over-diagnosis of abnormality in members of those cultures.

COULD know ...

Multiple perspectives on abnormality

Strupp and Hadley suggest three 'vantage points' from which to judge a person's abnormality.

These are: (1) the society of which the person is a member; (2) the mental health professional; (3) the individual him or herself.

Each 'judge' operates from a different perspective, often using different criteria to judge abnormality.

There is value in this approach ...

... as it overcomes the limitations of using just one single way of defining abnormality.

- **E** – However, some people who might be described as having a mental disorder by *society* (e.g. rapists) may not describe *themselves* as abnormal.
- **E** – A judgement of abnormality must be recognised as a product of one of the three vantage points.
- **L** – Without this, even greater confusion can arise.

CHOOSE THE RIGHT ANSWER

The following statements are all linked to different definitions of abnormality.

Tick the box next to the **two** statements that describe the 'failure to function adequately' definition of abnormality.

A	Involves repeatedly breaking unwritten societal rules concerning acceptable standards of behaviour. ☐
B	Exhibiting behaviour that interferes with normal daily functioning. ☐
C	Showing an absence of particular characteristics that would constitute healthy behaviour. ☐
D	May be subjectively experienced as a felling of not being able to cope. ☐
E	Determined solely on clinical characteristics determined by a mental health professional. ☐

Answers on page 198

 CIRCLE TRUE OR FALSE

T or F Judgements of deviation from social norms are dependent on the context of a behaviour.

T or F What is considered abnormal in one culture would also be considered abnormal in another.

T or F Those behaviours that appear abnormal can never be adaptive for an individual.

T or F Cultural differences in lifestyle can be misinterpreted as failure to function adequately.

T or F Only very few people fail to satisfy all of the criteria of ideal mental health.

T or F The criteria of ideal mental health apply mainly to individuals living in Western cultures.

Answers on page 198

 KEY PHRASES

Exam question:

Outline the deviation from social norms and deviation from ideal mental health definitions of abnormality. *(6 marks)*

On the facing page these definitions of abnormality are described for you.

For each definition select **three** key words or phrases.

Deviation from social norms			
Deviation from ideal mental health			

Now try to write an answer to the exam question using your key phrases. Your answer should be between 100–150 words in length.

See page 20 for an explanation of the 'two-pronged attack' needed to answer 'applying your knowledge' questions.

⚙ **APPLYING YOUR KNOWLEDGE**

Every time Anna leaves the house, she has to go round several times checking that all the lights are off and the windows closed and locked. This always makes her late for work or when she has arranged to meet friends.

Identify **one** definition of abnormality that could describe Anna's behaviour. Explain your choice. *(1 mark + 2 marks)*

One way of defining abnormality is to see whether or not someone meets the criteria for ideal mental health. Helen is highly independent and has a strong sense of identity.

Describe **two** other criteria that you would expect Helen to display if she were to be described as having 'ideal mental health'. *(2 marks)*

Cheryl is 35 years old. At a relative's funeral she laughed and made phone calls throughout the service. When she talks to people she stands very close to them, making them feel uncomfortable.

Identify **one** definition of abnormality that could describe Cheryl's behaviour. Explain your choice. *(1 mark + 2 marks)*

Identify:	**Criterion 1:**	**Identify:**
Explain:	**Criterion 2:**	**Explain:**

Answers on page 198

KEY WORDS

- Biological approach
- Concordance rates
- Depression
- Diathesis-stress model
- Genetic inheritance
- Neuroanatomy
- Neurochemistry
- Psychopathology
- Schizophrenia
- Ventricles
- Viral infection

Possible essay question ...

Outline and evaluate the biological approach to psychopathology. *(12 marks)*

Other possible exam questions ...

+ Outline the biological approach to psychopathology. *(6 marks)*
+ Explain **one** limitation of the biological approach to psychopathology *(3 marks)*
+ Apply this knowledge to ... *(6 marks)*

MUST know ...

The biological approach assumes that mental disorders are caused by physical factors.

Genetic inheritance

Mental illness may be inherited via genes so that people who are related are more likely to develop the same disorders.

If identical twins are more alike for a particular disorder than are non-identical twins, this suggests a genetic influence for that disorder.

Neuroanatomy

Abnormalities in the structure of the brain, caused by ageing, disease, etc. can lead to the development of abnormal behaviour.

Neurochemistry

Altered brain chemistry can also lead to abnormality, particularly changes in the levels or activity of neurotransmitters.

 There is inconclusive evidence ...

... for the role of genetic inheritance in the development of psychopathology.

- **E** – If genetic inheritance was the sole cause of psychopathology, then twins with the same genetic predisposition for a disorder such as schizophrenia would both become mentally ill.

 Biological factors are not necessarily the cause ...

... of an individual's psychopathology.

- **E** – Changes in neurochemistry could be the consequence of a mental disorder rather than a cause. Low levels of serotonin may be a consequence of becoming depressed instead of its cause.

 The biological approach has led to successful treatments ...

... for mental illness.

- **E** – For example, drug treatments are based on our understanding of the activity of neurotransmitters in the brain, and involve changing this activity in order to bring about changes in behaviour.

SHOULD know ...

Like physical illness, abnormality is related to change, illness or dysfunction in the body.

Genetic inheritance

There are low concordance rates for some disorders (e.g. phobias) but relatively high rates for others (e.g. schizophrenia).

Many of the genes for abnormal behaviours are the product of evolutionary adaptations despite the fact these are no longer useful.

Neuroanatomy

For example, some schizophrenics have enlarged ventricles in the brain, indicating shrinkage of brain tissue around the ventricles.0

Neurochemistry

Low levels of serotonin have been found in the brains of depressives and high levels of dopamine in the brains of schizophrenics.

- **E** – For example, Gottesman and Shields found that if one identical twin developed schizophrenia, there was only a 50% chance of the other twin also developing schizophrenia.
- **L** – The diathesis-stress model can explain this – individuals inherit a vulnerability for a disorder, but this only develops if the individual is exposed to stressful life conditions.

- **E** – In the research on enlarged ventricles, it is not clear whether the shrinkage in brain tissue is a *cause* of the schizophrenic symptoms or a *consequence* of them (e.g. the result of taking antipsychotic medication).
- **L** – This suggests that there isn't a simple cause-and-effect relationship between biological influences and mental disorders.

- **E** – There is evidence that such treatments are effective, e.g. WHO reports that there were higher relapse rates for schizophrenics treated with placebos than with antipsychotics.
- **L** – As altering neurochemistry with drug treatments is successful in ridding an individual of their abnormal symptoms, this suggests that the origin of those symptoms is also neurochemical.

COULD know ...

Viral infection

Some disorders may be explained in terms of exposure to viruses in the womb.

Mothers of some schizophrenics had contracted a strain of the influenza virus during pregnancy.

The virus appears to remain dormant until puberty, when other hormones may activate it, producing the symptoms of schizophrenia.

 An interaction of infection and genetics ...

... can increase the risk of developing schizophrenia.

- **E** – Børglum *et al.* scanned the genes of sick and healthy people to identify interaction between genes and viruses in schizophrenia.
- **E** – Women infected with cytomegalovirus during pregnancy were far more likely to have a child that went on to develop schizophrenia if both carried a particular gene defect.
- **L** – This suggests that an anti-viral medicine could be developed for these women to take during pregnancy, preventing the onset of schizophrenia in their offspring.

FILL IN THE BLANKS

The biological approach assumes that mental disorders are caused by

(1) .... factors. Mental illness may be inherited via

(2) .... so people who are related are more likely to

develop the same disorders. If (3) .... twins are

more alike for a disorder than are (4) .... twins, this

suggests a genetic influence for that disorder. Abnormalities in the structure

of the (5) ...., caused by ageing, disease, etc., can lead to the

development of abnormal behaviour, e.g. some schizophrenics have

(6) .... ventricles in the brain, indicating

(7) .... of brain tissue around the ventricles. Altered brain

chemistry can also lead to abnormality, particularly changes in the levels or

activity of (8) ...., e.g. low levels of

(9) .... have been found in the brains of people

suffering from depression and high levels of (10) ....

in the brains of those suffering from schizophrenia.

Answers on page 198

MATCH THEM UP

Match up the aspects of the biological approach in the table below.

1	Enlarged ventricles in the brain	**A**	Found in some people with depression.
2	High concordance rates in twins	**B**	Are more likely to develop the same disorders.
3	Altered brain chemistry	**C**	Suggests people only inherit vulnerability to a disorder.
4	Like physical illness, abnormality caused by	**D**	Found in some people with schizophrenia.
5	Low levels of serotonin	**E**	Contracted influenza during pregnancy.
6	People who are genetically related	**F**	Leads to change in activity of neurotransmitters.
7	Mothers of some schizophrenics	**G**	Suggests a genetic influence.
8	Diathesis-stress model	**H**	Change, illness or dysfunction in the body.

Answers on page 198

PRACTICE ELABORATION

On the facing page, there are a number of evaluative points for the biological approach to psychopathology. After reading these (and without looking back at them), try to expand the three points included in the table below.

Point	Elaboration	Conclusion (link back)
There is inconclusive evidence …		
Biological factors are not necessarily the cause …		
The biological approach has led to successful treatments …		

A MARKING EXERCISE

You can read marking guidelines on page 10.

Read the student answer to the following exam question:

Outline the biological approach to psychopathology and explain **one** limitation of this approach. *(3 marks + 3 marks)*

Hani's answer

The biological approach explains psychopathology in terms of genetics, in that characteristics are passed on from parents to the child through the genes. It can also be explained in terms of problems with brain chemicals that cause abnormality.

A limitation is that abnormality cannot be entirely inherited because otherwise there would be a 100% probability that one twin would develop schizophrenia if the other twin had this disorder.

TASK 1

What mark do you think this would get? AO1 _____ AO2 _____

TASK 2 Your turn

Write an improved answer here:

Answers on page 198

KEY WORDS

- Defence mechanism
- Depression
- Ego
- Id
- Meta-analysis
- Oedipal conflict
- Psychodynamic approach
- Regression
- Repression
- Superego

Possible essay question ...

Outline and evaluate the psychodynamic approach to psychopathology. *(12 marks)*

Other possible exam questions ...

+ Outline the psychodynamic approach to psychopathology. *(6 marks)*
+ Outline the psychodynamic approach to psychopathology and give **one** limitation of this approach. *(3 + 3 marks)*
+ Apply this knowledge to ... *(6 marks)*

MUST know ...

The psychodynamic approach assumes that mental disorders have psychological rather than physical causes.

Early experiences cause mental disorder

In childhood, the ego is not mature enough to deal with trauma such as the loss of a parent.

This can lead to repression of any emotions associated with that loss.

Later in life, further losses may cause the individual to re-experience this earlier loss, leading to depression.

The role of unconscious motivation

The unconscious mind exerts a powerful effect on behaviour through the influence of previously repressed emotions or trauma.

This frequently leads to distress, as the individual doesn't understand why they are acting in that particular way.

The underlying problem cannot be controlled until it is brought into conscious awareness.

 EVALUATION
There is a lack of research support ...

... for the psychodynamic explanation of psychopathology.

- **E** – The theory is difficult to prove or disprove using scientific methodology, therefore much of the support is restricted to individual case studies.

 EVALUATION
Many of the key concepts are abstract ...

... therefore are difficult to define or demonstrate.

- **E** – For example, the id, ego and superego are key aspects of this approach, yet they are abstract concepts rather than concrete entities.

EVALUATION
The psychodynamic approach has led to successful treatments ...

... for mental illness.

- **E** – Shedler's review of meta-analyses found that therapies based on the psychodynamic approach proved as effective as other forms of therapy.

SHOULD know ...

Freud believed that mental disorders were the result of unresolved childhood conflicts such as the Oedipal conflict.

The role of childhood conflicts

Conflicts between the id, ego and superego create anxiety for the individual, which can be reduced by use of defence mechanisms e.g.:

- *Repression* – moving unpleasant thoughts or desires into the unconscious.
- *Regression* – behaving like a child when faced with a difficult situation.

A defence mechanism becomes pathological when it is overused and its use leads to significant problems in everyday functioning

The Oedipal conflict – for boys, a wish for sexual possession of the mother countered by fear of punishment by the sexual rival – the father.

Resolution of this conflict in males leads to the development of the superego.

Lack of resolution of this conflict may lead to the development of anxiety disorders.

- **E** – However, Fisher and Greenberg reviewed over 2,500 experimental studies and found that many of Freud's major claims about the causes of abnormality received experimental support.
- **L** – Despite this, a major problem for this approach is that many of its claims cannot be disproved or falsified, which would be necessary for it to be regarded as a scientific explanation of abnormality.

- **E** – Similarly, there is no way to know for certain that a process such as repression is actually operating because it takes place at an unconscious level.
- **L** – This makes it difficult to conduct research to demonstrate these processes.

- **E** – Shedler suggests that psychodynamic treatments are effective because they enable therapists to gain awareness of previously inner thoughts and feelings rather than focusing on symptoms alone.
- **L** – The success of psychodynamic therapies offers further support for the validity of these concepts in explaining abnormality.

COULD know ...

Misuse of psychological energy and psychopathology

Psychodynamic theorists believe problems result from the way that an individual uses their psychological energy.

In cases of anxiety and depression, a person invests too much energy in defences, having less available energy for other, healthier, activities.

In more severe forms of psychopathology, e.g. schizophrenia, an individual may not invest enough energy in defences, and as a result becomes overwhelmed by their instinctual drives.

 EVALUATION
There are advantages of the psychodynamic approach ...

... as an explanation of abnormal behaviour.

- **E** – Because of the contribution of psychodynamic theorists, we have explanations of abnormal behaviour other than those based on biological processes alone.
- **E** – This approach was the first to demonstrate the potential of psychological rather than biological treatments for illnesses such as depression and anxiety.
- **L** – This suggests that, although the psychodynamic approach has been largely superceded by other approaches, it still has explanatory value.

CHOOSE THE RIGHT ANSWER

The following statements refer to different approaches to abnormality. Select **three** statements that describe the psychodynamic approach.

A Holding unrealistic and irrational beliefs about oneself and the world. ☐

B Behaviour is caused mainly by the unconscious. ☐

C Behaviour is shaped by forces in the environment. ☐

D There is a conflict between the id and the superego. ☐

E The mind is an information processor. ☐

F Abnormality is caused by unresolved childhood problems. ☐

Answers on page 198

 CIRCLE TRUE OR FALSE

T or F The psychodynamic approach assumes that mental disorders have primarily physical causes.

T or F Regression involves moving unpleasant thoughts or desires into the unconscious.

T or F Resolution of the Oedipal conflict leads to the development of the superego.

T or F An immature ego leads to repression of emotions associated with trauma during childhood.

T or F Anxiety is increased by the use of defence mechanisms.

T or F Underlying problems can be resolved while still in the unconscious.

Answers on page 198

 JUMBLED SENTENCES

On the facing page there are three criticisms related to the psychodynamic approach to psychopathology. Similar sentences are presented below in a jumbled order. Sort them into order by placing the number for each sentence in the correct square.

Criticism 1

| 3 | **1** Despite this, many claims cannot be disproved or falsified. |

| ☐ | **2** Many claims about the causes of abnormality supported experimentally. |

| ☐ | **3** The psychodynamic approach is difficult to research scientifically. |

| ☐ | **4** However, in a review of 2,500 studies by Fisher and Greenberg. |

Criticism 2

| ☐ | **1** It is difficult to show that a process such as repression is actually operating. |

| ☐ | **2** Makes it difficult to carry research to demonstrate scientifically. |

| ☐ | **3** Concepts such as id, ego and superego are abstract and difficult to define. |

| ☐ | **4** Difficult to demonstrate conflict between different parts at an unconscious level. |

Criticism 3

| ☐ | **1** Therapy effective because of focus on inner feelings rather than symptoms. |

| ☐ | **2** Their success supports the validity of these concepts in explaining abnormality. |

| ☐ | **3** The psychodynamic approach has led to successful treatments. |

| ☐ | **4** Shedler reviewed meta-analyses of the effectiveness of psychodynamic therapies. |

Answers on page 198

MATCH THEM UP

Match up the statements in the table below.

1	An immature ego	**A**	A wish for sexual possession of the mother by the male child.
2	Repression	**B**	Formed as a result of resolution of Oedipal conflict.
3	Regression	**C**	Cannot deal with trauma in childhood.
4	The unconscious mind	**D**	Can become pathological if overused by the individual.
5	The Oedipal conflict	**E**	Can be reduced by the use of defence mechanisms.
6	The superego	**F**	Reverting to childlike behaviour in difficult situations.
7	Conflict between id, ego and superego	**G**	Involves moving disturbing thoughts into unconscious.
8	Defence mechanisms	**H**	Contains repressed thoughts and desires.

Answers on page 198

An idea

1 Look back at the spread on memory improvement techniques on page 46. Select one of these techniques and use it to help you remember the material on the facing page.

2 Alternatively – concepts such as the id, ego, superego, unconscious, conflict, defence mechanisms, etc. are criticised as being too abstract. This also makes them more difficult to remember when revising. So, your task is to try and make these more concrete in your mind. On a separate piece of paper, create a 'story board' of cartoons (however amateurish) that turns the main concepts and processes into concrete images that will help you remember them.

Have fun!

KEY WORDS

- Agoraphobia
- Behavioural approach
- Classical conditioning
- Depression
- Obsessive-compulsive disorder (OCD)
- Operant conditioning
- Phobia
- Social learning

Possible essay question ...

Discuss the behavioural approach to explaining psychopathology. *(12 marks)*

Other possible exam questions ...

+ Outline the behavioural approach to psychopathology. *(6 marks)*
+ Evaluate the behavioural approach to psychopathology. *(4 marks)*
+ Apply this knowledge to ... *(6 marks)*

MUST know ...

The behavioural approach assumes that abnormal behaviours are acquired as a result of experiences in life, i.e. they are *learned*.

Only behaviour is important

The behavioural approach focuses only on the abnormal behaviour of the individual.

This is in contrast to approaches that focus on underlying psychological or physical causes.

Abnormal behaviours are learned

Abnormal behaviour is no different to normal behaviour in terms of how it is learned.

It is learned through the processes of classical and operant conditioning and social learning.

Learning environments

The environment may reinforce maladaptive behaviour by providing desired consequences.

Although it is usually disruptive (e.g. not being able to leave home), sometimes it is useful for the individual (e.g. receiving help from others).

 The behavioural approach is criticised ...

... for being a limited view of factors that might cause abnormal behaviour.

- *E* – Behaviourist explanations are limited because they ignore many important influences that might contribute to abnormal behaviour.

 There is counter evidence ...

... that challenges the behavioural approach to abnormality.

- *E* – Explanations of the acquisition of phobic behaviours focus on the role of conditioning, yet many people cannot recall any incident that may have led to such traumatic conditioning.

 Support for this approach comes from ...

... the success of therapies based on the behavioural approach.

- *E* – These include systematic desensitisation (based on the principle of classical conditioning) and modelling (based on the principle of social learning).

SHOULD know ...

Abnormality is seen as the development of learned behaviour patterns that are considered maladaptive for the individual.

Only behaviour is important

Someone with OCD displays compulsive behaviour such as constant hand washing.

Someone with a phobia displays anxious behaviour in the presence of the phobic object.

Abnormal behaviours are learned

A disorder may develop if maladaptive behaviour leads to some reward (operant conditioning).

Abnormal behaviours are also acquired by seeing others rewarded for behaviour (social learning).

Learning environments

For an individual with agoraphobia, not leaving home lowers their anxiety levels.

For individuals with depression, displaying depressive symptoms elicits help from others. As this is rewarding, the symptoms persist.

- *E* – These include cognitive factors such as thought processes, emotional influences, neurotransmitter imbalance and genetics, all of which have been shown to impact on the development of abnormality.
- *L* – This suggests that behavioural processes do not operate to the exclusion of other influences.

- *E* – By contrast, some basic anxieties (such as fear of heights) may be 'hard-wired' into the brain because they provided a survival advantage to our distant ancestors and so are learned more readily.
- *L* – This explains why some abnormal behaviours are learned easily (because of their potential survival advantage), while others tend never to be learned at all.

- *E* – However, they may not lead to long-term cures because simply removing symptoms may not deal with the *cause* of a disorder.
- *L* – Therefore, the illness returns because the underlying problem is still there, which casts doubt on the claim that the problem is purely a matter of maladaptive learning.

COULD know ...

This approach lends itself to scientific validation

The basic concepts of the behavioural model, e.g. behaviour, reward, etc. can be observed and measured in a way that psychodynamic concepts cannot.

As a result, this approach is open to scientific validation.

Experimenters have successfully used the principles of learning to create symptoms in participants, suggesting that real disorders may develop in the same way.

 However, an integrated approach may be better ...

... because it combines the best ideas and techniques from all the different approaches.

- *E* – Norcross argues that psychodynamic and behavioural approaches could offer a more complete understanding of psychopathology if they borrowed ideas from each other.
- *E* – Cognitive behaviourists stress the importance of cognitive factors (individual's perception of events) that mediate between a stimulus and its response.
- *L* – This suggests that traditional behavioural views of psychopathology may give way to a more integrated approach.

✓ CHOOSE THE RIGHT ANSWER

Which **two** of the following statements apply to the behavioural approach to psychopathology?

A Unresolved conflicts in childhood affect adult behaviour. ☐

B All behaviour is learned in the same way. ☐

C Abnormal behaviour is caused by faulty thought processes. ☐

D Abnormal behaviour may be the result of observing the actions of others. ☐

E Irrational thoughts lead to abnormal behaviour. ☐

Answers on page 198

✎ FILL IN THE BLANKS

The text below is an answer to the following exam question:
Outline the behavioural approach to psychopathology. *(4 marks)*

The behavioural approach assumes that abnormal behaviours are acquired as a result of (1) .... in life, i.e. they are *learned*. This approach focuses only on the abnormal behaviour of the individual. This is in contrast to approaches that focus on underlying (2) .... or (3) .... causes. Abnormal behaviour is no different to (4) .... in terms of how it is learned. It is learned through the processes of classical and (5) .... conditioning and (6) .... The (7) .... in which behaviour is learned may reinforce maladaptive behaviour. Although usually (8) .... (e.g. not being able to leave home), sometimes it is useful for the individual (e.g. receiving help from others).

Answers on page 198

✓ A MARKING EXERCISE

Read the student answer to the following exam question:

Outline the behavioural approach to psychopathology. *(6 marks)*

Aubrey's answer

The behavioural model states that abnormality is learned through classical conditioning, operant conditioning and by social learning. In classical conditioning an unconditioned stimulus and a conditioned stimulus are paired together so that eventually the conditioned stimulus produces the same response as the unconditioned stimulus. In operant conditioning a response becomes more frequent if it is reinforced by something the person wants or needs. Finally, in social learning, which is also known as observational learning, a person observes someone else behaving in a certain way and also observes what behaviours they are rewarded for carrying out. This is known as vicarious reinforcement, and means that an individual imitates behaviour that they have seen reinforced in others.

Your comments on Aubrey's answer:

....

....

....

....

....

Aubrey would get _____ out of 4 marks

Answers on page 198

◎ PRACTICE ELABORATION

Using the material on the facing page, complete the **AO2 evaluation** part of the following question in the table in your own words:
Outline and **evaluate** the behavioural approach to psychopathology. *(12 marks)*

Point	Elaboration	Conclusion (link back)
The behavioural approach is criticised for being a limited view …		
There is counter evidence to challenge the behavioural approach …		
Support for this approach comes from the success of therapies …		

161

Possible essay question …

Discuss the cognitive approach to explaining psychopathology. *(12 marks)*

Other possible exam questions …

+ Outline the cognitive approach to psychopathology. *(6 marks)*
+ Evaluate the cognitive approach to psychopathology *(4 marks)*
+ Apply this knowledge to … *(6 marks)*

MUST know …

The cognitive approach explains psychopathology in terms of irrational and negative thinking about the world.

Abnormality is caused by faulty thinking

Mental disorders arise out of distortions in the way that people think about a situation.

Faulty and irrational thinking prevents the individual from behaving in a rational manner.

The A-B-C model

A – an activating event.

B – the belief (which may be rational or irrational).

C – the consequence (which may be healthy or unhealthy).

The individual is in control

The individual is in control rather than being controlled by other factors, e.g. biological factors.

Abnormality is due to faulty control, because the individual controls their own thoughts.

 The patient is to blame …

… because the focus is exclusively on events in the patient's mind.

- *E* – The cognitive approach says that the fault lies with the patient – a mental disorder arises because of their faulty thinking, which they take sole responsibility for changing.

 Faulty thinking may be a consequence …

… rather than a cause of psychopathology.

- *E* – Faulty thinking may be a consequence of the mental disorder rather than its main cause. For example, it is possible that an individual develops a negative way of thinking *because* of their disorder.

Support for this approach comes from …

… the success of therapies based on the cognitive approach.

- *E* – They have been shown to be effective in the treatment of a range of different disorders, including panic disorders and depression.

SHOULD know …

Implicit in this approach is the belief that if the patient's thought processes can be changed it will bring about behavioural change.

Abnormality is caused by faulty thinking

For example, an irrational assumption – 'It is awful when things are not the way I want them to be'.

Depression may develop because the person holds an irrational belief about the cause of their failure.

The A-B-C model

An activating event such as an overheard comment from colleagues can lead to an irrational belief that they are talking about you. This leads to an unhealthy consequence of anxiety or depression.

The individual is in control

This implies that recovery from mental illness is only possible by changing the way an individual thinks about events in their life, not by the use of drugs or by looking for repressed conflicts.

- *E* – This is a weakness of the approach because blaming the patient overlooks other factors that are beyond the individual's ability to change.
- *L* – Understanding psychopathology must also include those factors not under the direct control of the individual. For example, the lives of depressed people are usually extremely stressful and deficient in financial and social resources.

- *E* – Lewinsohn *et al.* measured distorted cognitions in a large community sample. They found no difference between those who eventually developed depression and those that did not.
- *L* – This means that it is difficult, if not impossible, to demonstrate that negative thinking is the *cause* of mental disorders such as depression.

- *E* – Studies (e.g. Hollon *et al.*) have shown that people receiving cognitive therapy improve steadily in cognitive functioning over the course of their therapy. They became less pessimistic in their thinking, corresponding to improvements in their depression.
- *L* – This finding supports the claim that thought processes and mental disorders are connected.

COULD know …

Examples of distorted cognition

Arbitrary inference – people draw conclusions without sufficient information.

Magnification and exaggeration – people overestimate the personal significance of negative events.

Personalisation – people relate events to themselves even though there is no basis for such a connection.

Overgeneralisation – people may hold extreme beliefs on the basis of a single incident.

 However, the type of distorted cognition may differ …

… according to the *type* of mental disorder.

- *E* – For example, studies comparing depressed and anxious patients have found that the two types of patient tend to differ in the typical distorted cognitions that they display.
- *E* – Beck *et al.* found that depressed individuals tend to focus on personal inadequacy and worthlessness, while anxious people focus more on perceived future danger.
- *L* – This suggests that distorted cognitions may be specific to different types of mental disorder.

✓ CHOOSE THE RIGHT ANSWER

Which **two** of the following statements apply to the cognitive approach to psychopathology?

A Abnormal behaviour is learned in the same way as normal behaviour. ☐

B Abnormality is caused by distorted thoughts. ☐

C Abnormality is caused by unresolved childhood conflicts. ☐

D Abnormal behaviour is the result of irrational beliefs. ☐

E Abnormality is due to damage in the brain. ☐

Answers on page 198

✏ FILL IN THE BLANKS

The text below is an answer to the following exam question:
Outline the cognitive approach to psychopathology. *(4 marks)*

Mental disorders arise out of (1) .... in the way

that people (2) .... about a situation. This prevents

the individual from behaving in a rational manner. The A-B-C model

explains the connection between A – the (3) ....

event, B – the (4) ...., which may be

(5) .... or (6) ....

C – the (7) ...., which may be

(8) .... or (9) ....

In this approach, abnormality is seen as being due to

(10) .... control, as the individual controls their

own thoughts.

Answers on page 198

APPLYING YOUR KNOWLEDGE

Identify the psychology

Craig is convinced that wherever he goes, people are talking about him, and that whenever something goes wrong it is his fault. This makes him feel so bad he can no longer leave the house or meet friends.

Use your knowledge of the cognitive approach to psychopathology to explain why Craig feels the way he does. *(4 marks)*

Link to Craig

Answers on page 198

KEY PHRASES

Exam question:

Evaluate the cognitive approach to psychopathology. *(4 marks)*

On the facing page there are four evaluative points relating to the cognitive approach. Select **three** of these and then enter **three** key words or phrases for each point in the table below.

Point 1			
Point 2			
Point 3			

Now try to write an answer to the exam question using your key words. Your answer should be about 100 words in length.

KEY WORDS

- Anti-anxiety drugs
- Antidepressant drugs
- Antipsychotic drugs
- Benzodiazepines (BZs)
- Beta-blockers (BBs)
- Dopamine
- GABA
- Neurotransmitter
- Placebo
- Schizophrenia
- Selective serotonin re-uptake inhibitors (SSRIs)
- Synapse
- Tardive dyskinesia

Possible essay questions …

Outline and evaluate **one or more** biological therapies for the treatment of abnormality. *(12 marks)*

Outline and evaluate the use of drugs for the treatment of abnormality. *(12 marks)*

Other possible exam questions …

+ Outline the use of drugs in the treatment of abnormality. *(6 marks)*
+ Evaluate the use of drugs in the treatment of abnormality. *(4 marks)*
+ Apply this knowledge to … *(6 marks)*

MUST know …

Drug treatments target biological processes, such as the functioning of neurotransmitters and hormones.

Antipsychotic drugs

These are used to combat the symptoms of psychotic illnesses such as schizophrenia.

Antipsychotics block the action of dopamine and so alleviate symptoms of schizophrenia.

Antidepressant drugs

These are used to relieve the symptoms of mood disorders such as depression.

SSRIs prolong the action of serotonin at the synapse, relieving the symptoms of depression.

Anti-anxiety drugs

Benzodiazepines (BZs) enhance activity of GABA, the body's natural method of reducing anxiety.

Beta-blockers (BBs) lower the activity of the sympathetic nervous system and thus decrease anxiety levels.

 Drug therapies are effective …

… in the treatment of mental disorders.

- **E** – Research shows that drugs are an effective means of treating the symptoms of mental disorders such as schizophrenia and permitting sufferers to lead a normal life.

 Drugs are easy to use …

… compared to more time-consuming psychological treatments such as stress inoculation.

- **E** – Drug treatments require little effort from the patient, who does not have to do any thinking or spend hours attending therapy. For this reason many patients opt for drug treatment.

 Drugs have side effects …

… which interferes with the effectiveness of treatment.

- **E** – For example, SSRI antidepressants may cause anxiety, sexual dysfunction, nausea and even suicidal thoughts.

SHOULD know …

Drug treatments work on the assumption that if the causes of abnormality are biological then treatments should also be biological.

Antipsychotic drugs

Conventional antipsychotics bind to dopamine receptors without stimulating them.

Atypical antipsychotics temporarily bind to receptors allowing for normal dopamine transmission.

Antidepressant drugs

Antidepressants work either by reducing the rate of re-absorption of a neurotransmitter or blocking the enzyme that breaks down neurotransmitters in the synapse.

Anti-anxiety drugs

GABA causes changes within neurons in the brain making it harder for them to be stimulated.

BBs cause the heart to beat more slowly and blood pressure to drop, making the person feel less anxious as a result.

- **E** – For example, a WHO report (2001) found that antipsychotics were more effective than a placebo in treating schizophrenia.
- **L** – This suggests that drugs play an important role in the treatment of mental disorders, although treatment with drugs alone is less effective than drugs combined with psychological support.

- **E** – However, in reality, many clinicians advocate a mixture of drug treatments and some form of psychotherapy or community support.
- **L** – As a result, the patient is more likely to be motivated to continue treatment, which is then more likely to be effective.

- **E** – Antipsychotics also have worrying side effects, including tardive dyskinesia, which is characterised by involuntary bodily movements. This is found in 30% of patients taking antipsychotics.
- **L** – This problem is one of the main reasons why drug treatments do not work for all people, they simply decide not to take their medication because they can no longer tolerate the side effects.

COULD know …

Placebo effects

Drugs appear to have a psychological as well as a chemical effect, which contributes to their overall effectiveness.

Because doctors do not generally prescribe placebos, they have no way of comparing effects of the drugs to placebos.

Kirsch argues it is important to know if placebos work because if they do, improvement would be possible without reliance on drugs with potentially serious side effects.

 There is research support for the placebo effect …

… from a review of 38 studies of antidepressants.

- **E** – For example, Kirsch *et al.* found that patients who received placebos fared almost as well as those who received the real antidepressant drugs.
- **E** – However, other studies have found stronger effects for the real drugs. Mulrow *et al.* found a 60% success rate for antidepressants, 35% for the placebo.
- **L** – This suggests that for antidepressants, a proportion of their beneficial effects may be psychological.

CHOOSE THE RIGHT ANSWER

Which **three** of the following statements apply to drug treatments of psychopathology?

A Drug treatments focus on distorted thought processes. ☐

B Drug treatments target the underlying psychological causes of anxiety. ☐

C Drug treatments target neurotransmitters and hormones. ☐

D Drug treatments frequently suffer from side effects. ☐

E Drug treatments are easier to use than psychological therapies. ☐

Answers on page 198

 APPLYING YOUR KNOWLEDGE

Lydia has a fear of flying but her friend Freya has persuaded her to take a gap year and travel round the world together. As the time to depart gets closer, Lydia's anxiety about having to fly gets worse. She goes to see her GP, who gives her a drug prescription to deal with her anxiety.

Explain **one** strength and **one** limitation of this type of treatment for Lydia.

Strength:

Limitation:

Answers on page 198

 CIRCLE TRUE OR FALSE

T or F Antipsychotics are used in the treatment of depression and other mood disorders.

T or F Anti-anxiety drugs typically work by increasing activity in the nervous system.

T or F SSRIs prolong the action of serotonin in the synapse.

T or F Beta-blockers work by enhancing the action of GABA, the body's natural form of anxiety relief.

T or F Conventional antipsychotics bind to dopamine receptors, but do not stimulate them.

T or F Benzodiazepines reduce the activity of the sympathetic nervous system.

Answers on page 198

 MATCH THEM UP

Match up the drugs and the descriptions in the table below.

1	Antipsychotics	**A**	Reduce heart rate and blood pressure.
2	Antidepressants	**B**	Allow normal levels of dopamine transmission.
3	Anti-anxiety drugs	**C**	Reduce the reabsorption of serotonin at the synapse.
4	Conventional antipsychotics	**D**	Cause changes within neurons making them harder to stimulate.
5	Atypical antipsychotics	**E**	Make the person feel calmer.
6	SSRIs	**F**	Are used to treat disorders such as schizophrenia.
7	Benzodiazepines	**G**	Block dopamine receptors.
8	Beta-blockers	**H**	Are used to treat mood disorders.

Answers on page 198

 RESEARCH ISSUES

Researchers want to assess the effectiveness of a new type of antidepressant drug. They decide the best way of doing this is to test the drug (drug 1) against an existing drug of known effectiveness (drug 2) and also against a placebo, a tablet with no active constituent.

They ask for recruits from the university who would like help with their 'low mood'. They assess nearly 200 volunteers and select 20 for each of the three groups. These are randomly allocated into the three treatment conditions. They are then tested again after three months of taking the 'drug'.

Explain **one** ethical issue relevant to this study.

Answers on page 198

DRAWING CONCLUSIONS

	Mean severity of symptoms (%)	Mean severity score after three months
Drug 1	70	58
Drug 2	70	37
Placebo	70	56

State **two** findings and for each one draw a conclusion (state what the findings show):

Finding 1:

Conclusion 1: This shows that …

Finding 2:

Conclusion 2: This shows that …

Answers on page 198

KEY WORDS

- Cognitive impairment
- Depression
- Electroconvulsive therapy (ECT)
- Placebo
- Randomised controlled trials (RCTs)
- Schizophrenia
- Sham ECT

Possible essay question …

Outline and evaluate the use of ECT for the treatment of abnormality. *(12 marks)*

Other possible exam questions …

+ Outline how ECT (electroconvulsive therapy) is used to treat abnormality. *(4 marks)*
+ Evaluate the use of ECT in the treatment of abnormality. *(4 marks)*
+ Apply this knowledge to … *(6 marks)*

MUST know …

ECT is generally used for severely depressed patients for whom psychotherapy and drug treatments have proved ineffective.

How does it work?

ECT consists of passing an electrical current through the brain to produce a seizure.

A small amount of electric current, lasting about 0.5 seconds, is passed through the brain.

This produces a seizure, which lasts up to one minute and affects the whole brain.

The strength of current needed to produce a seizure varies from person to person.

Why does it work?

Neurotransmitter theory – ECT works by causing the release of neurotransmitters in the brain, which in turn reduces the symptoms of depression.

ECT releases neurotransmitters such as serotonin in a way similar to antidepressants, but ECT is much more powerful than antidepressants.

 ECT is effective …

… in the treatment of depression.

- *E* – Leiknes *et al.* reviewed data from 90 randomised controlled trials (RCTs). These showed that 'real' ECT was superior to 'sham' ECT and that ECT had greater benefits than antidepressants.

 ECT saves lives …

… in people whose depression is thought to be life-threatening.

- *E* – ECT can be an effective treatment, particularly in cases of severe depression that could lead to suicide.

 ECT has side effects …

… that cause considerable distress to patients.

- *E* – There is evidence that cognitive impairment (e.g. impaired memory) occurs after ECT. A DoH report found that 30% of people who had ECT claimed that it left them with fear and anxiety.

SHOULD know …

ECT can also be used in the treatment of some subgroups of schizophrenia, particularly those who are resistant to antipsychotic drugs.

How does it work?

ECT is delivered either unilaterally (electrode on temple of non-dominant side of the brain) or bilaterally (one electrode on each temple).

Unconscious patient is given a nerve-blocking agent to paralyse muscles during treatment.

ECT is usually given three times a week, with the patient requiring 3–15 treatments.

If the dose is too low there is no benefit, but with higher doses, the risk of side effects is greater.

Why does it work?

Anti-convulsant theory – seizures teach the brain to try to resist them. This dampens abnormally active brain circuits, which then stabilises mood.

Brain damage theory – the seizures damage the brain, causing memory loss and disorientation that creates the illusion that problems are gone.

- *E* – Rose *et al.* analysed studies of patients' experiences of ECT. The proportion of people who had found ECT to have been helpful ranged from 30 to 80%.
- *L* – However, studies that reported lower satisfaction levels were more likely to have been conducted by patients, those reporting higher satisfaction levels were more likely to have been carried out by doctors.

- *E* – Brådvik and Berglund analysed cases of patients with severe depression. They found suicide attempts were less common in patients who received ECT compared to those who had antidepressants without ECT.
- *L* – Because of this life-saving effect, the overall benefits would be considered greater than the risks.

- *E* – Leiknes *et al.* found that cognitive impairments were greater in individuals who received bilateral ECT than those who received unilateral ECT.
- *L* – Although the risk of cognitive impairment is significant in ECT, a reduction in the risk of side effects (i.e. by lowering the dose of ECT) also means a reduction in the effectiveness of treatment.

COULD know …

Placebo effect

The dramatic nature of ECT and the care received makes patients feel they are being taken seriously, i.e. ECT works because of the placebo effect.

Studies have compared standard ECT with 'sham' or placebo ECT. In placebo ECT, the patient has the same things done to them but no electrical current is given and there is no seizure. Patients who received real ECT were much more likely to recover than those receiving the placebo treatment.

 The placebo explanation has some support …

… although other studies suggest it is less important.

- *E* – Reed and Bentall found that ECT was only slightly more effective than a placebo and this difference disappeared after the treatment period was over.
- *E* – But Pagnin *et al.*'s meta-analysis of studies of ECT found a significant superiority for ECT versus placebo.
- *L* – However, the fact that some patients also recover after receiving placebo ECT suggests that attention from others during the therapy also plays a part in recovery, i.e. a *psychological* factor.

MATCH THEM UP

Match up the statements about ECT in the table below.

1	ECT	**A**	Electrodes on both sides of the brain.
2	Nerve blocking agent	**B**	For up to one minute.
3	Unilateral ECT	**C**	There is little benefit.
4	Bilateral ECT	**D**	For about 0.5 seconds.
5	Electrical current passed through brain	**E**	Are more likely to produce side effects.
6	The seizure lasts	**F**	Paralyses muscles during treatment.
7	With low doses	**G**	Electrodes on one side of the brain only.
8	High doses of ECT	**H**	Stands for electroconvulsive therapy.

Answers on page 199

 APPLYING YOUR KNOWLEDGE

You are employed by a local hospital to write a leaflet explaining about ECT for patients.

In about 100–150 words, and using non-technical language, explain what is involved in ECT, and what potential problems there may be for patients receiving this treatment.

CIRCLE TRUE OR FALSE

T or F ECT is mostly used in the treatment of severe depression.

T or F A small amount of current, lasting about five seconds, is passed through the brain.

T or F The electrical current is the aspect of ECT that has the main therapeutic benefit.

T or F In unilateral ECT, an electrode is attached to the temple on the dominant side of the brain.

T or F ECT is only used for patients for whom drug treatments have been effective.

T or F ECT is thought to be more powerful than antidepressants in its action.

Answers on page 199

 JUMBLED SENTENCES

On the facing page there is a description of how ECT is used. Similar sentences are presented below in a jumbled order. Place the number for each sentence in the correct square.

5	**1**	This causes a seizure, which affects the whole brain.
	2	A small amount of electrical current is then passed through the brain.
	3	A nerve-blocking agent is given to paralyse muscles to prevent injury.
	4	This is repeated for 3–15 treatments.
	5	The patient is given an anaesthetic so they are unconscious prior to treatment.
	6	Electrodes are attached to both temples or to just one temple (unilateral ECT).

Answers on page 199

DRAWING CONCLUSIONS

A researcher carried out a review of studies that had looked into the effectiveness of ECT at different levels of intensity in the treatment of severe depression. He noticed that studies reported a fairly wide range of shock levels (ranging from 35 to 225 millicoulombs). He converted the findings of each study into a rating scale where 100 meant no improvement at all after ECT and 0 meant a total absence of symptoms following treatment.

Each of the studies used in the review had also carried out a one-year follow-up where psychologists had interviewed the patients prior to treatment and again 12 months after treatment to assess the degree of cognitive impairment one year after ECT. This was also rated from 0–100, with 100 representing almost complete impairment and 0 representing no impairment after ECT.

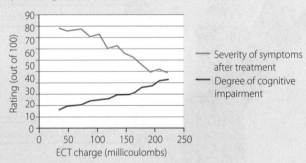

The above graph summarises the findings of this study. State **two** findings and for each one draw a conclusion (state what the findings show).

Finding 1:

Conclusion 1: This shows that …

Finding 2:

Conclusion 2: This shows that …

Answers on page 199

Key Words

- Cultural bias
- False memories
- Psychoanalysis
- Psychotherapy
- Repression
- Transference
- Unconscious

Possible essay question ...

Outline and evaluate psychoanalysis as a treatment for abnormal behaviour. *(12 marks)*

Other possible exam questions ...

+ Outline what is involved in psychoanalysis. *(4 marks)*
+ Outline **two** techniques used in psychoanalysis. *(4 marks)*
+ Evaluate psychoanalysis as a therapy *(6 marks)*
+ Apply this knowledge to ... *(6 marks)*

MUST know ...

Psychoanalysis aims to make the unconscious conscious and find the causes of a person's abnormal behaviour.

Repression and the unconscious mind

Many of the factors that cause behaviour operate at an unconscious level.

These are the result of repressed memories or unresolved conflicts from childhood.

The therapist traces these influences back to their origins and helps the individual to deal with them.

How does it work?

Free association – the patient expresses thoughts exactly as they occur, even though they may appear unimportant to them.

Therapist interpretation – the therapist draws tentative conclusions about the possible causes of the problem.

Working through – patient and therapist examine the same issues over and over again to gain greater clarity concerning the causes of their behaviour.

EVALUATION — There is research support ...

... for the effectiveness of psychoanalysis in the treatment of abnormal behaviour.

- *E* – DeMaat *et al.* carried out a review of studies and concluded that psychoanalysis produced significant improvements in symptoms that were maintained in the years after treatment.

EVALUATION — Psychoanalysis is culturally biased ...

... against people from non-Western cultures.

- *E* – Sue and Sue argue that members of Asian cultures tend to discuss intimate matters only with family and close acquaintances rather than with strangers (e.g. the therapist).

EVALUATION — The issue of false memories ...

... challenges the idea that what is recovered during therapy are *real* memories.

- *E* – Critics claim some therapists are not helping patients recover *repressed* memories but are unwittingly planting false memories, e.g. of sexual abuse.

SHOULD know ...

Individuals are generally unaware of many of the factors that influence their behaviour, some of which originate in the unconscious.

Repression and the unconscious mind

The therapist helps the patient to experience aspects of their inner life that were hidden because they are painful or guilt provoking.

Patients may experience the stress of insight as painful or embarrassing memories are brought into the conscious mind.

How does it work?

Free association reveals areas of conflict and brings repressed memories into consciousness.

Patients may offer resistance to the therapist's interpretations or display transference, where they recreate feelings associated with the problem and transfer them onto the therapist.

Working through is the process that produces the greatest changes in the patient, and is a distinguishing feature of psychoanalysis.

- *E* – Cogan and Porcerelli compared patients at the beginning of psychoanalysis with those at the end. The latter group had significantly lower scores for depression, anxiety, etc. *and* higher scores for strengths such as enjoyment of challenges and life satisfaction.
- *L* – This supports the effectiveness of psychoanalysis because it led to a decrease in negative and an increase in positive outcomes.

- *E* – Many cultural groups do not value insight in the same way that Western cultures do. In China, a person who is depressed or anxious avoids thoughts that cause distress rather than being willing to discuss them openly.
- *L* – This contrasts with the Western belief that open discussion and insight are always helpful in therapy.

- *E* – Research by Loftus has shown that it is possible to induce false memories through suggestion, and that these memories can become stronger and more vivid over time.
- *L* – Psychoanalysis assumes that patients are able to accurately recall memories that have been repressed. However, there is little evidence to support this.

COULD know ...

Longer treatment is better treatment

Research (e.g. Sandell *et al.*) has shown the benefits of long-term psychotherapeutic treatment generally.

Because the process of gaining insight and working through requires time, psychoanalysis tends to be a relatively long-term treatment.

As a result of this lengthy process, the patient's character is believed to develop toward greater maturity so they no longer 'need' their abnormal symptoms to handle their conflicts.

EVALUATION — There is supporting evidence for ...

... the greater benefits offered by long-term treatment.

- *E* – Tschuschke *et al.* found that psychodynamic therapies such as psychoanalysis were more effective in the long term.
- *E* – Wilczek *et al.* compared patients selected for long-term psychoanalytic therapy (mean = three years) with a control group who did not receive therapy. Those patients who completed their therapy showed a significant reduction in symptoms compared to those who did not engage in therapy.
- *L* – This supports the claim that long-term psychoanalytic treatment produces more favourable outcomes for patients.

SPOT THE MISTAKES

Read this student answer to the following exam question:

Outline what is involved in psychoanalysis. *(6 marks)*

There are six mistakes, draw a circle round each.

> In psychoanalysis, the therapist attempts to bring regressed thoughts and feelings into the unconscious mind where they can be dealt with in a supportive environment. In order to achieve this, the therapist may use the cognitive interview. In this technique, the client says the first relevant thing that comes into their mind. The therapist then offers an interpretation of the client's behaviour. The client may show resistance to this interpretation by changing the subject or transferring emotions onto the therapist. This is known as working through. Finally, the therapist and client go over the cause of their problems many times until the client experiences transference, and is able to deal with them more constructively.

Answers on page 199

DRAWING CONCLUSIONS

A researcher looked at the effectiveness of treatment in two groups of patients suffering from symptoms of depression.

One group received psychoanalytic therapy and the other group received cognitive behavioural therapy, both over a two-year period. These two groups were compared to a control group of patients who received no treatment over the same two-year period.

The graph below shows the percentage of patients who reported a 'significant improvement' in their depressive symptoms at three months, six months and one year.

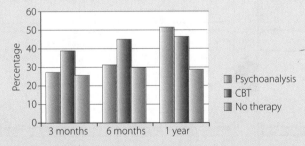

State **two** findings and for each one draw a conclusion (state what the findings show).

Finding 1:
Conclusion 1: This shows that ...
Finding 2:
Conclusion 2: This shows that ...

Answers on page 199

FILL IN THE BLANKS

To help prepare an answer to the exam question 'What is involved in psychoanalysis?', fill in the table below.

Component	Description
Free association	
Therapist interpretation	
Working through	

WRITE YOUR OWN EVALUATION POINT

Using the material on the facing page, write an evaluative point in your own words, underling the key words.

See page 14 for an explanation of how to SEEL.

S	
E	
E	
L	

KEY WORDS

- Aerophobia
- Agoraphobia
- Anxiety
- Aquaphobia
- Arachnophobia
- Counterconditioning
- Desensitisation hierarchy
- Modelling
- Phobia
- Relaxation
- Self-efficacy
- Systematic desensitisation (SD)

Possible essay question ...

Outline and evaluate systematic desensitisation as a treatment for abnormal behaviour.
(12 marks)

Other possible exam questions ...

+ Outline what is involved in systematic desensitisation.
(6 marks)

+ Evaluate the use of systematic desensitisation as a treatment for abnormal behaviour.
(4 marks)

+ Apply this knowledge to ...
(6 marks)

MUST know ...

Systematic desensitisation (SD) is used in the treatment of anxiety associated with phobias.

How does it work?

The patient is taught how to relax, and then works through their desensitisation hierarchy, with the aim of being able to relax and therefore reduce their anxiety at each stage.

Responses of relaxation and fear are incompatible and so the fear is gradually dispelled.

Step 1: Patient is taught how to relax their muscles completely.

Step 2: Therapist and patient together construct a desensitisation hierarchy – a series of imagined scenes, each one causing a little more anxiety than the previous one.

Step 3: Patient gradually works his/her way through desensitisation hierarchy, visualising each anxiety-evoking event while engaging in the competing relaxation response.

Step 4: Once the patient has mastered one step in the hierarchy (i.e. they can remain relaxed while imagining it), they are ready to move onto the next.

Step 5: Patient eventually masters the feared situation that caused them to seek help in the first place.

 ### SD is relatively quick ...

... and requires less effort on the patient's part compared to other psychological therapies.

- **E** – As a result, patients are more likely to persevere, making treatment more likely to succeed.

 ### SD is effective ...

... for a range of anxiety disorders.

- **E** – McGrath *et al.* estimate that SD is effective in about 75% of patients with specific phobias (such as arachnophobia), although it was less effective with social phobias such as agoraphobia.

SHOULD know ...

There are three main components to SD:

- *Relaxation training* – patients are taught how to relax, usually with a muscle relaxation method.
- *Desensitisation hierarchy* – stimuli are ordered according to the amount of anxiety they elicit.
- *Counterconditioning* – each item on the hierarchy is presented repeatedly while the person relaxes until it no longer elicits anxiety.

SD in action

Several means of confronting the feared situation can be used in SD. These include:

- *'In vitro' exposure* – exposure is through imagination and visualisation of the feared situation (e.g. imagining handling a spider).
- *'In vivo' exposure* – exposure involves actual encounters with the feared situation rather than just visualising it (e.g. handling a spider).
- *Modelling* – exposure is vicarious, i.e. the patient observes someone else undergoing SD treatment for the same phobia.

 ### In vivo exposure is the most effective ...

- **E** – Egan found 'in vivo' to be significantly more effective than 'in vitro' in the treatment of aquaphobia.
- **E** – Öst *et al.* found that 'in vivo' exposure produced significantly better than modelling in the treatment of arachnophobia.
- **L** – This shows that 'in vivo' desensitisation is more effective in the treatment of phobias than other forms of exposure.

- **E** – SD can also be self-administered using computer simulations. For example, Chandler *et al.* found that a computer-delivered SD programme was effective in the treatment of agoraphobics.
- **L** – This has the potential to make delivery of SD even more efficient for the patient.

- **E** – Capafons *et al.* found that people with aerophobia had less anxiety after SD treatment compared to a control group and showed lower physiological signs of fear during a flight simulation.
- **L** – This shows that SD is useful for a number of different problems, particularly those that have anxiety as their main symptom.

COULD know ...

Alternative views of why SD works

The cognitive view suggests that gradual exposure to the feared situation is helpful because it presents the individual with information that disconfirms the irrational beliefs which cause their anxiety.

The 'self-efficacy' explanation proposes that SD is effective because it promotes a sense of confidence in the individual that they can cope with the situation rather than being overwhelmed by it.

SD is not universally effective ...

... for phobias that have an adaptive basis.

- **E** – SD appears to be less effective in treating phobias that have an underlying adaptive component (e.g. fear of dangerous animals) than those acquired as a result of personal experience (e.g. fear of public speaking).
- **E** – The reason for this difference is most probably that these 'ancient fears' helped our ancestors to survive.
- **L** – As a result, these phobias are harder to remove, despite the fact they have less relevance for modern humans.

✏️ FILL IN THE BLANKS

Before systematic desensitisation can begin, the patient must

first be taught how to (1) .... This is usually

achieved using the technique of (2) ....

.... The next stage involves the therapist and

client together working out a desensitisation

(3) .... with stimuli that would elicit the

(4) .... anxiety ranked at the bottom and those

that would elicit the (5) .... anxiety at the top.

The patient may simply work their way through the hierarchy

while visualising the stimuli, known as (6) ....

exposure or by actually experiencing them in real life, i.e.

(7) .... exposure. When the patient can stay

(8) .... while imagining (or experiencing) a

particular stimulus, they move on to the next level in the hierarchy.

Answers on page 199

✔️ A MARKING EXERCISE

Read the student answer below to the following question:

Evaluate the use of systematic desensitisation as a treatment for abnormal behaviour. *(4 marks)*

Sophia's answer

Systematic desensitisation is based on the behavioural model of abnormality. An advantage of systematic desensitisation is that it can be used to reduce anxiety in people with different types of phobia. It is also quick and relatively easy to carry out, which means it is popular with patients. A final advantage is that it is effective in that it has been shown to help reduce anxiety in a range of different phobias, including arachnophobia (fear of spiders). It can do this quite quickly, which is one of the things that makes this such an effective form of treatment.

TASK 1

What mark do you think this answer would get? _____ out of 4 marks

---

TASK 2 Your turn

Write an improved answer here:

Answers on page 199

✔️✗ CIRCLE TRUE OR FALSE

T or F SD works on the basis that fear and relaxation are compatible emotions.

T or F 'In vivo' exposure involves visualising the feared situation.

T or F SD may also be achieved using vicarious exposure to the feared situation.

T or F Desensitisation hierarchy presents the most feared situation first, working toward the least feared.

T or F Each item in the desensitisation hierarchy is presented once only.

T or F Relaxtion training must take place before the first step of the desensitisation hierarchy.

Answers on page 199

⚙️ APPLYING YOUR KNOWLEDGE

Constructing a desensitisation hierarchy

Write down hierarchies for the two behaviours below. For each of these behaviours, begin at 1 (a situation that could be performed comfortably) and progress, in realistic and small steps, up to 10 (a situation causing the greatest anxiety).

Hierarchy 1

Target behaviour – anxiety when interacting with members of the opposite sex.

1	
2	
3	
4	
5	
6	
7	
8	
9	
10	

Hierarchy 2

Target behaviour – fear of flying.

1	
2	
3	
4	
5	
6	
7	
8	
9	
10	

Answers on page 199

KEY WORDS

- A-B-C model
- Cognitive behavioural therapy (CBT)
- Dodo bird effect
- Irrational thoughts
- Rational-emotive behaviour therapy (REBT)

Possible essay question ...

Outline and evaluate cognitive behavioural therapy as a treatment for abnormal behaviour. *(12 marks)*

Other possible exam questions ...

+ Outline what is involved in cognitive behavioural therapy. *(6 marks)*
+ Evaluate the use of cognitive behavioural therapy as a treatment for abnormal behaviour. *(4 marks)*
+ Apply this knowledge to ... *(6 marks)*

MUST know ...

Cognitive behavioural therapies such as REBT (rational emotive behaviour therapy) are based on the idea that many problems result from irrational thinking, which can be changed during therapy.

How does REBT work?

Irrational beliefs about activating events have unhealthy consequences (the A-B-C model).

REBT tries to change irrational beliefs into rational beliefs and so healthy consequences.

Negative event (A)	Negative event (A)
↓	↓
Rational belief (B)	Irrational belief (B)
↓	↓
Healthy emotion (C)	Unhealthy emotion (C)

During therapy, the patient is encouraged to dispute their irrational (self-defeating) beliefs.

They are then able to move to a more rational interpretation of events.

This leads to a healthier emotional state and more positive behaviours.

 A strength of REBT is ...

... its usefulness is not limited to people suffering from mental disorders.

- **E** – It is also useful for many non-clinical populations (e.g. students suffering from examination anxiety).

 REBT is effective ...

... in the treatment of different disorders.

- **E** – In a meta-analysis by Engels *et al.*, REBT was shown to be effective in treating different disorders, including OCD and agoraphobia.

REBT's influence may be limited ...

... because it cannot change *environments*.

- **E** – REBT fails to address the issue that the irrational environments in which clients exist (at home and at work) continue beyond the therapy.

SHOULD know ...

What is the aim of REBT?

REBT helps the client understand the irrationality of their thinking and the consequences of thinking in this way.

Enables them to change self-defeating thoughts (e.g. 'I cannot be happy unless everybody likes me') and as a result become happier and less anxious.

How is this achieved?

Change is achieved through:

- *Logical disputing* – client is shown that their beliefs do not follow logically from the information available.
- *Empirical disputing* – client shown that their beliefs are not consistent with reality.
- *Pragmatic disputing* – client is shown the lack of usefulness of their irrational beliefs.

Disputing (**D**) leads to a more effective (**E**) attitude to life and a new set of feelings (**F**).

This extends the **A-B-C** model by adding **D-E-F** components.

- **E** – REBT is effective even in the absence of an actual therapist. Yoichi *et al.* developed a computer-based counselling programme based on REBT that produced significant decreases in anxiety.
- **L** – This shows that REBT helps people change dysfunctional thoughts and behaviours in both clinical and non-clinical situations.

- **E** – REBT was also effective on 'non-targeted variables', e.g. blood pressure as well as 'targeted variables' such as feelings of anxiety.
- **L** – Because REBT can also influence physiological changes in the individual, this suggests that its effectiveness is not simply due to client compliance.

- **E** – Clients may be in a marriage with a bullying partner or work with an overly critical boss. These environments reinforce dysfunctional thoughts and behaviours within the individual.
- **L** – This shows that irrational thoughts may not always be irrational, in which case it is the environment that needs to change rather than the individual's way of thinking.

COULD know ...

The 'Dodo bird effect'

Luborsky *et al.* reviewed research into different types of psychological therapy, suggesting that, despite the differences in approach, all therapies work equally well.

This has become known as the 'the Dodo Bird Effect', referring to the claim that all therapies are roughly equivalent in their effects.

One explanation for this effect is that most types of psychotherapy (including CBT) share certain core features. These include a theoretical rationale for the therapy, close rapport between therapist and client and shared therapeutic goals.

 There is research evidence ...

... for the Dodo Bird Effect.

- **E** – Wampold *et al.* published a meta-analysis of 200+ studies in which psychological therapies were compared with no treatment.
- **E** – Differences in the treatments' effectiveness were minimal (and all were better than no treatment).
- **L** – Although psychotherapies may be broadly comparable in their effects, effectiveness may depend partly on the kinds of psychological problems that clients are experiencing.

✓ CHOOSE THE RIGHT ANSWER

The following statements refer to psychological therapies.
Select **three** statements that describe the cognitive behavioural approach.

A	Therapy is based upon the A-B-C model.	☐
B	The client visualises the feared situation in a non-threatening environment.	☐
C	Change is brought about by bringing repressed memories into consciousness.	☐
D	Positive change is brought about through the process of disputing.	☐
E	The client overcomes their fears following gradual exposure to the feared situation.	☐
F	The client is helped to change their self-defeating thoughts to more positive ones.	☐

Answers on page 199

⚙ APPLYING YOUR KNOWLEDGE

Jasmine's grandmother, who is originally from Hong Kong, is convinced she is going to be deported because she worries that the authorities will find out she gave the wrong date of birth when she first entered the UK 60 years earlier. She now refuses to leave the house because she thinks people are talking about her impending deportation. Jasmine, who is studying psychology, suggests what her grandmother needs is CBT.

What is meant by cognitive behavioural therapy (CBT)?
Why would it be suitable for Jasmine's grandmother?

Answers on page 199

◎ PRACTICE ELABORATION

On the facing page, there are a number of evaluative points relating to CBT. After reading these points (and without looking back at them), try to expand the three points included in the table below.

Point	Evidence	Conclusion (link back)
A strength of REBT is …		
REBT is effective …		
REBT's influence may be limited …		

💡 RESEARCH ISSUES AND DRAWING CONCLUSIONS

A researcher was recruited by a regional hospital trust who wanted to know the most effective form of treatment for the two most common forms of disorder dealt with by the mental health team – depression and anxiety.

She gathered data from therapists working across the region, representing three forms of therapy, CBT (REBT), psychoanalytic therapy and counselling. After six months of receiving therapy, clients were asked to rate (as a percentage) how much they felt they had improved as a result of receiving therapy (see graph, right). The researcher also interviewed each client in order to gather qualitative data on the effects of their therapy.

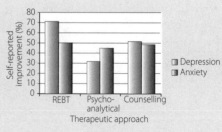

(a) Explain **one** advantage of gaining qualitative data in this study.

(b) Explain **two** factors that, unless they were controlled for, would make it difficult to compare the effectiveness of the different types of therapy in this study.

(c) State **two** findings and for each one draw a conclusion (state what the findings show).

Finding 1:
Conclusion 1: This shows that …
Finding 2:
Conclusion 2: This shows that …

173

MUST | Deviation from social norms

Abnormality = breaking social norms such as ... norms of sexual behaviour or politeness.

Failure to function adequately

I'm not coming out until he stops staring at me

BATH ROOM

Mentally healthy people operate within certain acceptable limits. Anything that interferes with this functioning is labelled as abnormal.

Deviation from ideal mental health

Johoda described criteria for ideal mental health. Absence of these criteria = possible abnormality.

SHOULD

These norms are implicit rules concerning ...

Individuals experience abnormality as ...

As a result they ...

Examples of these criteria are ...

I can't cope anymore · *I don't know who I am* · *I'm rubbish*

COULD | Multiple perspectives

she has an eating disorder · *I'm too fat* · *she's painfully thin*

Doctor   Individual   Society

EVALUATION

Deviation related to context and degree

Judgements of deviation dependent on the context of a behaviour.

Acceptability of a behaviour dependent on the context.

No clear line between a behaviour that is abnormal and harmless eccentricity.

Abnormal behaviours can help a person

They may lead to helpful intervention from others.

E.g. depression may elicit helpful support to overcome stress.

Suggests behaviours that appear abnormal may be adaptive.

Difficult to achieve all the criteria

Suggests everyone is abnormal to some degree.

Unusual to find people who satisfy all criteria all the time.

Need to establish how many need to be absent to be considered abnormal.

There is value in this approach

Doctor   SELF   Society

Overcomes limitations of using just one way of defining abnormality.

This explanation is limited because ...

Defining behaviour as abnormal pointless without considering cultural context.

For example ...

This means that ...

This explanation is limited because ...

'Adequate functioning' determined by culture in which individual lives.

This is likely to produce ...

This explains ...

This explanation is limited because ...

Most criteria apply mainly to people living in Western cultures.

It would be inappropriate to ...

This would lead to ...

TOPIC 51 — The biological approach

MUST — Genetic inheritance

Mental illness inherited via genes. Closely related individuals more likely to develop the same disorders. If MZ more alike than DZ — suggests genetic basis for disorder.

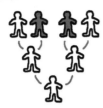

Neuroanatomy Abnormalities in the structure of the brain caused by ageing, disease, etc.

Neurochemistry Altered brain chemistry, e.g. changes in levels or activity of neurotransmitters.

SHOULD — Genetic inheritance

Concordance rates — High ... / Low ...

Some genes for abnormal behaviour are the product of evolutionary adaptations.

Neuroanatomy E.g. some schizophrenics	Neurochemistry E.g. some people with depression
↓	↓
Enlarged vesicles in the brain	Low levels of serotonin in the brain

COULD — Viral infection

I can't come in today. I have the flu

Exposure to viruses in the womb.

EVALUATION

Inconclusive evidence

 →

MZ twins (same genetics) but Only one develops schizophrenia

If genetic inheritance sole cause, then both MZ twins with same genetic potential would develop disorder.

E.g. Gottesman and Shields ...

Diathesis-stress model explains this ...

Cause or consequence

Biological factors → Psychopathology
OR?
Psychopathology → Biological changes

Changes in neuroanatomy might be the consequence rather than the cause of a mental disorder.

For example ...

This suggests that ...

Real-world application

Drugs → NEURO TRANSMITTER → Behaviour

Drugs change neurotransmitter activity which lead to changes in behaviour.

There is evidence ...

This suggests that ...

Interaction of infection and genetics

Gene defect — DNA

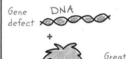

+ VIRUS = Greater likelihood of schizophrenia

TOPIC 52 — The psychodynamic approach

MUST — Early experiences

Early loss   Later loss

Repression of emotions → Re-experience of earlier loss → DEPRESSION

Unconscious motivation

Repressed into unconscious → TRAUMA EMOTIONS FEARS MEMORIES ← Repressed emotions or trauma influence behaviour. This leads to distress. To be controlled they must be brought into conscious awareness.

SHOULD — Childhood conflicts

Conflicts between id, ego, superego create anxiety — can be reduced by defence mechanisms, e.g.:

Repression ...

Regression ...

These become pathological when overused.

Oedipal conflict:
Successful resolution → ....
Lack of resolution → ....

COULD — Misuse of psychological energy

Too little energy on defences = schizophrenia

Too much energy on defences = depression and anxiety

EVALUATION

Lack of research support

DIFFICULT to prove or disprove

Using scientific methodology — support restricted to case studies.

However ...

A major problem for this approach is ...

Key concepts are abstract

Many key concepts are abstract and so they are difficult to demonstrate.

Superego? Ego? ID? Unconscious?

There is no way to know ...

This makes it difficult to ...

Real-life application

Tell me about your early experiences

Psychodynamic treatments as effective as other therapies (Shedler).

They are effective because ...

This offers further support ...

Advantage of this approach

FREUD Rocks!

Psychological causes rather than just biological ...

Psychological treatments ...

Still has explanatory value ...

MUST — Only behaviour is important

Focuses only on abnormal behaviour of individual rather than focusing on cognitive or physical causes.

Abnormal behaviours are learned

No different to how normal behaviour is learned. Learned through classical and operant conditioning and through social learning.

Learning environments

Maladaptive behaviour may be reinforced by others. Means it is sometimes useful for the individual.

SHOULD — Examples

Someone with phobia …

Someone with OCD …

Operant conditioning …

Social learning …

Agoraphobia …

Depression …

COULD — Scientific validation

EVALUATION

Criticised as a limited view

Approach is too limited as it ignores influences of other factors.

These include …

This suggests that …

Counter evidence

E.g. fear of riding in a car; fear of technology

HARD WIRED / LEARNED

E.g. fear of the dark; fear of snakes

The acquisition of some phobias (i.e. 'ancient fears') are not dependent on learning.

These phobias …

This explains why …

Support from success of therapies

ARACHNOPHOBIA LAB

Modelling — Systematic desensitisation

These include modelling and systematic desensitisation (classical conditioning).

However …

Therefore …

An integrated approach better

COMBINES

BEST IDEAS

AND TECHNIQUES

TOPIC 54 — *The cognitive approach*

MUST — Abnormality caused by faulty thinking

Mental disorders arise out of distortions in thinking. Prevents individual acting in rational manner.

The A-B-C model
A - Activating event
B – Belief (rational or irrational)
C – Consequence (healthy or unhealthy)

Individual is in control

Abnormality a product of faulty control (not biological factors), because individual controls their own thoughts.

SHOULD — Changing thought processes brings about behaviour change

Based on irrational assumptions, e.g …

Depression may develop because …

For example:
A …

B …

C …

This implies that recovery from mental illness is only possible if …

COULD — Examples of distorted cognition

Arbitrary influence …

Magnification and exaggeration …

Personalisation …

Overgeneralisation …

EVALUATION

Focuses only on events in person's mind

Bad luck
Financial problems
Situational factors
Biological factors

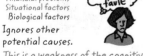

Ignores other potential causes.

This is a weakness of the cognitive approach because …

An understanding of psychopathology therefore requires …

Faulty thinking — cause or consequence of psychopathology?

Faulty thinking

Mental disorder

Faulty thinking may be a cause or the consequence of mental disorder, e.g. as in schizophrenia.

Lewinsohn et al. found …

This means that …

Support based on success of cognitive therapies

Therapies based on the cognitive approach have been shown to be effective for a range of disorders.

SUCCESSFUL THERAPIES SUGGEST A VALID EXPLANATORY APPROACH

E.g. Hollon et al.…

This finding supports the claim that …

Type of distortion differs according to type of disorder

MUST | Drug treatments

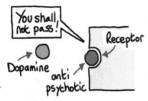

Antipsychotics
Combat symptoms of psychotic illnesses such as schizophrenia. Do this by blocking action of dopamine at receptor sites.

Antidepressants
Relieve symptoms of mood disorders such as depression. SSRIs prolong action of serotonin in synapse.

Anti-anxiety drugs
BZs enhance action of GABA.
BBs lower action of SNS and so decrease anxiety levels.

SHOULD

Antidepressants work by ...

Or by ...

GABA causes changes within neurons which ...

BBs cause changes such as ...

COULD

Drug effects versus placebo effects

EVALUATION

Drug therapies are effective

Antipsychotic drugs → Social support

Effective in treatment of disorders such as schizophrenia.
For example, a WHO report ...

This suggests that ...

Drugs are easy to use

Compared to more time-consuming psychological treatments, require little effort from patient.
However, in reality ...

As a result ...

Drugs have side effects

Side effects can interfere with the effectiveness of the treatment.
E.g. antipsychotics ...

This is one of the main reasons ...

Research support for placebo effect

However ...

This suggests that ...

MUST | How does it work?

Strength of current needed varies from person to person

Small amount of electrical current → Produces seizure

Lasts for 0.5 sec | Lasts for up to 1 min

Why does it work?

Neurotransmitter theory

ECT releases neurotransmitters in similar way to antidepressants but much more powerful.

ECT causes release of neurotransmitters. This reduces symptoms of depression.

SHOULD

Usually given three times a week, 3–15 treatments.

Patient given nerve-blocking agent to paralyse muscles.

Dose too low — no benefit; too high — the risk of side effects is greater.

Anticonvulsant theory ...

Brain damage theory ...

COULD | Placebo effects

ECT + AFTERCARE

SHAM ECT VERSUS **REAL ECT**

EVALUATION

Effective in treating depression

superior to **REAL ECT** greater benefit than
↓
SHAM ECT   **ANTI-DEPRESSANTS**

Leiknes et al. — review found ECT effective in treatment of depression.
Rose et al. ...

However ...

Saves people's lives

... when depression is life-threatening.
Effective form of treatment when severe depression could lead to suicide.
Brådvik and Berglund ...

Because of this life-saving effect ...

Has side effects

ECT
↓
Cognitive ← **SIDE** → Increased
impairment **EFFECTS** fear and anxiety

ECT has side effects that cause distress to patients.
Leiknes et al. ...

However, reducing the risk of side effects means ...

Placebo explanation has some support

ECT VERSUS **PLACEBO**

TOPIC 57 — Psychological therapies: psychoanalysis

MUST | Repression and the unconscious mind

Factors that cause behaviour may operate at an *unconscious* level. E.g. repressed memories and unresolved conflicts from childhood. Therapist traces these to their origins and helps individual deal with them.

How does it work?

Free association
(uncensored thoughts)

Therapist interpretation
(tentative conclusions)

SHOULD | Individuals unaware of unconscious influences

Free association ...

Therapist interpretation ...

Working through ...

COULD | Longer treatment = better treatment

Research has shown ...

As a result ...

EVALUATION

Research support

We reviewed many studies. We concluded that psychoanalysis produces significant improvements.

de Maat et al. ...

Cogan and Porcerelli ...

This supports the effectiveness of psychoanalysis because ...

Culturally biased

TOWARDS WESTERN CULTURES

Sue and Sue — members of Asian cultures do not discuss intimate matters with strangers.

Many cultural groups do not value 'insight' in the same way ...

This contrasts with ...

Recovered memories could be false

Therapists may unwittingly plant false memories during therapy.
Research by Loftus has shown ...

There is little evidence to support the assumption that ...

Supporting evidence for long-term treatment

LONG-TERM PSYCHOANALYTIC THERAPY MORE EFFECTIVE

(TSCHUSCHKE ET AL.)

TOPIC 58 — Psychological therapies: systematic desensitisation (SD)

MUST | How does SD work?

Patient taught to relax

Construction and desensitisation hierarchy

Patient gradually works through hierarchy

Relaxing at each stage allows progression

Patient masters feared situation

SHOULD | Components of SD

Relaxation training ...

Desensitisation hierarchy ...

Counterconditioning ...

SD in action

'In vitro'   'In vivo'   'Modelling'

COULD | Self-efficacy

CONFIDENCE

Darn... she's obviously had SD

EVALUATION

Quick and little effort

PHOBIA? Try SD. Quicker and easier than other therapies.

You are more likely to persevere. Makes SD more likely to succeed!

SD can also be self-administered ...

This has the potential ...

Effective for many disorders

Arachnophobia   Aerophobia

SD effective for specific phobias, less so for social phobias (McGrath et al.).
For example ...

This has the potential ...

In vivo exposure most effective

More so than 'in vitro' and modelling. SD most effective in treatment of arachnophobia and aquaphobia.
E.g. Öst et al. ...

This shows that ...

SD not universally effective

GRRRRR

Less effective for phobias with underlying adaptive component.
This is because ...

As a result ...

MUST	Irrational thinking can be changed during therapy

RATIONAL EMOTIVE BEHAVIOUR THERAPY

Negative event (A)   Negative event (A)

⬇   ⬇

Rational belief (B)   Irrational belief (B)

⬇   ⬇

Healthy emotion (C)   Unhealthy emotion (C)

Therapy attempts to change irrational beliefs into rational beliefs. Irrational beliefs disputed during therapy. Leads to more rational interpretation of events and healthier consequences.

SHOULD	The aim of REBT

REBT helps individual to ...

REBT enables them to change ...

Empirical disputing, e.g. ...

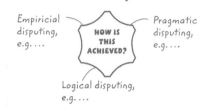

HOW IS THIS ACHIEVED?

Pragmatic disputing, e.g. ...

Logical disputing, e.g. ...

DISPUTING leads to a more EFFECTIVE attitude to life and a new set of FEELINGS.

COULD	The Dodo bird effect

Everyone has won and all must have prizes

EVALUATION

Usefulness not limited to mental disorders

EXAM STRESS

Useful for non-clinical populations, e.g. students with exam anxiety. REBT can even be effective ...

This shows that ...

Effective form of treatment

ENGELS ET AL. META ANALYSIS — EFFECTIVE IN THE TREATMENT — OCD AND AGORAPHOBIA

REBT also effective on ...

This suggests that the effectiveness of REBT is ...

Irrational environments

REBT fails to address the irrational environments that exist beyond therapy.
E.g. clients may have bullying partner or overly-critical boss. As a result ...

This shows that ...

There is research evidence

200 +
STUDIES   Wampold et al.

Compared psychological therapies with no treatment.
They found ...

Effectiveness may depend on ...

Section A Cognitive psychology and research methods

Answer all questions.

1 Psychologists have explained human memory using the multi-store model and the working memory model. Which **two** of the following statements (**A–E**) apply to the working memory model? Tick the **two** correct boxes. *(2 marks)*

A	The model was first proposed in the 1960s.	
B	Verbal rehearsal leads to the creation of long-term memories.	
C	Verbal rehearsal is managed by the articulatory process.	✓
D	There are three separate stores that differ in terms of duration and capacity.	
E	The central executive allocates resources to the other subsystems.	✓

2 (a) Explain what is meant by misleading information. *(2 marks)*

Misleading information refers to information that suggests a particular answer, which therefore might mislead a witness into giving inaccurate information. For example, a question that said 'How fast were the cars travelling when they smashed into each other?' suggests the cars were travelling fast and could lead someone to overestimate the speed of the cars.

2 (b) Outline how **one** research study investigated the effect of misleading questions on the accuracy of eyewitness testimony (EWT). *(4 marks)*

One study was by Loftus and Palmer in the 1970s. They used 45 student participants and showed them films of traffic accidents. Then they asked them some questions about the films. One question was called the critical question and was about how fast the cars were travelling. Each participant was assigned to one of five conditions: some participants had the word 'smashed' ('How fast were the cars travelling when they smashed into each other?') and others had 'hit', 'collided', 'contacted' or 'bumped'.

3 Beth is a keen supporter of her local animal charity, who looks after animals with no homes and tries to find them new ones. She has volunteered to do a school assembly about the charity to try to get more volunteers involved. She can't use any notes so has to remember everything she has to say.

Using your knowledge of psychology, explain **one** suitable method that she might use to help her remember the key points of her talk. *(4 marks)*

She could use the method of loci. In order to use this she would mentally place each item to be remembered along a familiar route, such as walking around her house. For example, her first point might be to tell everyone about the charity, so she would place the symbol for the charity on the fridge door. This would remind her that she should say something about the charity. Her next point might be to talk about the numbers of animals that were saved, so she would put the number in a frying pan on the cooker. The more unusual the association between items and places where they are stored, the more memorable they become.

4 A psychology teacher suggested that her class might conduct a study investigating eyewitness testimony and age. They decided to compare the performance of young adults (age 16–18) with older adults (aged 30–40). In order to test the accuracy of eyewitness testimony, they tested each participant by showing them a video clip of a rather unpleasant accident and then asking them questions to see how much information they could recall. The dependent variable was the number of correct responses given.

4 (a) Write a non-directional hypothesis for this experiment. *(2 marks)*

There is a difference in the number of correct answers given by younger (16–18) and older (30–40) participants.

Examiner's comments

1 This simple recognition task should be straightforward but there are still ways in which mistakes can be made.

The question asks for *two* boxes to be ticked. Ticking more than two would lead to 0 marks.

Although some of these statements may jog your memory you need to make sure they are attributes of the *working memory* model. For example, statement D is familiar only because it is an aspect of the multi-store model.

This answer would get both of the marks available because just the two statements have been ticked and they are both correct.

2 (a) When there are 2 marks available, it is always a good idea to say two distinct things in your answer. This helps the examiner discriminate between a 1 mark answer and a 2 mark answer.

This answer offers a clear and detailed explanation of the nature of misleading information. This is suitably detailed by the inclusion of an example so would get both of the marks available.

2 (b) It is easy to just focus on the headline terms in this question (misleading questions, EWT) and miss the *'how'* instruction and the qualifier *'one'*.

This answer has presented a number of discrete statements about the *procedures* used in this named study and avoided the temptation to include any information about the findings or conclusions of the study. The answer is sufficiently detailed for the full 4 marks.

3 Before answering a question of this type it is important to read the stem carefully (about remembering what she wants to say at a school assembly) *and* the psychology that would be appropriate.

The appropriate psychology would be 'strategies for memory improvement' so there are several possible strategies she could use, although only *one* should be used here.

This answer identifies the method of loci as an appropriate strategy. It goes on to unfold this method within the context suggested by the question stem.

There are two detailed examples of how information relevant to Beth's talk might fit into the method of loci technique and the answer is finished off with a suitable comment about unusualness. This is worth 4 marks.

4 It is wise to read through the study carefully before attempting any of the questions that follow. There is often information in the research study described that will inform your answers to the questions relating to it.

4 (a) There are a number of things to bear in mind for part **(a)** – to state there is 'a difference' in performance between the two conditions, to operationalise the IV and DV and to ensure the hypothesis is *non*-directional rather than directional.

All of these are present in this answer, including operationalisation of the IV (younger and older) and DV (number of correct answers) so the answer would be worth 2 marks.

4 (b) Explain why the students thought it would be a good idea to conduct a pilot study. *(3 marks)*

A pilot study would be a good idea because it is a way of checking whether your procedures will work. For example, it might be that there were too many questions for participants or that some questions were confusing, and these could be changed. It is better to do this with a small group of people before conducting the actual experiment, rather than just conducting the main study and finding out it didn't work very well.

4 (c) Explain why the study used an independent groups design rather than a repeated measures design. *(1 mark)*

In order to compare age they had to use an independent groups design because otherwise you would have to test someone when they are young and then wait about 15 years until they are older to test them again.

4 (d) Explain **one** limitation of using an independent groups design. *(2 marks)*

One limitation is that you don't control participant variables. It might be that the older participants were smarter and had better memories than the younger ones, and that would explain why they did better not because they are older.

4 (e) Identify **one** ethical issue associated with this experiment. Suggest how psychologists could deal with this ethical issue. *(3 marks)*

One ethical issue is deception because the participants would probably not be told that beforehand that they had to recall elements of the video clip. This can be dealt with by debriefing the participants at the end of the study and telling them the true aims (to investigate eyewitness testimony). They could also be offered the chance to withhold their data if they have been offended by the deception.

5 'The cognitive interview is used a means of improving the accuracy of eyewitness testimony.'

Describe and evaluate the use of the cognitive interview. *(12 marks)*

The first feature of the cognitive interview (CI) is 'report everything', where an eyewitness is asked to include every single detail they remember about the event. This should lead eyewitnesses to recall a lot more information especially details that they may have otherwise omitted because they seemed unimportant.

The second feature is 'mental reinstatement of original context', where the eyewitness tries to recreate the original scene in their own mind and imagine they are there again. Aspects of the original scene are encoded with the memories, so revisiting the scene triggers these memories.

The third feature is 'changing the order', where the eyewitness tries to recall things in different orders. By varying the route through memory this stops the witness predicting what might have happened next, so their memory is not affected by expectations.

The fourth feature is 'changing the perspective', trying to recall what happened by imagining how other witnesses might have viewed the scene. This builds up extra detail because of the multiple perspectives taken.

One way to evaluate this technique is to consider its effectiveness. Köhnken et al. conducted a meta-analysis of 53 studies that used the CI. They found a 34% increase in correct recall using CI compared with standard interview. This is quite a considerable improvement and supports the value of the CI.

Other research support comes from Milne and Bull. They found that just using one of the CI techniques didn't produce any better results. However, using techniques 1 and 2 together did lead to improved recall. This shows that there may be specific parts of the CI that are more valuable than others.

One problem with these studies is that there are many versions of CI that are used. This means that it is important to look at specific elements of the CI and compare their effectiveness, as Milne and Bull did. It could be that simply spending more time on interviewing is what matters, rather than the particular techniques of the CI.

Despite the apparent value of the CI it has not be adopted by all police forces. One problem is that it is more time consuming than the standard interview (Kebbell and Wagstaff). Also police often do not receive adequate training. Therefore police officers prefer to use their traditional methods.

Total for section = 36 marks

Examiner's comments

4 (b) Note that this question does not ask for a *definition* of a pilot study but an explanation of why one might have been used in this particular study.

For 3 marks it is a good idea to make three distinct points. There are three such points here, all suitably detailed and clearly set within the context of the intended study. It would get the full 3 marks.

4 (c) The answer shows a clear awareness of why the repeated measures design would be inappropriate for this study and so gets the 1 mark available.

4 (d) The answer identifies an appropriate limitation for 1 mark and offers suitable elaboration for the second mark.

4 (e) This question has two distinct requirements. First there is a need to identify one ethical issue in *this* experiment (for 1 mark). For the remaining 2 marks there is a requirement to show how this issue might be overcome.

An appropriate ethical issue is identified within the context of this particular experiment for the first mark. Two ways of dealing with that issue are described in detail for the remaining 2 marks. You could present only one way of dealing with the ethical issue but would need to elaborate this to gain the two available marks.

5 Essay questions such as this will sometimes contain a short piece of text prior to the question itself. It is important to remember that you are answering the *question* rather than the issues in any preceding text.

All questions that begin with 'describe and evaluate' require an answer with equal amounts of AO1 (description) and AO2 (evaluation). One way to ensure an appropriate balance between AO1 and AO2 is to divide your answer into two distinct halves, one AO1 and AO2 and insure that each are of equal length.

For the AO1 content, just a detailed exposition of the four stages would be appropriate. This could include either *how* each component works or *why* it works.

For the AO2 content, approximately four critical points, appropriately elaborated, would be enough to gain full marks.

The four components of the cognitive interview are described accurately and with an appropriate level of detail for each. At 167 words for this AO1 content, there is certainly sufficient detail for 6 marks.

A nice touch is the way the four components of the CI are each given their own paragraph, which also provides a handy visual check of how much detail has been included for each component.

The same neat approach is taken for the AO2 material. Four clear critical points are made and each is appropriately elaborated within its own paragraph.

Each critical point follows the S E E L rule (see page 14), where the critical point is stated, followed by evidence and elaboration and then finally a link back. Each AO2 point is about 50 words.

The AO2 material would also be worth 6 marks.

Overall, this is an answer worth the full 12 marks.

Section B Developmental psychology and research methods

6   Psychologists use the Strange Situation to assess strength of attachment in infants.

6   **(a)**   Outline the use of the Strange Situation. *(4 marks)*

The Strange Situation consists of a number of short episodes involving a parent and their infant child plus a stranger. At the beginning the parent and infant are playing. A stranger then arrives and the parent leaves. This allows the researcher to assess the child's response to the parent's departure (separation anxiety) and also to assess stranger anxiety. The parent returns and therefore greeting behaviour can be assessed. In a later episode the child is left on its own for a while.

6   **(b)**   Outline **one** limitation of the Strange Situation. *(3 marks)*

One limitation is that it may not apply to non-Western children. The Strange Situation was developed in the US and is based on Western assumptions. For example, the assumption that a well-attached child should only be mildly distressed when separated from their parent. This is not true in Japan where children are rarely separated from their parents and therefore become very distressed in the Strange Situation when left by their parent and are classified as insecurely attached when they aren't. This means that the Strange Situation is not a valid measurement of attachment in Japan.

7   **(a)**   Explain the difference between insecure-resistant attachment and insecure-avoidant attachment. *(4 marks)*

One difference is in terms of reunion behaviour. Insecure-resistant children resist the parent on reunion which is an active behaviour whereas as insecure-avoidant children are more passive and just avoid or ignore the parent.

Another difference is in terms of stranger anxiety. Insecure-resistant children become quite distressed when left with a stranger (high stranger anxiety) whereas insecure-avoidant children are again just avoidant or indifferent (low stranger anxiety).

7   **(b)**   Identify **one** other type of attachment. *(1 mark)*

Secure attachment.

8   A psychologist tests the belief that the amount of time a parent spends with a baby is related to security of attachment. In order to conduct this study the psychologist asks parents to estimate how much time both the mother and the father spend with the baby each week. The psychologist then observes each parent with the baby to calculate how securely attached the baby is to the parent.

8   **(a)**   Suggest **two** behaviours the psychologist might observe in order to determine whether the infant has a secure attachment to the parent. *(2 marks)*

Two behaviours could be willingness to explore and the baby's response to cuddles from the parent (to establish whether they are indifferent or resistant or enthusiastic).

8   **(b)**   Apart from ethical issues, identify **one or more** limitations with the design of this study. *(3 marks)*

One limitation might be that the parent might be just reading to the child throughout the observation. This means that you couldn't really assess the interaction between parent and child very well because they were only doing one thing.

Another limitation might be that the observer has certain expectations about which parent might be 'better' and this would influence what they record.

8   **(c)**   The psychologist finds that parents who spent more time with their children have a more secure attachment with that child (on a scale of 1 to 10 where 10 is very securely attached). What kind of correlation is this? *(1 mark)*

This is a positive correlation.

Examiner's comments

6   **(a)**   It is important to write the appropriate amount for the marks available and to include specific details to demonstrate the quality of your knowledge.

The answer on the right has included a good level of detail by explaining how the various episodes are used. The answer does not provide a list of all episodes but instead gives the sense of what is involved. There is clearly 4 marks of material here: it is relevant, accurate and reasonably detailed.

6   **(b)**   Questions on criticisms vary in terms of the marks available – they may be 2 marks or 3 marks or even, occasionally, 4 marks. As always, be prepared to write enough information for the marks available.

Also, when writing a critical point, aim to follow the SEEL rule (see page 14) – state your point, provide plenty of explanation/ elaboration and, where relevant, add a link back at the end.

The answer on the left does all of this and more – and is worth the full 3 marks.

7   **(a)**   There are two key tips for questions on differences. The first key tip is to always start by stating the difference and then demonstrate it.

The second key tip is to use the word 'whereas' to demonstrate the difference.

For 4 marks you probably need to look at two differences. The mark schemes tend to say '1 mark for a very brief or muddled explanation of the difference. Additional marks for further elaboration which makes the difference clear.'

This means you could get all 4 marks by providing an elaboration of one difference; or produce two differences with only some elaboration of each. You would not get full marks for a list of differences with no elaboration.

The answer here is worth 4 marks.

7   **(b)**   This is a 1 mark answer so you simply need to state the attachment type. Other answers that would be creditworthy include disinhibited attachment or disorganised attachment.

8   **(a)**   Any behaviour used in an observational study must be *observable*. The observer needs to be able to look at the infant and decide whether or not the infant is displaying the behaviour.

The behaviour selected must also be related in some way to attachment – most likely related to the Strange Situation.

Both behaviours given here are observable and related to attachment, so the full 2 marks.

8   **(b)**   It is important not to offer criticisms of the Strange Situation here because that is not being assessed. The question aims to assess your understanding of observational research.

A student could get full marks by giving just one limitation as long as there was sufficient elaboration (think of SEEL).

In the answer on the left two limitations are given, each with some elaboration. This is plenty for the 3 available marks.

8   **(c)**   When two variables increase together this is a positive correlation.

9 A Health Centre is planning to prepare a leaflet for prospective parents about how to offer the best care for their babies.

Suggest **two** pieces of advice they might include in this leaflet. Refer to psychological research on attachment in your answer. *(4 marks)*

One piece of advice would be that babies need to form an attachment by the time they are six months old. This period is very important for later development. Research by Rutter with Romanian orphans found that those adopted before the age of six months developed normally but the same was not true for those adopted later.

A second piece of advice would be that physical separation from a child's mother or father is not a problem as long as good substitute emotional care can be provided. The Robertsons showed this in their research where they looked after children who were separated from their mothers for a brief period. The children seemed very content and greeted their mothers enthusiastically when reunited.

10 Research on the effects of institutional care has looked at the behaviour of ex-institutional children later in their life. One study used in-depth interviews with a group of adults who had experienced institutional care for more than one year early in their lives.

10 (a) Write **one** suitable question which could be used in the interview to produce quantitative data. *(2 marks)*

How many years of your life were spent in institutional care?

10 (b) Explain **one** strength of using quantitative data rather than qualitative data. *(2 marks)*

Quantitative data is easier to analyse because you can show the data in a graph and calculate the mean etc. You can't summarise and analyse qualitative data in the same way.

10 (c) Explain why it might be preferable to use a questionnaire rather than an interview to collect data in this study. *(2 marks)*

Some people feel they can be more honest when answering a questionnaire because in an interview someone is listening as you speak and this might make you feel more embarrassed or ashamed.

11 Outline and evaluate research into the effects of day care on peer relations. *(8 marks)*

One study was the EPPE study, a longitudinal study conducted in the UK with over 3,000 children from the age of 3 to 11. The children attended a wide range of day care providers (e.g. attached to a school or not, low and high quality) and were compared with home-cared children. They found that pre-school day care was associated with improved social behaviour, e.g. independence, cooperation and peer relationships. The earlier the start in pre-school the more sociability was improved.

One criticism of this study is that such conclusions ignore individual differences. Some children feel more uncomfortable or distressed to be in the day care situation, away from home and with many other children. For example, shy children may find it overwhelming (Pennebaker et al.) and insecurely attached children may be more distressed (NICHD). This means that day care may not promote peer relations for all children.

Clarke-Stewart et al. studied 150 American children aged 2–4 years either in day care centres or home care (with mother or carer). They found that the day care children were better at negotiating with peers and settling disputes (both important for good peer relations). This suggests that day care provides opportunities to practise social skills.

However, day care may sometimes have negative effects on peer relations. Clarke-Stewart et al. found that when there were too many children (more than 20) the effects could be harmful. Children in large classes spent more time being aggressive and less time socialising. This shows that interacting with peers is not always beneficial to peer relations.

Total for section = 36 marks

Section A Biological psychology

1 Outline the pituitary-adrenal system. *(3 marks)*
  - *Activation of hypothalamus leads to release of CRF into the bloodstream.*
  - *CRF causes pituitary gland to release ACTH – transported to adrenal cortex.*
  - *Activation of adrenal cortex leads to release of the hormone cortisol.*

2 The scattergram below shows the relationship between stress and daily hassles.

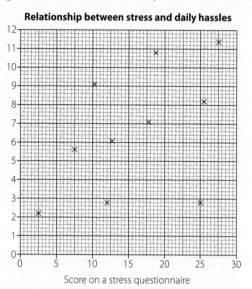

Relationship between stress and daily hassles

Score on a stress questionnaire

2 (a) What does the scattergram tell you about the relationship between stress and daily hassles. *(4 marks)*

There appears to be a positive correlation between the two variables.

This suggests that the more daily hassles a person experiences the more stress they experience.

However it is not a very strong correlation.

This means that you could conclude that daily hassles are unlikely to have that much of an effect on stress levels.

2 (b) How many people are represented in this scattergram? *(1 mark)*

Ten people.

3 Drug therapies are used as a form of stress management. Evaluate the use of drugs as a form of stress management. *(4 marks)*

Drugs are effective in combating the effects of stress. For example, Kahn et al. found that BZs were superior to a placebo in reducing the effects of patients' stress over an eight-week period. Other research shows that beta-blockers reduce anxiety and thus are an effective form of stress management.

Drugs are easy to use compared to other forms of treatment. Drug treatments require little effort from the patient compared to the significant investment in time and motivation required in psychological methods, e.g. stress inoculation. The relative ease of use of drug treatments means that people are more likely to continue with treatment. This increases the effectiveness of drugs as stress management.

Examiner's comments

1 It is perfectly acceptable to present your answer in bullet form as long as each bullet point contains sufficient detail. A diagram also would have been a good way to present this information – again, as long as enough information is included.

It is also acceptable (and creditworthy) to use common abbreviations such as CRF without spelling them out.

This answer would gain the full 3 marks because it is accurate and detailed and covers the key points.

2 (a) In questions that ask you to draw conclusions from a graph it is important that you do more than *describe* what is there. You then must state what this means.

In the scattergram for this question the scatter could be seen as a positive correlation but a weak one. These are two important pieces of information – the direction (positive) and the strength (weak). These facts are *descriptions* of what is there. You would get some credit for this information.

For full marks you must go on to interpret this in the context of this graph, in other words to state what the graph tells us about the relationship between stress and daily hassles.

For the full 4 marks you should state two findings and draw two conclusions from them. It may be helpful to organise your answer so you can see that you have done this – state the finding, then start a new line beginning with 'This suggests that …' or 'This means that …'.

2 (b) This answer is correct. A wise student knows when two words would be a sufficient answer!

3 Questions often require you to describe and evaluate a topic. Alternatively you might be asked to just describe the topic or just evaluate it. In the case of questions that only require evaluation students seem to find it difficult to plunge straight in and can't resist including some description. In an evaluation question (as here), description would not gain any credit so it is important not to waste time and just plunge straight in.

When providing evaluation or criticisms, either strengths or limitations are acceptable. Clearly if a question asks for 'limitations' then strengths would not be creditworthy – but the terms 'evaluation' and 'criticisms' mean that you can be positive and/or negative.

In evaluation questions there is also no requirement to be balanced – you can focus all on strengths or all on limitations if you wish – as is the case in the answer on the left.

In order to gain full marks you must always elaborate your critical points. Just providing a list of criticisms with very little explanation would be described as 'superficial' and, in a 4 mark question, would gain a maximum of 2 marks.

Providing one criticism with a lot of elaboration would also not be sufficient for full marks as a range of material is required.

On the left two points are covered in reasonable depth for the full 4 marks.

4 Discuss research into life changes as a source of stress. *(12 marks)*

Holmes and Rahe believed that life changes were related to stress-related illnesses. To conduct research they needed a tool to measure life changes. Their tool (the SRRS) is based on 43 life events. They asked people to rate these life events and then calculated an average rating for each life event. This gave them a number of life change units (LCUs) for each event which was a measure of the amount of readjustment required. The highest LCU for a life event was for 'death of a spouse' (LCU of 100).

Rahe et al. studied the effects of life changes using a group of 2,500 US Navy sailors. The men completed the SRE (similar to the SRRS) measuring life events over the two years prior to a six-month tour of duty. During the tour of duty a record was kept of any illnesses. Rahe et al. found a small but positive correlation between life events and illness.

Michael and Ben-Zur compared life satisfaction in recently divorced or bereaved men and women. After bereavement (a life change) people were less satisfied than they had been before their bereavement. For the divorced participants it was the other way around, satisfaction was higher after the divorce than before.

One problem is that most studies of life change produce only correlational data. A third variable, such as anxiety, may affect both life changes and stress-related illness. For example, Brown claims that people with high levels of anxiety would be more likely to report experience of negative life events and also be more prone to illness. This means that a causal assumption must be avoided.

Another criticism of life changes research is that there are individual differences. The SRRS ignores the fact that the impact of life changes such as pregnancy or retirement varies from person to person. For example, Sherbourne et al. found that the impact of bereavement was greater for younger than older individuals. This means the SRRS may not assess stress accurately.

Daily hassles may be more significant as a source of stress than life changes. Life-changing events are relatively rare in the lives of most people, whereas minor stressors such as a family argument (i.e. hassles) are commonplace. DeLongis et al. found no relationship between life events and health but did find a significant positive correlation between hassles and health problems.

Section B Social psychology

5 **(a)** Outline the difference between conformity and obedience. *(4 marks)*

The difference between conformity and obedience lies in the source of the social influence. In the case of conformity a person is influenced by a group of people – the majority. This majority don't instruct you in any way, it is their behaviour, attitudes and values that you adopt.

In contrast, obedience means a person acts in response to a direct order which may be just from one person. This order may be spoken or in written form, such as on a poster that tells you what to do or how to do something.

5 **(b)** Outline **one** study of obedience. *(6 marks)*

Milgram conducted the key study on obedience. He recruited 40 male volunteers who were told this was a study of how punishment affects learning. After drawing lots, the real participant was always the 'teacher' and the confederate was always the 'learner'.

The teacher's job was to administer a learning task and to deliver shocks (in 15 volt increments up to max of 450 volts) when the learner made a mistake. The learner was in a different room to the teacher. The control was the remote condition as Milgram conducted similar studies with slightly altered conditions.

Milgram found that all participants went to at least 300 volts. At this point 12.5% of participants refused to continue giving shocks but 65% of participants continued to obey the authority figure all the way to the maximum shock level (450 volts). These results were contradictory to predictions made prior to the study that only 4% would go as far as 300 volts.

Examiner's comments

4 On page 183 we commented on an 8 mark question that also required an outline and evaluation of research. In a question worth 12 marks it is necessary to cover three pieces of research.

Note that the word 'research' refers to studies as well as explanations, i.e. you don't have to restrict yourself to the description of a study (though in general that's what we have covered in this book). The first paragraph here is an explanation arising from a study.

The answer here is nicely structured so that each of the three pieces of research is presented in a separate paragraph. Descriptions include both what was done and the results of the research. Important details are included but kept to an appropriate level – too much detail of any one study would mean insufficient time for the other studies and for the evaluation.

If a student did present just one study in considerable detail this would not gain the full 6 AO1 marks because that would not demonstrate 'sound' knowledge of the research area.

This answer has been arranged so all the description (AO1) comes first followed by all the evaluation (AO2). Again, paragraphs are used to separate these points and make each one clear. In this case only three critical points have been covered. However, each of them follows the full four-point rule (S E E L). This would just about be sufficient for the full 6 AO2 marks – but note that this means doing a very high level of elaboration and including the 'link back' at the end.

Overall the essay is worth the full 12 marks.

5 **(a)** You have to be very careful in a question like this to avoid just writing a definition of conformity and a definition of obedience – that is not what the question requires. The focus must be on how they are different.

This answer identifies one difference and then explains that in relation to each term. The amount of elaboration of each means that one difference is enough for the full 4 marks.

5 **(b)** It is safest, when answering a question about a study, to include information on how it was conducted and information about the results, though these don't have to be balanced.

It is possible that such questions could be worth as much as 6 marks, but they are more likely to be worth 4 or 5 marks. But just to be sure, you should always know one study in each topic area in considerable detail so you could answer a question worth 6 marks.

In the case of Milgram's study, students often know too much information. The amount on the left is just about right for a 6 mark question (about 150 words) and is more or less the same as we have given for all of our key studies.

The answer has been divided into paragraphs to make it easier to read than one long chunk of text.

Examiner's comments

5 **(c)** A researcher interviews students on their attitudes about conformity. Give **one** advantage of collecting information using an interview. *(3 marks)*

One advantage of using an interview is that you can adapt the questions as you go along. For example, you might ask someone whether they would feel uncomfortable dressing in a different way to everyone else and if they answer 'no', you could follow this up with another question such as 'Can you think of a situation where you would be uncomfortable being different to other people'. This means you might be able to get more information than in a questionnaire because you can ask a question appropriate to that person.

5 **(c)** This answer is a bit on the long side but fits the requirements of a 3 mark question. The three key elements are: (1) state the advantage; (2) provide some context, i.e. give an example in the context of conformity; and (3) provide a link back explaining why this is an advantage.

6 Outline **one or more** explanations of independent behaviour. *(5 marks)*

One explanation for independent behaviour is having social support. Asch found that the presence of social support enables an individual to resist pressure from the majority for them to conform. They do not necessarily conform to their allies (which wouldn't be independent behaviour); the presence of allies enables them to behave independently and follow their own beliefs.

Milgram also found that social support is linked to greater independence. In Milgram's study, when two confederates refused to continue giving shocks, only 10% of participants continued to the 450 volt shock level, i.e. they behaved independent of the orders from the authority figure.

Presence of a like-minded ally makes an individual feel more confident and better able to stand up to the majority or unjust authority.

6 When answering questions on independent behaviour you can draw on research related to resisting pressure to conform, resisting pressure to obey and/or locus of control – all are explanations for independent behaviour.

However, you must take especial care so that you are focusing on independence rather than not conforming or not obeying. Being independent is not quite the same as, for example, not conforming.

The answer here just presents one explanation (having social support) but explains this in the context of conformity and obedience. One explanation, with plenty of detail can be sufficient for full marks – 'one or more' means that one is sufficient but a candidate can write more than one if they wish.

7 Attitudes towards women's rights changed in this country over a hundred years ago. In some parts of the world such attitudes are still changing.

Using your knowledge of research into social influence, explain how social change related to woman's rights occurs. *(6 marks)*

Social change often begins with minority influence. A single person or small group of people express strong views, in this case about women's rights. This draws people's attention to the kind of things that women have to endure, such as lower pay and fewer opportunities.

The fact that the women's rights groups have strong views and they are passionate and consistent creates conflict in the minds of the majority who start to think about the points they are making. This may cause the majority to change their views.

This is especially true if the women's rights campaigners appear to suffer – in the case of women's rights in the UK before the World War I many women risked imprisonment or even death by hunger strike to advance their cause. This is called the augmentation principle.

The final part of the process is sometimes called the snowball effect. Gradually, more and more people change their views and agree that women should have equal rights. What was a minority has become a majority. Majority influence takes over and social change has occured.

7 In application questions, such as this, you should remember the two-pronged attack. You must explain the behaviour of women's rights groups but ensure this is linked to psychological research.

Remember that 'research' doesn't just include studies but also explanations. In this answer it is explanations of minority influence that have been used as 'research'.

Having said this, questions on social change are a bit different to other application questions. You won't be expected to know how the women's rights groups behaved or the kind of activities the Green movement has used to attract attention. So the emphasis in these social change questions is more on the psychology than the stem of the question.

Section C Individual differences

8 Describe and evaluate the deviation from social norms definition of abnormality. *(6 marks)*

The deviation from social norms definition suggests that we can define abnormality by looking at social norms, the standards of acceptable behaviour that all societies have. Examples include politeness, appropriate sexual behaviour, etc. People who behave in a socially unacceptable or deviant way (e.g. they shout in the street or hit people) are considered anti-social or undesirable, and therefore abnormal.

One limitation of this definition is that deviance is not an absolute. Judgements of deviance are dependent on the context of a behaviour. Some behaviours are considered acceptable in one context but not in another. There is also no clear line between what is an abnormal deviation and what is harmless eccentricity. This means that it is impossible to say that any behaviour is always abnormal because it is relative to other factors.

8 The question begins with the words 'describe and evaluate' which advises you that the 6 marks for this question are divided evenly into AO1 and AO2 – 3 marks for each.

In the first paragraph the definition is described, using examples to provide detail. For 3 marks you would be expected to give a basic definition plus some further explanation – essentially making three distinct points. The description here is worth 3 marks.

In the second paragraph the definition is evaluated by looking at one limitation in depth. As always, the SEEL rule (see page 14) has been followed to give enough for 3 marks.

Alternatively, for 3 marks, you might look at two limitations (and/or strengths) in less depth.

9 (a) One psychological approach to the explanation of abnormality is the psychodynamic approach. Outline this approach to abnormality. *(5 marks)*

Freud's psychodynamic approach to psychopathology suggests that mental disorders have psychological not physical causes.

Freud suggested that conflicts between the id, ego and superego create anxiety. This can be relieved by the use of ego defences such as repression where unpleasant thoughts are moved into the unconscious.

The unconscious mind exerts a powerful effect on behaviour through the influence of previously repressed emotions. This frequently leads to distress, as the individual does not understand why they are acting in that particular way.

Such distress can only be resolved if the repressed material it is brought into conscious awareness.

Freud believed that mental illnesses had their origins in unresolved childhood conflicts. In childhood, the ego is not mature enough to deal with traumas such as the loss of a parent, so this may lead to repression of any associated emotions.

9 (b) Psychoanalysis is the therapy related to the psychodynamic approach. Outline **one** technique that may be used in psychoanalysis. *(2 marks)*

One technique is free association. A patient expresses thoughts exactly as they occur, even though the thoughts may appear unimportant to the individual.

9 (c) Another therapy that is used in the treatment of abnormality is systematic desensitisation. Explain **one** criticism of this method of treatment. *(3 marks)*

One problem is that the underlying problem is not dealt with. Systematic desensitisation may appear to resolve a problem, but simply eliminating symptoms (rather than dealing with the cause of a disorder) may result in other symptoms appearing later on. This means that the therapy, in the long term, could be ineffective.

10 Selma has been having many difficulties at home and at work. She feels she has become very depressed and doesn't want to go back to work. Her doctor suggests that cognitive behavioural therapy (CBT) may help her recover.

What information might the doctor give about this kind of therapy? *(4 marks)*

The doctor might tell her what would be involved in the therapy. For example, he would say that the aim of the therapy is to teach her how to dispute the irrational beliefs that she holds. Cognitive behavioural therapists do this because they believe that problems such as depression occur because people think irrationally.

The doctor might also tell her that CBT is a very effective therapy but it does require quite a lot of effort on the patient's part because they have to work consciously and deliberately to change the way they think. An alternative might be drug therapy which requires much less effort but has the disadvantage of unpleasant side effects. In contrast, CBT has no side effects.

11 A psychologist investigated which methods of treatment were most effective. Thirty depressed patients were given one of three different treatments for six weeks after which their improvement was assessed on a scale of 1–30 where 0 = no improvement. They were assessed again after one year to see if the improvements had continued. Improvement rates are shown in the table below.

	Mean improvement score after six weeks	**Mean improvement score after one year**
ECT	11	12
Drug therapy	17	10
Psychoanalysis	13	23

Explain what these results show about the effectiveness of different therapies. *(4 marks)*

The results show that drug therapy was the most effective treatment after six weeks.

This suggests that depressed patients might do best by taking drugs to improve their depression rather than other forms of treatment.

However, the results also show that drug therapy was the least effective of the three therapies after one year.

This suggests that drug therapy doesn't have long-term benefits and therefore patients might, overall, be better off with psychoanalysis which is a more lasting treatment.

Introduction

AO1: descriptive skills (page 11)

How many marks? Alice's answer contains many details (e.g. 18 seconds) and is all relevant. However not all elements have been sufficiently detailed, so 5 out of 6 marks. Tom's answer seems very competent but lacks those specific details and finishes with an uncreditworthy criticism. 3 out of 6 marks.

AO2: evaluation skills, the beginner's guide (page 13)

Fill in the blanks: For example, *(S) One problem with eating an apple is* it hurts your teeth. *(E) This is because* apples are quite firm and you have to bite hard. *(S) One limitation of (name a theory)* multi-store *theory is* it is oversimplified. *(E) This is because* it just has three stores that each are supposed to do just one thing. *(S) One strength of the research study by* Baddeley *is* it was well controlled. *(E) This is because* it was conducted in a lab where extraneous variables could be controlled.

Mark these 2 mark answers: Aled states the criticism and offers some further elaboration, 2 out of 2 marks. Naomi's elaboration really doesn't add anything so 1 out of 2 marks. Alison has stated and elaborated sufficiently for 2 out of 2 marks.

Clear and coherent: *First thing that is wrong*: Rita has given two answers. *Second thing that is wrong*: neither answer is sufficiently clear (for example, why is the need for informed consent a limitation?). Got 0 marks.

Mark these 3 mark answers: Jack's answer is good because he makes a comparison with interviews but last bit isn't really linked, 2 out of 3 marks. Shaheen has provided two clear elaborations so 3 out of 3 marks.

AO2: evaluation skills, expert level (page 15)

Superficial consideration or reasonable depth or greater depth? Sahil: greater depth. Anthony: reasonable depth.

Extended writing skills – theories (page 17)

Rebecca's answer: AO1: The answer contains some detail but is a bit brief i.e. limited = 5 out of 6 marks. AO2: There are 4 AO2 points. However the meaning/elaboration is not always clear. More elaboration is given for the limitations than the strengths = 4 out of 6 (a range in limited depth).

Eric's answer: AO1: Contains very little detail, a lot of waffle and flawed in places, basic = 2 out of 6 marks. AO2: There are 3 points and none of them make much sense (worse than superficial) = 1 out of 6 marks.

Bruce's answer: AO1 = Detail is closer to basic = 3 out of 6 marks. AO2: 3 points plus summary, generally in greater depth = 5 out of 6 marks.

Extended writing skills – studies (page 19)

Tony's answer: *Number of studies* = 3 (own age findings comes from a study), detail is basic as studies are not identifiable by name or detail. AO1 = 3 out of 6 marks. *Number of AO2 points* = 4 but they are all superficial, even rudimentary. The same points could be used almost anywhere. AO2 = 1 out of 6 marks.

Wei's answer: *Number of studies* = 4. The first two (Kebble and Rattner) are not relevant whereas the Yarmey study is reasonable. The Gordon study contributes very little. So overall this is basic = 3 out of 6 marks. *Number of AO2 points* = 0, therefore 0 out of 6 marks.

Emily's answer: *Number of studies* = 2, both are reasonably detailed so 6 out of 6 marks. *Number of AO2 points* = 4, depth is superficial/limited (see breakdown of AO2 points below), so 4 out of 6 marks.

(S) On the other hand a range of psychologists found children are more inclined to change their views of an event when misleading questions are used as compared with adults.

(S) Therefore it is hard to draw up conclusions as to how EWT is affected as there is contradictory evidence. (E) However conclusions can be made regarding having worse memory and therefore EWT accuracy is worse.

(S) There are also many problems in the way in which research on age and eye witness testimony is carried out. (E) For example Brassard and Memon's research took place in a lab experiment with a video of an event being shown. (E) This situation means that the real anxiety of witnessing an event is lost and (L) so EWT may be different if the event is witnessed in the real world so the studies lack ecological validity.

(S) Also individual differences play a big part in the accuracy of EWT as some people have better memories than others and (L) so age may not be the defining factor.

Applying your knowledge (page 21)

Amalia's answer: There is sufficient context for 3 out of 4 marks, but most of the answer lacks reference to the stem.

Melissa's answer: Excellent context (reference to stem). The answer does more than use the name 'Jenny' – the steps of the cognitive interview have been shaped to this particular incident (e.g. They could ask 'If you were standing on the other side of the road what would you have seen?'), 4 out of 4 marks.

Pedro's answer: There is some attempt to refer to Jenny but the description of the interview isn't all relevant (e.g. explaining why it works is not creditworthy), 2 out of 4 marks.

Roy's answer: The reference to the stem is minimal and the answer is not all relevant (final two sentences on schemas), 1 out of 4 marks.

Chapter 1

Topic 1 Research on the duration of memory (page 29)

Drawing conclusions: For example, *Finding 1*: After 3 seconds recall was almost 100%. *Conclusion 1*: This shows that there is very little decay after 3 seconds. *Finding 2*: After 18 seconds almost nothing could be remembered. *Conclusion 2*: This shows that within a short period of time information disappears from STM if rehearsal is prevented.

Circle true or false: F, F, T, T, T, F, F

Jumbled sentences: 4, 3, 2, 5, 1   9, 7, 8, 10, 6   11, 14, 12, 13, 15

Topic 2 Research on the capacity of memory (page 31)

A marking exercise: *Celeste's answer*: LTM information relates to duration not capacity and STM comment could apply to anything, not clearly capacity = 1 out of 3 marks (rudimentary). *Jennifer's answer*: Detailed answer for STM, reasonable for LTM but just two definitions rather than a difference = 2 out of 3 marks (limited).

Applying your knowledge: For example, *Identify the psychology*: The capacity of STM is only about 7 items (and might be as little as 4 items).

Link to a method they could use: This means that it might be good to try to remember small bits of text at a time where there are only 7 chunks of information. Rehearse this and then move on to something else. *Identify the psychology*: One way to increase the capacity of STM is by chunking. *Link to a method they could use*: You can apply chunking to learning by grouping things together and having one word to represent a whole chunk.

Fill in the blanks: (1) Miller, (2) the span of STM, (3) seven notes on musical scale or seven days of the week, (4) seven, (5) 15, (6) chunking.

Topic 3 Research on encoding in memory (page 33)

Match them up: 1B, 2C, 3A

Fill in the blanks: (1) quite artificial, (2) different kinds of memory task, (3) encoding in STM/LTM, (4) 20 minutes, (5) months and years.

Drawing conclusions: For example, *Finding 1*: There was a clear difference for STM memory between acoustically similar and semantically similar words. *Conclusion 1*: This shows that STM is mainly acoustic. *Finding 2*: In LTM the semantically similar words caused more difficulty with recall. *Conclusion 2*: This shows that semantic coding is used in LTM.

Topic 4 The multi-store model (page 35)

Complete the diagram: A = sensory memory. B = long-term memory. C = rehearsal loop.

Match them up: 1B, 2A, 3C, 4E, 5D

Spot the mistakes: [mistakes are in bold; correct material in brackets] The multi-store model consists of **two** (three) stores. One store is short-term memory. Information in short-term memory has a very limited duration of less than **5 seconds** (18 seconds). Short-term memory also has a limited capacity. It is said to hold 7 plus or minus 2 items. Once information is in the short-term memory it can be rehearsed and then passed into long-term memory. Long-term memory holds information for weeks, months or years. **It never disappears** (it may disappear but is potentially forever). An important difference between short-term and long-term memory is that information is usually in a **semantic** (auditory) form in short-term memory though it may also be visual.

Applying your knowledge: For example, *Identify the psychology*: The MSM proposes that people remember things by rehearsing them in short-term memory; increasing rehearsal turns this into long-term memories. *Link to Mr Bill*: This means that Mr Bill should encourage his clients to repeat what he says; for example, he could make a joke of asking them to see if they can list the advantages he told them. *Identify the psychology*: The MSM suggests that LTM is mainly semantic. *Link to Mr Bill*: This means that Mr Bill should emphasise the meaning of what he is saying; for example, he could explain the underlying evidence for each advantage so the client thinks about the advantages more deeply.

Topic 5 The working memory model (page 37)

A marking exercise: *David's answer*: Has listed the components of the WMM and explained some of them but not enough for full marks = 3 out of 4 marks. *Betty's answer*: The first two sentences are not creditworthy, does little more than list the components except for some creditworthy information about the episodic buffer = 2 out of 4 marks.

Fill in the blanks: (1) brain-damaged patients, (2) Shallice and Warrington, (3) visual stimuli/letters, (4) verbal material/sounds, (5) word length, (6) a list of long words/three syllable words, (7) short words, (8) well defined, (9) central executive.

Applying your knowledge: For example, *One component of the WMM*: The visuo-spatial sketchpad (VSS), which processes visual information. *This links to the stem*: Because doing two visual tasks would mean that both have to

be processed by this limited capacity store and therefore performance on both is slower. *Another component of the WMM*: The phonological loop (PL) which processes auditory/verbal information. *This links to the stem*: Because doing a second task which was verbal would be performed by this second component and there would be no interference.

Topic 6 EWT and misleading information (page 39)

Match them up: 1D, 2G, 3H, 4F, 5A, 6B, 7C, 8E

True or false: F, T, T, F, T, F

Drawing conclusions: For example, *Finding 1*: More participants in the control condition said 'no' there was no broken glass. *Conclusion 1*: This suggests that the leading question about speed did affect participants' memory of the accident. *Finding 2*: The 'smashed' group were most likely to answer 'yes' to the question about broken glass. *Conclusion 2*: This suggests that the misleading question (suggesting the car was travelling fast) lead them to remember it was a serious accident where there may well have been broken glass.

Applying your knowledge: For example, the question suggests the desired answer – in this case saying it was a man suggests the gender of the thief.

Topic 7 Effect of anxiety on EWT (page 41)

Fill in the blanks: (1) heard an argument in the adjoining room, (2) two, (3) a pen covered in grease, (4) a knife covered in blood, (5) high, (6) 49%, (7) 33%, (8) reduces, (9) weapon, (10) weapon focus.

Jumbled sentences: 2, 4, 3, 5, 1   7, 6, 9, 8   10, 12, 11, 14, 13

A marking exercise: It got this mark because the information provided about procedures (how) is basic and there is nothing about the findings (both procedures and findings must be included). Examples of further information that could be included would be more procedural detail (e.g. interviews were 4–15 months later, those who were threatened were the bank tellers) and include information about the findings (e.g. all victims had better than 75% recall, bank tellers had best recall).

Fill in the boxes:

Anxiety reduces accuracy of EWT. Evidence: Johnson and Scott study. *This suggests that* people who are more anxious are less accurate when asked to identify faces.

Anxiety enhances accuracy of EWT. Evidence: Christiansen and Hubinette (the bank tellers). *This suggests that* people who are very anxious may have even better recall than those who are not very anxious.

Anxiety may sometimes reduce and sometimes enhance the accuracy of EWT. Explanation: Yerkes–Dodson. *This suggests that* there isn't a simple linear relationship between anxiety and accuracy – moderate levels of anxiety do not enhance accuracy.

Topic 8: Effect of age on EWT (page 43)

A marking exercise: [paragraphs inserted and AO2 material highlighted]

A study was undertaken where participants on the street were asked to describe a young woman who had just walked past. Each participant had to recall the woman and the youngest adults did best, therefore showing that age affected immediate recall.

Although this study was a natural experiment participants may have been aware when being asked to describe a woman as this isn't an everyday task therefore it lacks ecological validity.

It also has low ecological validity because it was difficult to control the extraneous variables so it would be difficult to replicate.

Throughout many studies a factor called own-age bias was discovered. This would affect recall on eyewitness testimony because if the witness was 17 then they are more likely to recognise a criminal of age 17 due to own-age bias. Again if a 75 year old saw a criminal age 75 they would be more likely to identify them accurately than a 17 year old due to own-age bias.

In another study participants watched a video of a car accident and were told to come back a week later. They recalled information accurately.

This study lacked ecological validity because the participants watched a video and therefore weren't emotionally involved. Also it didn't take into account individual differences.

AO1: Study by Yarmey described accurately but lacking detail. In this essay the own-age bias is *described* and is therefore AO1. The final study that is mentioned (about a car accident) is not made relevant to age = 3 out of 4 marks (range of research but lacks detail).

AO2: The points are rudimentary and repetitive = 1 out of 4 marks.

Applying your knowledge: For example, *Explanation 1*: Her age means she might be less accurate at identifying a young person. *This is supported by research* on the own-age bias (Anastasi and Rhodes). *Explanation 2*: Older woman might be less confident and therefore provide fewer and less accurate details. *This is supported by research* by Yarmey that found older adults lacked confidence and this might explain their reduced accuracy.

Drawing conclusions: For example: *Finding 1*: In each age group the greatest accuracy was for identifying photographs of their own age group. *Conclusion 1*: This shows that people are better at identifying people of their own age. *Finding 2*: Older participants were least accurate when identifying younger participants, and the reverse was true for younger participants. *Conclusion 2*: This shows that people are least accurate the bigger the age gap between the witness and the person they are identifying.

Topic 9 The cognitive interview (page 45)

Circle true or false: T, F, T, T, F, F, T, T, F

Applying your knowledge: For example, *One technique is* changing the order in which information is recalled (e.g. starting at the end point and working back to the beginning), *this could be used with the students by* asking them to think about the events in reverse starting from when the man left the room or even before that. *Another technique is* report everything, *this could be used with the students by* encouraging them to think of every little detail including things that don't appear to be directly relevant such as what the teacher was doing.

Topic 10 Strategies for memory improvement (page 47)

A marking exercise: YES, NO

Two memory strategies have been described but neither have been well applied, therefore just 1 out of 4 marks.

Applying your knowledge: For example: *Identify* **one** *memory strategy*: Method of loci. *Material to be remembered*: Might be Loftus and Palmer's study. *Explain how Mary would use the identified memory strategy*: Mary would mentally place the items in familiar places around her house, for example she would go into her kitchen and imagine having 45 students sitting round the table, in front of them would be three bowls one with each of the verbs. She would then go to the living room and the numbers 40.8 and the word smashed would be on the TV. To remember these details she would mentally walk around her house while practising her talk.

Jumbled sentences: 6, 16, 4   5, 10, 13, 9   3, 1, 15   11, 12, 8   2, 14, 7

Drawing conclusions: *Finding 1*: The mean score for strategy B is higher. *Conclusion 1*: This shows that strategy B may be the most effective learning strategy. *Finding 2*: The standard deviation for strategy B is larger. *Conclusion 2*: This shows that there was a greater spread of scores which means that some students did very well but others did poorly, and therefore strategy B may not be as good as strategy A overall.

Chapter 2

Topic 11 Explanation of attachment: learning theory (page 55)

Match them up: 1B, 2C, 3A

Spot the mistakes: [mistakes are in bold; correct material in brackets] An infant may develop an attachment through operant conditioning. In this case food is a **secondary** (primary) reinforcer. Food **increases** (decreases) the infant's sense of discomfort. One criticism of this explanation comes from **Barlow's** (Harlow's) research with **cats** (monkeys). In this study he showed that the animals spent **most** (least) time with the wire mother with a feeding bottle. Another study with human babies also showed that food **matters** (doesn't matter) in attachment. The babies were observed in their own home.

Drawing conclusions: For example, *Finding 1*: The infant monkeys spent more time with the cloth covered 'mother' than the 'mother' with the feeding bottle. *Conclusion 1*: This shows that attachments were not related to food but more related to contact comfort. *Finding 2*: This effect was slightly smaller for the younger monkeys who spent less time with the cloth covered 'mother' than the older ones. *Conclusion 2*: This shows that the younger monkeys may have been less interested in contact comfort and perhaps more interested in exploring or just being on their own (they didn't spend more time feeding).

A marking exercise: *AO1: Has material been appropriately selected?* NO (introduction not relevant). *Is the material accurate?* YES. *The material is* LESS DETAILED (main points covered but could have included some of the 'technical terms' such as 'conditioned response'). *What mark would this answer get for AO1?* 3 marks out of 4. **AO2**: *The evaluation is* A RESTRICTED RANGE (only one point but in some depth, therefore better than 'rudimentary'). *What mark would this answer get for AO2?* 2 marks out of 4.

Topic 12 Explanation of attachment: Bowlby's theory (page 57)

Circle true or false: T, F, F, T, T, F, T, T

Fill in the blanks: (1) Lorenz, (2) Tronick *et al.*, (3) moves, (4) cultural, (5) primary, (6) monotropy.

Applying your knowledge: For example, *One new strategy* might be to develop important secondary attachments. *Link*: This is important because, in the absence of having their primary attachment figure present, the young children need secondary attachments for healthy psychological development. *A second strategy* would be to ensure that all carers understood the importance of being sensitive and accepting in the way they respond to the children. *Link*: Bowlby suggested that this is important in the formation of secure attachments.

Topic 13 The Strange Situation (page 59)

Fill in the table:

	1	2	3	4	5	6	7	8
Parent	✓	✓	✓		✓			✓
Stranger			✓	✓			✓	✓

Applying your knowledge: For example, *Element of Strange Situation*: Stranger enters. *How it would be used*: Arrange for someone who Omar had never met to enter the room where Omar and his father are playing and observe Omar's reactions. *Element of Strange Situation*: Parent leaves. *How it would be used?* This would involve Omar's father leaving the room for a short period of time (leaving Omar with the stranger or just on his own). *Element of Strange Situation*: Parent returns. *How it would be used?* This would involve Omar's father coming back in the room to observe how Omar greeted his father.

Jumbled sentences: 5, 8, 2, 6, 7, 3, 1, 4

A marking exercise: The answer shows some components of the S E E L rule but not enough for 4 marks. The criticism is stated and there is some elaboration/explanation and the final link back. The answer could gain 4 marks if there had been some further elaboration OR if a second point of evaluation was included.

Topic 14 Types of attachment (page 61)

Match them up: 1A, 2D, 3B, 4C

Drawing conclusions: For example, *Finding 1*: The majority of infants are securely attached. *Conclusion 1*: This shows that secure attachment is the dominant type of attachment. *Finding 2*: There were similar numbers of infants categorised as insecure-avoidant and disorganised. *Conclusion 2*: This shows that the disorganised type is a relatively important category.

A marking exercise: Tanya starts with similarities instead of differences but then does identify two differences, but they are brief (lack detail) = 2 out of 4 marks. Bethany's answer clearly identifies two differences and gives details of each = 4 out of 4 marks. Corey's answer also clearly identifies two differences but with a bit less detail, for example he only says the insecure-resistant child will cry on the parent's return = 3 out of 4 marks.

Topic 15 Cultural variations in attachment (page 63)

Circle true or false: F, F, T, T, T, T, T, F

Spot the mistakes: [mistakes are in bold; correct material in brackets]
The **Special** (Strange) Situation (SS) may not be a valid measure of attachment in all cultures. It was developed in the **UK** (US) and therefore may not apply to other cultures. In some cultures, such as Japan, infants are rarely separated from their mothers and therefore show **little** (more) distress in the Strange Situation. Another criticism of the research on cultural variations is that it often assumes that 'country' is the same as 'culture'. The study by van IJzendoorn and **Kroonenberg** (Sagi) showed that different cultural groups in Japan differed in terms of attachment type. In rural Japan there were **more** (less) securely attached infants than in urban cities.

Applying your knowledge: For example, *Identify the psychology*: In some cultures insecure attachment is more common than in the US because of different child rearing practices (e.g. in collectivist cultures 'dependence' is encouraged whereas in individualist cultures 'independence' is desirable and encouraged). *Link*: Yuna may get more distressed than would be expected because she has experienced less separation because she was raised in a traditional Japanese family. *Identify the psychology*: There are cultural similarities as well as differences in attachments. *Link*: Yuna probably still has one important primary attachment to her mother as that is universally the most common thing.

Topic 16 Disruption of attachment (page 65)

Fill in the blanks: (1) residential nursery, (2) two, (3) four, (4) physical, (5) emotional, (6) Hart, (7) insecure, (8) hospital.

Applying your knowledge: For example, *Suggestion for Sally*: Ask the staff what they do to provide emotional support. *Link to psychological research*: The Robertsons showed that when John was left with little emotional care he became very upset over a period of a week. *Suggestion for Sally*: When she isn't there try to find someone else who can provide appropriate emotional care or leave him with a special teddy bear. *Link to psychological research*: The Robertsons provided substitute emotional care for Jane, Lucy, Thomas and Kate and this helped them cope with the emotional separation from their mother.

Fill in the boxes: For example, *Initially*: withdrawn emotionally, crying, being distressed, refusing to eat. *Later*: rocking back and forth, sucking his thumb, despair, apathy, being quiet, detachment, indifference.

Topic 17 Failure to form attachment (privation) and institutional care (page 67)

Circle true or false: T, T, F, F, F

Applying your knowledge: For example, *Identify the psychology*: Hodges and Tizard found that children who failed to form attachments had many social difficulties later in life. *Recommendation*: This suggests that it is very important to ensure that children are adopted to good homes where secure attachments can be formed. *Identify the psychology*: Rutter *et al.* found that adoptions before the age of six months were less likely to lead to developmental social problems than those after six months. *Recommendation*: This suggests that it is important to make adoptions as early as possible to avoid a failure to form attachment.

Constructing an answer: For example, *Difference*: Whether an attachment has been formed. *Example of disruption*: In the Robertsons' study John had formed an attachment to his mother. *Example of failure to form attachment*: In the study by Hodges and Tizard the children in the institution had not formed attachments. *Difference*: Long-term effects. *Example of disruption*: Robertsons showed that disruption need not have long-term effects if there is good substitute emotional care. *Example of failure to form attachment*: Hodges and Tizard found that even with good substitute emotional care the children had difficulty in peer relationships later in life.

A marking exercise: *Mario's answer*: AO1 – a reasonably detailed and accurate account of one study covering both procedures and findings = 3 out of 3 marks. AO2 – an elaborated criticism, made specific to this study and clearly explained = 3 out of 3 marks. *Radu's answer*: AO1 – a muddled version of Rutter *et al.*'s study, the babies were adopted before the age of six months not 'put in' (to the institution). The reference to Bowlby's work is creditworthy as 'research' therefore 2 out of 3 marks. AO2 – this is a superficial point that has very little context and could almost be used in any essay, therefore 1 out of 3 marks.

Topic 18 The impact of day care on aggression (page 69)

Jumbled sentences: 4, 2, 3, 1   6, 7, 5, 8   9, 12, 11, 10, 13

Drawing conclusions: For example, *Finding 1*: There is a positive correlation between hours spent in day care and levels of aggression. *Conclusion 1*: This shows that time spent in day care may contribute to increased aggression. *Finding 2*: The correlation is weak. *Conclusion 2*: This shows that it is likely that many other factors may be involved which dilutes or moderates any effect (day care may make children more aggressive but other factors counteract this).

Spot the mistakes: [mistakes are in bold; correct material in brackets] The EPPE study was conducted in the **US** (UK) and involved over 3,000 children from the age of **5** (3) to 11. There were two groups of children: those in day care and those home-cared. Cognitive and social development was assessed and teacher ratings were used. The results showed that the longer time children spent in day care the **less** (more) aggressive they were. It was also found that starting pre-school at an early age was associated with increased aggression. This effect had **increased** (decreased) by age 10. The quality of care was important – **high**- (low-) quality care was associated with increased aggressiveness.

Topic 19 The impact of day care on peer relations (page 71)

Constructing an answer: *Effect*: Positive, e.g. increased sociability, independence – give relevant study. *Effect*: Negative, e.g. greater aggression, shy children withdrawn, insecure attachment – give relevant study.

Match them up: 1D, 2C, 3B, 4A, 5E

Applying your knowledge: For example, *Benefits for Mark's daughter*: She may learn how to cooperate and make friendships with other children better. *Link to research*: The EEPE study found that pre-school day care improves all aspects of social behaviour, e.g. independence, cooperation and peer relationships. *Benefits for Mark's daughter*: She may learn to be less distressed and timid in new situations. *Link to research*: Clarke-Stewart *et al.* found that this was a benefit of day care because the interaction with other children provides opportunities to practise social skills.

A marking exercise: *Bill's answer*: The study is not identifiable (no researcher's name and no detail included which indicates what study it is) = 0 out of 4 marks. *Betsy's answer*: The first sentence is general scene-setting and not creditworthy. The final sentence is evaluation and again not creditworthy. The relevant information is basic at best = 2 out of 4 marks.

Topic 20 Influence of research into attachment on child care practices (page 73)

Fill in the blanks: (1) emotionally, (2) primary, (3) alternative or secondary or substitute, (4) three, (5) visiting, (6) emotional.

Drawing conclusions: For example, *Finding 1*: There were more adopted children who were securely attached in the 'before six months' group than the 'after six months' group. *Conclusion 1*: This shows that adoption before six months is better for attachment. *Finding 2*: In both groups there were more securely attached children than insecurely attached children. *Conclusion 2*: This shows that adoption after six months wasn't universally negative, so other factors must be important aside from age of adoption.

Constructing an answer: For example, *Suggestion:* Ensure emotional care provided. *Link to attachment research:* Robertsons showed importance of substitute emotional care in avoiding effects of disruption of attachment. *Suggestion:* Provide early attachment to avoid failure to form attachment. *Link to attachment research:* Rutter *et al.* have found that social and cognitive development is 'normal' if adoptions take place early enough (before six months).

Research issues: For example, *Definition of validity*: The extent to which a study and its findings represent the 'real' world. *Argument suggesting that the validity of attachment research is high*: Some of the research is conducted in everyday settings with good ecological validity. *Support for this argument*: The research by the Robertsons. *Argument suggesting that the validity of attachment research is low*: Many of the studies were poorly controlled. *Support for this argument*: Tronick *et al.'s* study of women in Africa was an observational study with few controls.

Topic 21 Influence of research into day care on child care practices (page 75)

Applying your knowledge: For example, *Advice*: Don't have too many children to look after. *Reference to psychological research*: NICHD study found that day care staff can only provide sensitive care if the ratios were as good as one member of staff to three children. *Advice*: Take some training/qualification. *Reference to psychological research*: Sylva *et al.* found that the higher the qualifications of day care staff the better the day care children's social development was.

Choose the right answer: A, C, D

A marking exercise: Answer A = 0 marks (not a characteristic of day care). Answer B = 1 mark (no appropriate elaboration). Answer C = 2 marks ('one to one' identified and elaborated 'so the child could form an attachment').

Practice elaboration: For example, *Characteristic of high-quality day care*: Good staff-to-child ratio. *Elaboration*: 1:3 would be good enough according to NICHD. *Characteristic of high-quality day care*: Experienced staff. *Elaboration*: This means having good qualifications and time spent doing the job.

Chapter 3

Topic 22 Experiments (page 83)

Fill in the blanks: (1) independent, (2) dependent, (3) extraneous, (4) confound, (5) validity.

A marking exercise: *Kerry's answer*: 1 + 1 mark (neither variables are operationalised). *Megan's answer*: 1 + 0 marks (second answer is not a variable). *Rohan's answer*: 2 + 2 marks (both variables are operationalised).

Circle true or false: T, F, T, T, T

Applying your knowledge: For example, (a) The aim is to see whether rewards affect performance. (b) IV = receiving £1 or not for doing the test, DV = score on the test. (c) Children who are offered £1 do better on the test than those who receive nothing. (d) Directional hypothesis. (e) The children who got the reward might be smarter anyway. Therefore they would do better on the test, not because they got the reward but because they were smarter and this would confound the results. (f) One demand characteristic would be that the offer of a reward might make the children in the no reward group realise what the experiment was about and they would try very hard. (g) One strength is the experimenter could repeat this study if he had controlled all the variables carefully such as using the same test and the same reward. One limitation is that the situation was contrived so the children might have behaved differently to how they would behave when tested at school – they probably wouldn't be offered money so it isn't very realistic.

Topic 23 Experimental design (page 85)

Choose the right answer: A, D, E

Match them up: 1E, 2A, 3B, 4F, 5D, 6C

Jumbled sentences: 4, 2, 9, 7, 3, 6, 1, 5, 8

Applying your knowledge 1: For example, (a) Because there are two separate groups of participants, one for each of the experimental conditions (being left- or right-handed). (b) You could not put one person in both conditions unless they were ambidextrous; most people are either right- or left-handed. (c) One strength is you avoid order effects (e.g. no effect from doing the same task twice), one limitation is participant variables (e.g. having more experience with art activities) may reduce validity. (d) There is a difference between the creativity score (on a test of creativity) of people who are right- or left-handed.

Applying your knowledge 2: For example, one reason is that it controls the participant variables. If you used independent groups then one group might have faster reaction times in general and then the superior performance of one group would be due to this rather than the coffee. A second reason is that repeated measures means you don't have to use as many participants because you would need twice as many in an independent groups design.

Topic 24 Field and natural experiments (page 87)

Fill in the blanks: (1) dependent, (2) laboratory, (3) practical, (4) internal, (5) external/ecological, (6) laboratory.

Circle true or false: T, F, F, T, T, T, T

Fill in the boxes:

What is unique about a lab experiment?	High level of control over extraneous variables.
What is unique about a field experiment?	The DV is tested in a 'natural' environment (this *may* be true for a natural experiment but not necessarily).
What is unique about a natural experiment?	Uses an IV that varies 'naturally' – not controlled by the experimenter.
What do all types have in common?	An IV and a DV.

Applying your knowledge: For example, (a) It is a field experiment because the environment in which the study was conducted was the students' everyday environment and the IV was manipulated by the experimenter. (b) One strength is that participants act like they normally do which makes the results more generalisable to everyday life. (c) Independent groups, one limitation is that people in one group could have better memories. (d) One other limitation is that extraneous variables may not be controlled, for example some participants may not use the strategy they were told to use. This could be corrected by randomly allocating participants to groups which should ensure the two groups are similar. (e) In a natural experiment the IV would not be controlled by the experimenter so the experimenter could just ask people what strategy they use and assign them to an experimental group on that basis. (f) They could repeat the study and see if the results were consistent (or could check the test that they used and see if people got the same result twice in a row.)

Topic 25 Selection of participants (page 89)

Choose the right answer: *Opportunity sample*: C, D. *Volunteer sample*: B, E. *Random sample*: A, F.

A marking exercise: *Dylan's answer* = 3 out of 3 marks (two criticisms each with some elaboration). *Carrie's answer* = 2 out of 3 mark (first sentence not really an evaluation, second sentence is a criticism with some elaboration). *Charlotte's answer* = 1 out of 3 marks (mention of 'bias' gains one mark, the rest is not relevant).

Spot the mistakes: [mistakes are in bold; correct material in brackets] Psychologists need to select participants for their research studies. One way to do this is by using a **voluntary** (volunteer) sample. This means you ask people if they want to take part. Such a sample is likely to be **unbiased** (biased). Another technique that can be used is the random sample. To do this you identify your **main** (target) population and then put all the names in a machine like they use for the lottery and randomly select the number you require. A third method is the opportunity sample. The people who are chosen are the ones most **willing** (available).

Applying your knowledge: For example, (a) Could be any of the 3 methods plus an explanation of how, e.g. one method would be an opportunity sample. You could just go up to people in the street and ask them how many calls they make per day and also rate their friendliness. (b) Strength as appropriate to part (a) but should include some context related to the stem as the question says '… in this study', e.g. this is the easiest method you could do because you can straight away go get your 30 people in the street rather than waiting for volunteers or contacting a random sample. (c) Independent groups. (d) Mobile phone use (1 mark), number of calls per day (1 mark for operationalisation). (e) It is a natural experiment because the IV has not been controlled by the experimenter. People are put in categories according to their existing behaviour.

Topic 26 Data analysis (page 91)

Match them up: 1C, 2G, 3H, 4B, 5D, 6F, 7I, 8E, 9A

Drawing conclusions 1: For example, *One finding*: Group A were slower on visual task 1 than Group B. *This suggests that* doing a second visual task at the same time interferes with the first visual task. *Second finding*: Group A were slower on visual task 1 than visual task 2. *This suggests that* interference doesn't affect both tasks equally.

Drawing conclusions 2: For example, *One finding*: In general the day care children had higher social development scores than the home care children. *This suggests that* day care had a positive effect on social development. *Second finding*: There was an increase in social development score at age six in the day care children. *This suggests that* the effect was most marked when children started school and perhaps were better able to cope with peers having been in day care.

Fill in the blanks: *Data set 1* = median, because there are extreme values. *Data set 2* = mode, because the data are in categories.

Topic 27 Ethical issues (page 93)

Simple selection: B, E, C, D, A

Fill in the boxes: For example, *Lack of informed consent*: (S) Debriefing (E) Do this after the study and discuss any ill feelings. *Deception*: (S) Debriefing (E) tell participants the true aims, might allow them to withdraw their data. *Protection from harm*: (S) Debriefing (E) Ask participants if they experienced any psychological harm and assure them that, e.g. any embarrassment was normal. *Confidentiality*: (S) Provide anonymity (E) Do not ask for participants' names and assure them that all information is stored securely. *Lack of privacy*: (S) Only observe in public places (E) Ask for presumptive consent to see if it is acceptable.

Applying your knowledge: For example, (a) It is a laboratory experiment because the participants are tested with contrived materials in a controlled environment. (b) If you used repeated measures you would have to use the same participants as children and adults and have to wait a long time. (c) One issue is deception and another issue is informed consent. She could deal with deception by debriefing participants at which time she would tell them the real aims and might offer that they could withhold their data. She would discuss any concerns they had. A second issue is informed consent. She would deal with this by seeking some outline consent before the study began, especially to gain consent from the children's parents. She would give an outline of what will be involved (e.g. tell them they would be watching a film of a robbery and answering a questionnaire). (d) Children may be impatient and not pay attention very closely to the task. This means their results would lack validity. (e) The purpose is to advise psychologists about what is not permissible ethically, and also about how they should deal with any situations where ethical issues arise. (f) The mean is a measure of central tendency where all the values of the data are taken into account in the final calculation. (g) Younger children performed less well than adults. This suggests that they wouldn't be as good as eyewitnesses. The spread of the data (standard deviation) is bigger for the adults. This suggests that some of the adults were less accurate than the children. The children were more consistent in terms of accuracy.

A marking exercise: Ahmed's answer gets the full 3 marks as he has stated the point (don't identify) and then said two further pieces of information (don't use photos/names, or change them). Christian's answer only receives 1 out of 3 marks. Only the third sentence is creditworthy. The final sentence is too vague.

Topic 28 Studies using correlational analysis (page 95)

Match them up: 1A, 2E, 3D, 4B, 5F, 6C

Drawing conclusions: (a) 18. (b) See scattergram below; this is a zero correlation. (c) This suggests that there is not a genetic basis for aggression.

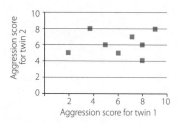

Write your evaluation point: For example, S = A correlation cannot show a causal relationship. E = People often misinterpret correlations and assume that a causal relationship has been demonstrated. E = They would think that a positive correlation means that day care *causes* increased aggression. L = The correlation only shows that the two variables increase together; an intervening variable may be involved that is a causal factor, such as the fact that their mothers work more and are more stressed.

Research issues: For example, it would be appropriate to use a pilot study to check that key aspects of the design worked. For example, to check the standardised instructions are clear enough for the participants to understand what they are required to do. Also to check the method of assessing how many hours a week children were in nursery to see if the method was reliable.

Applying your knowledge: For example, (a) Ask teachers to rate each child on a scale of 1 to 10 where 10 is very aggressive. (b) There is a correlation between hours spent in day care per week and aggressiveness. (c) A correlational analysis only demonstrates a relationship, cannot tell us whether one variable caused the change in the other. In this case whether day care caused aggressiveness.

Topic 29 Observational techniques (page 97)

A marking exercise: Robbie's answer would receive 2 out of 4 marks because he only mentions creating a checklist and also ticking these off. Anne's answer receives 3 out of 4 marks because she does what Robbie did but also adds some examples of the categories that might be used. Pierre's answer receives 0 marks because he has focused on what he might do with the results rather than *how* the content analysis would be done.

Applying your knowledge 1: For example, (a) Avoiding a stranger (stranger anxiety), closeness to mother on her return (reunion behaviour). (b) The observations may not be reliable because the observer may misinterpret a behaviour and think a child was avoiding someone when they might have been playing a game. (c) It means you can arrange the setting to be able to test what you are interested in, such as arranging for the stranger to come and go.

Fill in the blanks: (1) structured, (2) coding, (3) checklist, (4) time, (5) event.

Research issues: For example, one ethical issue is lack of informed consent. You could deal with this by asking other people if they thought this study is acceptable. If they think it is then you could take that as presumptive consent.

Applying your knowledge 2: For example, (a) Playing with other children. (b) The list of behavioural categories would be used to record the behaviour of individual children by watching each child for a period of time (e.g. an hour) and ticking the behaviours observed in a behaviour checklist. This could be used to calculate a score for social development. (c) (S) One limitation is that the behavioural categories might not include every behaviour that the children do. (E) Therefore the record would not accurately reflect what they were actually doing. (E) This means that the results would lack validity. (L) It might be better to do a pilot study at the beginning to get the behavioural categories right.

Topic 30 Self-report (page 99)

Circle true or false: T, F, T, T, T, F, F

Applying your knowledge: For example, (a) The psychologist might want to check whether the questions were easy to understand and could also check the standardised instructions. (b) How many years did you attend day care? (numerical answers only) (c) What is your worst memory of day care? (d) The psychologist can give the questionnaire out to a lot of children so you get a lot of replies to analyse. If you were conducting interviews each would take a lot more time than questionnaires which would reduce the number of participants that could be involved. (e) It might be better to use an interview so you could encourage the children to elaborate and explain their answers. Children also might find it difficult to write their answers down so an interview would be better.

Simple selection: Questionnaire: A, D, F. Interview: B, C, E.

Research issues: For example, one issue would be confidentiality. People who answered would not want their identities to be recognisable because then other people might link what they said to their families. A second issue is informed consent. People should be given information before they agree to take part about what kind of data will be collected and how it will be used, so they can decide whether or not to take part.

Drawing conclusions: For example, *Finding*: The largest number of respondents identified just one primary attachment figure. *Conclusion*: Bowlby's idea of monotropy continues into adolescence.

Topic 31 Case studies (page 101)

Match them up: 1E, 2C, 3I, 4A, 5F, 6B, 7K, 8D, 9G, 10J, 11H

Applying your knowledge 1: For example, (a) One technique would be interviewing. The psychologists would interview people arrested for rioting and also people who had been affected. (b) One limitation would be that people don't tell the truth, especially the people who had committed crimes, who would try to put themselves in a good light (social desirability bias). The people affected might also not tell the truth, they might exaggerate the effect the riots had had. Another limitation would be that it is retrospective recall and people don't always remember past events accurately. (c) One strength is the rich detail that could be collected, which might give new insights into rioting behaviour and change our views about the causes and effects of rioting.

Research issues: For example, the psychologist would not reveal the adopted woman's name nor the names of any other people involved. Any information that is stored should be protected so it cannot be accessed by other people. The psychologist should also ensure that any details that would identify the adopted woman are not included in the study.

Applying your knowledge 2: For example, (a) They might use psychological tests to assess the emotional development of some of the children who had been there. (b) They might use a volunteer sample where they advertise for an institution who would be willing to take part.

Chapter 4

Topic 32 The body's response to stress (page 109)

Fill in the blanks: (1) sympathetic, (2) immediate (acute), (3) an increase, (4) adrenal medulla, (5) adrenaline, (6) oxygen, (7) parasympathetic nervous system, (8) reducing.

Match them up: 1F, 2C, 3E, 4B, 5A, 6D

Applying your knowledge: *Identify the psychology*: The SNS prepares the body for activity in the presence of a sudden stressor. It does this through the action of adrenaline and noradrenaline. Noradrenaline activates internal body organs necessary for fight or flight. *Link to Ian's response*: Ian's response during the 'scary bits' of the film is typical of a SNS reaction because his heart is beating faster and his hands are clammy, both typical of the actions of noradrenaline.

A marking exercise: Thomas has produced a suitably detailed response to the question. It is accurate and making three very distinct points makes it easier for the examiner to decide to award full marks = 3 out of 3 marks. Ellie's answer is not as detailed and mainly centres around ACTH and cortisol, although she doesn't really explain their action = 2 out of 3 marks.

Topic 33 Stress-related illness and the immune system (page 111)

Jumbled sentences: 3, 7, 5, 2, 1, 6, 4

Circle true or false: F, F, F, T, F, F

Applying your knowledge: *Identify the psychology*: When the individual is under high levels of stress, the immune system may find it hard to cope, resulting in more minor illnesses as the body becomes less able to fight off infection. This was what Kiecolt-Glaser *et al.* found in their study of students facing an important examination. Their immune systems were least effective during the stress of the exam period itself. *Link to Laura*: Because Laura's staff are under considerable stress (heavy workloads, etc.), it seems likely that their immune systems are not functioning that effectively, which would account for the high levels of absence due to illness.

Topic 34 Life changes (page 113)

Fill in the blanks: (1) Holmes and Rahe, (2) stress-related illnesses, (3) 43, (4) readjustment, (5) life change units, (6) 50, (7) death of a spouse, (8) 100.

Applying your knowledge: *Identify the psychology*: Holmes and Rahe's SRRS lists various life changes such as marriage and a large mortgage as contributing to stress-related illness. The more life change units a person experiences in a given time, the more likely they are to become ill. *Link to David's illness*: David has experienced four major life changes in a relatively short period of time: marriage, birth of a child, promotion at work and a large mortgage, which would give him a high LCU score and a greater likelihood of developing stress-related illness.

Topic 35 Daily hassles (page 115)

Jumbled sentences: 3, 5, 6, 7, 1, 2, 4

Circle true or false: F, T, T, F, T, F

A marking exercise: This answer starts by addressing the 'how' instruction in the question. However, Devon then gets sidetracked by a description of what the study has *shown* (i.e. its findings). These are not required so would get no credit. The only creditworthy part of this answer is the first sentence, so this would be worth just 1 out of 4 marks.

Topic 36 Workplace stressors: workload (page 117)

Applying your knowledge: *Identify the psychology*: Research by Johansson *et al.* showed that workers who have high levels of workload and responsibility are more likely to have lower feelings of well-being and higher absence rates due to illness than workers with lower levels of workload. *Link to Jackie's stress*: Because Jackie always feels under time pressure to produce work within a limited time schedule, she is likely to experience high stress levels. Her boss could offer her stress management support (e.g. relaxation classes) to help her cope with the stress she is under.

A marking exercise: Parveen has started well, and her description of both studies is accurate and suitably detailed. However, the last five lines of this answer are irrelevant as there is no requirement to evaluate the research, therefore she has wasted her time doing so = 3 out of 4 marks.

Topic 37 Workplace stressors: control (page 119)

Circle true or false: F, T, F, T, F, F

Applying your knowledge: *Identify the psychology*: Research has shown that people find lack of control to be particularly stressful at work. Marmot *et al.* found that job demands were not as important as job control in determining levels of stress among civil servants. *Link to Rick*: Rick's lack of control over what news goes into the newspaper or how the news is collected is probably the main cause of his stress, particularly as he is clearly competent as a media graduate. His job demands, being at a basic grade, are likely to be fairly low, therefore are not likely to be a contributory factor in his stress.

Fill in the blanks: (1) low, (2) CHD, (3) high, (4) smoking, (5) coronary, (6) lower, (7) more, (8) angina, (9) protective, (10) older.

Topic 38 Personality factors: Type A (page 121)

Drawing conclusions: For example, *Finding 1*: In the Indian sample, drivers with the Type A behaviour pattern showed more evidence of braking and horn blowing than did drivers with the Type B behaviour pattern. *Conclusion 1*: This shows that in this sample, people with a Type A behaviour pattern are more aggressive and impatient in their driving behaviour. *Finding 2*: There was no difference in terms of braking or horn blowing behaviour between the Type A and Type B drivers in the US sample. *Conclusion 2*: This suggests there are cultural differences in the impact of Type A behaviour on driving, with Type A people in India demonstrating more aggression and impatience in their driving behaviour than those with the same Type A behaviour pattern in the US.

Circle true or false: F, T, F, T, F, T

Applying your knowledge: (a) Karl is more likely to have the Type A behaviour pattern. (b) Differences would include impatience (Karl would be more likely to be impatient with his work colleagues) and competitiveness (compared to Max, Karl would be more likely to strive for promotion and want to recognised as being the best in his department).

Choose the right answer: A, D

Topic 39 Personality factors: hardiness (page 123)

Drawing conclusions (a): For example, *Conclusion 1*: The graph suggests that males score higher on hardiness than females, although the difference between males and females is less among teachers than it is among students. *Conclusion 2*: There is little difference between students

Activities: suggested answers

and teachers in terms of hardiness, although male students appear to be more hardy than male teachers and female teachers more hardy than female students.

Research issues (b): *Problem:* Questionnaires suffer from the problem of the social desirability bias. In this study, it is possible that males in particular would have responded in a way that would make them appear more hardy than they actually were.

Applying your knowledge: *Identify the psychology:* Research on the hardy personality suggests that people who are high in hardiness are more resistant to the negative effects of stress. *Link to Kenzi and Cynthia's responses:* The fact that Kenzi and Cynthia react so differently to the stress of teaching suggests that Cynthia would score higher on hardiness than Kenzi, which would explain why she is less affected by the stress of the job. *Identify the psychology:* People high on hardiness score highly on control, challenge and commitment. *Link to Kenzi and Cynthia's responses:* Cynthia shows more evidence of challenge in her attitude to reorganisation, whereas Kenzi sees reorganisation as a threat.

A marking exercise: Jon's answer is clear, focused, accurate and suitably detailed. He has stuck to the task without being tempted about anything other than 'how' the research was carried out. It covers two studies so has a suitable amount of depth *and* breadth = 4 out of 4 marks. Sam's answer promises more than it delivers. It is all rather general and a little vague in that it doesn't focus on any specific research students. There is certainly some creditworthy material, particularly the middle section, but it lacks focus and detail = 2 out of 4 marks.

Topic 40 Psychological methods of stress management (page 125)

Spot the mistakes: [mistakes are in bold; correct material in brackets] Stress inoculation training aims to **raise individuals' hardiness levels** (enhance individuals' coping repertoires and empower existing coping skills) to make them more resistant to stress. The main phases of SIT are conceptualisation, **focusing** (skills acquisition) and application. In the first phase individuals are taught how to think differently about stressors, and to break these down into what they might achieve in the short, medium and long-term. In the second phase individuals are taught a range of coping skills, including problem solving and **avoidance** (using social support systems). In the final phase, application, these skills are put to the test in real-world situations. SIT usually consists of somewhere between 8 and 15 one-hour sessions. After treatment, clients are expected to practise their newly acquired coping skills **without** (with) further input from the SIT therapist. This is because relapse prevention skills are built into the initial SIT sessions.

Choose the right answer: B, C, F

Applying your knowledge *Identify the psychology:* The three phases of stress inoculation training are: conceptualisation, e.g. thinking differently about a stressor; skills acquisition, e.g. being taught how to use social support systems; and application, e.g. applying these skills in increasingly stressful situations. *Link to Kelda:* Kelda could be taught to think differently about her job, for example breaking down what she finds stressful into small, changeable components (conceptualisation). She could be taught to delegate and to use the support offered by her colleagues (skills acquisition) and then she can rehearse these new skills at work, with booster sessions from the therapist.

Topic 41 Biological methods of stress management (page 127)

Spot the mistakes: [mistakes are in bold; correct material in brackets] Benzodiazepines (BZs) combat the symptoms of stress by **reducing the actions of noradrenaline** (enhancing the action of GABA). This slows down action in the CNS, making it harder for neurons to be stimulated

and consequently making the person feel more relaxed. Beta-blockers work by **increasing levels of** (reducing the activity of) adrenaline in the brain, which reduces anxiety levels and makes the person feel calmer. BBs **stimulate** (block) special receptors on the surface of the heart, **increasing** (reducing) their activity. This makes the heart beat **faster** (slower) and makes it harder for blood vessels to contract. This causes blood pressure to fall, which makes the person feel calmer.

Applying your knowledge: *Identify the psychology:* Beta-blockers reduce anxiety levels by blocking the action of adrenaline and noradrenaline. As a result, the heart beats slower, blood pressure falls and the person feels calmer and less anxious. *Link to Kelda's use of drug therapy:* Because BZs can only be prescribed for short periods and Kelda's stress is likely to be more long-term, beta-blockers would be more suitable. By reducing some of the physiological symptoms of her stress, such as her heart beat and blood pressure, that would make her less anxious, and more confident about being able to do the job well.

A marking exercise: The first part of Cleo's answer covers a *strength* of drug therapies. The answer is not specific to drug therapies, it could be referring to any form of stress management. This has minimal merit as a result of this lack of specific content, but as the statements themselves are accurate, it would still get some credit for that = 1 out of 3 marks. The limitation is slightly better as there is some content that does apply specifically to drug therapies. However, this is not really elaborated and the lack of detail detracts from the overall quality of the answer = 2 out of 3 marks, so 3 out of 6 marks overall.

Chapter 5

Topic 42 Conformity (page 135)

Choose the right answer: Internalisation: D; Compliance: B

Drawing conclusions: *Conclusion 1:* Based on the data, this suggests that both boys and girls are influenced by the behaviour of others when judging the number of marbles in a jar. *Conclusion 2:* The data also suggests that boys are influenced more than girls are, with a greater tendency to make more extreme estimations when guided by the judgements of others.

Topic 43 Why people conform (page 137)

Circle true or false: F, T, T, F, T, T

Applying your knowledge: (a) Matt's behaviour can be explained in terms of normative social influence. By doing what others do this shows that he is motivated by the desire to be liked by his co-workers. (b) Matt's behaviour can now be explained in terms of informational social influence. He has taken on the attitudes to work that are present within his co-workers, because he appears to accept that is the appropriate way to behave in his new role.

A marking exercise: *Wesley's answer:* Although Wesley has shown evidence of understanding, he has made the error of including *two* explanations, when the question only asked for one. Therefore, his description of normative social influence (which gets the credit) lacks sufficient elaboration and would be worth 2 out of 3 marks. *Lucy's answer:* This answer is accurate and sufficiently detailed for the full 3 out of 3 marks.

Topic 44 Obedience (page 139)

Drawing conclusions: There are a number of possible findings from this graph. *Finding 1:* These include the finding that obedience levels drop from 40% to 30% when the teacher has to have physical contact with the learner when delivering shocks. *Conclusion 1:* This shows that victim proximity is an important factor when determining obedience, with greater proximity being associated with less obedience. *Finding 2*: When the experimenter is no longer in the same room as the teacher, obedience levels drop from 65% to 21%. *Conclusion 2*: This shows that authority proximity is an important factor in determining obedience, with greater proximity being associated with greater obedience.

Match them up: 1G, 2H, 3E, 4F, 5C, 6A, 7B, 8D

Circle true or false: F, T, F, T, F, T

Topic 45 Explanations of why people obey (page 141)

Choose the right answer: Gradual commitment: B; Agentic shift: D; The role of buffers: E

Research issues: *Identify an ethical issue*: The most obvious ethical issue is that of deception (deceiving other shoppers into thinking she was really asking for directions). *How should she deal with this*: Given that she has already deceived the participants, she should attempt to make up for this in a debriefing session, where she would apologise for the deception, explain the meaning of the research, offer the chance for participants to withdraw any data gathered from them and deal with any issues arising from the deception.

Applying your knowledge: *Identify the psychology:* The role of buffers. People find it easier to obey when there are buffers (e.g. they cannot see the consequences of their action) between them and their 'victim'. *Link to pilot's experiences:* The pilot admits that when the orders were for high altitude bombing (when they did not have to witness the consequences of their bombing), it was easier to obey orders. However, when they were bombing from much lower altitudes, and could see their victims, obeying orders became much more difficult. *Identify the psychology:* Agentic shift. People will shift from an autonomous state to an agentic state when they are given an order from someone in authority. In this state, they believe the responsibility for their actions lies within the authority figure rather than within themselves. *Link to pilot's experiences:* The pilot takes the attitude that he (and other bomber pilots) were not ultimately responsible for the consequences of their actions, but that this responsibility lay with the people who had issued them with their orders.

Circle true or false: F, T, T, T, T, F

Topic 46 Resisting pressure to conform (page 143)

Match them up: 1E, 2C, 3F, 4A, 5D, 6B

Applying your knowledge: *Identify the psychology*: Research has shown that people are better able to resist the urge to conform when they have a supporter who resists. This gives them more confidence to resist themselves. *Link to Sophie and Jasmine*: Because Jasmine tends to conform to the rest of the group when on her own but not when Sophie is around, this suggests that Sophie gives her confidence to resist her friends because Sophie acts as a role model for resisting conformity.

A marking exercise: There are two ways in which someone might resist conformity offered here. The first is appropriate (gaining social support) and there is some detail offered, so this would receive 2 out of 3 marks. The second way is a little vague as there is no suggestion of how someone might 'improve their morality'. There is some credit for this suggestion, but the difficulty of defining *how* this might be achieved would restrict this to 1 out of 3 marks. Total = 3 out of 6 marks.

Topic 47 Resisting pressure to obey (page 145)

Match them up: 1F, 2E, 3D, 4B, 5A, 6C

Applying your knowledge: *Identify the psychology*: People have a tendency to obey anyone who projects a commanding presence. By questioning the legitimacy of an order, or the person's right to give it, people are more able to resist obedience. *Link to Jason*: Because Jason is used to obeying orders from those he regards as having legitimate authority in the Royal Marines, he is less likely to obey orders from authority figures that he regards as lacking that legitimacy. This is an example of resisting obedience through questioning authority.

Research issues: *Finding 1*: The percentage of people who obeyed relatively minor requests from a smartly dressed confederate was generally higher than the percentage of people who obeyed the same requests from a casually dressed confederate. *Conclusion 1*: This suggests that people are more likely to obey someone who appears to have status than they are someone who appears to have less status. *Finding 2*: The percentage of people who obeyed dropped as the magnitude of the request increased regardless of whether the person was smartly or casually addressed. *Conclusion 2*: This suggests that people are more willing to resist requests that may be costly for them than they are to resist requests that are less personally costly.

Circle true or false: F, T, F, T, T, F

Topic 48 Locus of control (page 147)

Fill in the blanks: (1) control, (2) ability, (3) effort, (4) less, (5) independent, (6) external, (7) luck, (8) passive, (9) less, (10) independent.

Spot the mistakes: [mistakes are in bold; correct material in brackets] People who have an internal locus of control tend to see themselves as responsible for whatever happens to them. This is seen as a product of their ability or **their good luck** (effort). People who are high in internality are **more** (less) likely to rely on the opinions of others to determine how they behave. They are also more likely to take responsibility for their behaviour. Externals, in the other hand, believe that whatever happens to them is a product of **their own effort** (luck) or the effort of others. People who are high in externality are **more** (less) likely to display independent behaviour. They are also less likely to take responsibility for their behaviour.

Applying your knowledge: (a) Jack shows evidence of an internal locus of control. He believes that he can make a difference in his potential role on the student council and so uses his ability and effort to get people to vote for him. This active attitude is a characteristic of an internal locus of control. (b) Leanne shows evidence of an external locus of control. She does not believe that anything she does will make much difference to the outcome, and trusts instead to luck. This passive attitude is a characteristic of an external locus of control. (c) Jack is more likely to display independent behaviour because he has an internal locus of control. Internals rely less on the opinions of others and take more responsibility for what they do. This is evident in Jack's behaviour because he wants to change the way things are at his university rather than accept the status quo. He also believes that he can 'make a difference', which indicates he takes personal responsibility for bringing about this change.

Topic 49 Social change (page 149)

Match them up: 1C, 2D, 3A, 4E, 5B

Drawing conclusions: For example, *Finding 1:* The graph shows that, from 1960 onwards, non-violent minorities have been more successful than violent minorities in bringing about social change. *Conclusion 1:* This suggests that minorities who adopt non-violent ways of getting their message across are more successful in changing the views of the majority and bringing about social change. *Finding 2:* The largest difference in percentage success rates for violent and non-violent minorities in bringing about social change is most pronounced in recent years, with over 60% of non-violent minorities being successful in the years 2000–2006, whereas in the same period, only 12% of violent minorities were successful in bringing about social change. *Conclusion 2:* This shows that as well as factors such as consistency and augmentation being important factors in whether minorities change the views of the majority, it appears that the way in which they do it is also important, with non-violence being more successful than violence.

Applying your knowledge 1: *Identify the psychology*: Minorities must first gain the attention of the majority in order to create a conflict between what they accept to be the case and the point of view the minority is putting forward. *Link to healthy eating*: Celebrity TV chefs and TV campaigns have drawn our attention to the unhealthy ingredients of junk food. This creates a conflict for the majority because of their desire for good health and the realisation they are eating foods that are harmful. *Identify the psychology*: Research has shown that minorities have a greater influence if they are consistent in their message. *Link to healthy eating*: Celebrity chefs such as Jamie Oliver have used the media to try to change people's attitudes toward healthy eating, and have consistently tried to change school meals policy through classroom education. *Identify the psychology*: The influence of minorities is increased if they are seen to suffer to get their message across. *Link to healthy eating*: Chefs such as Jamie Oliver have faced hostility from parents and education chiefs and have had to endure great personal cost and stress, which means that people take the message more seriously and are more likely to be influenced by it.

Circle true or false: F, F, T, T, T, T

Chapter 6

Topic 50 Definitions of abnormality (page 155)

Choose the right answer: B, D

Circle true or false: T, F, F, T, F, T

Applying your knowledge: Anna's behaviour is most likely to be defined in terms of a 'failure to function adequately'. This is because her behaviour interferes with her ability to carry on with her daily routine, in this case being able to leave the house without undue anxiety.

Topic 51 The biological approach (page 157)

Fill in the blanks: (1) biological, (2) genes, (3) identical, (4) non-identical, (5) brain, (6) enlarged, (7) shrinkage, (8) neurotransmitters, (9) serotonin, (10) dopamine.

Match them up: 1D, 2G, 3F, 4H, 5A, 6B, 7E, 8C

A marking exercise: *AO1:* Two relevant points made, with a little elaboration would be worth 2 out of 3 marks. *AO2:* An appropriate point made with some elaboration, although this should mention the obvious conclusion that this figure is not 100%, therefore other factors must be operating. 2 out of 3 marks. Total = 4 out of 6 marks.

Topic 52 The psychodynamic approach (page 159)

Choose the right answer: B, D, F

Circle true or false: F, F, T, T, F, F

Jumbled sentences: Criticism 1: 3, 4, 2, 1. Criticism 2: 3, 4, 1, 2. Criticism 3: 3, 4, 1, 2.

Match them up: 1C, 2G, 3F, 4H, 5A, 6B, 7E, 8D

Topic 53 The behavioural approach (page 161)

Choose the right answer: B, D

Fill in the blanks: (1) experiences, (2) conflicts, (3) biological, (4) normal behaviour, (5) operant, (6) social learning, (7) environment, (8) disruptive.

A marking exercise: Although this looks like a very competent answer to the question, its relevance is strictly limited. Why is this the case? Aubrey focuses only on describing the three main types of learning that make up the behavioural model *without* applying this specifically to abnormality. There is some relevance in the first sentence, but the rest is implicit only. 2 out of 4 marks.

Topic 54 The cognitive approach (page 163)

Choose the right answer: B, D

Fill in the blanks: (1) distortions, (2) think, (3) activating, (4) belief, (5) rational, (6) irrational, (7) consequence, (8) healthy, (9) unhealthy, (10) faulty.

Applying your knowledge: *Identify the psychology*: Activating events can lead to irrational beliefs which in turn can lead to unhealthy consequences. *Link to Craig*: The activating event for Craig is the sight of people talking to each other, while perhaps looking at him. This leads to an irrational belief that they must be talking about him because they blame him for things going wrong. This leads to an unhealthy consequence in that he feels upset and depressed, with the result that he removes himself from social interactions.

Topic 55 Biological therapies: drugs (page 165)

Choose the right answer: C, D, E

Applying your knowledge: *Advantage*: An advantage for Lydia is that drug treatment are easy to use, which would mean that her treatment would not take up her time in the same way that psychological therapies would. Given that she is about to travel round the world, this would be far more convenient for her. *Disadvantage*: A disadvantage of drug treatments for Lydia is that they can have side effects. These can be unpleasant, which would make her trip less enjoyable, which may make her less motivated to continue her treatment, lowering its effectiveness.

Circle true or false: F, F, T, T, T, T

Match them up: 1F, 2H, 3E, 4G, 5B, 6C, 7D, 8A

Research issues: Appropriate ethical issues would include issues relevant to any experimental manipulation of this type, such as deception (participants would not have been told which condition they were in) and informed consent (by withholding this information, participants are denied the opportunity to give their consent). It seems unlikely that people suffering from depression would give their consent to receive a placebo instead of an effective drug. Alternatively, ethical issues might focus on the more specific ethical problems associated with this type of investigation. This would include the fact that, because investigators have a duty of care to their participants, withholding the antidepressant (in the placebo condition) from patients who need it would be to ignore this duty of care.

Drawing conclusions: *Finding 1:* There was a greater reduction in symptoms for participants on drug 2 than on drug 1. *Conclusion 1:* This suggests that the new drug (drug 1) is not as effective as the existing drug for the treatment of depressive symptoms. *Finding 2:* The reduction in symptoms for participants on the new drug was less than for those in the placebo condition. *Conclusion 2:* This suggests that any improvement over the three months for those on drug 1 could be solely due to a placebo effect rather than any effect due to the drug.

Topic 56 biological therapies: ECT (page 167)

Match them up: 1H, 2F, 3G, 4A, 5D, 6B, 7C, 8E

Circle true or false: T, F, F, F, F, T

Drawing conclusions: *Finding 1:* There is a decrease in the severity of symptoms as the level of the ECT charge increases. *Conclusion 1:* This suggests that there is a positive correlation between the level of ECT charge and its effectiveness. *Finding 2:* There is a decrease in the level of cognitive impairment as the level of ECT charge increases. *Conclusion 2:* This suggests that there is a positive correlation between the level of ECT charge and the likelihood of cognitive impairment.

Jumbled sentences: 5, 6, 3, 2, 1, 4

Topic 57 Psychological therapies: psychoanalysis (page 169)

Spot the mistakes: [mistakes are in bold; correct material in brackets] In psychoanalysis, the therapist attempts to bring **regressed** (repressed) thoughts and feelings into the **unconscious** (conscious) mind where they can be dealt with in a supportive environment. In order to achieve this, the therapist may use **the cognitive interview** (free association). In this technique, the client says the **first relevant thing** (first thing, no matter how irrelevant) that comes into their mind. The therapist then offers an interpretation of the client's behaviour. The client may show resistance to this interpretation by changing the subject or transferring emotions onto the therapist. This is known as **working through** (transference). Finally, the therapist and client go over the cause of their problems many times until the client experiences **transference** (insight), and is able to deal with them more constructively.

Drawing conclusions: *Finding 1:* The graph shows that there was less improvement in terms of symptom reduction for patients undergoing psychoanalysis for the first six months compared to CBT, but at one year psychoanalysis was superior. *Conclusion 1:* This suggests that psychoanalysis is more effective in the long term as a treatment for depression, whereas CBT is more effective in the short term. *Finding 2:* Both psychoanalysis and CBT show more improvement at all three points compared to a placebo group. *Conclusion 2:* This shows that there is a real therapeutic benefit to both therapies, as both have been shown to reduce depressive symptoms more effectively than a placebo condition.

Topic 58 Psychological therapies: systematic desensitisation (page 171)

Fill in the blanks: (1) relax, (2) muscle relaxation, (3) hierarchy, (4) least, (5) most, (6) in vitro, (7) in vivo, (8) relaxed.

Circle true or false: F, F, T, F, F, T

Applying your knowledge: *Hierarchy 1:* This could begin (step 1) with being in the same room as a member of the opposite sex, to smiling at them, to saying hello and so on. The 10th step in the hierarchy could then be asking them out on a date. *Hierarchy 2:* This could begin (step 1) with looking at a photograph of a plane, to going to an airport for coffee, to watching planes take off and so on. The 10th step in the hierarchy could then be going on a long-haul flight. Note that these steps could also be achieved 'in vitro' with the client visualising each of these steps.

A marking exercise: The first sentence is not AO2 so receives no credit. Two other points are made – that it helps reduce anxiety in a range of different phobias (this point is repeated) and that it is quick and easy (this is not elaborated). This answer would therefore receive just 2 out 4 marks.

Topic 59: Psychological therapies: CBT (page 173)

Choose the right answers: A, D, F

Applying your knowledge: *What is meant by CBT?* CBT is based on the idea that many problems are the result of irrational thinking. CBT attempts to help the person understand the irrationality of their thinking and the consequences of thinking in this way. Therapy enables them to change any self-defeating thoughts and become happier and less anxious as a result. *Why would it be suitable for Jasmine's grandmother?* Jasmine's grandmother's fears about deportation are clearly irrational, therefore her anxiety about deportation is unfounded. CBT would help because during therapy, the therapist would use disputing techniques to challenge her beliefs, for example using empirical disputing would show how there was no evidence that she was about to be deported or that people were talking about her.

Research issues: (a) An advantage of gaining qualitative data is that it offers the researcher the chance to gain in-depth information that would not be possible with a simple rating scale. For example, the patients receiving CBT could give information about the specific areas in which they felt the greatest improvement. (b) *Factor 1:* The different therapies would have been delivered by different therapists. Research has shown that the qualities of the individual therapist are every bit as important as the qualities of the therapies in the study therefore these would have a strong effect on any potential outcomes for the patient. *Factor 2:* Patients may well have been referred to the different types of therapies based on the severity of their symptoms or other factors that would make one type of therapy more suitable than the others. This would also influence the speed at which they would improve, or even the amount of improvement that might be reasonably expected.

Drawing conclusions: *Finding 1:* The level of self-reported improvement reported by patients with depression who received REBT was significantly greater than for the other two therapies. *Conclusion 1:* This suggests that REBT is a more effective treatment for depression than either psychoanalysis or counselling. *Finding 2:* The level of self-reported improvement reported by patients with anxiety who received REBT was approximately the same as that reported for the other two therapies. *Conclusion 2:* This suggests that all three therapies are moderately and equally effective in the treatment of anxiety.

Glossary

A-B-C model Refers to the three components of experience that can be used to judge whether an individual's belief system is distorted. A (activating event) leads to B (belief) and ultimately C (consequences).

Abnormality In psychology, behaviour that is neither typical or usual.

Acoustic Refers to sounds or the sense of hearing.

Acronyms A word or phrase formed from the initial letters of the item to be remembered.

Acrostics A sentence in which the first letter of each word spells out the message to be remembered.

ACTH *see* Adrenocorticotrophic hormone.

Activating event In REBT, something that is believed to happen, to have happened or to be about to happen and that triggers irrational beliefs leading to emotional problems.

Adaptive Any physical or psychological characteristic that enhances an individual's survival and reproduction, and is thus likely to be naturally selected.

Adrenal cortex A region of the adrenal gland, located above the kidneys. The adrenal cortex (outer region) manufactures glucocortoids (such as cortisol) and sex hormones, such as testosterone.

Adrenal medulla A region of the adrenal gland, located above the kidneys. The adrenal medulla (inner region) produces adrenaline and noradrenaline.

Adrenaline A hormone associated with arousal of the autonomic nervous system (e.g. raised heart rate). It is also a neurotransmitter. Americans use the term 'epinephrine'.

Adrenocorticotrophic hormone (ACTH) A hormone produced in the pituitary gland as a response to stress. Its principal effect is the release of cortisol from the adrenal cortex.

Aerophobia The fear of flying.

Agentic shift People may move from being in a state where they take personal responsibility for their actions (an autonomous state) to a state where they believe they are acting on behalf of an authority figure (an agentic state).

Agentic state A state where people believe they are acting on behalf of an authority figure.

Agoraphobia Fear of being in places or situations from which escape might be difficult.

Aim A statement of what the researcher(s) intend to find out in a research study. Often confused with a hypothesis.

Anonymity An important aspect of confidentiality, a participant remains anonymous, i.e. their name is withheld or simply not recorded.

ANS *see* Autonomic nervous system.

Anti-anxiety drugs The group of drugs that aim to reduce anxiety. They may do this by enhancing the neurotransmitter GABA or by reducing activity in the sympathetic nervous system.

Antidepressant drugs A group of stimulant drugs that increase the production of serotonin and/or noradrenaline, and thus reduce symptoms of depression.

Antipsychotic drugs Drugs that are effective in the treatment of psychotic illnesses, such as schizophrenia.

Anxiety A nervous emotional state where we fear that something unpleasant is about to happen. People often become anxious when they are in stressful situations. Anxiety tends to be accompanied by physiological arousal (e.g. a pounding heart and rapid shallow breathing).

Aquaphobia An extreme fear of water.

Arachnophobia An extreme fear of spiders.

Articulatory process A component of the phonological loop which acts as an 'inner voice', i.e. words/sounds are verbally repeated.

Articulatory suppression task An activity that prevents rehearsal of words in the articulatory loop.

Attachment An emotional bond between two people that endures over time. Leads to certain behaviours such as clinging and proximity-seeking. Serves the function of protecting an infant.

Attachment disorder A psychiatric disorder characterised by an individual's inability to identify a preferred attachment figure.

Attachment type Refers to whether a person is securely or insecurely attached, i.e. the way you relate to others in the context of intimate relationships.

Attrition The loss of participants from a study over time. This is likely to leave a biased sample or a sample that is too small.

Autonomic nervous system (ANS) Governs the body's involuntary activities (e.g. stress, heart beat) and is self-regulating (autonomous). It is divided into the sympathetic branch (fight or flight) and the parasympathetic branch (rest and digest).

Autonomous state A state where people take personal responsibility for their actions.

Bar chart The height of each bar represents the frequency of that item. The categories are generally placed on the horizontal (x axis) and frequency is on the vertical (y axis). Bar charts are suitable for words and numbers (nominal or ordinal/interval data).

BBs *see* Beta-blockers.

Behaviour checklist A systematic method for recording observations where a list of behavioural categories is used. The observer(s) can note every time any behaviour on the checklist is observed.

Behavioural approach to psychopathology Behaviourists believe that normal *and* abnormal behaviours are acquired as a result of the experiences we have in life. Abnormal behaviours are learned through the processes of conditioning and social learning.

Behavioural categories Dividing a target behaviour (such as attachment or sociability) into a subset of component behaviours to enable objective and reliable observations of the target behaviour.

Benzodiazepines (BZs) A group of drugs that have a tranquillising effect and are used to treat anxiety and stress. They work by slowing down the activity of the central nervous system.

Beta-blockers (BBs) A drug that decreases anxiety by blocking the action of adrenaline and noradrenaline during sympathetic arousal.

Biological approach to psychopathology Explains behaviour in terms of physiological and/or genetic causes. A mental disorder represents the consequences of a malfunction of biological processes.

Boredom effect An example of an order effect. In a repeated measures design, participants may do less well on a later condition because they have lost interest.

BPS Code of Ethics Ethical guidelines produced by the British Psychological Society. This includes information defining the ethical issues and information about how to deal with ethical issues.

Brain scanning A variety of techniques used to investigate brain functioning by taking images of a living brain. This makes it possible to match regions of the brain to behaviour by asking participants to engage in particular activities while the scan is taking place.

Buffer Something (e.g. a physical barrier or an ideological justification) that protects an individual from perceiving the true impact of their actions.

Burnout A psychological term referring to the emotional exhaustion and diminished interest in work that is a result of the chronic stress found in many occupations.

BZs *see* Benzodiazepines.

Capacity A measure of how much can be held in memory. Measured in terms of bits of information such as number of digits.

Cardiovascular problems Disorders of the heart or circulatory system, including hypertension (high blood pressure and heart disease).

Case study A research method that involves a detailed study of a single individual, institution or event.

CBT *see* Cognitive behavioural therapy.

Central executive A component of the working memory model, a hypothetical construct in working memory that monitors and coordinates all other mental functions in working memory.

Central nervous system (CNS) Comprises the brain and the spinal cord.

CHD *see* Coronary heart disease.

Child care The caring for and supervision of a child or children, usually from newborn to age 13.

Chunking Miller proposed that the capacity of short-term memory can be enhanced by grouping sets of digits or letters into meaningful units or 'chunks'.

Classical conditioning In classical conditioning, the neutral stimulus (NS) becomes the conditioned stimulus (CS) after the NS has been paired with the unconditioned stimulus (UCS). The NS now takes on the properties of a CS so that it produces a learned or conditioned response (CR).

Closed question A question that has a resitricted range of answers from which respondents select one; produces quantitative data.

CNS *see* Central nervous system

Co-variable A variable in a correlational analysis that is believed to vary systematically with another co-variable.

Coding system A systematic method for recording observations in which individual behaviours are given a code for ease of recording.

Cognitive approach to psychopathology Psychological disorders are explained in terms of irrational and negative thinking about the world. If this faulty thinking can be changed, the problem should disappear.

Cognitive behavioural therapy (CBT) A combination of cognitive therapy (to change dysfunctional *thoughts* and *beliefs*) and behavioural therapy (to change *behaviour* in response to these thoughts and beliefs).

Cognitive impairment The inability to think, e.g. concentrate, comprehend, formulate ideas, reason, remember and so on.

Cognitive interview (CI) A police technique for interviewing witnesses to a crime. The method is based on what psychologists have found out about memory.

Cognitive therapy A form of psychological therapy that aims to change dysfunctional thoughts and beliefs, based on the cognitive approach.

Cohort effect An effect caused because one group of participants has unique characteristics due to time-specific experiences during their development, such as growing up during the Second World War.

Collectivism An approach that places more value on the 'collective' rather than on the individual, and on interdependence rather than on independence. The opposite is true of individualist culture.

Compliance Going along with others to gain their approval or avoid their disapproval. This is a result of social comparison, and enables an individual to adjust their behaviour to that of the group. There is no change in the person's underlying attitude; only their public behaviour.

Concordance rates A measure of similarity between two individuals or sets of individuals on a given trait, usually expressed as a percentage.

Conditioned response (CR) In classical conditioning, the response elicited by the conditioned stimulus (CS), i.e. a new association has been learned so that the neutral stimulus (NS) produces the unconditioned response (UCR) which is now called the CR.

Conditioned stimulus (CS) In classical conditioning, the neutral stimulus (NS) becomes the CS after the NS has been paired with the unconditioned stimulus (UCS). The NS now takes on the properties of the UCS and produces the unconditioned response (now a conditioned response, CR).

Confederate An individual in a study who is not a real participant and has been instructed how to behave by the investigator/experimenter.

Confidentiality A participant's right to have personal information protected. The Data Protection Act makes confidentiality a legal right.

Conformity A form of social influence that results from exposure to the majority position and leads to compliance with that position. It is the tendency for people to adopt the behaviour, attitudes and values of other members of the group.

Content analysis A kind of observational study in which behaviour is observed indirectly using written or verbal material such as interviews, conversations, books, diaries or TV programmes.

Continuity hypothesis The view that there is a link between an infant's attachment relationship and later behaviour (including later relationships).

Continuous variable Any variable that is not in categories, e.g. number of children in a family would be continuous.

Control In the context of workplace stress, the degree to which workers perceive that they have direction over important aspects of their work, such as deadlines, procedures, etc.

Controlled observation A form of investigation in which behaviour is observed but under structured conditions, as opposed to a naturalistic observation.

Coronary heart disease (CHD) A medical condition where the blood vessels fail to supply adequate blood to the heart.

Correlation coefficient A number between −1and +1 that tells us how closely the co-variables in a correlational analysis are related.

Correlational analysis Determines the extent of a relationship between two co-variables.

Corticotrophin-releasing factor (CRF) A neurotransmitter involved in the stress response. It is released by the hypothalamus and triggers production of ACTH in the pituitary gland.

Cortisol A hormone released by the adrenal glands that is produced when an animal is stressed.

Counterbalance An experimental technique used to overcome order effects. Counterbalancing ensures that each condition is tested first or second in equal amounts.

Counterconditioning Being taught a new association that is the opposite of the original association, thus removing the original association.

Covert observation Observing people without their knowledge, e.g. using one-way mirrors. This is done because participants are likely to change their behaviour if they know they are being observed.

CRF *see* Corticotrophin-releasing factor.

Critical period A limited window in biological development during which certain characteristics can only develop.

Cross-sectional study One group of participants representing one section of society (e.g. young people or working-class people) are compared with participants from another group (e.g. old people or middle-class people).

Cultural bias The tendency to judge all people in terms of your own cultural assumptions. This distorts or *biases* your judgement.

Cultural relativism The view that ideas of normal and abnormal behaviour differ from culture to culture.

Culture The rules, customs, morals and ways of interacting that bind together members of a society or some other collection of people.

Curvilinear correlation A non-linear relationship between co-variables. For example, arousal and performance do not have a linear (straight line) relationship. Performance on many tasks is depressed when arousal is too high or too low, but it is high when arousal is moderate. The result is a U-shaped relationship (i.e. curved).

Daily hassles Frustrating, irritating everyday experiences that occur regularly in our work, home and personal life.

Daily uplifts The minor positive experiences of everyday life that often counter the negative effects of daily hassles.

Day care A form of child care that is not overnight. Offered at a non-home location or by an adult providing care in their own home or in the child's own home. Includes childminding and day nurseries.

Debriefing A post-research interview designed to inform participants about the true nature of a study, and to restore them to the state they were in at the start of the study. It may also be used to gain feedback about the procedures used in the study.

Decay An explanation for forgetting – the memory trace in our brain disintegrates over time.

Glossary

Deception This occurs when a participant is not told the true aims of a study (e.g. what participation will involve). Thus, the participants cannot give truly informed consent.

Defence mechanisms In psychoanalytic theory, unconscious strategies (such as repression, denial and projection) used by the ego to defend itself against anxiety.

Demand characteristics A cue that makes participants aware of what the researcher expects to find or how participants are expected to behave.

Dependent variable (DV) Depends in some way on the independent variable (IV). The DV is measured to assess the effects of the IV.

Depression A mental disorder characterised by a lowering of mood, often accompanied by difficulty thinking, concentrating and sleeping, as well as feelings of anxiety.

Desensitisation hierarchy In systematic desensitisaton therapy, a list of anxiety-provoking situations arranged in order from least to most distressing. Working through these should result in a reduced sensitivity to the anxiety-provoking situation.

Deviation from ideal mental health Abnormality is seen as deviating from an ideal of positive mental health. This includes a positive attitude towards the self and an accurate perception of reality.

Deviation from social norms Abnormal behaviour is a deviation from unwritten rules about how one 'ought' to behave. Violation of these rules is considered abnormal.

Diathesis-stress model In the case of certain disorders, individuals inherit a vulnerability for the disorder (diathesis) which develops only if such individuals are exposed to difficult environmental conditions (stress). The greater the underlying vulnerability, the less stress needed to trigger the disorder.

Digit span A way of measuring the capacity of short-term memory in terms of the maximum number of digits that can be recalled in the correct order.

Directional hypothesis States the direction of a difference (e.g. bigger or smaller) or correlation (positive or negative).

Disinhibited attachment A type of insecure attachment where children do not form close attachments. Such children will treat strangers with inappropriate familiarity (overfriendliness) and may be attention-seeking.

Disorganised attachment Characterised by a lack of consistent patterns of social behaviour. Such infants lack a coherent strategy for dealing with the stress of separation. For example, they show very strong attachment behaviour which is suddenly followed by avoidance or looking fearful towards their caregiver.

Displacement An explanation for forgetting, where existing information is displaced out of memory by new information.

Disruption of attachment Children who have formed an attachment with a primary attachment figure may experience some temporary or long-term break. Such a break may be physical (which causes emotional separation) or just emotional, for example if the child's mother is depressed.

Dodo bird effect The observation that all psychotherapies share common factors (e.g. attention from the psychotherapist, chance to express one's feelings) and therefore there are only small differences between different therapies in terms of success. The term 'dodo bird' is taken from *Alice in Wonderland* where the dodo declared that everyone has won and should have prizes.

Dopamine A neurotransmitter involved in the sensation of pleasure. Unusually high levels are associated with schizophrenia.

Double blind Neither the participant or researcher are aware of the research aims or other important details of a study, and thus have no expectations that might alter a participant's behaviour.

Dual-task performance Refers to a research procedure where an individual is asked to perform two tasks simultaneously. If participants are slower doing these tasks at the same time than when doing them separately (i.e. these two tasks interfere with each other), it is assumed that both tasks compete for the same resources in the brain. For example, reading outloud and walking are two tasks that can be performed just as well separately as simultaneously. However, reading outloud while writing a letter at the same time leads to reduced performance on each task.

Duration A measure of how long a memory lasts before it is no longer available.

DV *see* Dependent variable.

Ecological validity A form of external validity. The ability to generalise a research effect beyond the particular setting in which it is demonstrated to other settings.

ECT *see* electroconvulsive therapy

Effective Pre-School Primary Education (EPPE) A longitudinal study of the effects of pre-school on later development. Now called EPPSE (Effective Pre-School, Primary & Secondary Education) because the original children are now being studied at secondary school age.

Ego The conscious, rational part of the personality. It develops because a young child must deal with the constraints of reality and so is governed by the reality principle.

Electroconvulsive therapy (ECT) The administration of an electrical current through electrodes on the scalp. This induces a seizure, which has been shown to sometimes be effective in relieving major depression.

Encoding The way information is changed so it can be stored in the memory. Information enters the brain via the senses (e.g. eyes and ears) and is then stored (encoded) in various forms, such as visual codes (like a picture), acoustic forms (sounds) or a semantic form (the meaning of the experience).

Episodic buffer In the working memory model, a store that receives input from many sources, temporarily stores this information, then integrates it in order to construct a mental episode of what is being experienced right now.

EPPE *see* Effective Pre-School Primary Education

Ethical guidelines Concrete, quasi-legal documents that help to guide conduct within psychology.

Ethical issues Arise in research where there are conflicting sets of values between researchers and participants concerning the goals, procedures or outcomes of a research study.

EV *see* Extraneous variable

Event sampling An observational technique: counting the number of times a certain behaviour (event) occurs.

Experiment A research method to investigate causal relationships by observing the effect of an independent variable on the dependent variable (see laboratory, field and natural experiment).

Experimental condition In an experiment with a repeated measures design, this is the condition containing the independent variable.

Experimenter effect *see* Investigator effect.

External validity Concerns the degree to which a research finding can be generalised to, for example, other settings (ecological validity), or other groups of people (population validity), and over time (historical validity).

Externality (external control) Individuals who tend to believe that their behaviour and experience is caused by events outside their own control.

Extraneous variable (EV) Any variable, other than the IV, that may potentially affect the DV and thereby confound the findings of a research study. Order effects, participant variables and experimenter effects may act as EVs.

Eyewitness testimony (EWT) The evidence provided in court by a person who witnessed a crime, with a view to identifying the perpetrator of the crime. The accuracy of eyewitness recall may be affected during initial encoding, subsequent storage and/or eventual retrieval.

Failure to function adequately Mentally healthy people are judged as being able to operate within certain acceptable limits. If abnormal behaviour interferes with daily functioning, it may be considered abnormal.

False memory Remembering events, especially traumatic events, that have not actually occurred. Such recall may be prompted by suggestions made of a therapist.

Faulty thinking Dysfunctional or irrational mental activity.

Field experiment A controlled experiment that is conducted outside a laboratory (i.e. not in a specially designed environment). The experimenter goes to the participant rather than vice versa. The IV is still manipulated by the experimenter, and therefore causal relationships can be demonstrated.

Fight or flight A term meaning an animal is energised to either fight or run away in response to a sudden stressor.

Free recall A method of testing memory. Participants are given a list of items to be remembered, one at a time. Later the participant is asked to recall the items (e.g. by writing down as many items from the list as possible in any order they choose).

GABA (gamma-amino-butyric-acid) A neurotransmitter that reduces excitement in the nervous system, thus acting as a natural form of anxiety reducer.

Genetic inheritance Receiving genetically coded traits as a result of transmission from parent to offspring.

Gradual commitment The process of agreeing at first to a small request and then to larger and larger requests.

Graph A pictorial representation of the relationship between variables.

Group norm The standards that govern behaviour within a group.

Hardiness A personality characteristic that provides a defence against the negative effects of stress. A person with a hardy personality is high in control, commitment and challenge.

Hardiness training The aim of hardiness training is to acquire the characteristics of a 'hardy' personality; to increase self-confidence and a sense of self-control within an individual's life.

Heroic imagination A mental orientation that makes people more likely to act 'heroically' when an opportunity arises.

Hippocampus A structure in the subcortex (i.e. 'under' the cortex). It is present in each hemisphere of the forebrain and is part of the limbic system, therefore involved in motivation, emotion and learning.

Holocaust The systematic, bureaucratic, state-sponsored persecution and murder of approximately six million Jews by the Nazi regime and its collaborators. 'Holocaust' is a word of Greek origin meaning 'sacrifice by fire'.

Hormones Chemical substances that circulate in the blood and only affect target organs. They are produced in large quantities but disappear very quickly. Their effects are slow in comparison to the nervous system, but very powerful.

Hypothalamus A structure in the subcortex (i.e. 'under' the cortex). It is present in each hemisphere of the forebrain. It functions to regulate bodily temperature, metabolic processes such as eating and other autonomic activities, including emotional responses.

Hypothesis A precise and testable statement about the assumed relationship between variables.

Id The irrational, primitive part of the personality. It demands immediate satisfaction and is ruled by the pleasure principle.

Immune system Designed to defend the body against antigens (bacteria, viruses, toxins, etc.) that would otherwise invade it. White blood cells (leucocytes) identify and eliminate foreign bodies (antigens).

Independent behaviour Behaving in a way that shows freedom from any control or influence of other group members.

Independent groups design An experimental design where participants are allocated to two (or more) groups, each one receiving a different treatment.

Independent variable (IV) An event that is directly manipulated by the experimenter in order to observe its effects on the dependent variable (DV).

Indigenous theory A theory developed within a culture and applied to that cultural group, as opposed to using a theory that was developed in relation to another cultural group.

Individualism An approach that values independence rather than reliance on others. This is typical of Western cultures, in contrast to many non-Western cultures that could be described as collectivist.

Informational social influence The result of wanting to be right, i.e. looking to others for the right answer, and conforming to their opinion.

Informed consent In terms of ethics, participants must be given comprehensive information concerning the nature and purpose of a study and their role in it. This is necessary in order that they can make an informed decision about whether to participate.

Innate Behaviours that are a product of genetic factors. These may be apparent at birth or appear later through the process of maturation.

Inner scribe In the working memory model, a component of the visuo-spatial sketchpad that deals with spatial relations, such as the arrangement of objects in the visual field.

Insecure attachment Develops as a result of a caregiver's lack of sensitive responding to an infant's needs. May be associated with subsequent poor cognitive and emotional development.

Insecure-avoidant attachment Infants who are willing to explore and are unresponsive to mother's return. They generally avoid social interaction and intimacy with others.

Insecure-resistant attachment Infants are less interested in exploring and show distress on mother's return. Generally they both seek and reject intimacy and social interaction.

Institutional care An 'institution' is a place dedicated to a particular task, such as looking after children awaiting adoption, caring for the mentally ill or looking after patients in hospital. Institutional care refers to situations where people are looked after for a period of time, as opposed to day care or outpatient care where people go home every day. In the past, such institutions had fairly strict regimes and offered little emotional care.

Inter-observer reliability The extent to which there is agreement between two or more observers involved in conducting an observation.

Internal validity Concerns whether a study or measurement has tested what it set out to test.

Internal working model A cluster of concepts about relationships. In the short term it gives a child insight into their caregiver's behaviour. In the long term it acts as a template for future relationships because it generates expectations about how people behave.

Internalisation Going along with others because of an acceptance of their point of view. This is a result of an examination of the group's position, which may lead to *validation* of the person's own views or acceptance of the group's views both in public and in private.

Internality (internal control) Individuals who tend to believe that they are responsible for their behaviour and experience (as distinct from external influences).

Intervening variable A variable that comes between two other variables that can explain the relationship between those two variables.

Interview A research method or technique that involves a face-to-face, 'real-time' interaction with another individual and results in the collection of data.

Interviewer bias The effect of an interviewer's expectations on a respondent's behaviour. Such expectations may be communicated unconsciously.

Investigator effect Where the investigator directly or indirectly has an effect on a participant's performance, other than what was intended.

Irrational belief/thoughts *see* Faulty thinking.

IV *see* Independent variable.

Job control *see* Control.

Job strain The suggestion that workplace stress is a combination of low control and high job demand.

Keyword method A technique for improving memory, where a word to be remembered (such as 'Canberra', a city in Australia) is linked to some known words (can of berries). A visual image can be formed, for example a map of Australia on the can of berries, and this should improve recall of the link between the word and its meaning (that Canberra is a city in Australia).

Glossary

Laboratory experiment An experiment carried out in a controlled setting. Lab experiments tend to have high experimental (internal) validity and low ecological (external) validity, although this isn't always the case.

LCU see Life change units

Leading question A question that, either by its form or content, suggests what answer is desired or leads to the desired answer.

Learned helplessness Occurs when an animal finds that its responses are ineffective, and then it learns that there is no point in responding and behaves passively in the future.

Learning theory The name given to a group of explanations, i.e. classical and operant conditioning. Essentially, these explain behaviour in terms of learning rather than any inborn tendencies (the biological/evolutionary approach) or higher order thinking (the cognitive approach).

Legitimate authority A person or organisation who has been given command through legislation or general agreement.

Leucocytes White blood cells, the cells of the immune system that defend the body against infectious disease and foreign bodies.

Life change units (LCU) A measure of the stress levels of different types of change experienced during a given period, e.g. the death of a spouse is scored at 100; divorce at 73.

Life changes Events (e.g. divorce or bereavement) that require a significant adjustment in a person's life, thus they are a significant source of stress. They may be positive as well as negative, e.g. getting married.

Line graph A graph displaying continuous variables. Shows information as a series of data points connected by straight line segments.

Linear correlation A systematic relationship between co-variables that is defined by a straight line. *See also* Curvilinear correlation.

Locus of control An aspect of our personality. People differ in their beliefs about whether the outcomes of their actions are dependent on what they do (internal control) or on events outside their personal control (external control).

Long-term memory (LTM) Memory for events that have happened in the past. Lasts anywhere from two minutes to 100 years and has potentially unlimited duration and capacity.

Longitudinal study Observation of the same items over a long period of time.

Majority influence A form of social influence; where a person follows the norm established by more than 50% of the people (the majority).

Maladaptive behaviour Behaviours that inhibit a person's ability to cope with, or adjust to, particular situations.

Matched pairs design An experimental design where pairs of participants are matched in terms of key variables such as age and IQ. One member of each pair is placed in one experimental group and the other member is placed in the other experimental group.

Maternal reflexive thinking Being able to understand what someone else is thinking.

McCarthyism The practice of making accusations of disobedience and treason without proper regard for evidence, based on the activities of American Senator McCarthy in the 1950s.

Mean Calculated by adding up all the numbers and dividing by the number of numbers.

Measures of central tendency A descriptive statistic that provides information about a 'typical' number for a data set.

Measures of dispersion A descriptive statistic that provides information about the spread of a set of scores.

Median The middle value in an ordered list.

Meta-analysis A researcher looks at the findings from a number of different studies in order to reach a general conclusion about a particular hypothesis.

Method of loci A technique for improving memory, based on placing items to be remembered at key locations (loci). The items are remembered by mentally walking around the locations.

Mind maps A technique for improving memory where a diagram represents the key concepts and the links between them. The distinctiveness of the images aids recall.

Minority influence A form of social influence where members of the majority group change their beliefs or behaviour due to the actions of one or a few people (a minority group).

Misleading information Information that might suggest a particular answer to an eyewitness, thus leading them to provide a different answer than they might otherwise have given.

Mode The value that is most common.

Modelling The process of imitating another's behaviour, which involves cognitive representations of the modelled activities as well as abstractions of the underlying rules of the modelled behaviours.

Monitoring/challenging (lack of) Accepting an authority figure's definition of a situation without further checking (lack of monitoring). Failing to challenge the authority or doing so in a hesitant way that is easily overruled (challenging errors).

Monotropy The idea that the one relationship an infant has with his/her primary attachment figure is of special significance in emotional development.

Moral dilemma A conflict over the appropriate decision to make over questions of right and wrong.

Morality Rules about right and wrong that guide our behaviour, based on socially agreed principles.

Multi-store model (MSM) An explanation of memory based on three separate memory stores, and how information is transferred between these stores.

Mundane realism Refers to how a study mirrors the real world. The experimental environment is realistic to the degree to which experiences encountered in the experimental environment will occur in everyday life (the 'real world').

Natural experiment A research method in which the experimenter cannot manipulate the independent variable directly, but where it varies as a consequence of some other action, and the effect on a dependent variable can be observed.

Naturalistic observation A research method carried out in a naturalistic setting, in which the investigator does not interfere in any way, but merely observes the behaviour(s) in question (likely to involve the use of structured observations).

Negative affectivity A tendency to experience negative emotions, such as anger, contempt, disgust, guilt, fear and nervousness.

Negative correlation As one co-variable increases, the other decreases.

Neuroanatomy The branch of anatomy that deals with the structure of the brain and other parts of the nervous system.

Neurochemistry The action of chemicals (e.g. neurotransmitters) in the brain and the drugs that influence neural activity.

Neuron A specialised cell in the nervous system for transmission of information.

Neurotransmitter Chemical substances, such as serotonin or dopamine, that play an important part in the workings of the nervous system by transmitting nerve impulses across a synapse.

Neutral stimulus (NS) In classical conditioning, the stimulus that initially does not produce the target response, i.e. it is neutral. Through association with the unconditioned stimulus (UCS), the NS acquires the properties of the UCS and becomes a conditioned stimulus (CS) producing a conditioned response (CR).

NICHD Stands for National Institute for Child Health and Human Development who have sponsored an American longitudinal study of the effects of early child care on development.

Non-directional hypothesis Predicting that there will be a difference between two conditions or two groups of participants, without stating the direction of the difference.

Non-psychotic illness A psychotic illness is one where a patient loses touch with reality, such as schizophrenia. Neurotic illnesses are non-psychotic.

Noradrenaline A hormone associated with arousal of the autonomic nervous system (e.g. raised heart rate), and also a neurotransmitter.

Normative social influence The result of wanting to be liked and be accepted as part of a group by following its norms.

NS *see* Neutral stimulus.

Obedience A type of social influence whereby somebody acts in response to a direct order. There is also the implication that the person receiving the order is made to respond in a way that they would not have done without the order.

Observation A study that only uses observational techniques as opposed to a study that uses them to measure one of the variables.

Observational learning Learning through observing others and imitating their behaviour.

Observational techniques The use of systematic methods to record behaviour by watching or listening to what people do. Such techniques may be used in an observational study, an experiment (to measure the DV) or other study.

Observer bias The tendency for observations to be influenced by the expectations or prejudices of the observer.

Obsessive-compulsive disorder (OCD) A mental disorder where anxiety arises from both obsessions (persistent and intrusive thoughts) and compulsions (means of controlling these thoughts).

Oedipal conflict Incestuous feelings that a young boy develops for his mother, coupled with rivalry with his father for her affections, leading to castration anxiety (fear that his penis will be removed). Resolution of this conflict leads to the development of the superego.

Open question A question that invites respondents to provide their own answers rather than to select an answer that has been provided. Tends to produce qualitative data.

Operant conditioning Involves reinforcement. Any behaviour that results in a pleasant consequence is increasingly 'stamped in' (reinforced). It becomes more probable that you will repeat that behaviour in the future. If you do something and it results in an unpleasant consequence (punishment), it becomes less likely that you will repeat that behaviour.

Operationalise Providing variables in a form that can be easily measured, i.e. the constituent operations are identified.

Opportunity sample A sample of participants produced by selecting people who are most easily available at the time of the study.

Order effects In a repeated measures design, an extraneous variable arising from the order in which conditions are presented. For example, participants do better the second time because they have had some practice.

Overt observation An observational technique where observations are 'open', i.e. the participants are aware that they are being observed.

Own-age bias The tendency to recognise or remember things more easily if they relate to your own age group.

Participant variables Characteristics of individual participants (such as age, intelligence, etc.) that might influence the outcome of a study.

Peer relations The social relationships and interpersonal interactions between people of a similar age.

Phobia A mental disorder characterised by high levels of anxiety that, when experienced, interfere with normal living. Includes specific phobias (e.g. fear of heights) and social phobias (anxiety in social situations).

Phonological loop (PL) A component of the working memory model that encodes speech sounds, involving maintenance rehearsal (repeating the words over and over, i.e. a *loop*). It is divided into a phonological store (inner ear) and an articulatory process (inner voice).

Phonological store A component of the phonological loop that acts as an 'inner ear', i.e. storing sounds.

Pilot study A small-scale trial of a study. Run to test any aspects of a research design for a proposed research study, with a view to making improvements.

Pituitary gland Known as the 'mastergland', the pituitary releases a variety of hormones that act on other glands throughout the body.

Pituitary-adrenal system Stress response involving the pituitary gland and adrenal cortex. It helps the body cope with chronic stressors.

Placebo A drug or treatment that contains no active ingredient or therapeutic procedure.

Pleasure principle In Freudian psychology, the id's primitive desire to seek instant gratification and avoid pain at all costs.

Positive correlation Co-variables increase together.

Post-event information In eyewitness testimony, information supplied after the event, such as a leading question or misleading information.

Post-traumatic stress disorder (PTSD) A condition triggered by a terrifying event (such as combat or rape). Symptoms may include flashbacks, nightmares and severe anxiety, as well as uncontrollable thoughts about the event.

Practice effect In a repeated measures design participants may do better on one condition rather than another because they have completed one already and therefore may have improved their ability to perform the task.

Prefrontal cortex The anterior part of the frontal lobe, involved in 'executive functions', such as complex cognitive behaviours, moderating socially appropriate behaviours, personality and goal-directed behaviour (motivation).

Presumptive consent A method of dealing with lack of informed consent or deception by asking a group of people who are similar to the participants whether they would agree to take part in a study. If this group of people consent to the procedures in the proposed study, it is *presumed* that the real participants would agree as well.

Primary attachment The most import emotional bond for an individual.

Primary attachment figure The person who has formed the closest bond with a child. Demonstrated by the intensity of the relationship. Usually a child's biological mother, but could be an adoptive mother, a father, grandmother, etc.

Primary reinforcer A reinforcer is any experience (such as food) that is rewarding (reinforcing). Some rewards are learned through experience (secondary reinforcers) whereas others are innate (primary reinforcers).

Privacy A person's right to control the flow of information about themselves. If privacy is invaded, confidentiality should be protected.

Privation The failure to develop any attachments during early life. This is contrasted with 'deprivation' or 'disruption' where attachment bonds have formed, but may be disturbed either through physical or simply emotional separation.

Prospective study A research study where participants of interest are identified (e.g. those with high blood pressure or who were adopted) and then followed over time to observe the outcome. The 'opposite' is a retrospective study where people, for example, who are adopted are studied to consider events that occurred in their past.

Protection from harm During a research study, participants should not experience negative physical effects, such as physical injury, nor psychological effects, such as lowered self-esteem or embarrassment.

Psychoanalysis A therapy developed by Sigmund Freud to bring unconscious emotions and memories into the conscious mind and enable a person to deal with them.

Psychodynamic approach to psychopathology Any approach that emphasises the dynamics of behaviour. In other words, what *drives* us to behave in particular ways. Psychoanalysis is an example of the psychodynamic approach.

Psychological test The measurement of any psychological ability, such as personality or intelligence or emotional type.

Glossary

Psychopathology The study of psychological disorder. 'Pathology' is the study and diagnosis of illness.

Psychotherapy Any psychological form of treatment for a mental disorder, as distinct from medical forms of treatment.

PTSD *see* Post-traumatic stress disorder

Punishment In operant conditioning, the application of an unpleasant stimulus such that the likelihood of the behaviour that led to it reoccurring is decreased.

Qualitative data Expresses 'quality'. This includes descriptions, meanings, pictures and so on. The data cannot be counted or quantified but they can be turned into quantitative data by placing qualitative information in categories and counting instances.

Quantitative data Represents how much, how long, how many, etc. there are of something. Data that are measured in numbers or quantities. This includes questions with yes/no answers because these can be counted.

Questionnaire Data are collected through the use of written questions.

Quota sample Groups of participants are selected according to their frequency in the population. Selection is done from each group using opportunity sampling.

Random allocation Allocating participants to experimental groups using random techniques.

Random sample A sample of participants produced by using a random technique.

Random technique Method of selection that ensures each member of the population has an equal chance of being selected. For example, placing all names in a hat and drawing out the required number, or by assigning each person a number and using a random number table.

Randomised controlled trials (RCTs) A research method using an independent groups design where participants are randomly allocated to groups. The gold standard in clinical research.

Range The difference between the highest and lowest score in a data set.

Rating scale A means of assessing attitudes or experiences by asking a respondent to rate statements on a scale of 1 to 3 or 1 to 5, etc.

Rational-emotive behaviour therapy (REBT) A cognitive behavioural therapy that helps a person change dysfunctional emotions and behaviours. It does this by making the person aware of their self-defeating beliefs and replacing them with more constructive ones.

Reality principle In psychoanalytic theory, the drive by the ego to accommodate the demands of the environment in a realistic way.

REBT *see* Rational-emotive behaviour therapy.

Reference group The group to which an individual or another group is compared.

Regression A form of ego defence whereby a person returns psychologically to an earlier stage of development rather than handling unacceptable impulses in a more adult way. Anxiety-provoking thoughts can thus be temporarily pushed into the unconscious. Often confused with repression.

Reinforcement If a behaviour results in a pleasant state of affairs, the behaviour is 'stamped in' or reinforced. It is then more probable that the behaviour will be repeated in the future. There is both positive and negative reinforcement – both lead to an increased likelihood that the behaviour will be repeated. Negative reinforcement is the escape from an unpleasant stimulus.

Relaxation A state of inner calm; decreased muscle tension, lower blood pressure, slower heart and breath rates.

Reliability A measure of consistency.

Repeated measures design An experimental design where each participant takes part in every condition under test.

Replication The opportunity to repeat an investigation under the same conditions in order to test the validity and reliability of its findings.

Representative A sample or research environment that accurately stands for, or represents, the population being studied.

Repression A form of ego defence whereby anxiety-provoking material is kept out of conscious awareness as a means of coping.

Retention interval The period of time during which you have to remember something.

Right to withdraw A participant should be able to drop out of a study at any time if they are uncomfortable in any way. They should also have the right to refuse permission for the researcher to use any data they produced.

Role play A controlled observation in which participants are asked to imagine how they would behave in certain situations, and then asked to act out the part. This method has the advantage of permitting the study of behaviours that might be unethical or difficult to study in the real world.

Sample A selection of participants taken from the target population being studied and intended to be representative of that population.

Sampling The process of taking a sample. All sampling techniques aim to produce a representative selection of the target population.

Scattergram A graphical representation of the relationship (i.e. the correlation) between two sets of scores.

Schedule of Recent Experience (SRE) An adapted form of the SRRS.

Schizophrenia A mental disorder where an individual has lost touch with reality and may experience symptoms such as delusions, hallucinations, grossly disorganised behaviour and flattened emotions.

Scientific method The method used in scientific research where scientists start by observing natural phenomena and then develop explanations and hypotheses that are tested using systematic research methods.

Secondary attachment The most important emotional bond is a primary attachment but other emotional bonds are formed of lesser importance but still important for emotional development.

Secondary attachment figure Acts as a kind of emotional safety net and is therefore important in emotional development. Also contributes to social development.

Secondary reinforcer A reinforcer is any experience that is rewarding (reinforcing). Some rewards are learned through experience (secondary reinforcers such as money) whereas others are innate (primary reinforcer such as food).

Secure attachment An infant who is willing to explore, easy to soothe and displays high stranger anxiety. The infant is comfortable with social interaction and intimacy. Such attachments have been related to healthy subsequent cognitive and emotional development. Develops as a result of sensitive responding by the infant's primary attachment figure to the infant's needs.

Self-efficacy A person's belief that they can perform competently in a given situation.

Self-report A research method that relies on the participant answering questions – either verbally (in an interview) or in writing (in a questionnaire).

Semantic The meaning of something, such as a word.

Semi-structured interview An interview that combines some pre-determined questions (as in a structured interview) and some questions developed in response to answers given (as in an unstructured interview).

Sensitive period A biologically determined period of time during which a child is particularly sensitive to a specific form of stimulation, resulting in the development of a specific response or characteristic.

Sensory memory (SM) Information at the senses – information collected by your eyes, ears, nose, fingers and so on. Information is retained for a very brief period by the sensory registers (less than half a second). Capacity of sensory memory is very large. The method of encoding depends on the sense organ involved, i.e. visual for the eyes, acoustic for the ears.

Separation Being parted from something or someone.

Separation anxiety Distress shown by an infant when separated from his/her attachment figure.

Serotonin A neurotransmitter found in the central nervous system. Low levels have been linked to many different behaviours and physiological processes, including aggression, eating disorders and depression.

Sham ECT A form of imitation ECT. A patient is anesthetised and electrodes are connected to the scalp. However, unlike ECT, no electric current is administered and therefore no convulsion is generated.

Short-term memory (STM) Memory for immediate events. Lasts for a very short time and disappears unless rehearsed. Limited duration and limited capacity. Sometimes referred to as working memory.

Single blind A type of research design in which the participant is not aware of the research aims or of which condition of the experiment they are receiving.

SNS *see* Sympathetic nervous system

Sociability The extent to which a person engages in, and enjoys, relationships with other people.

Social change Occurs when a society as a whole adopts a new belief or way of behaving, which then becomes widely accepted as the norm.

Social desirability bias The tendency for respondents to answer questions in a way that presents them in a better light.

Social learning/social learning theory The basic assumption of this theory is that people learn through indirect as well as direct rewards, by observing the behaviour of models (observational learning) and imitating such behaviour in similar situations if the model was rewarded for such behaviour (vicarious reinforcement).

Social Readjustment Rating Scale (SRRS) Developed by Holmes and Rahe to test the idea that life changes are related to stress-related illnesses, such as anxiety and depression.

Social releasers A social behaviour or characteristic that elicits a caregiving reaction.

Social support Care and assistance from other people.

Spontaneous decay The disappearance of the physical memory trace over time where there is no external cause.

SSRIs (selective serotonin re-uptake inhibitors) A class of drug used in the treatment of depression (an antidepressant).

Standard deviation Shows the amount of variation in a data set. It assesses the spread of the data around the mean.

Standard interview An interview that lacks the four components of the cognitive interview.

Standardised instructions The instructions given to participants to tell them how to perform a task.

Standardised procedures A set of procedures that are the same for all participants in order to be able to repeat a study. This includes standardised instructions.

Strange Situation (SS) Method to assess strength of attachment, conducted in a novel environment and involving eight episodes. An infant's behaviour is observed as mother leaves and returns, and when with a stranger. The method measures attachment in terms of stranger anxiety and separation anxiety and reunion behaviour.

Stranger anxiety Distress shown by an infant when approached by an unfamiliar person.

Stratified sample Groups of participants are selected according to their frequency in the population. Selection is done randomly from each strata.

Stress Experienced when the perceived demands of a situation are greater than the perceived ability to cope.

Stress inoculation training (SIT) A type of CBT that trains people to cope with stressful situations more effectively by learning skills to protect them from the damaging effects of future stressors.

Stress management Techniques intended to help people deal more effectively with the stress in their lives so that they are less adversely affected by it.

Structured interview Any interview in which the questions are decided in advance.

Studies using a correlational analysis *see* Correlational analysis.

Suffragettes Women seeking the right to vote by means of organised protest.

Superego This develops between the ages of three and six. It embodies the conscience and our sense of right and wrong, as well as notions of the ideal self.

Sympathetic nervous system (SNS) The part of the autonomic nervous system that is associated with physiological arousal and 'fight or flight' responses.

Sympathomedullary pathway A stress response, involving the sympathetic nervous system and adrenal medulla, which helps the body prepare for fight or flight.

Synapse A small gap separating neurons. It consists of the presynaptic membrane (which discharges neurotransmitters), the postsynaptic membrane (containing receptor sites for neurotransmitters) and a synaptic gap between the two. The synaptic gap between a transmitting and receiving neuron is about 10 nanometres wide.

Systematic desensitisation Based on classical conditioning (the behavioural approach), a therapy used to treat phobias and problems involving anxiety. A client is gradually exposed to the threatening situation under relaxed conditions until the anxiety reaction is reduced and ultimatey extinguished.

Tardive dyskinesia 'Dyskinesia' refers to involuntary repetitive body movements, 'tardive' refers to a slow onset. It is a common side effect of antipsychotic drugs.

Target absent line-up Police often identify a criminal by showing an eyewitness a parade of people in which the suspected criminal may or not be present. 'Target absent' refers to the suspect being absent. This enhances the validity of the line-up procedure because otherwise an eyewitness feels they have to identify someone.

Target population The group of people that the researcher is interested in. The group of people from whom a sample is drawn and about whom generalisations can be made.

Temperament hypothesis The view that attachment type can be explained in terms of an infant's innate emotional type rather than the sensitivity of the attachment figure.

Tend and befriend A response to stress that is more associated with females. It involves protecting the young (the 'tend' response) and seeking social contact and support from others (the 'befriend' response).

Terrorism Any act intended to cause death or serious bodily harm to civilians with the purpose of intimidating a population or compelling a government to do, or abstain from, any act.

Test–retest A method used to check reliability. The same test or interview is given to the same participants on two occasions to see if the same results are obtained.

Time sampling An observational technique in which the observer records behaviours in a given time frame, e.g. noting what a target individual is doing every 30 seconds, or some other time interval.

Tolerance In relation to drugs, the fact that the body increasingly adapts to the drug and needs increasingly larger doses to achieve the same desirable effect. These increases eventually level off.

Transference Displacing the feelings about one person onto another. It is a problem that occurs during psychoanalysis when a patient may transfer their feelings about others onto the therapist. The therapist then has to deal with this as an additional 'problem'.

Type A behaviour A tendency to approach life in a certain way, characterised by competitiveness and impatience, for example. It is believed to increase the risk of coronary heart disease.

Type B behaviour Characterised by an easygoing, relaxed and patient approach to life. It is believed to decrease the risk of coronary heart disease.

Type D behaviour An aspect of personality, describing a person who tends to think negatively (e.g. worrying) and who is also socially inhibited (e.g. shy).

Glossary

Unconditioned response (UCR) In classical conditioning, the innate reflex response to a stimulus, such as salivating when presented with food.

Unconditioned stimulus (UCS) In classical conditioning, the stimulus that inevitably produces an innate reflex response, such as food producing a salivation response.

Unconscious Lacking consciousness or awareness. In psychoanalytic theory, the unconscious part of your mind contains information that is either very hard or almost impossible to bring into conscious awareness. However, such material exerts a powerful influence over behaviour.

Unstructured interview An interview that starts out with some general aims and possibly some questions, and lets the interviewee's answers guide subsequent questions.

Validity The extent to which a study and its findings are legitimate or true.

Ventricles Spaces or cavities found, for example, in the brain and filled with cerebrospinal fluid.

Vicarious reinforcement Learning that is not through direct reinforcement of behaviour, but through observing someone else being reinforced for that behaviour.

Viral infection Illness caused by a virus rather than bacteria. Viral infections tend to affect the whole body whereas bacterial infections are more localised.

Visual cache In the working memory model, a component of the visuo-spatial sketchpad that deals with the storage of visual information, such as the arrangement of objects.

Visuo-spatial sketchpad In the working memory model, a component that encodes visual information. Divided into the visual cache (stores information) and inner scribe (spatial relations).

Volunteer bias A form of sampling bias. Occurs because volunteer participants are usually more highly motivated than randomly selected participants.

Volunteer sample A sample of participants produced by asking for volunteers. Sometimes referred to as a 'self-selected' sample.

Weapon focus effect In violent crimes, an eyewitness' attention may be drawn to the weapon held by a criminal, reducing their ability to remember other details, such as the criminal's face.

Withdrawal symptoms Abnormal physical or psychological reactions to the abrupt discontinuation of a drug to which an individual has developed a physical dependence.

Word-length effect People remember lists of short words better than lists of long words, governed by the capacity of the phonological loop.

Working memory model (WMM) An explanation of short-term memory, which is also called 'working memory'. Based on four components, some with storage capacity.

Workload The demands of a person's work role. This can be stressful because it is repetitive, high intensity, monotonous or high volume.

Workplace stressors Aspects of our working environment that create anxiety and cause a stress reaction in our body.

Yerkes–Dodson effect The curvilinear relationship between arousal and performance – people do not perform well when they are very relaxed, they perform best when moderately aroused and performance drops again at high levels of arousal.

Zero correlation Co-variables are not linked.